D0616777

Future Farm Programs

Comparative Costs and Consequences

Iowa State University
Center for Agricultural
and Rural
Development

Future
Comparative

The Iowa State University Press
Ames, Iowa, U.S.A.

HD
1765
.H4

Farm Programs
Costs and Consequences

EARL O. HEADY C. F. Curtiss Distinguished Professor in Agriculture; Professor of Economics; Executive Director, Center for Agricultural and Rural Development. Iowa State University

LEO V. MAYER Associate Professor of Economics; Associate Director, Center for Agricultural and Rural Development. Iowa State University

HOWARD C. MADSEN Associate in Economics; Program Specialist, Center for Agricultural and Rural Development. Iowa State University

OTHER PUBLICATIONS of the Center for Agricultural and Rural Development are available as follows:

BOOKS FROM THE IOWA STATE UNIVERSITY PRESS (HARD-BOUND)

Sociological Perspectives of Domestic Development, 1971
Benefits and Burdens of Rural Development: Some Public Policy Viewpoints, 1970
A North American Common Market, 1969
Food Goals, Future Structural Changes and Agricultural Policy: A National Basebook, 1969
Alternatives for Balancing World Food Production Needs, 1967
Roots of the Farm Problem, 1965
Economic Development of Agriculture, 1965
Family Mobility in our Dynamic Society, 1965
Farmers in the Market Economy, 1964
Our Changing Rural Society: Perspectives and Trends (Developed by the Rural Sociological Society under editorship of James H. Copp), 1964
Farm Goals in Conflict: Family Farm, Income, Freedom, Security, 1963
Adjustments in Agriculture—A National Basebook, 1961

REPORTS FROM THE CENTER FOR AGRICULTURAL AND ECONOMIC DEVELOPMENT

CARD 39	Bargaining Power Programs: Estimated Effects on Production, Net Farm Incomes and Food Costs for Specified Price Levels
CAED 38	Food Costs, Farm Incomes, and Crop Yields with Restrictions on Fertilizer Use
CAED 37	Policy Choices for Rural People
CAED 36	Trade-offs in Farm Policy
CAED 34	Analysis of Some Farm Program Alternatives for the Future
CAED 33	Role of the Universities in Social Innovation
CAED 32	Farm Programs for the 1970's
CAED 31	Abundance and Uncertainty . . . Farm Policy Problems
CAED 30T	Capacity and Trends in Use of Land Resources
CAED 29	Implications of Changes (Structural and Market) on Farm Management and Marketing Research
CAED 28	A Recipe for Meeting the World Food Crisis
CAED 26	Weather Variability and the Need for a Food Reserve
CAED 25	International Home Economics
CAED 10	New Areas of Land-Grant Extension Education

Library of Congress Cataloging in Publication Data

Heady, Earl Orel, 1916–
    Future farm programs.

    At head of title: Iowa State University Center for Agricultural and Rural Development.
    Includes bibliographical references.
    1. Agriculture and State—U.S. 2. Simulation methods. 3. Linear programming. I. Mayer, Leo V., joint author. II. Madsen, Howard C., 1944– joint author. III. Title.
HD1765 1972.H4   338.1'0973   79–137095
ISBN 0-8138-0675-5

© 1972 The Iowa State University Press, Ames, Iowa 50010. All rights reserved.
Composed and printed by The Iowa State University Press. First edition, 1972.

INDIANA
PURDUE
LIBRARY
AUG 28 1978

FORT WAYNE

WITHDRAWN

Contents

Preface vii

1. The Background of Demand, Productivity,
   and Supply Control Programs 3
2. Future Capacity and Resource Requirements of Agriculture . 24
3. Short and Intermediate Term Compensation
   Policies for Agriculture 105
4. Long Term Land Retirement Programs 142
5. Land Retirement and Alternative Levels
   of Farm Product Prices 175
6. Resource Adjustment in Rural Areas 204
7. Net Cost of Demand Expansion under Public Law 480 . . . 225
8. A Simulation Model for Agricultural Policy 275
   Collaborator: Mordechai Schechter
9. Agriculture under Historic Programs, Reduced
   Technical Change, and Free Markets 326
   Collaborator: A. Y. Lin
10. Potentials for Improvements and Equity in
    Land Retirement Programs 384

Index 405

Preface

THIS BOOK deals with the problems of farm programs for the commercial sector of U.S. agriculture. It provides an in-depth analysis of alternative land retirement or diversion programs which use price support, direct payments, and other methods for supply control or restraint. Hence it provides analyses of a restricted set of agricultural policy alternatives since it relates mainly to the use of land retirement, withdrawal, or conversion as basic policy mechanisms.

For the major and most geographically dispersed crops, some form of land retirement or diversion has been the basic mechanism of farm policy in the United States over the last forty years. Land retirement or diversion programs have been implemented under such labels as the AAA, feed grain, wheat and cotton programs, conservation reserve, soil bank, acreage quotas, and similar names. However, the fact remains that these programs all emphasize a reduction of crop acres to control or lessen output of the major field crops—cotton, feed grains, wheat, and tobacco. The emphasis has never been on restraining capital or labor inputs for these crops, but always on lessening the input of land. Neither has the historic emphasis been on placing a direct restraint on output or marketing quotas for these crops, although marketing orders and quotas have been used for certain vegetable, fruit, and dairy commodities.

The authors do not view land retirement or diversion as either the best or worst mechanism for supply control and farm income improvement. In terms of various economic criteria, there are many policy alternatives which could be implemented on behalf of commercial farmers. Certainly this type of program does little or nothing for that part of the labor force replaced from agriculture by rapid technical change, for older persons and families with few resources and low incomes who are stranded on farms, or for nonfarm persons in rural communities who suffer declining economic and employment opportunities as farms and farm people become fewer in number. Programs for the latter groups are urgently needed. However, they are discussed elsewhere (see *Benefits and Burdens of Rural Development,* Iowa State University Press, 1970). Here we have focused on farm programs centering around land diversion of various levels and types.

Future Farm Programs incorporates several analyses dealing with various facets of land retirement programs. These programs have been the foundation of U.S. agricultural policy over several decades and have promise of so serving for the next decade or two. Under these prospects, it seems useful that added detail and data be made available relating changes in "output" variables to changes in "input" variables. The output variables or effects which compete with or substitute for each other include government costs, net farm income, land retirement, secondary social costs, and related items. The input or "control" variables are payment levels, price support levels, regional restraints on land retirement, and similar items.

The following sequence is utilized: First, the outlook for future farm structure, productivity, and supply is analyzed. Next, the effect of various land retirement programs, bargaining power through acreage quotas, and free markets are compared in their expected effect on farm income, government payments, location of farm adjustments, and rural community income problems. Several land retirement alternatives are then examined in terms of price levels and supply control to be attained, and the extent of regional concentration allowed in land diversion. Farm income, government costs, and interregional adjustments in crop production are detailed for each of these. A comparison is also made of the relative costs of international food aid and land retirement as means of solving surplus problems. Finally, two methodological studies are presented. The first uses simulation and response models in estimating the effects of input variables on substitutions among output variables in land retirement programs. The second uses long-run regression and simulation models to examine the level of employment, resource structure, and net farm income under programs prevailing in the past, a free market regime, and a slower rate of technical change.

EARL O. HEADY
LEO V. MAYER
HOWARD C. MADSEN

Future Farm Programs

Comparative Costs and Consequences

CHAPTER ONE

The Background of Demand, Productivity, and Supply Control Programs

AMERICAN AGRICULTURE has been faced with the same basic set of structural problems for the last forty-five years. These problems have been temporarily accentuated or alleviated during periods of depression and war, but they have returned each time and brought with them the same effects in price and income depression, farm labor migration, and pressures on the rural community. The basic forces underlying these problems have been partially offset by various government programs initiated in the 1930s and continued over the past four decades. While the relative emphasis given to various elements of agricultural policy has changed with time, the main program instruments to restrain production and improve prices and income are the same as we move into the 1970s as they were in the 1930s. The major instrument used to control supply and bolster farm prices and income is land retirement (with payments to farmers to encourage participation), supplemented by short-run commodity storage programs by the Commodity Credit Corporation. The major instrument used to increase demand is the food aid program. During the 1930s, this aid concentrated on domestic consumers through the Food Stamp Plan. In recent times, international food aid has been the focus of emphasis and has entirely overshadowed publicly assisted domestic food programs.

Largely, legislation and funding relating to basic commodities such as wheat, feed grains, and cotton have been on a definite but short-term basis. Similarly, farmer participation has generally been on the basis of annual contracts. Since its basic initiation in the 1930s the combination of land retirement (supply control), commodity storage (price support), and food distribution programs has appeared and reappeared under different names throughout several administrations. While the titles given the programs have differed under the temporary legislation of different administrations, programs have remained fundamentally the same as the basic farm policy instruments enacted in the 1930s. Short-term programs were appropriate in the initial periods of experimentation in the early 1930s when the nation was caught in a deep depression, and emergency measures were necessary to protect people, farms, and other sectors from severe hardships. At that early time, short-term programs could be justified because economic knowledge of their effects was very limited. The belief at that time was that the large supplies of farm products relative to demand and the low farm prices and income were the result of unemployment and low consumer income. Relatively little was known about the magnitudes of potential demand elasticities and the rate of farm technological progress and supply increase. It was not unreasonable, given the existing paucity of knowledge, to suppose the major solution to the basic farm problem was national policy to restore full employment.

Later, World War II and the large temporary spurt in the world demand for U.S. food commodities, along with a continuation of these conditions in the restoration period, gave a false feeling of proof to the temporary nature of the basic farm problem. However with a return to greater normalcy in the late 1940s and early 1950s, and the reconstruction of the food supply in war-damaged countries, the same symptoms of the U.S. farm problems as in the 1920s and 1930s again appeared. Food supply increased faster than the growth in domestic and export demand. The improved income and savings position of farmers during the 1940s provided a capital base wherein they could more rapidly invest in the new technologies forthcoming from private and public research. These new technologies, communicated through extension education and the promotional efforts of private industry, were the vanguard of an avalanche of farm innovations serving as the societal pay-off from previous investments in farm technological research. But at the same time, the rising per capita incomes of American consumers brought declining demand elasticities for food at the farm gate. Consumers became so well fed they simply did not consume a greater physical quantity of food. Their preferences included upgrading the quality of the food mix and the incorporation of more services such as freezing, packaging, and ease of food preparation. Price elasticities of demand for food had fallen so low that a 1 percent increase in output could be marketed only with a price reduction of about 2.5 percent for many basic commodities.[1] Consequently, increases in output at rates higher than the growth in population and exports caused the greater ouput to have a smaller market value than previous levels of output. Similarly, income elasticities of demand for food in its "farm form" had dropped practically to zero.

1. For an elementary explanation of the magnitude and consequences of food demand elasticities, see Earl O. Heady, *A Primer on Food, Agriculture and Public Policy.* (New York: Random House, 1967), pp. 3–22.

This state of domestic demand faces American food producers over future decades. Food demand will grow at approximately the rate of population growth and expansion of foreign demand. Increases in production exceeding growth in demand will cause short-run depressions of farm prices and incomes in the absence of offsetting storage and price support programs.

While malnutrition in the United States may still prevail to some extent, programs to alleviate this problem will not result in aggregate demand increments great enough to offset existing or near-term "surplus" supply capacity.[2] Most malnutrition among certain low-income and ethnic groups is more a function of deficiencies in vitamins, protein, and minor nutritional components rather than aggregate food intake. In this form, it also prevails somewhat even in higher income groups. But its elimination, a need of high priority, does not pose a demand increase which will even begin to absorb the nation's long-run overcapacity in supply of food.

Still, even with low demand elasticities, increasing population would cause the problem to be temporary if we were approaching limits in our ability to improve farm technology and increase food supply at "reasonable" real prices; or it would be temporary if the population explosion and economic development of other nations were to be rapidly translated into effective demand for U.S. farm crops. These eventualities may occur. Perhaps unexpected world and national policies will be implemented to cause this sudden world food demand to burst upon our farm markets. If so, it would change the outlook tremendously, and the basic farm problem could still be considered of temporary nature. Short-run programs to tide us over until this flood in world food demand occurs would be appropriate and perhaps even most efficient; but this is not the immediate prospect, even if it can be considered imminent in several decades. Hence, we must consider prospects in technological advances, food supply capacity, and farm programs in the context of the next one or two decades. There is even the potential that developing nations will progress much more rapidly in increasing supply to meet their own domestic food demands. The "green revolution" underway in Asia is an indication of this possibility.[3]

SUBSTITUTION OF CAPITAL TECHNOLOGY ● The commercial farming sector is confronted with two basic structural problems. Both of these structural problems stem from the rapid substitution of capital technology for other resources used in agriculture. Because rural

2. J. M. Wetmore et al., Policies for Expanding the Demand for Farm Food Products in the United States, pt. 1, History and Potentials, *Agricultural Experiment Station Technical Bulletin* 231, Univ. of Minnesota, April 1959.

3. Willard W. Cochrane, *The World Food Problem, A Guardedly Optimistic View* (New York: T. Y. Crowell, 1969); CAED, *Alternatives for Balancing World Food Production and Needs* (Ames: Iowa State Univ. Press, 1967).

towns serve as the origin and destination of commodities and inputs for commercial farming, the majority of them also face difficulties based on these two structural developments: substitution of capital for land, and substitution of capital for labor. Capital constituted 20 percent of all inputs in agriculture in 1900. By 1950, the percentage of capital had grown to 45. It now approaches 70 percent. Capital input takes biological forms such as improved seed, fertilizers, pesticides, breeds, rations, etc. It also takes mechanical forms such as new types or higher capacities of machines and equipment.

Capital-Land Substitution ● Capital in the form of biological inputs especially serves as a substitute for land. As yield per acre increases, the same output can be grown on fewer acres. As the capital-land substitution process takes place, total production or supply capacity increases. In the absence of storage programs, these shifts in supply cause market prices to decline with corresponding depression of farm income. The "surplus" capacity problem of U.S. agriculture results from this type of capital-land substitution, especially through the introduction of biological innovations, but also by mechanical innovations which have biological effects of greater timeliness and improved cultural practices. In an attempt to offset this substitution process and restore or maintain farm price and income objectives, supply control was implemented with land retirement as the basic policy instrument.

The magnitude of technological advance in production of basic field crops is indicated in Table 1.1. The rate of percent increase in yields has been increasing over the past three decades. There is, of course, a question of whether these rates can continue or must decline as inputs representing modern technologies are used on more farms and at higher levels. Typically, the marginal productivity of a technical input declines as it is used on more and more land. Its marginal rate of substitution for land also declines. However, over the past three decades, continuous introduction of innovations has offset these effects and maintained the productivity and substitution rates of capital technology for land.

Under the capital-land substitution process of the past, the nation has been able to reduce the acres of land used for crops (Table 1.2). Acreages of all crops have declined by 10 percent from 1934–38 to the present while crop output increased by 72 percent. Acreages of wheat, feed grains, and cotton have decreased by 5, 21, and 64 percent respectively. During the same period wheat and feed grains production increased by 100 and 132 percent respectively and cotton production decreased by 15 percent.

Even with growing nonagricultural demand and uses for land, food supply capacity has outpaced domestic and export demand at prices acceptable to the farm sector. Land retirement programs to control supply have been at levels indicated in Table 1.3 over recent years. The Conservation Reserve Program was a longer-term program, initiated dur-

Table 1.1 ● Average Yields Per Acre and Increases in Principal Field Crops, 1950–54 and 1965–69

Crop	Unit	1950–54	1965–69	Increase (%)	Annual compound increase (%)
Corn	bu	39.4	77.4	96	4.3
Rice	lb	2,411.0	4,365.0	81	3.8
Cotton	lb	297.0	481.0	62	3.1
Wheat	bu	17.3	27.6	60	3.0
Tobacco	lb	1,292.0	1,957.0	51	2.6

Source: U.S. Dept. of Commerce, Statistical Abstract of the United States, 1958–70, Bureau of the Census.

Table 1.2. ● Acreages and Production of Major Field Crops for Selected Years

		1909-13	1924-28	1934-38	1955-59	1965-69
All crops	acreage (millions)	379	359	334	327	300
	output (1957-59 = 100)	64	72	68	98	117
Wheat	acreage (millions)	48	56	55	49	52
	output (million bu)	682	826	716	1,096	1,437
Feed grains	acreage (millions)	145	136	123	140	97
	output (million tons)	95	86	72	145	167
Cotton	acreage (millions)	33	42	28	14	10
	output (million bales)	13	15	13	13	11

Sources: U.S. Dept. of Commerce, Statistical Abstract of the United States, 1960-70, Bureau of the Census; U.S. Dept. of Commerce, Historical Statistics of the United States, Colonial Times to the Present, 1960, Bureau of the Census; U.S. Dept. of Agriculture, Agricultural Statistics, USDA SRS, 1969; U.S. Dept. of Agriculture, Changes in Farm Production and Efficiency, USDA ERS Statistical Bulletin 233.

Table 1.3 ● Land Diverted from Crops under Various Supply Control Programs 1956–69

Year	Total	Program (million acres)						
		Wheat	Feed grains	Cotton	Acreage reserve	Conservation reserve	Cropland conversion	Cropland adjustment
1956	13.6	...	...	...	12.2	1.4	...	...
1957	27.8	...	...	...	21.4	6.4	...	...
1958	27.1	...	...	...	17.2	9.9	...	...
1959	22.5	...	...	...	...	22.5	...	...
1960	28.7	...	...	...	...	28.7	...	...
1961	53.7	10.7	25.2	...	...	28.5	...	...
1962	64.7	7.2	28.2	...	...	25.8	0.1	...
1963	56.1	5.1	24.5	0.5	...	24.3	0.1	...
1964	55.5	7.2	32.4	1.0	...	17.4	0.4	...
1965	57.4	8.3	34.8	4.6	...	14.0	0.4	...
1966	63.3	...	34.7	4.9	...	13.3	0.4	2.0
1967	40.8	...	20.3	3.0	...	11.0	0.6	4.0
1968	47.8	...	31.0	...	...	9.2	0.6	4.0
1969	58.0	11.5	38.5	...	...	3.4	0.6	4.0

Source: U. S. Dept. of Agriculture, Agricultural Statistics, 1969.

ing the 1950s for periods up to ten years. The wheat, feed grains, and cotton programs are annual programs with cash payments made to farmers for withdrawing cropland from production.

The long-term retirement initiated during the 1950s was not of sufficient magnitude to reduce supply to a level consistent with price supports provided during that period. The difficulty was the magnitude of the program and not its longer-run nature. The program tended to be concentrated in lower-producing areas. Since output per acre is less on lower quality land, more acres must be withheld from production to achieve a given level of output reduction. The amount of land out of production under the Conservation Reserve in 1960 was only half the amount out of production under all programs in the mid-1960s. The larger amount of more productive land retired under short-term contracts was great enough to restrain supply. Even then the larger amount of land withdrawn under government programs in the 1960s did not actually reduce total production enough to lower stocks. It only brought production in line with ongoing utilization. The large stocks built up during the 1950s through high support prices and inadequate land retirement were liquidated by food aid and other publicly assisted export programs during the 1960s. The buildup of stocks under the CCC during the 1950s occurred because land retirement programs were too small to mesh annual supply with effective demand. Public Law 480 legislation was one means of solving the surplus farm commodity problem in the United States.

Food aid under PL 480 has had purposes other than solely liquidating U.S. stocks. The American population also has humanitarian orientation toward lessening the misery of hunger in other peoples. Even private groups have made vigorous efforts to gather funds and food for individual shipments which might serve these purposes. But even though this is true, the overriding forces which gave rise to PL 480 and large direct and indirect budgets for food aid were the presence and cost of storing public stocks of surplus grains.

It is apparent that food aid as a demand mechanism is a more expensive way to handle domestic surplus capacity problems than are land retirement or other types of supply control. If the instrument is food aid, the government must pay the producer the gross value per acre of his crop output—the value of production costs plus his normal profit margin—plus the costs of storage, handling, and shipment. To remove the same amount from the market with land retirement, the farmer needs only a payment to cover his normal profit margin; the outlay covering his production costs, storage, handling, and transportation can be deleted. The farmer will be as well off and the taxpayer will be better off, but only from the standpoint of removing a given amount of supply from the domestic market.

Capital-Labor Substitution ● A major problem in the structural adjustment of agriculture stems from the second substitution process, namely, the substitution of capital technology for labor. Forms of biological capital which substitute for land also substitute for labor. Just as higher yields result in the need for fewer crop acres, less labor also is needed in filling the nation's food basket. But even more important are the mechanical forms of capital which replace labor from agriculture and greatly extend the number of acres and animals one worker can handle. This substitution of capital for labor is encouraged by two developments: (1) the new forms of machines and equipment which increase the productivity and raise economic returns of the remaining labor, and (2) economic development which lowers the real price of capital relative to labor through (a) accumulation of capital which increases its supply relative to labor, and (b) greater capital investment in education of the human agent so that it is less available as a source of energy and physical manipulation as it migrates more to occupations based on skill and intellect.

The capital-labor substitution not only reduces the work force and population in agriculture, but it is also the basic force in reducing the number and enlarging the size of farms. As capital comes to dominate the input or resource structure, the fixed costs of farming increase. Hence larger volumes, represented by more crops and animals per farm, are needed to reduce unit costs and create an acceptable profit margin. Typically, too, the greater capitalization and larger size of enterprises encourage more specialization in agriculture. The capital-labor substitution which encourages fewer and larger farms has a greater impact on the rural community than does the capital-land substitution which increases supply capacity and tends to create surpluses which depress farm prices and income. The latter forces are reflected in the commerce of rural towns as the savings and purchasing power of farm families are affected. However, supply control and price support programs which maintain farm incomes can offset these latter forces in their impact on the rural community. They do not have similar effects in offsetting the capital-labor substitution process. Even in the absence of surplus capacity and burdened farm prices, capital technology which replaces labor and encourages larger farms would prevail with its impact on labor employment in agriculture and economic opportunity in the rural community. The persons who bear the brunt of declining employment and reduced business in rural areas through capital-labor substitution on farms are in no way compensated by supply control and land retirement programs.

Table 1.4 summarizes the nature of structural changes taking place in agriculture under the introduction of capital representing new technological forms. Farm numbers have been more than halved and farm size has more than doubled since 1930. The addition of $32.4 billion in non-real-estate capital has been accompanied by replacement of 8.2 million workers and 46 million acres of cropland, the substitution rate being even greater since output has increased 99 percent since 1930.

Being replaced from employment in agriculture and having the volume of business reduced for the country merchants are important

Table 1.4 ● Number and Sizes of Farms, Resources Employed, and Total Output of Agriculture, Selected Years 1930–69

Year	Number of farms (million)	Average size of farms (acres)	Persons employed in farming (million)	Acres used for all crops (million)	Non-real estate capital[a] ($ billion)	Index of output
1930	6.3	157	12.5	382	10.1	100
1940	6.1	175	11.0	368	8.3	115
1950	5.4	216	9.9	377	25.1	141
1960	3.7	303	7.1	355	37.9	174
1969	3.0	360	4.3	336	42.5	199

Sources: U.S. Dept. of Agriculture, Agricultural Statistics, 1967, 1969; U.S. Dept. of Commerce, Statistical Abstract of the United States, 1970, Bureau of the Census; U.S. Dept. of Agriculture, Changes in Farm Production, 1964, 1970, supplements to USDA ERS Statistical Bulletin 233; U.S. Dept. of Agriculture, The Balance Sheet of the Farming Sector, USDA ERS, 1969.

[a] Value of livestock, machinery, and equipment in constant 1960 dollars.

and very personal effects of farm structural changes for the persons involved. They are as personal as reduction in prices and income of farmers resulting from technical advances outpacing demand. But while the first are as important as the second and involve even more people since the farm population has been more than halved and the rural town population has declined about as rapidly, we have had no programs for those people leaving agriculture, or rural merchants with reduced sales. Farm policy implemented through land retirement has little promise of alleviating these aspects of farm structural changes.

PROSPECTS IN THE FUTURE ● Even though short-run land retirement programs could be desirable and efficient options if the problems created by the capital-land substitution process promised to be short lived, they would do little to relieve those problems of structural change resulting in the replacement of labor from agriculture and the trend to fewer and larger farms. But is this likely? Is the problem of surplus capacity only of temporary duration? Research results presented in the next chapter attempt to answer this question. Results show that excess cropland is still in prospect for 1980. If production is on an optimal interregional basis, the nation could meet its domestic food demand (considering population and per capita income growth) and still export 2 billion bushels of wheat in 1980 from the present cropland base. It could also make large increases in exports of feed grains, soybeans, and cotton. The exportable amounts greatly exceed the practical expectations in foreign market growth over the next decade. With exports at expected trend levels, the nation's posed surplus capacity in 1980 appears to parallel that of 1970. These results from research reported in the next chapter are similar to those forthcoming from other studies. The results of Daly and Egbert, similar to our own, show that total output could increase to 160 percent of the 1957–59 average by 1980.[4] A study by Abel and Rojko shows that if less developed countries only increased their grain production at historic rates (a rate now being questioned in light of the "green revolution" being posed for Asia), the United States could meet its share of developing countries' total import needs with 186 million acres of grain.[5] The United States has been harvesting 165 million acres of grain, with around 55 million acres withheld from production. In addition Upchurch estimates that 150 million additional acres could be cropped (and some of this land moves into crop production each year).[6] Tweeten estimates continued excess

4. R. F. Daly and Alvin C. Egbert, Statistical Supplement to A Look Ahead for Food and Agriculture. Agricultural Economics Research, Jan. 1966.

5. Martin E. Abel and Anthony S. Rojko, World Food Situation: Prospects for World Grain Production, Consumption and Trade, USDA *Foreign Agriculture Economic Report* 35, 1967.

6. L. M. Upchurch, The capacity of the United States to supply food for developing countries, pp. 215–23, in *Alternatives for Balancing World Food Production and Needs*, CAED (Ames: Iowa State Univ. Press, 1967).

capacity of 50 million acres in 1980. His estimates are based on projections of annual increases of 2.0 percent in per capita incomes, 1.4
percent in exports, 1.6 percent in domestic demand reflecting mainly
population growth, 2.0 percent increase in total demand, 1.7 percent increase in agricultural productivity, and 0.3 percent in total farm inputs.[7]
Hence prevailing evidence suggests that the surplus capacity problem is
not temporary in nature. It appears to be of long-run or minimally of
intermediate-term duration.[8]

THE COMPENSATION AND WELFARE BASIS FOR PROGRAMS
● While land retirement and supply control have been the basic
instruments of U.S. farm policy since the 1930s, they represent only one
of a broader set of possible policies which might be used in solving problems of agriculture and rural communities. Similarly land retirement
is only one of numerous supply control mechanisms that could be used.
There are many alternative types of land retirement programs that might
be employed to solve the problems of surpluses, low farm income, and
depressed resource returns in agriculture. Among various efficiency,
equity, and other criteria which might be used as the gauge, neither land
retirement nor supply control are the worst or the best of policy instruments which might be used to solve the ills of agriculture and farm communities; but these are the basic policy mechanisms which have long had
public political concurrence and societal financial support in the United
States.

Policies for commercial farmers have an important logical and economic basis. A conflict arises however because programs which are best
suited to solve problems of commercial farming are not well adapted to
similarly solve the several other problems plaguing agriculture: problems
of chronic poverty, workers replaced from employment by improved farm
technology, or nonfarm persons in rural communities who bear the in-
cidence of decreased business and employment as commercial farms enlarge and invest in more productive technologies. Hence we examine
here only the equity basis for commercial farm programs, that basis which

7. Luther G. Tweeten, Objectives and Goals for Farm Commodity Programs after 1969,
CAED Report 31, Iowa State Univ., 1968.

8. We use the terms "surplus capacity" and "surplus supply" in the rather popular
meaning of these words. The "man on the farm" meaning of these words is as follows:
Supply is so large relative to demand that it results in prices and farm incomes at low
levels which are generally unacceptable for farmers. In this sense, also, surplus capacity may be used to reflect supply potential on normally cropped land but which is
withheld from production if publicly accepted price support levels are attained. More
specifically, of course, surplus supply is only a relative term because it is not easy to
imagine output greater than demand in the sense of a zero price. A more logical definition of "surplus" would refer to output levels which cause farm resource returns to
fall below market or opportunity employment levels. Conceptually, we have this more
logical definition in mind but continue the more popular usage of the term in the
text.

grows out of a national goal of sharing the benefits of increased farm efficiency between consumers and commercial farmers.

Both the private and public sectors invest increasing amounts in developing new capital technologies for agriculture. Individual farmers calculate these technologies to be profitable and invest in them. For the single farmer, when he makes his decision, price is a constant. However when masses of farmers decide similarly and the greater supply reaches the market, the aggregate result is a reduced price. Since demand for food is inelastic, price falls by a greater percentage than the increase in aggregate output, and total revenue declines below its previous level in the absence of price support mechanisms or marketing restraints. The individual farmer cannot escape this problem by refusing to adopt new technologies however. If he tries this escape, he simply markets less at the reduced price, and his position is worse than if he innovated and produced more to sell at the lower price. In markets with price elasticities of demand as low as those for farm products, only a few producers who expand output by a greater proportion than the price decline can benefit from this environment. (The word *few* is used because the total or majority of the industry cannot escape the revenue or income-reducing effects of an inelastic demand by greatly increasing output.)

For such commodities as food with an inelastic demand, consumers gain directly from larger production and reduced prices, although it is doubtful that consumers-at-large directly wish to gain at the expense of farmers. Since demand is inelastic, that part of food originating on the farm (in contrast to the modern processing and service aspects which consumers do not differentiate from food per se) requires a smaller consumer outlay. With respect to the farm-originated portion of food, consumers can buy the same amount with a smaller expenditure; or they can upgrade the quality with the same expenditure by purchasing a different mix of grades and commodities. Although the decline in real food price has been fairly well hidden by the increased cost of added services and processing of food for which consumer demand elasticity has been high, the real price of food has fallen sharply over recent decades, and is now only about a third of the 1929 level.[9]

In addition the consuming and nonfarm sectors gain as labor is released from agriculture and migrates to produce the commodities and services in other sectors. Consuming society has both more food produced with less labor and more of other products produced from the transferred labor. Further, with a net migration of people from agriculture, capital also flows from farms and rural communities in the form of investment in the skills and education of the migrants and the capital inheritances accumulated in agriculture taken with them. These forms of capital, estimated at $16 to 20 billion annually, represent a net one-way flow simply because few people migrate occupationally and geographically from metropolitan centers into farming.

9. Heady, *Food, Agriculture and Public Policy*, p. 29.

Thus rapid technological progress and supply advances in farming would bring two types of gains to consumers but would bring reduced incomes to commercial farmers under the inelastic demand for food in a competitive market. Numerous methods could be used to compensate farmers and replaced farm workers to make them as well or better off while leaving gains from the process with consumers. From the standpoint of various criteria, some would be more efficient and others less efficient than land retirement as the basic policy mechanisms. However it can be shown that private and public investments to advance farm technology can bring simultaneous gains to consumers and commercial farmers through higher net income, given appropriate supply restraint programs. If, under technological advance, supply is let out slowly relative to growth in population and demand, a greater quantity can be sold without a proportionately greater reduction in price. Consumers can still gain from a reduced price for food, a reduced input to output ratio on farms, and labor and land released from farms for other employment and uses. Farmers can gain from a greater revenue and reduced real costs of production.[10] But without appropriate policies, the combination of rapid farm technical advance and inelastic food demand results in gain for consumers-at-large, but loss for the mass of farmers (although selected small groups of consumers may not gain, and equally selective small groups of farmers may gain). Policies to meet the market environment of the commercial farm sector thus have an equity basis; but particular policies which can be justified on an equity basis and attain these goals for commercial farmers need not guarantee similar economic equity for replaced farm workers and nonfarm rural people with reduced incomes. Commercial farm policies employed to date have made few contributions to rural communities affected by the same technological advances which give rise to the need for policies which attain or restore equity for commercial farmers.

Compensatory policies to offset the rapid effects of developmental policies in agriculture can bring equity to producers of the major farm commodities. If they are so used, it is inconsistent that they should restore equity or gain to some strata of farmers but cause sacrifices for other farmers and groups of the rural community. It seems no more acceptable that consumers should gain through a sacrifice by commercial farmers than that policies should be used to bring gains to farmers of one region or commodity through a sacrifice in income by farmers of other regions or commodities, or losses to other groups in rural communities. A variety of agricultural policies could do so; even a variety of agricultural supply control programs could do so; and even more specifically, individual types of land retirement programs could have this out-

10. For an algebraic illustration of these conditions, see: Earl O. Heady, *Agricultural Policy under Economic Development* (Ames: Iowa State Univ. Press, 1962), pp. 157–84; Earl O. Heady, Productivity, farm policy and income, pp. 170–89, in *Farmers in the Market Economy*, CAED (Ames: Iowa State Univ. Press, 1964).

come. The potential of gains to some groups through sacrifices by others causes restraints on the types of agricultural programs which are feasible, desirable, or publicly acceptable. Perhaps it is this potential that causes a particular policy format to become embedded and rather inflexible after it has been in effect for a period of time. The benefits of a particular program such as a specific land retirement pattern soon become capitalized in the value of land and other fixed assets. A newly formulated program may bring gains to others previously bypassed in agricultural policies, but cause a loss in capitalized gains to still others and thus upset the balance in the distribution of gains and sacrifices of a past policy. For example, a land retirement program which transferred large surplus acreages from field crops to grass for grazing would bring gain to crop-livestock farmers at the expense of range cattle producers. A shift in programs to reduce wheat and cotton acreage but allow expansion of feed grains on the same acreage poses the same redistribution of benefits among various commodity groups. Or a shift from a dispersed pattern of land retirement, such as characterized by current programs, to a regionally concentrated program could leave farmers as well or better off, through various compensation schemes, but cause merchants and other nonfarm persons in the regions of retired farms to sacrifice in employment and income.

These are the types of considerations which place restraints on the economic and political acceptability of variously proposed agricultural policies. They are important and should not be neglected when other criteria such as public costs, decision freedom, and market orientation are applied in evaluating farm programs.

LAND RETIREMENT ALTERNATIVES ● As previously outlined, land retirement as a means of supply control and price restoration has been the basic policy instrument used in attempts to guarantee equity to commercial farmers under the technological and demand conditions summarized above. As a policy means, land retirement does not have unanimous consent among all farm organization and commodity groups and political parties, nor has it been first choice as the preferred policy format by all farm-related groups or recent federal administrations. One major farm group has pressed for free markets or long-term land retirement in preference to short-term land diversion programs. Another farm organization has placed priority on restricted farm marketings in contrast to a reliance on supply control through land retirement. Some producer groups have voted marketing quotas rather than acreage reductions upon themselves. Secretary of Agriculture Clinton Anderson proposed direct payments and unrestrained marketings. Secretary Ezra Taft Benson emphasized subsidized food exports, commodity storage, and unrestrained marketings. Secretary Orville Freeman proposed marketing quotas and put the proposal to the test at the polls. Still, even with this variety of priorities and proposals by different farm groups and administrations, land retirement as a means of supply control and price restoration has been, and has prospects of being the continuing foundation of U.S. agricultural policy. Hence later studies emphasizing quantitative aspects of land retirement programs are brought together to extend knowledge and understanding of their alternatives, consequences, and potentials. Land retirement is not proposed as an optimal and composite farm policy format; neither is it condemned as being "among the worst of the lot." It is selected for particular analysis since it has had political acceptance, has long been the foundation of domestic policy, and has prospects of continuing in this role.

Land retirement is only one of many instruments which could be used in solving the income problems for commercial agriculture which stem from the one type of substitution, namely the substitution of capital technology for land. It is a mechanism to solve problems revolving around this substitution but has little to contribute to solving problems which stem from the other type of substitution—the substitution of capital technology for labor. As mentioned previously, land retirement is neither the "worst" nor the "best" of a longer list of policy alternatives which might include direct subsidies to farmers (such as the deficiency payments to English farmers), marketing quotas (as used for some fruits and vegetables in the United States), farmer marketing boards with legislated power to bargain in prices and establish producer quotas (as used in several countries), exports of publicly purchased surpluses, direct payments to individuals rather than those related to the inputs and outputs of farming, transfer payments to assist reemployment of disadvantaged farmers in other occupations, and early retirements (as exercised in Sweden and Holland), or use of the market to bring equilibrium to prices, incomes, and numbers of farmers, and other types of programs. Along with land retirement, any individual program or combination of programs in this group could absorb as many farmer and public funds as are now spent on farm programs.

It is true however that land retirement used to control supply and provide price and income restoration has been the basic policy instrument. There are two reasons why this is the likely format for several years: first, the general public is willing to provide treasury funds at the level required for these types of programs; and second, the several farm groups seem to be better able to agree on and accept land retirement over many other alternatives that they individually propose. While a few scattered complaints are expressed, any organized or massive move on the part of the public or its representatives to reduce the Treasury costs of farm programs and remove the modest restraints on supply are lacking. It is even possible that if an effective coalition were formed among farm organizations, the rural community population, and farm operators, society-at-large would be willing to invest even more in achieving a broader equity throughout the rural sector and in enlarging economic opportunities for its members. As among competing farm and commodity groups, political and economic conflict over programs makes it easier to add a few patches here and there but continue the same general format than to agree on a wholly new program.

While some program elements have been expanded greatly relative to others, this has been the mold for the last four decades. The existing policy format apparently is not considered "first best" by the current or previous administration or by the majority of commodity and organizational groups that represent segments of agriculture. Yet in the same strategy context, it has been a "saddle point" which various political and economic groups accepted "as one of the better of the worst things that could happen to us." It is clear that to most groups these programs are optimal to none, but better than the potential payoffs of numerous other policy alternatives. But one additional point seems clear: The "game" may be much more among commodity, agribusiness, and farm organization groups as competitors than between consumers or taxpayers and farmers aggregately as the antagonists. With appropriate effort it is likely that consumers (taxpayers) and the farm public could arrive at unanimous consent in improved farm policies which better guarantee (1) market returns on resources used in agriculture, (2) equity within agriculture, and (3) improved economic opportunities for those of rural communities who prefer either or both occupational and geographic migration. But infighting among farm groups themselves will likely prevent this more optimal outcome.

TYPES AND TRADE-OFFS IN LAND RETIREMENT ● Land retirement programs are not "black and white" and "either, or" choices. Many types of programs are possible. They can be selected singly or in combination. They can be of short-run or long-run duration. They can be meshed to promote interests of both consumers (more land for recreation, etc.) and farmers (restricted output and higher prices) or one group alone. They can be implemented at higher or lower levels, regardless of their type, to bring greater or more modest farm prices and income. They can be on a whole-farm or a partial-farm basis. They can be concentrated regionally in consistency with land productivity and markets, or they can be dispersed interregionally regardless of comparative advantage. They could be on a voluntary basis as with feed grains in the 1960s or on a compulsory basis as with tobacco for several decades. As with the feed grains, wheat, and cotton programs of the 1960s they can be tied to allotments and bases for individual crops. Or, as under the set-aside program of the 1970s, they can relate to an aggregation of the farm's crop production potentials. They can be phased in quickly or in a lagged manner. The United States has combined most of these alternatives in some "mix" over time. Examples include compulsory acreage quotas for tobacco and voluntary participation for feed grains, whole-farm participation under the Conservation Reserve Program and partial-farm engagement under the original Agricultural Adjustment Act, long-term contracts under the Cropland Adjustment Program, and annual contracts for recent diversion programs. However, major reliance has been placed on voluntary land retirements on a partial-farm basis dispersed interregionally under annual contracts in recent programs.

Among land retirement possibilities, government costs for payments and community social costs for adjustments follow a fairly definite pattern depending on the nature of the program. While other types (and "degrees" or variations of the same) of programs could be listed, government costs for land retirement are generally of descending magnitude from first to last of the following: (1) annual land retirement on a partial-farm basis dispersed over all major crop-producing regions, (2) annual land retirement on a whole-farm basis interregionally dispersed, (3) whole-farm retirement allowed to concentrate partly on a regional basis but restrained to some interregional dispersement, and (4) whole-farm retirement concentrated by regions of least comparative advantage in production on a long-time basis. The public costs of land retirement and the consequent degree of supply control and price improvement suggested can vary considerably among such alternatives with the first being most costly. Costs decline as participation shifts from a partial-farm to a whole-farm basis for these reasons: With only part of the farm retired, the usual fixed costs of operation continue and the farmer must cover these along with his normal profit margin in the level of payment. But if he retires the entire farm, he can eliminate the fixed costs of operation, transfer the capital so represented to investment elsewhere, and take alternative employment. Older farmers can simply retire their farms instead of renting them out. For similar reasons, program costs decline as the length of the contract increases. Under a ten-year arrangement, fixed costs of operation cease for at least this period if the entire farm is "put in." The certainty under a long-term contract lowers the cost of participation over the uncertainty of annual contracts. As land retirement is allowed to concentrate on more marginal land or that of lowest comparative advantage the cost to attain a given reduction in output declines because yields are not in proportion to operational costs. Aside from level of fertilization and such intensification variables, the operational costs are about the same for an acre of one-hundred-bushel corn as for an acre of fifty-bushel yield. The margin above costs for the latter is less than proportional to yield, and if it serves as the formulation of payment, the cost per bushel of supply control therefore is less on land of low yield.[11]

In contrast to public costs of participation, however, the community

11. Also, other items such as age, the margin of profit between the last increment of fertilizer inputs on productive land, the proximity of alternative employment, the existence of underemployment in farming, consideration of farming opportunities for tenants, and other factors can also affect the ratio of payments for participation to the amount of production control obtained for the payment.

(social) costs of adjustment generally have a reversed magnitude: namely they increase from the first through the fourth of the types of land retirement previously discussed. If land is retired on a partial-farm, annual basis in all regions, farm enlargement is not speeded up, nor is the exodus of the farm population (but neither do these programs do much to stop the process). On the other hand, if all the land in a region is taken out of crops on a whole-farm basis for a long period, the impact in the short run is enormous. The ongoing process of farm consolidation and labor replacement is accentuated. Under more extensive organization, farms have to be larger, and fewer farm families prevail in the community. The result is a multiplier effect throughout the community as the farm-based volume of capital and consumption purchases declines. Employment and economic opportunities in the nonfarm sector of the rural community diminish accordingly. These are the secondary costs, already going on with the structural adjustment of farming under advancing technology, which could be speeded up with more extensive land retirement or cropland shifts in particular regions or areas. Other secondary or social costs are also implied, although they are already involved as farms become larger and fewer, and a smaller farm labor force prevails. Whole-farm retirement of course poses the possibility that landowners can be made as well or better off by land retirement, but that tenant farming opportunities are eliminated.

Competing and Complementary Variables ● Each type of land retirement program has one set of conditions or features which we could call the "control" or "input" variables. It also has a set of effects which we could call the "result" or "output" variables. The control or input variables include the payment rate per acre, the time period of the contract, the number of acres retired, the location of land retired, and similar items. The result or output variables include the level of prices attained, the magnitude of supply, the income of participating farmers, the income of nonparticipating farmers, the total government program costs, amount of surplus going into storage or public exports, and gains or losses to nonfarm persons in rural areas. A change or rearrangement in the input variables will cause the output variables to move in different directions. Some will increase and some will decrease; never will they all move in the same direction. A lower national payment rate per acre for long-term contracts on a regional basis can make participating landowners better off, control supply, and lessen government payments. But it will generally concentrate the secondary costs of farm adjustment on particular nonfarm groups in the rural community affected. These are the types of substitutions or trade-offs involved among the output variables as the input variables are changed to give rise to different types or combinations of land retirement programs. The farm and general public must decide on the value or weights to be attached to the output variables, and thus on the combination which will be selected. Taking any two of the output variables (although the whole set should be considered simultaneously), the relationship will usually be that illustrated schematically in Figure 1.1. If programs are rearranged (the input variables are altered) to lessen social costs to the nonfarm population in rural communities and minimize disturbances in income distribution among regional and commodity groups (i.e., as we move down the curve), increasing rates of sacrifice must be made in Treasury costs of programs. On the other hand, if they are rearranged to lessen Treasury costs (i.e., a movement up the curve) an increasing sacrifice must be made in the form of adjustment costs forced on the nonfarm population of rural communities. Land retirement programs of the kind used in the 1930s or the 1960s provide two points on this curve. "Conservation Reserve" types of programs fall at a higher point and certain long-term regional programs of another type would fall even higher. The optimal point (combination of programs) on this curve can be determined only by the general society of farmers, nonfarm rural people, and taxpayers (i.e., through their collective welfare function if such a function can even be reflected through the political process). But for an optimal choice to be made, information must be provided on the costs, income distribution effects, rural community costs, and other impacts of many alternative land retirement programs, as well as on the magnitude of changes required in the corresponding input variables.

Even for a given format of regionally dispersed, annual land retirement program, a different pattern of output variables will be involved as the input variables are arranged in different magnitudes and patterns. For example, a lowering of two input variables, per acre payment rates and acreage diverted, is expected to have the following effects on out-

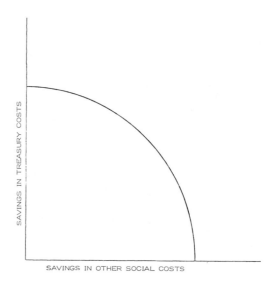

Fig. 1.1. Trade-offs between Treasury costs and other costs (social costs of nonfarm population in rural communities, etc.) for land retirement programs to attain given levels of supply control and commodity prices.

SAVINGS IN TREASURY COSTS

SAVINGS IN OTHER SOCIAL COSTS

put variables: reduction of farmer participation, reduction of income of participants, and increase in stocks moving into storage. An increase in per acre payments and land diverted would push these same output variables in the opposite directions but would also increase government costs. Even with an interregionally dispersed program such as we have at the present, a change of input variables to allow whole-farm participation on a long-term basis would have these expected effects on output variables: increase in income of participants, reduction of farming opportunities for tenants, reduction of government costs of farm programs, and some speedup of farm outmigration.

We have little knowledge of the amount, and even of the direction in some cases, in which different results or output variables change as the control variables are altered within a given program or among programs. Or given some final decision on the optimal mix of output variables, a state not yet attained, we still know little about changes in input variables necessary to reach this combination or objective. In general this is the state of policy making and decision. It must be initiated in the absence of relevant and appropriate quantitative analysis. Accordingly the studies which follow have been drawn together to provide greater quantitative knowledge on the trade-offs involved in alternative kinds and application levels of land retirement programs. By no means do they provide all the details on the inputs and outputs involved and useful for final policy selection. Neither are they posed as systematic models of the input and output variables, as compared to other approaches which might be possible. They do however provide more detail than previously available on land retirement programs. It is from data such as these that the interested public must establish the respective weights or values to be attached to the different effects (output variables) and relate these weights to the rate at which the effects substitute for or replace each other in the trade-offs involved in policy selection. Along with these weights, information for decision also relates to the magnitude of input or control variables. The studies provide conformation in these respects which has not been available previously, but not in the final degree which would be useful.

Many aspects and results of land retirement programs remain to be studied. Possibilities for detailed study would include the effects of current and alternative land retirement programs on land values, the distribution of payments among individual farmers, and the effect of payments and price guarantees for land retirement in encouraging farm enlargement. The current studies do not deal with these facets of land retirement programs. Instead we examine characteristics and results such as effects of the location, term of contract, payment rates, and level of participation or supply control on government costs, farm income, regional concentration of supply control, community costs of land retirement, and similar items.

Future Capacity and Resource Requirements of Agriculture

DESIGNING APPROPRIATE AGRICULTURAL POLICIES for the future depends partly on the prospective supply and demand conditions for agriculture. During the mid-1960s a belief suddenly evolved that by the 1970s governmental control policies for agriculture would no longer be needed. This expectation was based on projected increases in world population and the possibility that it might become translated into demand for U.S. farm products. The most optimistic persons even considered the possibility that growth in domestic population and per capita incomes and elimination of malnutrition in the United States could lift demand to levels where supply control and other price support programs would no longer be necessary.

Projections of a doubling of world population between 1965 and 2000 to around 7 billion people and the potential elimination of hunger for that majority of the world's people who now suffer malnutrition imply either great increases in food production in the developing countries or greatly enlarged international trade in food commodities. Whether this projected large increase in world demand for food ever becomes a reality depends on the following: (1) policies of population control exercised in developing countries, (2) their own national ability to increase food production and meet the food demand, (3) the pace of economic development and trade enabling them to finance greater imports, and (4) whether or not the United States or other countries and organizations are willing to finance food shipments to them. How these four variables will move over the next twenty years cannot be predicted accurately at this time. It depends on the population and food production policies implemented by nations with rapid population growth and lagging food production. Unfolding evidence suggests that population control could be successful if pursued vigorously.[1] Also developing trends in food production and the surge of the "green revolution" in Asia provide hope on the food supply side.[2] The important point is of course that the only sensible thing is for the less developed countries to initiate and implement effective policies on both the demand and supply sides. To let population growth progress unabated and fill the food gap through U.S. or other assistance does not solve these problems and only postpones the day of calamity. Eventually the capacity of U.S. agriculture would be exhausted and there would be even more people in the world to starve or suffer the misery of hunger. It is unlikely that citizens of the United States are going to commit themselves to finance ever larger food shipments to countries with ineffective population policies.

Even with the ongoing PL 480 program, U.S. publicly assisted exports have been declining in recent years. The total of government assisted wheat exports reached a peak of 569 million bushels in 1965 (43 percent of U.S. production) but declined to 471 million (31 percent of production) in 1967 and 240 million (16 percent of production) in 1969. Government assisted feed grain exports reached 4.6 million tons in the 1966 export year, but declined to 2.0 million tons in the 1968 export year.

From the standpoint of U.S. farm income, it would be better to underestimate world food demand in the decade ahead and gear domestic farm policies accordingly, than to overestimate demand and legislate an end to domestic policies. If the latter approach were used but an avalanche of world demand did not develop, U.S. farmers would find themselves with a mammoth flow of output, inadequate markets, and depressed prices and income. On the other hand, if the first approach is used and demand proves to be much larger than expected, retired land can quickly be put back into crop production. A year of lag might prevail in gearing up for the unexpected large demand, but farm prices would similarly rise to a high level. In two or three years the land could be back in operation and prices would turn toward a new equilibrium level.

SUPPLY CAPACITY AND POLICY NEEDS ● If world food demand were to explode year after next, the preferable farm policy would certainly be to maintain present policies. The need for these policies would soon expire and there would be little justification for the expense and bother of shifting to completely new programs or even of modifying existing ones. On the other hand, since present policies are essentially short run, inaugurated at earlier times when farm supply-demand imbalances

1. Donald J. Bogue, The prospects for world population control, pp. 72–85, in *Alternatives for Balancing World Food Production and Needs*, CAED (Ames: Iowa State Univ. Press, 1967).

2. Willard W. Cochrane, *The World Food Problem: A Guardedly Optimistic View* (New York: T. Y. Crowell, 1969).

were temporary, a shift to an outlook based on expected long-term "surplus" capacity would change the policy situation. The public might prefer modifications of programs to better achieve long-run solutions to the capacity problem. Such a shift could allow the nation to attack the economic and social problems of rural communities which result from (1) capital-labor substitution and reduction in farm numbers, (2) inadequacy of vocational training and education in rural areas, (3) the relative concentration of poverty in rural communities, and (4) increasing costs and declining supply of certain health, education, and welfare services in rural communities.

Hence this chapter deals with prospective food production in the United States over the next decade. We estimate the nation's ability to produce food in 1980 and attempt to provide the basis for answering the following questions: Will the American farm industry continue to be faced with large surplus capacity, or will its ability to produce soon be absorbed by growing international trade in foodstuffs? How long must the nation wait for world food demand to absorb our reserve capacity? What amount of reserve production capacity will be returned to production under alternative levels of world food aid and exports or under alternative domestic policies? Will the structure of agriculture continue to change? What farm size and capital investment are in prospect? More specifically, the foci of the analysis are these:

1. To determine regional and national land requirements for grain and cotton production under several projected levels of export demand for 1980
2. To determine national levels and regional allocation of livestock and poultry production necessary to meet projected domestic meat, poultry, milk, and egg requirements for 1980
3. To determine the regional labor requirements for farm labor associated with each alternative level of crop and livestock production in 1980
4. To determine the regional capital needs for agriculture under each farm policy model and demand level
5. To evaluate the comparative efficiencies of various types of farm policies and programs in producing the total quantity of agricultural output projected for 1980

To estimate the effect of different programs on production capacity, surplus acreage, and export potentials, we make the analysis under the simulation of several types of farm programs including both land retirement and other types of programs. The specific types of farm programs analyzed are (1) a simulated free market with and without cotton quotas, (2) a simulated feed grain program, (3) acreage quotas with continuation of export subsidies, and (4) acreage quotas assuming termination of export subsidy programs. The effect of each of these programs on regional allocation of crop production is also analyzed. Readers not interested in the following detail of the models used may turn to the sections on results which can be understood without a review of the methods used.

METHODS OF STUDY ● While emphasis is on grain and cotton production, the scope of this study includes the total agricultural economy of the United States. A summary of the methods used follows.

Crop Acreages ● Production and location of major crops are estimated through the use of a multi-regional linear programming model which minimizes the cost of producing and transporting projected levels of crop output for future years. For application of the model, the United States is divided into 160 producing regions and 31 consuming regions. Five possible crop-producing activities are defined for each region. These activities include production of such crops as wheat, feed grains, feed grains-soybean rotation, soybeans, and cotton (including both cotton lint and cottonseed). To reduce the computation burden, regions which have characteristically planted less than 25 percent of their available cropland to these crops are excluded from the multi-regional model, and the estimated production from the excluded regions is deducted from the total demand for each commodity. As a result, the model contains 144 producing regions and 31 consuming regions. These regions are shown in Figures 2.1 and 2.2.

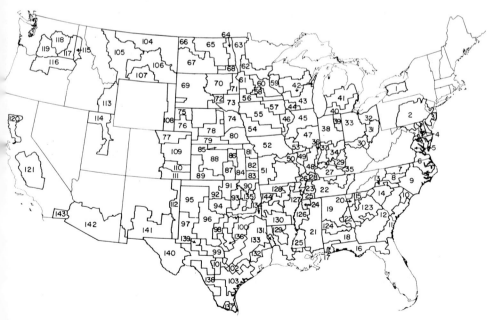

Fig. 2.1. Spatial location of producing regions.

Fig. 2.2. Spatial location of consuming regions.

The mathematical model used in this study can be summarized as follows:

$$\text{Minimize } f(c) = \sum_{i=1}^{144} \sum_{j=1}^{5} c_{ij} X_{ij} + \sum_{k=1}^{31} s_k W_k$$

$$+ \sum_{g=1}^{3} \sum_{k=1}^{31} \sum_{k'=1}^{31} z_{gkk'} T_{gkk'} \qquad (2.1)$$

where

c_{ij} = the cost per unit of the j-th crop activity in the i-th producing region; i represents the 144 crop-producing regions shown in Figure 2.1; and j represents the five crop-producing activities:

j = 1 = wheat
j = 2 = feed grains
j = 3 = feed grains–soybean rotation
j = 4 = soybeans
j = 5 = cotton

X_{ij} = level of the j-th activity in the i-th producing region
s_k = cost of transferring wheat to feed grains in the k-th con-

Note: Typewriter composition has been used for the more complex notation in this book.

suming region; k represents the 31 consuming regions shown in Figure 2.2.

W_k = quantity of wheat transferred into feed grains in the k-th consuming region

$z_{gkk'}$ = cost of transporting a unit of the g-th commodity from the k-th consuming region to the k'-th consuming region; k represents the 31 consuming regions as before; k' is defined likewise except that $k \neq k'$; and g represents the three commodities:

$$g = 1 = \text{wheat}$$
$$g = 2 = \text{feed grains}$$
$$g = 3 = \text{oilmeals}$$

$T_{gkk'}$ = level of the g-th commodity transported from (or to) the k-th consuming region to (or from) the k'-th consuming region

Given the above objective function, the model is subject to a total cropland restraint in each of the 144 crop-producing regions as follows:

$$a_{ij}X_{ij} \leq L_i \qquad (2.2)$$

where

a_{ij} = input-output coefficient which designates the amount of the restraint L required per unit of the j-th activity in the i-th crop-producing region

L_i = total acres of cropland available for crop production in the i-th region

X_{ij} = same as above

Under this particular model, crop production in each region is restrained only by total cropland. Within this particular set of restraints, production of each crop is allocated among the 144 regions according to the per unit costs for producing a unit of the j-th crop activity. The five crop activities compete on a cost basis for the given acres of cropland in each region.

To add more realism to the model, other restraints are included. To meet the agronomic requirement (as discussed later) that cropland cannot be continuously planted to soybeans, the following restraint is placed on soybeans:

$$a_{i4}X_{i4} \leq l_i \text{ for } i = 1, 2, \ldots, 144 \qquad (2.3)$$

where

l_i = acres of cropland available for soybeans in the i-th region
where $l_i = 0.5L_i$
a_{i4} = input-output coefficient for soybeans in the i-th region
X_{i4} = level of the soybean activity in the i-th region

In addition to meeting agronomic requirements, certain policy models require restrictions on acreages of individual crops. To simulate these restrictions, the following restraints are added to the model:

$$a_{ij}X_{ij} \leq Q_{ij} \text{ for } i = 1, 2, \ldots, 144; \text{ and all } j \neq 4 \qquad (2.4)$$

where

Q_{ij} = acres of allotment or quota in the i-th region for the j-th crop under a particular farm program
a_{ij} = quantity of restraint Q required per unit of X
X_{ij} = level of the j-th crop activity in the i-th region

In addition, the levels of output (the projected demands are discrete quantities) required of each policy model form the following additional set of restraints:

$$D_{ik} \leq \sum_{i=1}^{n_k} y_{i1}X_{i1} - q_kW_k \pm \sum_{k=1}^{31}\sum_{k'=1}^{31} b_{1kk'}T_{1kk'} \qquad (2.5)$$

$$D_{2k} \leq \sum_{i=1}^{n_k} y_{i2}X_{i2} + \sum_{i=1}^{n_k} y_{i3}X_{i3} + q_kW_k$$

$$\pm \sum_{k=1}^{31}\sum_{k'=1}^{31} b_{2kk'}T_{2kk'} \qquad (2.6)$$

$$D_{3k} \leq \sum_{i=1}^{n_k} y_{i3}X_{i3} + \sum_{i=1}^{n_k} y_{i4}X_{i4} + \sum_{i=1}^{n_k} y_{i5}X_{i5}$$

$$+ \sum_{k=1}^{31}\sum_{k'=1}^{31} b_{3kk'}T_{3kk'} \qquad (2.7)$$

$$D_c \leq \sum_{i=1}^{144} y_{i5}X_{i5} \qquad (2.8)$$

where

D_{1k} = demand for wheat in the k-th consuming region
D_{2k} = demand for feed grains in the k-th consuming region
D_{3k} = demand for oilmeals in the k-th consuming region
D_c = national demand for cotton lint
n_k = number of producing regions in the k-th consuming region
y_{ij} = output per unit (yield per acre) of the j-th crop activity in i-th producing region
$bg_{kk'}$ = quantity of the g-th commodity transported from (or to) the k-th consuming region to (or from) the k'-th consuming region per unit of T-th transportation activity
q_k = quantity of wheat transferred to feed grains in the k-th consuming region per unit of the W-th wheat activity

All other notation is as defined above. Finally, the following conditions must hold:

$$X_{ij} \geq 0 \tag{2.9}$$
$$W_k \geq 0 \tag{2.10}$$
$$T_{gkk'} \geq 0 \tag{2.11}$$

In abbreviated form, the programming model used in this study can be shown as

$$f(x) = cx' \tag{2.12}$$

where the x's are subject to the restraints

$$Ax' \geq b' \tag{2.13}$$
$$x \geq 0 \tag{2.14}$$

Minimizing $f(x)$, a set of x's exists such that the total value of $f(x)$ is a minimum where the elements of the vector x represent the activity levels of production, transfer, and transportation of grain and fiber activities and the elements of vector c represent the costs of each of the various activities included in the problem. As indicated previously, the vector x includes elements to represent (1) potential acreages of the 5 specified crop-producing activities in 144 crop-producing regions, (2) quantities of wheat transferred to feed grains in each of the 31 consuming regions, and (3) quantities of grains and oilmeals in each of the 1,336 transportation activities for transporting wheat, feed grains, and oilmeals between the 31 consuming regions. When this model is solved for a unique x, the acreage and location of each major crop in the 144 producing regions are specified for a given level of output.

Product Prices ● For each solution of the preceding set of equations, a valuable by-product is a set of programmed equilibrium prices for each of the four commodities. In this model, programmed prices are determined for wheat, feed grains, and oilmeals for each of the thirty-one consuming regions of the United States. These prices are shadow prices in a least-cost linear programming context and represent the cost of producing a unit of the commodity in the highest cost-producing region supplying a given consuming region. If in-shipments of the commodity are required to satisfy the level of demand in a consuming region, transportation costs are included in the product price. In addition, if cropland in the highest cost-producing region supplying a given demand region represents a scarce factor of production, there will be an accrual of land rent as a result of the scarcity; this land rent will also be included in the product prices. If the scarcity is artificially created by restraints for a specific farm program, this additional cost will increase the price of the product. In sum, the programmed product price (P) for the i-th commodity in the j-th region is equal to

$$P_{ij} = \frac{c_p + c_i + l_r + q_r}{Y_{ij}} \tag{2.15}$$

where

c_p = cost per acre of producing the j-th crop in the highest cost-producing region

c_t = transportation cost (if any) of transporting Y units (where Y_{ij} is the yield of the j-th crop in the highest cost-producing region) of the commodity from the k-th consuming region to the k'-th consuming region $(k \neq k')$

l_r = land rent (if any) in the highest cost-producing region

q_r = rent on quotas (if existent) in the highest cost-producing region

A set of programmed crop prices, land rents, and quota rents is derived simultaneously in each solution to the mathematical model. Solving for the magnitude of these variables completes the first phase of this study.

Labor Man-Hours ● In phase two of the study, labor requirements are estimated for (1) producing the acreages of crops specified in phase one, (2) producing the quantities of livestock and livestock products specified for a projected 1980 population of 243.4 million persons in the continental United States, and (3) producing crops other than those in the formal model, minor classes of livestock, and labor for overhead purposes.

Labor requirements are estimated by two methods: for food grains, feed grains, oilcrops, cotton, and tobacco, a per acre labor input require-

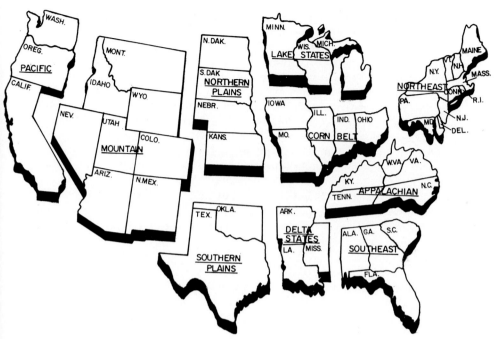

Fig. 2.3. The ten farm production regions of the United States.

ment for 1980 is estimated for each of the ten farm production regions shown in Figure 2.3.[3]

Labor requirements (L) per acre for wheat, feed grains, soybeans, cotton, and tobacco are projected with 1944–65 regional data using the functional form

$$L = at^b \qquad (2.16)$$

where t represents time and, in logarithmic form, becomes

$$\log L = \log a + b \log t \qquad (2.17)$$

For the above data, the function decreases at a decreasing rate.

Labor requirements for meat animals, dairy products, poultry and eggs, and other crops, including hay and forage, fruits and nuts, vegetables, and sugar, are estimated by using a system of ratio estimates based on (1) total output for each commodity, (2) output per man-hour for each commodity, and (3) total man-hours used for the commodity in

3. For a breakdown of states in each region and background data, see U.S. Dept. of Agriculture, Changes in Farm Production and Efficiency, USDA ERS *Statistical Bulletin* 233, supplements 1–4, 1966.

a base period. The estimates of total output and output per man-hour are reduced to an index form.

In addition to labor requirements for major uses, future labor required for minor crops, minor livestock commodities, and overhead needs are estimated by projecting past trends to continue to 1980.

Capital Requirements ● The third phase of this study involves estimating capital requirements for the agricultural sector in 1980. Estimates are made for three major categories of capital: (1) land and buildings, (2) machinery and equipment, and (3) livestock inventories, including cattle and calves, sheep and lambs, and hogs.

REAL ESTATE VALUES. The value of land and buildings is projected to 1980 under each of the various policy models. First, a base set of land and building values is developed for each of the ten farm production regions under the assumption that the same types of land retirement programs are continued in 1980 as were in effect in 1970. This set of estimates is then functionally related to the set of shadow prices for land in the linear programming (policy) model which also assumes continuation of 1970 type of land diversion programs. This particular set of shadow prices forms a base for calculating an index of cropland value using shadow prices from each of the other policy models.

Since only major cropland on farms is included in the programming models, but land values are projected for all land in farms, estimates are required of the proportion of total farmland affected by a change in land rent for each crop and given policy model. For this purpose, the proportion of total farmland in major crops under each policy model is calculated for each farm production region. These proportions are then used as estimates of the proportion of total land in farms affected by a particular farm program.

The algebraic form used to compute regional real estate values is the following:

$$V_i = [(r_n/r_o - 1.0)\ (P) + 1.0]v_i \qquad (2.18)$$

where

V_i = value of land and buildings for the i-th farm production region, with a particular farm program and level of ouput
r_n = new rent
r_o = old rent
P = proportion of total farmland in major crops for each of the ten farm production regions
v_i = value of land and buildings for the i-th farm production region in the base model

This formulation makes changes in the value of land and buildings a function of economic rent to cropland.[4] As an example of the computational form used, let us assume that under continuation of present programs in 1980 the total value of land and buildings in region A is projected to be $4,000; land rent per crop acre is $5.00; and the crops in the model use 50 percent of the total land in farms in the region. These data provide the base set of estimates for calculating the change in land and building values for the remaining policy models. Now let us assume that land rent is $7.50 per acre under a different policy model. The equation for calculating the new land and building values is as follows:

$$V_{lb} = [(7.50/5.00 - 1.0) (.50) + 1.0] (4,000) \qquad (2.19)$$

where V_{lb} is the value of land and buildings in region A under the alternative policy model. In this example, the increase in land rent is 50 percent $(7.50/5.00 - 1.0)$; and, since only 50 percent of the land in the region is affected, the expected change in average land and building values is 25 percent $[(.50) (.50)]$. Adding this increase to the base period value of land and buildings, the new value of land and buildings is $[(\$4,000) (125)] = \$5,000$. Each of the ten farm production regions is calculated similarly, and all regions are added for a total value of land and buildings in the United States.

MACHINERY VALUES. The investment in machinery and equipment on farms in 1980 is estimated from a set of demand equations in which the quantity of machinery used by farmers is a function of (1) the ratio of machinery prices to farm wage rate, (2) the man-hours of labor used for all farm work, (3) the acres of cropland harvested, (4) the number of farms, and (5) the time or level of technology. By including the cropland-harvested variable, it is possible to use acreages from the policy models of phase one. In addition, the number of man-hours of labor associated with each of the models is an independent variable in the demand equations. Capital requirements for machinery are estimated for each of the output levels and policy models in the study.

LIVESTOCK VALUES. Estimated livestock inventory values are based on the total hundredweight of red meat produced in each of the ten farm production regions in 1980, multiplied by the average 1963–65 investment per hundredweight of red meat produced. These values assume that capital intensity in livestock production remains the same through 1980 in each production region.

4. Other factors affecting real estate values are also recognized but are not evaluated in this study. For such an analysis, see John E. Reynolds and John F. Timmons, Factors Affecting Farmland Values in the United States, *Research Bulletin* 566, Iowa State Univ., Ames, February 1969.

After completing the individual estimates, capital requirements for land and buildings, machinery and equipment, and livestock inventories are then summed within each region and over all farm production regions to give an estimate of total capital requirements for these farm inputs in 1980. Estimates are based on 1965 prices for all inputs. Total capital requirements for 1980 are estimated under the different demand levels and alternative farm programs used in the study. The capital estimates also are computed on a per farm basis for each of the ten regions.

Resource Parameters ● Parameters for the basic linear programming model are estimated for both the 144 crop-producing regions and the 31 consuming regions. The following parameters are estimated for 144 crop-producing regions of the United States: (1) total cropland available for production or nonuse, (2) crop yields for each of the specified crops, and (3) production costs for each of these crops. Domestic demand levels and transportation costs between regions for each of the grain commodities are estimated for the 31 consuming regions. The analysis concentrates on the effects of changing the following variables: (1) export levels for wheat, feed grains, soybeans and soybean oilmeal, cottonseed meal, and cotton lint, and (2) variation in the type of farm programs used to control or stimulate production of major crops.

CROPLAND AVAILABLE. Land available for each of the specified crops is assumed to equal the maximum acreages which have been harvested in past years. Since not all crops are included, it is necessary to estimate available acreage for only those crops which are included in the study. Other crops are allocated a land base similar to that occupied in the past years.

Harvested acres and land idled from production under government programs for the seven crops included in the model totaled 252 million acres in 1965. This base acreage is used as a maximum potential acreage for the crops listed. Summer fallow land is not included in the above figures because it is not used for crops in the year of fallow. Acreages for the 144-region model, as well as for the regions not included in the formal model, are shown in aggregate form in Table 2.1 for each of the 10 farm production regions. Data for 1950 and 1965 are included for comparison.

Land available in a given region depends on agronomic characteristics of individual crops. For example, in some regions present land-use practices allow continuous cropping of land for certain crops, notably wheat and corn. In other cases, land must be rotated among crops to preserve the productivity of the soil and to prevent (or as a result of) disease problems. In most states soybeans cannot be grown continuously; in the models, soybeans are restricted to 50 percent of the available cropland in any region.

Table 2.1 ● Cropland Available for Major Field Crops by Regions, Past and Projected

Region	1950	1965 (million acres)	1980
United States	226.3	252.3	251.1
Northeast	5.8	5.8	5.7
Lake States	20.7	24.7	24.7
Corn Belt	60.0	70.4	70.3
Northern Plains	56.8	60.7	60.6
Appalachian	11.7	11.7	11.6
Southeast	11.3	11.5	11.5
Delta States	10.1	11.4	11.3
Southern Plains	27.6	30.8	30.7
Mountain	14.3	17.0	16.4
Pacific	8.0	8.3	8.3

NOTE: Land base is for wheat, corn, oats, barley, grain sorghum, soybeans, and cotton. Other cropland used for fruits, vegetables, and minor crops is not included in the total. The figures do not include land devoted to tame hay in rotation with other crops or grown alone. However, the figures do include cropland idled under government programs in 1965.

Crop Yield Trends ● In making estimates of potential crop production for 1980, yields for the various crops had to be projected for that time. The methods used in projecting yields are explained below.

WHEAT YIELDS. As is evident from Figure 2.4, wheat yields for the United States have followed a fairly definite upward trend over the last twenty years, with some indication of a more rapid rise since 1953. Wheat acreage and production especially have been affected by government supply control programs. Planted acreage of wheat was reduced from 79 million acres in 1953 to 62 million acres under the control program of 1954. After 1954, legislative requirements reduced wheat acreage to a maximum of 55 million acres. As a result of legislation in 1961 which further reduced wheat acreage, planted acreage in 1962 dropped to 49 million acres. However, yields increased as acreage was decreased under government programs.

Two linear regression forms were fitted to 1940–65 wheat yield data for each of thirty-nine wheat states and the average yield for the United States. The first regression used was a simple linear equation with wheat yield as a function of time.

$$Y = a + bT \qquad (2.20)$$

where

Y = yield per acre of wheat
T = time, with 1941 = 1

The second linear regression included a dummy variable as

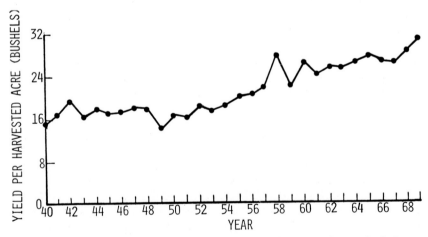

Fig. 2.4. *Yield per harvested acre of wheat in the United States, 1940–69.*

$$Y = a + bT + cD \qquad (2.21)$$

where

Y and T are defined as above
D = dummy variable to account for the increased slope of the
trend line since 1953 (i.e., 1940, . . . , 1953 = 0; 1954 = 1,
1955 = 2, . . . , 1965 = 12)

The latter function thus has the purpose of determining whether, in a practical sense, government programs have affected the per acre yield of wheat since 1953.

For the U.S. data, Equation (2.20) had an R^2 of 0.70 whereas Equation (2.21) had an R^2 of 0.84. All correlation coefficients were significant at the 0.01 level of probability, and the D variable explained a significant proportion of the variance in wheat yield over the period 1940–65.

Although Equation (2.21) gave a better fit for U.S. data, the results varied for the thirty-nine individual wheat-producing states. For twenty-two states, the regression coefficient for D was not significant at the 0.05 probability level; for nine states, it was at a borderline level; and for eight states it was significant. (The states which had a significant coefficient for the dummy variable were the more arid areas of the United States: North Dakota, South Dakota, Kansas, Oklahoma, Texas, Idaho, New Mexico, and Arizona.) These results suggest that government acreage programs which reduced wheat acreage after 1953 had an upward effect on yields in drier areas, but did not affect states with greater rainfall.

Since the dummy variable did not explain a significant proportion of variance of wheat yields in a majority of states, it was excluded in final projections. However, the results of the projection suggest that if acreage of wheat is again expanded in response to increased demand, states with limited rainfall may have lower yields as land less adapted to production is brought back into production. Since these more arid states produce a large proportion of the wheat crop, the national yield may likewise be affected. Equation (2.20) projects a national wheat yield of 32.3 bushels per acre in 1980.

FEED GRAINS YIELDS. The upward trend in feed grains yields has been rather sharp since 1954. Figure 2.5 shows that the average yield per acre for all feed grains increased from 0.70 tons in 1940 to 1.58 tons in 1965. The upward trend in yields evidently accelerated after 1954. Various studies have attempted to explain this trend. Shaw and Durost indicate that technology raised corn yields 1.34 bushels per acre between 1929 and 1962, and 1.46 bushels per acre over the period 1949–62.[5] Al-

5. L. H. Shaw and D. D. Durost, The Effect of Weather and Technology on Corn Yields in the Corn Belt, 1929–62, USDA ERS *Agricultural Economics Report* 80, 1965.

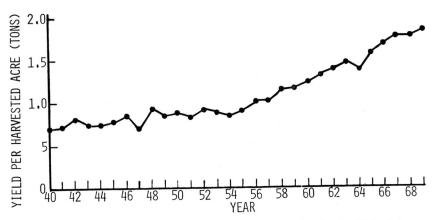

Fig. 2.5.   Yield per harvested acre of feed grains in the United States, 1940–69.

though the weather was normal for the total period, the corn yield was 0.7 bushels per acre above normal for the period 1949–62. Heady and Auer, in a study of the 1939–60 period, concluded that higher fertilizer application and variety improvement explained 69 percent of increased feed grains yields.[6] Location change, other technological improvements, and weather explained the remaining yield variance over this period.

From these studies, it appears that most of the upward trend in feed grains yields in recent years can be explained by new technology, and that weather was above normal over most of the 1960s. In projecting yields, it seems reasonable to assume that normal weather will prevail over any long period of time, and that technological innovations will continue. Thus the yields of corn, oats, and barley are projected to 1980 on the basis of yield trends for the period 1948–65; grain sorghum yields are projected on the basis of trends for the period 1940–65. The national projections for 1980 are corn, 99.4 bushels per acre; oats, 60 bushels per acre; barley, 48.9 bushels per acre; and grain sorghum, 61.8 bushels per acre.

SOYBEAN YIELDS. The national yield for soybeans was 16.2 bushels in 1940 and 24.6 bushels in 1965—approximately a 50 percent increase. As is evident from Figure 2.6, even the expanding acreage of recent years has not greatly affected the yield trend.

Yield projections for soybeans in 1980 are based on yields experienced in the 1940–65 period. The 1980 national yield is projected at 29.3 bushels per acre.

6. Earl O. Heady and Ludwig Auer, Imputations of Production to Technologies, *Journal of Farm Economics* 48:309–23.

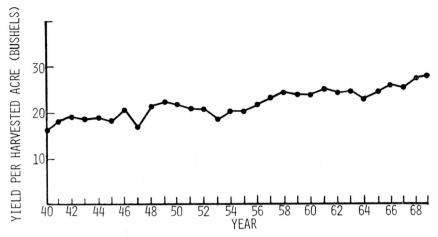

Fig. 2.6. Yield per harvested acre of soybeans in the United States, 1940–69.

COTTON YIELDS. The national trend of cotton yields per acre is shown in Figure 2.7. Cotton yields in the United States have shown a sizeable increase over the last two decades. Much of the increase in national yield has resulted from the shift of cotton acreage from the Southeast to the Southwest where per acre yields are higher. Yields have increased at a fairly steady rate within each major production area (Fig. 2.7).

The 1980 cotton yields are projected on the basis of 1945–65 trends. The projected national yield for 1980 is 754 pounds of cotton lint per acre as compared to 532 pounds in 1965. Projected state and national yields of all crops included in the study are shown in Table 2.2.

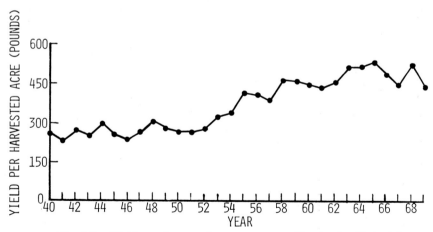

Fig. 2.7. Yield per harvested acre of cotton lint in the United States, 1940–69.

Table 2.2 ● Yields of Major Field Crops, Actual 1969 and Projected 1980

Area	All wheat		Soybeans		Corn		Oats		Barley		Grain sorghum		Cotton	
	1969	1980	1969	1980	1969	1980	1969	1980	1969	1980	1969	1980	1969	1980
	(bu per acre)												(lb per acre)	
United States	30.7	32.3	27.3	29.3	83.9	99.4	52.8	59.1	44.4	48.6	55.2	61.8	433	754
New York	40.0	43.6	21.0	19.2	75.0	73.4	56.0	73.0	48.0	47.5	...	...	...	...
New Jersey	38.0	41.7	28.0	28.9	81.0	90.8	40.0	44.9	55.0	59.7	...	...	...	...
Pennsylvania	35.5	39.9	30.0	26.5	84.0	79.4	51.0	60.7	51.0	48.8	...	...	...	...
Ohio	37.0	40.2	29.0	30.5	85.0	95.2	58.0	79.4	46.0	41.1	...	...	...	...
Indiana	39.0	48.5	32.0	35.4	96.0	116.1	59.0	69.6	38.0	50.2	65.0	87.1	...	...
Illinois	37.0	49.0	33.5	34.0	98.0	115.2	61.0	69.7	40.0	38.9	60.0	75.1	460	...
Michigan	40.0	45.6	23.0	28.8	74.0	87.9	57.0	65.5	47.0	51.1	...	...	...	...
Wisconsin	34.4	45.3	19.0	19.8	83.0	95.0	61.0	77.4	55.0	55.3	...	...	...	...
Minnesota	29.4	31.6	24.0	26.6	85.0	80.3	56.0	64.0	46.0	45.2	...	...	...	...
Iowa	32.0	30.2	33.0	34.3	98.0	109.2	50.0	63.3	46.0	53.3	82.0	83.2	...	...
Missouri	32.0	43.7	26.0	30.8	70.0	87.0	37.0	48.7	35.0	41.6	64.0	70.3	511	793
North Dakota	30.0	25.7	16.5	17.9	55.0	45.6	56.0	60.7	42.5	46.3	...	...	...	...
South Dakota	21.9	19.5	24.5	20.5	57.0	48.0	46.5	48.5	35.0	40.9	44.0	53.2	...	...
Nebraska	31.5	29.3	33.0	34.3	93.0	89.9	43.5	45.4	34.0	34.8	76.0	78.5	...	...
Kansas	31.0	30.0	33.0	23.3	74.0	76.4	38.0	40.8	37.0	35.9	56.0	53.4	...	...
Delaware	38.0	40.0	29.0	29.6	78.0	86.4	53.0	28.6	48.0	58.1	...	...	...	...
Maryland	39.0	36.5	33.0	32.3	81.0	84.0	55.0	57.1	48.0	51.8	55.0	47.6	...	...
Virginia	43.0	36.2	25.0	25.0	77.0	71.9	49.0	40.7	50.0	58.7	...	...	201	367
West Virginia	30.0	34.7	...	...	63.0	57.5	42.0	52.2	44.0	46.9	...	...	...	...
North Carolina	42.0	36.5	26.0	34.4	68.0	90.5	51.0	44.8	49.0	49.1	56.0	31.4	287	423
South Carolina	37.0	34.2	22.5	30.1	47.0	73.1	47.0	45.6	45.0	47.9	36.0	36.8	342	527
Georgia	34.0	39.0	24.0	26.5	33.0	71.0	52.0	56.8	46.0	49.3	40.0	37.3	351	629
Florida	28.0	...	27.0	28.2	39.0	64.4	45.0	54.0	...	...	...	...	360	489

Table 2.2 ● (Continued)

Area	All wheat		Soybeans		Corn		Oats		Barley		Grain sorghum		Cotton	
	1969	1980	1969	1980	1969	1980	1969	1980	1969	1980	1969	1980	1969	1980
	(bu per acre)												(lb per acre)	
Kentucky	34.0	40.3	28.0	31.2	77.0	89.8	44.0	52.0	50.0	44.2	49.0	54.9	516	...
Tennessee	32.0	35.7	24.0	31.3	46.0	68.6	44.0	48.6	36.0	39.0	47.0	52.4	505	836
Alabama	28.5	35.1	23.0	34.0	28.0	58.9	38.0	46.0	...	...	33.0	33.7	405	632
Mississippi	31.0	30.1	22.0	28.3	31.0	55.3	50.0	54.0	...	...	48.0	45.2	537	930
Arkansas	30.0	44.1	20.5	26.3	32.0	49.1	67.0	68.9	31.0	39.9	40.0	39.9	518	817
Louisiana	23.0	35.5	19.0	31.2	29.0	48.0	40.0	41.5	...	...	34.0	40.0	551	775
Oklahoma	28.5	29.8	17.0	24.4	65.0	47.6	41.0	40.2	35.0	36.1	47.0	41.2	288	448
Texas	24.0	24.6	29.0	32.4	44.0	45.1	38.0	31.0	35.0	28.9	50.0	62.1	294	583
Montana	26.6	25.9	...	...	70.0	100.3	50.0	44.9	42.0	35.7	...	...	...	...
Idaho	45.7	47.9	...	...	85.0	112.7	55.0	68.2	52.0	53.0	...	...	...	...
Wyoming	20.2	21.8	...	...	65.0	112.0	37.0	43.5	51.0	47.0	...	...	...	...
Colorado	21.0	18.6	...	...	91.0	111.3	43.0	49.0	44.0	43.8	36.0	39.1	...	...
New Mexico	32.0	27.0	...	...	62.0	84.5	...	61.0	58.0	73.6	56.0	76.7	517	960
Arizona	62.0	61.6	...	...	27.0	39.9	55.0	55.4	71.0	94.3	78.0	89.9	979	1,330
Utah	26.5	27.4	...	...	...	97.4	55.0	59.4	54.0	61.9	...	...	...	...
Washington	38.7	46.4	...	...	105.0	129.0	56.0	55.1	46.0	56.1	...	...	...	...
Oregon	38.1	43.9	...	...	78.0	111.9	56.0	69.9	43.0	49.0	...	...	...	...
California	34.0	34.2	...	...	92.0	129.3	50.0	53.7	47.0	72.0	69.0	97.9	893	1,314

Source: U. S. Dept. of Agriculture, Crop Production Annual Summary 1969, USDA ERS, 1970.

43

Production Costs ● Production costs per acre for the seven crops included in the study are based on initial estimates by Egbert and other reports.[7] Included in these costs are charges for power and machinery, seed, chemicals, fertilizers, labor inputs, and miscellaneous inputs. Land services, management, selling, purchasing, and other similar costs are not included in these estimates.

Production costs are projected to 1980 by developing ratio estimates which measure the relative cost of producing a specified unit of crop output. State-by-state data are used on the aggregate value of crop production for the seven specified crops, the estimated cash expenditures by farmers for all crop production, and national price deflators to remove effects of changes in prices paid and received by farmers. These projections are completed in the following manner:

1. The gross value of production for the seven crops included in the study was summed by states for the years 1949–64. To remove the effect of changes in crop prices received by farmers from the gross value of production, the data were deflated by the national index of prices received for crops for the appropriate year. The deflated value of production for the years 1949–64 was then converted to an index by dividing each year's value by the 1957–59 average value of crop production. The result was a state-by-state index of gross value of crop production with 1957–59 = 100.
2. Cash expenditures for crop production by states were gathered for 1949–64 by taking total farm cash expenditures and subtracting live-stock purchases and feed purchases. To remove the effect of changes in prices paid by farmers, the remaining cash expenditures for crop production for each state were deflated by the national index of prices paid by farmers for items used in production. The latter index was adjusted to remove the effect of changes in the prices paid for livestock and feed purchases. These deflated cash expenditures were then converted to an index by dividing each year's expenditures by the 1957–59 average expenditure. The result is an index of cash expenditures for crops with 1957–59 = 100.
3. The index of total cash expenditures for each year in a given state was divided by the index of gross value of crop production for that year. The resulting index is a ratio of deflated production cost per unit of output, all measured in index form with 1957–59 = 100. The ratio describes the relationship of production costs per unit of crop output.
4. If the average units of output per crop acre remained constant over time, this ratio index for the years 1949–64 would be adequate to project costs per acre of crop production. However since the gross

7. A. C. Egbert, Programming Regional Adjustment in Resource Use for Grain Production, Ph.D. thesis, Iowa State Univ., Ames, 1958.

value of production per acre (measured in constant prices) has been increasing, an additional step was necessary. This step was to weight the ratio index of production cost per unit of output by the changing number of units of output per acre for each crop in each state. To complete this final step, state yields of each of the seven major crops were developed into indices, again with 1957–59 = 100. These indices measure the units of output per acre for each crop. By multiplying these per acre crop output indices by the above ratio, indices of production costs per unit of output, an index of costs of production per acre for each crop results. Completing this step for each year in the period 1949–64 provides a time-series index of production costs on which to project actual costs of production to 1980.

Projected Levels of Commodity Demand ● The aggregate level of demand for agricultural commodities in the United States is made up of two major components, domestic consumption and export consumption.

DOMESTIC CONSUMPTION. Projected levels of U.S. domestic demand are based on state population estimates for 1980, published in 1966 by the Commerce Department,[8] and consumption projections for major agricultural commodities published by Daly and Egbert in January 1966.[9] These aggregate data were then divided into the thirty-one consuming regions of the model based on past proportions of livestock production in each region. The projected 1980 per capita consumption estimates for livestock and livestock products and the levels of domestic consumption are shown in Table 2.3.

The 1980 per capita and total domestic consumption levels include estimates for each major class of livestock. The total quantities of grain required in 1980 consider projected levels of livestock production by consuming regions.

Estimates of feed conversion rates were projected to 1980 to estimate required quantities of grain and oilmeals for each class of livestock. These conversion rates are presented in Table 2.4, and the quantities of grains and oilmeals required for livestock production in 1980 are reported in Table 2.5. The sum of grain fed to livestock and the quantities used directly in human consumption provide estimates of total domestic demand for grains in 1980.

ESTIMATES OF EXPORT DEMAND. Export demand is projected to 1980 for four major categories of commodities: wheat, feed grains, oilmeals, and

8. U.S. Dept. of Commerce, Current Population Reports: Illustrative Projection of the Population of States, 1970–85, Bureau of the Census, Ser. P–25, no. 326 (Washington, D.C.: GPO, 1966).

9. R. F. Daly and A. C. Egbert, A Look Ahead for Food and Agriculture, USDA ERS Agricultural Economics Research 18:1–19, and the unpublished statistical supplement, 1966.

Table 2.3 ● Estimated Per Capita and Total Domestic Consumption of Food and Fiber Products, Projected 1980 with Actual 1964 Consumption

Commodity	Per capita consumption (lb)		Total quantity consumed (million lb)	
	1964	1980[a]	1964[b]	1980
Livestock products:				
Beef & veal	183.8	203.5	34,999	49,525
Pork	107.5	97.0	20,469	23,606
Lamb & mutton	8.6	7.2	1,637	1,752
Broilers	31.2	50.2	5,941	12,217
Turkeys	7.2	11.8	1,371	2,872
Dairy products (milk equivalent)	628.0	570.0	119,580	138,718
Eggs (number)	314.0	290.0	59,790	70,576
Grain products:				
Wheat	160.0	142.8	30,608	27,191
Corn	53.0	51.1	10,092	9,730
Oats	7.8	8.0	1,485	1,523
Barley	1.4	1.1	267	210
Fiber products:				
Cotton	22.1	21.6	4,245	5,250

[a]Per capita consumption estimates for livestock products are taken from R. F. Daly and A. C. Egbert, A Look Ahead for Food and Agriculture, USDA ERS Agricultural Economics Research 18:1-9.
[b]A 48-state population of 190,413,000 was used for 1964 estimates.

Table 2.4 ● Feed Conversion Rates for Feed Grains and Oilmeals, Projected 1980 with Actual 1964 Consumption

Class of livestock[a]	Oilmeals required[b]		Feed grains required	
	1964	1980	1964	1980
	(lb of feed units[c])			
Beef & veal	244.5	315.4	1,302	1,417
Pork	264.0	311.8	4,666	4,764
Lamb & mutton	658.0	570.9	966	973
Dairy cattle	51.8	63.7	322	317
Turkeys	...	...	2,626	2,451
Hens & pullets	...	...	297	237
Broilers	...	...	1,752	1,482

[a]Quantities are number of feed units per 1,000 pounds of liveweight for beef, pork, lamb, turkeys, and broilers; for dairy cattle, per 1,000 pounds of milk; and for hens and pullets, per 1,000 eggs.
[b]Not estimated by individual class of poultry.
[c]One pound of feed units is defined as equal to one pound of corn.

Table 2.5 ● Domestic Feed Demand for Feed Grains and Oilmeals by Class of Livestock Projected 1980 with Actual 1964

Class of livestock	Oilmeals required[a]		Feed grains required	
	1964	1980	1964	1980
	(lb of feed units)			
Beef & veal	4,136	4,968	22,020	28,632
Pork	2,481	3,702	43,890	56,527
Lamb & mutton	435	707	637	857
Dairy cattle	3,264	4,417	20,318	21,808
All poultry	7,780	7,792	20,430	20,779
Eggs	...	...	9,572	8,333
Broilers	...	...	8,369	8,961
Turkeys	...	...	2,490	3,485
Horses & mules[b]	...	...	2,889	2,500
Other	674	700	5,843	6,000
Total	18,770	22,286	116,027	137,103

[a]Not estimated by individual class of poultry.
[b]Oilmeals required are included in "Other."

cotton lint. Two types of export programs are assumed for the study: under one, the government continues the present policy of subsidizing exports with the quantity varying with world requirements and the magnitude of export subsidies; under the other program used, the government terminates programs of export expansion, and world demand alone determines the movement of grain into export channels.

Three levels of exports are projected to 1980 under the policy of subsidizing exports: under level one, 1980 projected exports are at the 1965–66 levels; under level two, they increase at the 1950–65 trend level and are well above the 1965–66 level; under level three, we simply assume that exports are as large as allowed by the available land base if yields follow the trends to 1980, and if domestic consumer demand is met. Quantities of each major commodity for each level are shown in Table 2.6.

Under the final level of exports considered, government programs of export expansion are terminated and commercial exports are projected to 1980 on past trends. This trend level of exports projects quantities for both commercial sales and sales under government programs. Commercial exports in 1980 are then assumed to make up the same proportion of this total export demand as in 1964, when commercial export sales were 43 percent of total wheat exports, 90 percent of total feed grains exports, 99 percent of total oilmeal exports, and 79 percent of total cotton exports. Export level four (Table 2.6) presents estimates of the quantities of wheat, feed grains, and oilmeals moving without subsidy in 1980.

Policy Models Analyzed ● In addition to four different levels of exports, the study includes four alternative types of farm programs which are outlined below.

FREE MARKET. The first policy alternative simulates a free market and assumes that institutional restraints are removed from crop production. All acreage restrictions except cotton quotas are removed. Cotton quotas are set at a level equal to the average acreage grown in each region of the United States between 1950 and 1960. Exports are set at approximately 1965 levels (level one). This model assumes that production is freed from all restraints by counties and states so that it is distributed over the 144 producing regions of the model in a manner to minimize costs in meeting domestic and export demand. This is the pattern which would be expected in the long run under competition and free market prices.

The second free market model also assumes production restraints only on cotton, but export levels are raised to levels approximating the projected 1980 trend export level (level two), based on the rate of increase over the last fifteen years.

The third free market model eliminates restraints on cotton production. Cotton and other crops are produced in the regions of minimum

Table 2.6 ● Demand Levels for Major Grain Commodities and Cotton Lint, Actual 1965 Level and Projected Levels for 1980

Commodity	Actual level 1965			Projected consumption for 1980			
					Alternative export levels for 1980		
	Domestic	Export	Domestic	Level 1	Level 2	Level 3	Level 4
				(million)			
Wheat (bu)	587.0	867.0	720.0[a]	857.0	1,302.0	2,157.0	560.0
Feed grains[b] (tons)	130.0	29.0	154.0	29.0	40.0	70.0	36.0
Oilmeals[c] (tons)	17.0	11.0	20.0	11.0	24.0	37.0	17.0
Cotton (bales)	9.5	3.0	10.5	4.0	6.0	6.8	4.7

[a]Not including wheat used for feed.
[b]Feed grains are measured in tons of corn equivalent.
[c]Oilmeals are measured in tons of soybean equivalent although demand is supplied by both soybeans and cottonseed.

cost without regard to historical patterns of production. The projected trend level of exports (level two) is again used for this model.

The fourth free market model is based on maximum levels of exports (level three) possible in 1980 after projected domestic demand levels are met. As in the case of the other three models termed "free market" (but which also could be simulated by farm programs designed for this purpose), the production pattern is distributed among 144 regions to allow minimum resource inputs or costs to attain specified output levels. Hence, production is expedited to form a pattern by regions based on comparative advantage in technology, climate, location, and resources.

FEED GRAIN PROGRAM. The second type of farm program analyzed assumes that land retirement programs of the type for wheat and feed grains in the 1960s are continued and broadened to include cotton; base acreages are used for each crop. Farmers are assumed to retire enough land to just balance output with domestic and foreign demand to maintain prices at approximately their 1964–66 level. The trend level of exports (level two) is used. This program allows land to be retired from production in a manner to minimize both the costs of crop production and land retirement programs.

ACREAGE QUOTAS. Mandatory acreage quotas are an alternative to voluntary output control or land retirement programs. This would be a compulsory land retirement program. Hence the next farm program assumes trend level of exports (level two) and acreage quotas in each region for wheat, feed grains, and cotton. Soybeans are produced on land which acreage quotas free from other crops, if economically and agronomically feasible. This model analyzes the economic costs involved in controlling production with acreage quotas compared to the previous voluntary programs or free market models studied.

As under previous models, costs of producing the specified level of output are minimized. But in this model the costs are minimized within a smaller land base in each region for the crops included. Thus the model simulates a program for major field crops similar to tobacco programs of recent years. Quotas or acreage allotments are reduced in all regions to lessen total output. By reducing the acreage available in regions with a comparative advantage, other less advantageous regions continue production or are encouraged to return to production.

ACREAGE QUOTAS AND UNSUBSIDIZED EXPORTS. The last program examines the effect of terminating government programs of export expansion. In addition to acreage quotas, export bases for 1980 are set equal to the commercial export demand (level four). The program includes an estimate of the quantities of wheat, feed grains, oilmeals, and cotton which might be exported if government subsidies are terminated.

EMPIRICAL RESULTS ● For each of the seven alternative farm policy models analyzed in the following sections, the basic parameters are total available crop acres, yields of major crops, a specified set of demands for domestic and export use, crop production costs, and transportation costs. Each of the models supposes that the national parameters affecting agriculture in 1980 are as follows: domestic population is 243.4 million persons; food consumption per capita follows trends established over the past twenty-five years; livestock-feed conversion efficiency continues on trends established since 1940; and yields of crops and costs of production per acre follow trends established since the end of World War II.

A set of least-cost spatially located crop acreages are determined for each model. Also, a set of programmed equilibrium prices based upon variable production and transportation costs is derived for each commodity in each demand region. If land for crops represents a scarce factor as a result of all croplands being in use, land rent results in the particular region. These land rents are also specified for each model. Since the cost of transporting commodities from producing regions to final demand regions enters into the programmed prices of commodities, graphic summaries of quantities transported are presented for some models.

The acreage specified for each model serves as a partial basis for estimating regional and national requirements for labor in 1980. The man-hour requirements presented are considered to be a conservative set of estimates because they are based on past trends in labor use. The man-hour requirements decrease with time but the projected downtrend will be an underestimate if adoption rates of labor-saving technology increase.

Finally total capital values for land and building, machinery and equipment, and livestock inventories are specified for each of the ten farm production regions of the United States.

In the sections which follow, we measure surplus capacity in terms of the acreage which would be retired or idled under various land diversion programs and under the free market models. For results under the free market models, we term the acreage *converted,* because prices would actually fall to lower levels and cause the land to be shifted to grass or trees (or to produce more surplus of field crops—not actually allowed in the details of the model, yet the expected outcome in the short run). Here idle or converted land refers to cropland from the nation's crop base. In later chapters we also estimate pasture and other land which would be expected to "move out" with idled cropland under certain programs. But in this chapter, idle land refers only to cropland retired.

Simulated Free Market ● To provide a benchmark for the study, four models are discussed which incorporate various degrees of a free market along with various levels of exports. However, as used in this chapter for purposes of brevity, the term *free market* has a special meaning or use. Under the so-called free market models, we suppose that only the "discrete" demand levels mentioned earlier for the production mix are specified. Then the distribution of land is that which we would expect under long-run equilibrium where each region shifts to a crop pattern wherein the discrete demand levels are met at lowest cost (long-run competitive equilibrium). In a truly free market, greater supply would interact with demand to lower prices received by farmers and paid by food consumers, thus causing consumption to be greater than the discrete demand used for the model (which is the same as for other models). This latter concept of the free market is used in the next chapter wherein we let prices decline to affect total consumption and land requirements, and we also estimate income under these conditions of supply and demand interaction. Finally, under the supply-demand relationships estimated from a time-series simulation model in a later chapter, we also suppose the interaction of supply and demand to give market equilibrium prices. However, we use the more qualified notion of free market in this chapter (only the discrete demand levels are met and production meshes at this level) to measure what would be the level of cropland idled or converted to other uses under these conditions (i.e., the concept of a free market and the land shifted by comparative advantage).

MODEL A: FREE MARKET, COTTON QUOTAS, AND 1965 LEVEL EXPORTS IN 1980. With this type of farm economy in 1980, wheat production requires 59.7 million acres of cropland, feed grains require 73.9 million acres, soybeans use 29.3 million acres, cotton 10.0 million acres, and 78.4 million acres of cropland are converted. Land resources are in substantial "surplus" (i.e., large areas would need to be converted) and a large amount of excess capacity exists for this level of demand in 1980. (Under free markets, this land would not actually lie idle as under land retirement programs but would be converted to other uses or be used for the same crops at lower prices.)

Regional and national acreages of each crop for this level of demand are presented in Table 2.7. The regional acreages are presented for the ten farm production regions indicated previously in Figure 2.3. In addition the acres of converted land or excess capacity for each region are shown in the right-hand columns.

Under this model and level of demand, the Southern Plains and Mountain regions show substantial increases in wheat acreage while the Northern Plains show a significant decrease. Feed grains acres decrease in most regions as a result of a 25-million-acre decline in total acres compared to 1965. Soybean production remains centered in the Corn Belt, although the Northern Plains, mainly Nebraska, show some increase. Soybean production in the Delta States shows a million-acre decline, whereas the Lake States show a 2-million-acre decrease when

Table 2.7 ● Acreages of Major Crops and Converted Land by Regions, Actual 1965 and Projected 1980 Levels under Model A

Region[a]	Wheat		Feed grains		Soybeans		Cotton		Converted land	
	1965	1980	1965	1980	1965	1980	1965	1980	1965	1980
					(thousand acres)					
United States	49,313	59,673	98,956	73,859	34,551	29,283	13,621	10,010	55,950	78,448
Northeast	786	2,045	3,267	2,485	443	61	0	0	1,334	1,119
Lake States	1,671	3,303	13,857	11,607	3,781	1,481	0	0	5,428	8,318
Corn Belt	5,181	6,053	35,027	27,985	19,024	18,437	336	3	10,820	17,829
Northern Plains	21,776	13,283	21,633	14,239	2,178	3,443	0	0	15,111	29,749
Appalachian	687	1,046	4,668	4,908	2,247	634	891	670	3,230	4,395
Southeast	200	240	3,883	4,109	1,314	522	1,898	32	4,257	6,581
Delta States	559	4	1,103	380	5,300	4,248	3,133	411	1,255	6,222
Southern Plains	7,975	15,059	8,304	4,331	264	457	6,120	7,962	8,146	6,222
Mountain	7,105	12,672	4,342	2,381	0	0	518	48	5,084	2,903
Pacific	3,373	5,968	2,872	1,434	0	0	725	884	1,285	1,332

[a]States in each region are shown in Figure 2.3.

compared to 1965 acreages of soybeans. Cotton production continues to shift toward the Southwest, with both the Southern Plains and the Pacific regions increasing their acreage. The Southeast shows a significant decline in cotton acreage compared to 1965.

Converted land or "excess capacity" increases by large amounts under this level of demand and competitive market model. In the Northern Plains excess capacity almost doubles from levels of 1965. Acres of converted capacity also increase from 1965 levels in the Delta region. The Mountain and Southern Plains regions show a substantial decline in idle crop acres primarily because of increases in wheat acreage in the two regions. Increases in cotton acreage also affect crop acres used in the Southern Plains.

With this level of demand, large excess capacity is denoted, as indicated by the 78.4 million acres of cropland which must be converted when demand levels are just met in the qualified manner of this free market model. Given this large acreage and the free market economy, as simulated here, substantial concentration of converted land would result. Particular regions of the United States would be severely affected by the concentrated converting of crop acres of this magnitude. Figure

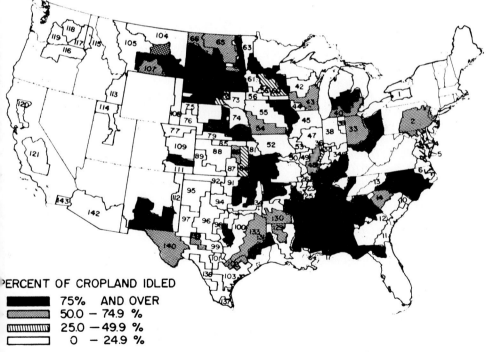

Fig. 2.8. *Proportion of total cropland converted in each of the 144 crop-producing regions for major crops under the free market model with 1965 level exports in 1980.*

2.8 shows the proportion of total cropland converted in each of the 144 producing regions of the model. As is evident, regions in the Southeast generally show a high proportion of cropland converted. The Northern Plains also show a high proportion of cropland converted under this level of demand. These regions would substantially reduce their agricultural plant under a free market economy as simulated in this particular model. The result of such large excess capacity would be severe adjustments not only for direct agricultural interests, but also for the adjacent rural businesses which are located in and dependent upon the rural farm sector.

Programmed prices and land rents resulting from this level of demand and this type of model are presented in Table 2.8. This model produces a low level of programmed commodity prices. There is also a large variation among regions in the cost of producing each of the crops. Prices received by farmers in 1965 (shown in Table 2.8) were supported in varying degrees by government programs. These programs provided a national support price for a commodity, and then adjusted state prices on the basis of transportation costs to the nearest major market. The substantial difference in the per unit cost of producing the crop in different regions is left out of these price calculations. As a result, the average price received by farmers varies only modestly between regions. In contrast, the programmed prices derived for this model show substantial variation by regions. At the national level, wheat price is $1.11 in 1980 under this model; feed grains price in corn equivalent is $0.69 per bushel. Programmed crop prices are presented in Table 2.8 for the ten farm production regions.

In addition to programmed crop prices, Table 2.8 includes the programmed rents to cropland in each region. Rents are computed from the linear programming shadow prices and have a corresponding meaning to prices: Rents result from the scarcity of additional acres of cropland on which to grow crops or from acreage quotas which restrict the acres of a crop to be grown. In regions without an acreage quota and with idle cropland the rents would be zero. In this particular model, only cotton production is restrained by acreage quotas; thus rents accruing to acreage quotas result entirely from cotton quotas. Later models apply quotas to other crops as well.

Under the programming model used here, the value of rent to an acre of cropland represents the opportunity cost of an additional unit of cropland. For example, in the Appalachian region, an additional acre of cropland would lower the total cost of producing the specified level of demand by $1.12. An additional unit of cotton quota would lower total costs by $1.19, and together, total cost of cotton production could be lowered by $2.31 for each additional acre of cropland and cotton quota. Since there is a restraint on these two resources, a rent of $2.31 per acre occurs on the available acres of cotton land and quota.

The Pacific region shows the largest programmed rents. These are

Table 2.8 ● Programmed Prices of Major Crops and Programmed Rents Per Acre by Farm Production Region for a Free Market with Acreage Quotas for Cotton and 1965 Level Exports in 1980

Region	Wheat 1965	Wheat 1980	Feed grains 1965	Feed grains 1980	Soybeans 1965	Soybeans 1980	Cotton[a] 1965	Cotton[a] 1980	Total crop rent	Source of rent: cropland	Source of rent: acreage quotas
	($ per bu)		($ per bu)		($ per bu)		(¢ per lb)		($ per acre)		
United States	1.34	1.11	1.10	.69	2.49	1.13	28.0	25.9	...	...	...
Northeast	1.35	1.35	.30	.86	2.43	1.24	...	...	6.29	6.29	0
Lake States	1.43	.97	1.01	.57	2.49	1.04	...	...	3.19	3.19	0
Corn Belt	1.35	.97	1.08	.47	2.50	.92	...	...	3.77	3.77	0
Northern Plains	1.36	.67	1.13	.55	2.35	1.03	...	...	2.51	2.51	0
Appalachian	1.38	1.32	1.24	.83	2.44	1.17	...	...	2.31	1.12	1.19
Southeast	1.42	1.40	1.24	.91	2.49	1.11	...	...	.08	.08	0
Delta States	1.29	1.37	1.27	.86	2.50	1.08	...	...	1.31	.83	.49
Southern Plains	1.34	1.20	1.25	.61	2.28	.83	...	...	22.08	8.32	13.76
Mountain	1.26	1.04	1.28	.83	...	1.32	...	...	7.28	7.22	.06
Pacific	1.34	1.13	1.44	1.06	...	1.44	...	...	24.61	23.37	1.24

aRegional prices were not calculated.

caused by the small acreages of land available for major field crop production in this region. The limited acreages of land result in large
quantities of grains being shipped into these regions, and the resulting
higher programmed price provides a rent to the acres of locally raised
grains.

Labor requirements for this model are presented in Table 2.9.
However, the quantity of labor required for this level of demand is not
substantially different from other levels of demand, as a review of the
additional models will indicate. For the United States, the projected
total quantity of labor for farm work in 1980 is 34 percent less than the
man-hours of labor used for farm work in 1965. Labor required for
crops falls 35 percent while labor for livestock decreases by 28 percent.
Lower overhead labor requirements also account for some of the decrease in total man-hours.

On a regional basis, the Delta region would decrease man-hours
used by 53 percent. The Pacific region has the smallest decrease—18 percent. In terms of regional groupings, the Southern Plains, Mountain,
and Pacific regions each indicate approximately a 20 percent decrease in
labor required. The Northeast, Lake States, Corn Belt, and Northern
Plains show approximately a 30 percent decrease, whereas the Appalachian, Southeast, and Delta regions indicate approximately a 40 percent
or greater decrease in man-hours of labor required for agricultural activities. Overall, the quantity of labor in agriculture is expected to decline
more than one-third by 1980 for this level of demand.

Fixed capital inputs are the third major resource analyzed. For the
United States as a whole, capital requirements for the major inputs listed
in Table 2.10 are expected to increase by approximately 29 percent between 1965 and 1980. Even under this level of demand, large increases
(40 percent or above) will take place in the Southern Plains, Mountain,
and Pacific regions. The Corn Belt shows the least change, an indication
of the large proportion of land in farms used for the specified crops in
the model and the low feed grains prices which result from this level
of demand. Looking at individual categories, land and building values
are projected to increase 17 percent between 1965 and 1980 (valued in
constant 1965 dollars). The value of machinery and equipment is projected to increase by 52 percent and livestock inventories by 56 percent
under this model.

Figure 2.9 portrays the quantity of wheat moving from excess-supply
to deficit-demand areas. At this level of demand only a small quantity
of wheat moves between regions. Many states are self-sufficient. The
Great Plains states show some out-movement, primarily to export markets. Montana and Idaho also produce and ship quantities of wheat,
mainly for feed, into Washington and Oregon. The states with large
deficits—Texas, Louisiana, and Mississippi—are mainly exporting centers
and funnel wheat into world markets.

An estimated 155 million bushels of wheat were used for feed in

Table 2.9 ● Labor Requirements by Regions, Actual 1965 and Projected 1980 Needs under Model A

Region	Percentage change All farm work 1965-80	All farm work		All livestock		All crops	
		1965	1980	1965	1980	1965	1980
		(million man-hours)					
United States	-33.6	7,976	5,272	3,066	2,210	3,798	2,479
Northeast	-35.9	627	402	314	202	226	154
Lake States	-30.2	849	593	452	320	284	210
Corn Belt	-36.6	1,309	803	658	474	448	248
Northern Plains	-34.0	630	416	290	225	240	134
Appalachian	-38.3	1,157	714	341	226	658	407
Southeast	-41.1	801	472	219	169	484	257
Delta States	-52.9	594	280	179	135	340	118
Southern Plains	-23.4	709	543	247	156	353	315
Mountain	-21.5	470	369	174	143	230	183
Pacific	-18.1	830	680	192	160	535	453

Table 2.10 ● Capital Requirements in 1980 for Major Categories of Inputs under Model A

Region	Percentage change total capital 1965–80	Total capital		Projected 1980 value of		
		1965	1980	land and buildings	machinery and equipment	livestock inventories
				($ billion)		
United States	+29.4	198.9	257.4	187.3	38.3	21.8
Northeast	+15.0	10.9	12.6	7.9	3.5	1.2
Lake States	+28.6	16.1	20.7	12.9	5.5	2.2
Corn Belt	+ 5.9	45.0	47.7	33.9	8.9	4.9
Northern Plains	+24.6	23.0	38.7	19.1	6.1	3.6
Appalachian	+13.7	15.0	17.1	12.1	3.6	1.4
Southeast	+11.0	12.6	14.0	11.9	1.0	1.1
Delta States	+15.2	9.2	10.6	8.4	1.3	.9
Southern Plains	+40.0	24.2	33.8	28.7	2.9	2.2
Mountain	+45.7	17.0	24.7	19.5	2.7	2.5
Pacific	+44.9	25.9	37.5	32.9	2.8	1.8

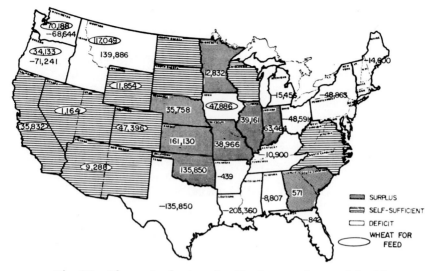

Fig. 2.9. *Flows of wheat under the free market model with cotton quotas and 1965 level exports.*

1965. Under this model, with similar levels of exports in 1980, but different levels of wheat production technology and a different type of farm program, 375 million bushels of wheat are indicated for feed in 1980. Most of this wheat is fed in the Far West.

Feed grains flows are shown in Figure 2.10. Many areas satisfy their

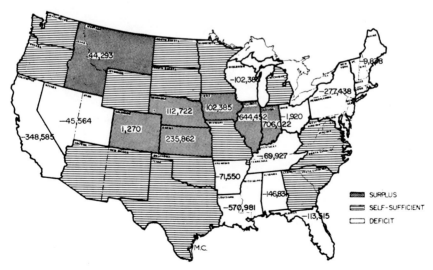

Fig. 2.10. *Flows of feed grains under the free market model with cotton quotas and 1965 level exports.*

own needs at the specified level of demand. The surplus corn states of Iowa, Illinois, and Indiana ship corn through ports mainly in Wisconsin, Louisiana, and Mississippi for the export market. Nebraska, Kansas, and Colorado also have out-movement of feed grains, mainly grain sorghum, which move to Utah, Nevada, and California. A total of 1.8 billion bushels of feed grains (measured in bushels of corn) are transported among regions with this model.

Figure 2.11 shows the movement of oilmeals from excess-supply to deficit-demand areas. The Corn Belt states of Iowa, Illinois, and Missouri, along with Arkansas, Tennessee, and Kentucky, have exports of oilmeals. Kansas also exports some soybeans while Texas and Oklahoma export cottonseed to other states. All other states import oilmeals, either for livestock feed or to move through their port facilities into foreign markets.

MODEL B: FREE MARKETS, COTTON QUOTAS, AND TREND LEVEL EXPORTS IN 1980. This model is the same as the previous one, except that it assumes a higher level of exports. Wheat exports total 1,302 million bushels; feed grains—40 million tons; oilmeals—24 million tons; and exports of cotton total 6.0 million bales. Production is allocated under least-cost criteria for all crops except cotton, which has acreage quotas. As a result, total costs of production for grain and oilmeals are minimized for this level of output.

Given this set of parameters and the nature of free market models as explained earlier, the analysis indicates an increase in wheat and

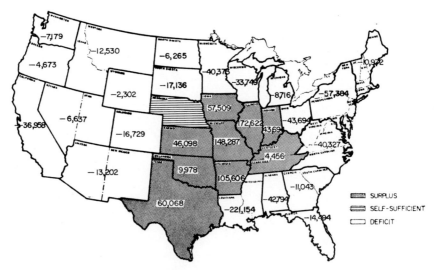

Fig. 2.11. Flows of oilmeals under the free market model with cotton quotas and 1965 level exports.

soybean acreages compared to 1965, but decreases in feed grains and cotton acreages. To satisfy domestic needs for 720 million bushels of wheat, feed demand of 241 million bushels, and an export demand of 1,302 million bushels requires a total of 69.5 million acres with the 1980 level of production technology (Table 2.11). On a regional breakdown, the Southern Plains increase wheat production by over 7 million acres. The increase includes large areas in both Oklahoma and Texas. The Mountain region also increases acreage by 6 million acres, located mainly in eastern Colorado, eastern New Mexico, and both eastern and and western Montana; both the eastern areas of the United States and the Far West areas increase wheat acreage. In the East wheat acreage increases because of the nearness to large population centers with sizeable quantities of wheat consumed for food. In the Far West a large quantity of wheat is used as livestock feed under this free market economy. The Mountain and Pacific regions use 241 million bushels of wheat for livestock—the only regions to use wheat for feeding purposes under this model.

Feed grains acreage shows a substantial decrease from 1965 levels, although total tons produced increase from 158 million tons to 195 million tons in 1980, a 24 percent increase. Almost all regions show a decrease: the Corn Belt almost 5 million acres, the Northern Plains over 4 million acres, and the Southern Plains over 4 million acres; other regions show shifts of smaller magnitude.

With the increased level of demand in 1980 soybean acreage increases by almost 8 million acres from the 1965 figure. The total quantity of oil-meals produced increases from 28 million tons to 44 million tons, of which 24 million tons are exported in 1980. Oilmeals include both soybeans and cottonseed. The largest increase in acreage of soybeans shows up in the Corn Belt; most other regions show some decline from 1965 levels.

Cotton acreage declines from 1965 levels. Production however increases to 16.5 million bales compared to approximately 12.5 million bales in 1965. Total acreage decreases by over 2 million acres. On a regional basis, the Southern Plains and Pacific regions show increases while the Southeast and Delta regions show decreases. The magnitude of shifts is reduced because acreage quotas on cotton are retained in this model. The full impact of unimpeded shifts in cotton production is analyzed in the next model.

Excess capacity is still large for the farm economy of 1980 simulated by this model. Although exports increase by sizeable amounts, 47.0 million acres of cropland remain to be converted to other uses after domestic and export demands are satisfied. Acreage of converted land of this magnitude provides a firm basis for increasing output to meet additional food needs. Under this market economy model, substantial shifts are indicated in the location of converted acres when compared to 1965 idle or retired acres. The Northern Plains increase idle or con-

Table 2.11 ● **Acreages of Major Crops and Unused Land by Regions, Actual 1965 and Projected 1980 Levels under Model B**

Region	Wheat		Feed grains		Soybeans		Cotton		Converted land	
	1965	1980	1965	1980	1965	1980	1965	1980	1965	1980
					(thousand acres)					
United States	49,313	69,455	98,956	81,016	34,551	42,493	13,621	11,329	55,950	46,979
Northeast	786	2,110	3,267	2,485	443	1,116	0	0	1,334	0
Lake States	1,671	3,904	13,857	13,332	3,781	2,602	0	0	5,428	4,871
Corn Belt	5,181	7,710	35,027	30,389	19,024	28,103	336	3	10,820	4,101
Northern Plains	21,776	18,386	21,633	17,565	2,178	2,682	0	0	15,111	22,080
Appalachian	687	1,323	4,668	4,838	2,247	1,257	891	670	3,230	3,564
Southeast	200	497	3,883	4,109	1,314	1,915	1,898	32	4,257	4,930
Delta States	559	673	1,103	361	5,300	4,361	3,133	1,690	1,255	4,180
Southern Plains	7,975	15,569	8,304	4,122	264	457	6,120	8,002	8,146	2,563
Mountain	7,105	13,315	4,342	2,381	0	0	518	48	5,084	690
Pacific	3,373	5,968	2,872	1,434	0	0	725	884	1,285	0

verted land by 7 million acres even though total wheat acreage for the United States increases. The Delta region also shows increased idle land. The Southern Plains and Mountain regions, by contrast, decrease idle land 5.5 and 4.5 million acres respectively. The Corn Belt also shows less idle land under the competitive pressures of this model.

Programmed prices of crops and programmed rents per acre under this model are presented in Table 2.12. Compared to model A, the general level of prices increases with the higher level of demand of model B. Wheat price rises from $1.11 to $1.27, nearly the 1965 level. Feed grains prices are also above the previous model but still substantially lower than 1965 levels—an indication of the effect which the substantial reduction in acreage might allow. Production under a free market concentrates in the most efficient producing areas, and the per unit cost of production is reduced. Since programmed prices in these models do not include all fixed costs of production, lower equilibrium prices result. Actual market prices which by necessity must cover fixed costs would be somewhat higher. Only in the Pacific region is the feed grains price above $1 per bushel, and this results from added transportation costs of importing large quantities of grain. United States' average soybean and cotton prices are also slightly higher than in the previous model.

Programmed rents per acre increase with the higher level of demand and consequent greater production. The necessity of using cropland acres with higher per unit production costs causes the general price level to rise and higher land rents to accrue. The acreage quotas on cotton also cause a substantial contribution to total rent in cotton-producing regions. The Southern Plains show the greatest effect of this particular policy (Table 2.12). Cropland with a cotton quota in this region would have a substantially higher value than cropland without such a quota.

As indicated in Table 2.13, labor man-hours required for this level of demand are 32 percent lower than the actual 1965 requirements. The largest decrease is in the Delta region where 43 percent fewer man-hours are required for agricultural production. Although this decrease is still large, it is 10 percent smaller than model A which assumed 1965 level exports. The Pacific region shows the smallest decrease in man-hours of farm work, 18.1 percent. The Mountain and Southern Plains regions follow closely, and then come the Lake States with their labor-intensive fruit crops. All other regions exceed a one-third decline in total man-hours required.

Capital inputs increase by 35 percent over 1965 levels with the higher level of demand. The largest increase, 48 percent, is indicated for the Pacific region; the smallest increase, 17 percent, is in the Southeast. Other regions show an increase which falls between these two (Table 2.14).

The quantities of each major crop which are transported among

Table 2.12 ● **Programmed Prices of Major Crops and Programmed Rents Per Acre by Farm Production Regions under Model B**

Region	Wheat		Feed grains		Soybeans		Cotton[a]		Total crop rent	Source of rent	
										crop-land	acreage quotas
	1965	1980	1965	1980	1965	1980	1965	1980			
	($ per bu)						(¢ per lb)		($ per acre)		
United States	1.34	1.27	1.10	.76	2.49	1.25	28.0	27.2	...	...	...
Northeast	1.35	1.46	1.30	.90	2.43	1.41	...	...	10.21	10.21	0
Lake States	1.43	1.05	1.01	.61	2.49	1.18	...	...	5.16	5.16	0
Corn Belt	1.35	1.08	1.08	.52	2.50	1.07	...	...	8.01	8.01	0
Northern Plains	1.36	.78	1.13	.60	2.35	1.16	...	...	4.31	4.31	0
Appalachian	1.38	1.46	1.24	.89	2.44	1.38	...	...	5.84	4.04	1.80
Southeast	1.42	1.48	1.24	.93	2.49	1.28	...	...	.18	.18	0
Delta States	1.29	1.49	1.27	.94	2.50	1.27	...	...	4.55	2.90	1.65
Southern Plains	1.34	1.38	1.25	.66	2.28	1.01	...	...	27.07	11.56	15.51
Mountain	1.26	1.16	1.28	.93	...	1.46	...	...	11.85	11.75	.10
Pacific	1.34	1.34	1.44	1.16	...	1.62	...	...	34.02	30.38	3.64

aRegional prices were not calculated.

Table 2.13 ● Labor Requirements by Regions, Actual 1965 and Projected 1980 Needs under Model B

Region	Percentage change all farm work 1965-80	All farm work (million man-hours)		All livestock		All crops	
		1965	1980	1965	1980	1965	1980
United States	-31.8	7,976	5,442	3,066	2,210	3,798	2,604
Northeast	-35.2	627	406	314	202	226	157
Lake States	-29.1	849	602	452	320	284	218
Corn Belt	-33.3	1,309	873	658	474	448	285
Northern Plains	-31.6	630	431	290	225	240	146
Appalachian	-38.0	1,157	717	341	226	658	409
Southeast	-40.0	801	481	219	169	484	265
Delta States	-42.9	594	339	179	135	340	170
Southern Plains	-23.4	709	543	247	156	353	316
Mountain	-21.3	470	370	174	143	230	185
Pacific	-18.1	830	680	192	160	535	453

Table 2.14 ● Capital Requirements for Major Categories of Inputs under Model B

Region	Percentage change total capital 1965-80	Total capital		Projected 1980 value of		
		1965	1980	land and buildings	machinery and equipment	livestock inventories
				($ billion)		
United States	+34.6	198.9	267.6	202.9	42.7	21.9
Northeast	+21.2	10.9	13.2	8.1	3.9	1.2
Lake States	+44.6	16.1	23.2	14.5	6.6	2.2
Corn Belt	+29.7	45.0	58.4	42.5	11.0	4.9
Northern Plains	+32.8	23.0	30.7	20.3	6.7	3.6
Appalachian	+18.1	15.0	17.7	12.7	3.6	1.4
Southeast	+17.8	12.6	14.8	12.4	1.2	1.1
Delta States	+26.5	9.2	11.6	9.4	1.3	.9
Southern Plains	+42.5	24.2	34.4	29.2	2.9	2.2
Mountain	+48.5	17.0	25.2	20.0	2.7	2.6
Pacific	+48.3	25.9	38.4	33.8	2.8	1.8

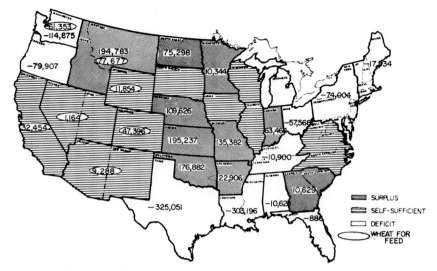

Fig. 2.12. Flows of wheat under the free market model with cotton quotas and trend level exports.

regions are shown in Figures 2.12, 2.13, and 2.14. The figures show the major surplus and deficit regions for each crop considered.

MODEL C: FREE MARKET, NO COTTON QUOTAS, AND TREND LEVEL EXPORTS IN 1980. Model C features the removal of cotton quotas, allowing cotton

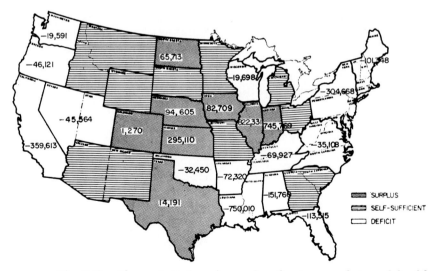

Fig. 2.13. Flows of feed grains under the free market model with cotton quotas and trend level exports.

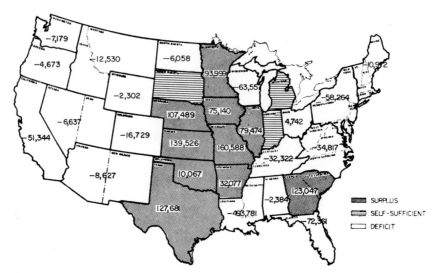

Fig. 2.14. Flows of oilmeals under the free market model with cotton quotas and trend level exports.

production to concentrate in areas of lowest production cost. Other parameters of the model remain the same as the last model analyzed: wheat production satisfies domestic demand of 720 million bushels and exports of 1,302 million bushels; feed grains demand is specified at 154 million tons for domestic use and 40 million tons for export; soybean and cottonseed demand is set at 20 million tons of oilmeals for domestic use and 24 million tons for exports; and cotton lint demand remains at 10.5 million bales for domestic consumption and 6.0 million bales for export.

Acreages of cropland for producing these levels of wheat, feed grains, and soybeans are only slightly affected by the removal of cotton quotas. Evidently there is little competition between cotton acreages and other crops. Total acreage for cotton declines by 2 million acres from 11.3 million to 9.3 million acres; acreages in the Southern Plains increase from 6.1 million acres in 1965 to 9.1 million acres under a policy of unrestrained production. According to these estimates, under a policy of producing cotton at a minimum cost, 98 percent of the cotton acreage is located in the Southern Plains. Even the Pacific region reduces acreage of cotton as acreage quotas are removed. Crop acreages and idle land are shown in Table 2.15.

Excess capacity increases with the removal of cotton quotas. Converted idle land under this model increases by 1.2 million acres to 48.2 million acres. The smaller number of acres of cropland required for crop production represents a saving to society in terms of the expenditures necessary to produce the food and fiber needs of the nation.

Table 2.15 ● Acreages of Minor Crops and Converted Land by Regions, Actual 1965 and Projected 1980 Levels under Model C

Region	Wheat		Feed grains		Soybeans		Cotton		Converted land	
	1965	1980	1965	1980	1965	1980	1965	1980	1965	1980
					(thousand acres)					
United States	49,313	69,987	98,956	81,167	34,551	42,606	13,621	9,300	55,950	48,219
Northeast	786	2,124	3,267	2,485	443	1,101	0	0	1,334	0
Lake States	1,671	3,976	13,857	13,605	3,781	2,602	0	0	5,428	4,526
Corn Belt	5,181	7,710	35,027	30,660	19,024	27,832	336	3	10,820	4,101
Northern Plains	21,776	17,784	21,633	17,013	2,178	3,269	0	0	15,111	22,646
Appalachian	687	1,323	4,668	5,064	2,247	1,060	891	12	3,230	4,194
Southeast	200	497	3,883	4,109	1,314	1,915	1,898	32	4,257	4,930
Delta States	559	673	1,103	380	5,300	4,358	3,133	96	1,255	5,758
Southern Plains	7,975	15,697	8,304	4,051	264	469	6,120	9,135	8,146	1,360
Mountain	7,105	13,362	4,342	2,366	0	0	518	1	5,084	704
Pacific	3,373	6,831	2,872	1,434	0	0	725	21	1,285	0

As compared to model A, which postulated 1980 exports equal only to 1965 quantities, this model shows substantially less cropland converted when demand levels are filled (48.2 versus 78.4 million acres). However, the concentration of converted land by regions remains high. As indicated in Figure 2.15, the Northern Plains and Southeast regions of the United States still show a large proportion of total cropland idled or converted. Adjustment problems would be severe for regions with over 75 percent of total cropland idled from crop production. The major difference between models A and C is that fewer regions fall into this category.

Programmed crop prices show almost no change from model B; wheat, feed grains, and soybeans remain quite similar (Table 2.16). Programmed cotton price however drops substantially. With the removal of production restraints, the programmed price of cotton lint falls 10 cents per pound. The large shift of production toward the Southwest has a substantial effect on the cost of producing cotton.

As might be expected, the effects of eliminating cotton quotas concentrate in the regions which produce cotton. Total rent per acre drops in the Southern Plains by $10.01. The Pacific, Delta, and Appa-

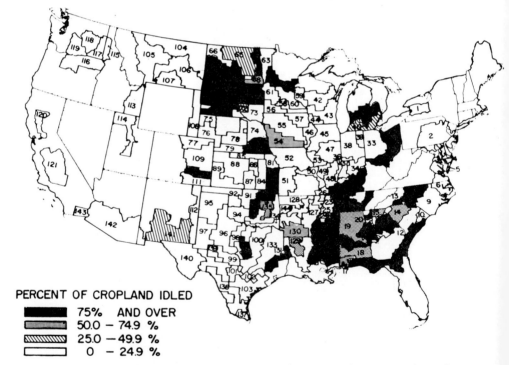

PERCENT OF CROPLAND IDLED

■ 75% AND OVER
▨ 50.0 − 74.9 %
▨ 25.0 − 49.9 %
□ 0 − 24.9 %

Fig. 2.15. Proportion of total cropland unused for crops in each of the 144 crop-producing regions under the free market model without cotton quotas and with trend level exports in 1980.

Table 2.16 ● Programmed Prices of Major Crops and Programmed Rents Per Acre by Farm Production Region for Model C

Region	Wheat		Feed grains		Soybeans		Cotton[a]		Total crop rent	Source of rent	
	1965	1980	1965	1980	1965	1980	1965	1980		crop-land	acreage quotas
			($ per bu)				(¢ per lb)			($ per acre)	
United States	1.34	1.27	1.10	.75	2.49	1.23	28.0	17.2	...	...	...
Northeast	1.35	1.45	1.30	.90	2.43	1.40	...	...	10.13	10.13	0
Lake States	1.43	1.04	1.01	.61	2.49	1.16	...	...	5.00	5.00	0
Corn Belt	1.35	1.08	1.08	.52	2.50	1.06	...	...	7.69	7.69	0
Northern Plains	1.36	.76	1.13	.59	2.35	1.15	...	...	3.94	3.94	0
Appalachian	1.38	1.45	1.24	.89	2.44	1.36	...	...	2.93	2.93	0
Southeast	1.42	1.48	1.24	.93	2.49	1.27	...	...	.18	.18	0
Delta States	1.29	1.47	1.27	.94	2.50	1.25	...	...	2.70	2.70	0
Southern Plains	1.34	1.34	1.25	.86	2.28	1.00	...	...	17.06	17.06	0
Mountain	1.26	1.15	1.28	.91	...	1.45	...	...	11.25	11.25	0
Pacific	1.34	1.32	1.44	1.14	...	1.60	...	...	29.58	29.58	0

aRegional prices were not calculated.

lachian regions also show declines. In each case the removal of the limiting factor on production, the cotton quota, causes a decline in the total rent per acre.

Labor requirements for this model are only slightly lower than they are with a policy of controlling cotton production with acreage quotas. Nationally, man-hours for all farm work show a decrease of 33 percent from 1965 levels without cotton quotas, compared to a 32 percent decline with quotas. Individual regions are affected more; the Delta region shows a decline of 54 percent in man-hours from 1965 levels, and a decline of an additional 11 percent with the elimination of cotton quotas. The Appalachian and Pacific regions also show slight additional declines in man-hours used. Labor requirements are shown in Table 2.17.

Capital used under this model shows only a modest change from model B. The Delta region, which decreases man-hours significantly, also shows a decrease in capital use. The elimination of cotton quotas appears to decrease the value of land and buildings nationally by approximately $4 billion. Machinery values increase slightly, partly as an offset to the greater decline in man-hours of labor used. All capital requirements are shown in Table 2.18.

Transportation of wheat, feed grains, and oilmeals is similar to the previous model and consequently is not repeated.

MODEL D: FREE MARKET AND MAXIMUM LEVEL OF EXPORTS IN 1980. Model D supposes that the United States adopts a policy of exporting all quantities of major crops above domestic needs which the agricultural sector is able to produce. Such a policy presumes that either subsidy programs might be increased in a humanitarian effort to feed nations which are in a food-short status, or that per capita incomes in underdeveloped countries increase and allow large quantities of foodstuffs to be purchased. Under such a situation, the nation's agriculture could be turned loose to produce at maximum levels compatible with available quantities of resources. The limiting resource with such a policy is presumed to be cropland. Export levels are 2,157 million bushels of wheat, 70.0 million tons of feed grains, 37.0 million tons of oilmeals, and 6.8 million bales of cotton.

A policy of all-out production to satisfy these export requirements and domestic demand levels requires 88.7 million acres of wheat; feed grains require 94.4 million acres; soybeans expand to 58.6 million acres; and cotton requires 9.7 million acres. Cotton acreage continues at a low level as production is centered in the higher yielding areas of the Southwest in the absence of acreage quotas. There are no idle acres under this production policy.

Regionally, Table 2.19 shows the cropland changes which such a policy encourages. Wheat acreage increases in all regions from 1965 acreages, with large increases in the Lake States, Northern Plains, Southern Plains, and Mountain regions. For feed grains, shifts in acreage

Table 2.17 ● Labor Requirements by Regions, Actual 1965 and Projected 1980 Needs under Model C

Region	Percentage change all farm work 1965-1980	All farm work		All livestock		All crops	
		1965	1980	1965	1980	1965	1980
		(million man-hours)					
United States	-33.0	7,976	5,347	3,066	2,210	3,798	2,519
Northeast	-35.2	627	406	314	202	226	157
Lake States	-29.0	849	603	452	320	284	219
Corn Belt	-33.3	1,309	873	658	474	448	285
Northern Plains	-31.9	630	429	290	225	240	145
Appalachian	-41.1	1,157	682	341	226	658	378
Southeast	-40.0	801	481	219	169	484	265
Delta States	-54.2	594	272	179	135	340	110
Southern Plains	-19.5	709	571	247	156	353	340
Mountain	-21.5	470	369	174	143	230	184
Pacific	-20.4	830	661	192	160	535	436

Table 2.18 ● Capital Requirements in 1980 for Major Categories of Inputs under Model C

Region	Percentage change total capital 1965-80	Total capital		Projected 1980 value of		
		1965	1980	land and buildings	machinery and equipment	livestock inventories
				($ billion)		
United States	+32.7	198.9	263.8	199.2	42.8	21.6
Northeast	+21.1	10.9	13.2	8.1	3.9	1.2
Lake States	+44.6	16.1	23.2	14.3	6.6	2.2
Corn Belt	+28.2	45.0	57.7	41.9	10.9	4.9
Northern Plains	+31.5	23.0	30.3	20.0	6.7	3.6
Appalachian	+14.6	15.0	17.2	12.2	3.6	1.4
Southeast	+17.8	12.6	14.8	12.4	1.3	1.1
Delta States	+20.2	9.2	11.1	8.8	1.3	.9
Southern Plains	+37.5	24.2	33.2	28.1	2.9	2.2
Mountain	+48.2	17.0	25.2	20.0	2.7	2.3
Pacific	+46.7	25.9	37.9	33.4	2.9	1.8

Table 2.19 ● Acreages of Major Crops and Unused Land by Regions, Actual 1965 and Projected 1980 Levels under Model D

Region	Wheat 1965	Wheat 1980	Feed grains 1965	Feed grains 1980	Soybeans 1965	Soybeans 1980	Cotton 1965	Cotton 1980	Converted land 1965	Converted land 1980
					(thousand acres)					
United States	49,313	88,673	98,956	94,381	34,551	58,563	13,621	9,654	55,950	0
Northeast	786	2,110	3,267	1,656	443	1,945	0	0	1,334	0
Lake States	1,671	9,078	13,857	7,318	3,781	8,312	0	0	5,428	0
Corn Belt	5,181	5,470	35,027	45,782	19,024	19,051	336	3	10,820	0
Northern Plains	21,776	29,369	21,633	20,177	2,178	11,167	0	0	15,111	0
Appalachian	687	934	4,668	6,109	2,247	4,599	891	12	3,230	0
Southeast	200	1,667	3,883	3,723	1,314	6,061	1,898	32	4,257	0
Delta States	559	3,625	1,103	1,532	5,300	6,012	3,133	96	1,255	0
Southern Plains	7,975	16,740	8,304	3,657	264	1,416	6,120	8,899	8,146	0
Mountain	7,105	12,929	4,342	2,994	0	0	518	511	5,084	0
Pacific	3,373	6,751	2,872	1,433	0	0	725	101	1,285	0

are toward the Corn Belt; this particular region increases feed grains acreage by 10 million acres over 1965 levels. The Southern Plains region shifts out of sorghum grain production and into wheat production. Soybean production expands into more marginal soybean-producing areas: the Lake States, Northern Plains, Appalachian, Southeast, and Delta regions. Cotton production is centralized in the Southern Plains with a small acreage in other regions.

Programmed crop prices (Table 2.20) for wheat, feed grains, and soybeans show large increases. Cotton price remains low but is substantially higher than the 17.2 cents per pound of model C even though total production increases only 0.8 million bales. The increased opportunity cost of using land for cotton production (or increased return to land from non-cotton uses) causes the cotton price to increase.

Programmed rents per acre also rise under this level of demand. Landowners would gain greatly from a policy of all-out production. Although fixed costs (taxes) have not been deducted from these rents, the level would still be substantially above any of the previous models.

Labor requirements for model D are presented in Table 2.21. Even under this higher level of demand, labor required for agricultural production is estimated to be 31 percent lower by 1980 when compared to 1965 statistics. However, man-hours used for crops decrease only 30 percent which is the least decline in any policy analyzed. The Delta and Appalachian regions are projected to decline substantially from the man-hours used in 1965. The Northeast, Southeast, and Corn Belt also reduce man-hour requirements for farm production. In general these results suggest that even with substantially increased levels of production the number of man-hours required for farm work will fall over the next decade. This kind of result is expected, of course, if increased efficiency in agriculture is to continue. The basic process of improving the efficiency of the production process requires that over a period of time, fewer man-hours be used to carry out the same activities.

Offsetting the reduction in labor which accompanies the process of economic development is the increase in capital which takes place. Under a maximum level of output, capital inputs increase greatly. For the United States, total capital inputs would increase by 187 percent (in constant dollars) (Table 2.22). The Corn Belt leads other regions in the percent of increase (371 percent) and is followed by the Lake States (314 percent). The extremely large programmed land rents cause land and building values to shoot upward. Likewise the increased demand and output causes the value of machinery and equipment to increase. The result is sharply higher capital values in agriculture.

The quantities of wheat, feed grains, and oilmeals shipped between regions are shown in Figures 2.16, 2.17, and 2.18. With this demand level, the number of excess-supply regions increases for wheat under this type of policy; feed grains and oilmeals also show some change.

Table 2.20 ● Programmed Prices of Major Crops and Programmed Rents Per Acre by Farm Production Region for Model D

Region	Wheat		Feed grains		Soybeans		Cotton[a]		Total crop rent	Source of rent	
	1965	1980	1965	1980	1965	1980	1965	1980		crop-land	acreage quotas
	($ per bu)		($ per bu)				(¢ per lb)		($ per acre)		
United States	1.34	4.40	1.10	2.53	2.49	6.19	28.0	23.6	...	...	...
Northeast	1.35	4.44	1.30	2.63	2.43	6.42	...	...	63.05	63.05	0
Lake States	1.43	3.89	1.01	2.42	2.49	6.02	...	...	59.42	59.42	0
Corn Belt	1.35	4.18	1.08	2.23	2.50	6.13	...	...	83.43	83.43	0
Northern Plains	1.36	3.93	1.13	2.40	2.35	5.81	...	...	46.52	46.52	0
Appalachian	1.38	4.46	1.24	2.61	2.44	6.10	...	...	59.71	59.71	0
Southeast	1.42	4.35	1.24	2.70	2.49	6.15	...	...	51.77	51.77	0
Delta States	1.29	4.54	1.27	2.65	2.50	6.26	...	...	57.78	57.78	0
Southern Plains	1.34	4.55	1.25	2.59	2.28	6.00	...	...	49.65	49.65	0
Mountain	1.26	4.18	1.23	2.81	...	6.38	...	...	68.26	68.26	0
Pacific	1.34	4.39	1.44	2.90	...	6.55	...	...	68.26	68.26	0

[a] Regional prices were not calculated.

Table 2.21 ● Labor Requirements by Regions, Actual 1965 and Projected 1980 Needs under Model D

Region	Percentage change all farm work 1965-80	All farm work		All livestock		All crops	
		1965	1980	1965	1980	1965	1980
		(million man-hours)					
United States	-31.0	7,976	5,501	3,066	2,210	3,798	2,654
Northeast	-35.2	627	406	314	202	226	157
Lake States	-27.6	849	615	452	320	284	230
Corn Belt	-32.6	1,309	882	658	474	448	293
Northern Plains	-25.4	630	470	290	225	240	180
Appalachian	-39.5	1,157	700	341	226	658	394
Southeast	-36.6	801	508	219	169	484	289
Delta States	-48.8	594	304	179	135	340	139
Southern Plains	-19.5	709	571	247	156	353	340
Mountain	-18.7	470	382	174	143	230	195
Pacific	-20.1	830	663	192	160	535	437

Table 2.22 ● Capital Requirements in 1980 for Major Categories of Inputs under Model D

Region	Percentage change total capital 1965–80	Total capital		Projected 1980 value of		
		1965	1980	land and buildings	machinery and equipment	livestock inventories
				($ billion)		
United States	+187.3	198.9	571.6	501.9	48.0	21.8
Northeast	+ 49.9	10.9	16.4	11.2	4.0	1.2
Lake States	+313.8	16.1	66.5	56.2	8.1	2.2
Corn Belt	+371.1	45.0	212.2	195.7	11.6	4.9
Northern Plains	+167.5	23.0	61.6	49.5	8.6	3.6
Appalachian	+ 84.8	15.0	27.8	22.7	3.7	1.4
Southeast	+292.9	12.6	49.5	46.2	2.2	1.1
Delta States	+216.7	9.2	29.1	27.0	1.3	.9
Southern Plains	+ 57.0	24.2	38.0	32.8	2.9	2.2
Mountain	+ 69.5	17.0	28.8	23.5	2.8	2.5
Pacific	+ 61.1	25.9	41.7	37.1	2.8	1.8

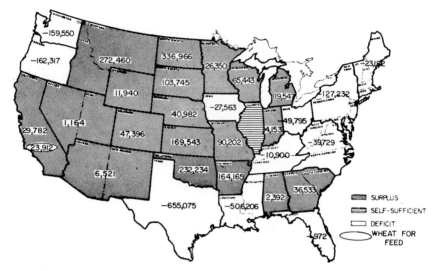

Fig. 2.16. *Flows of wheat under the free market model, no cotton quotas, and maximum level exports.*

Acreage Restraint Models ● All previous models included acreage restraints only for cotton. As a result, feed grains, wheat, and soybean production is allocated among crop-production regions on the basis of the lowest cost per unit of production. The resulting allocation of production results in the lowest cost for producing the given level of output.

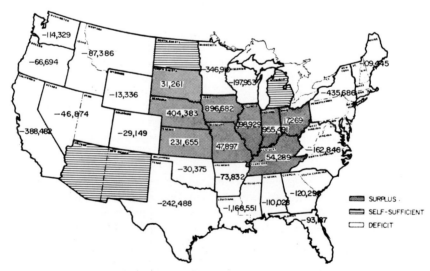

Fig. 2.17. *Flows of feed grains under the free market model, no cotton quotas, and maximum level exports.*

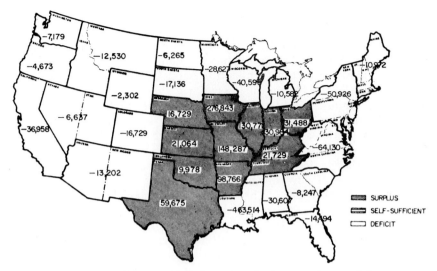

Fig. 2.18. Flows of oilmeals under the free market model, no cotton quotas, and maximum level exports.

Acreages of land which are not required for production at a given level of demand remain idle or are converted to other uses according to the above production plan. Given a time period of adequate length, possibly two or three decades, these acreages of land might return to grass or be utilized in other less intensive ways. In a shorter period of time, however, these marginal acreages have the potential of producing surplus commodities at lower prices and lowering the average returns to all resources in the industry. In general, society as expressed through the institution of government has been unwilling to allow average returns to land resources to remain depressed while marginal land resources slowly transfer from intensive crop production to less intensive use. As a result, federal programs were developed which immediately removed these acreages from production. The length of time for which these acres remain idle has varied; however over the last decade there have been continued annual land retirement programs for agriculture.

Given any policy other than all-out production, it is evident from the models analyzed that the agricultural economy will continue to have surplus capacity for the foreseeable future. Unless society changes its views on appropriate types of programs and what constitutes equitable returns to landowners, it is probable that programs for removing land from production will continue. Therefore a realistic look at the future structure of agriculture must include the possibility of farm policies other than a free market economy for agriculture. As a result we include three models which assume controls on crop production as explained below.

84   CHAPTER TWO

MODEL E: A FEED GRAIN PROGRAM WITH TREND LEVEL EXPORTS IN 1980.
The following model of the farm economy includes production controls
on wheat, feed grains, and cotton. This model assumes that the 1960s
type feed grain and wheat programs are continued and that a similar
program exists for cotton. Under this model, base acreages are calculated for each of the 144 producing regions. Production is then allocated
among the regions within the reduced land base so that total costs of
producing the specified level of demand are minimized. Farmers are
assumed to participate in the programs which retire the quantities of
land necessary to balance supply and demand for each commodity. Thus
the major change from previous models is that supply is controlled
through the use of government land retirement programs, rather than
through the marketplace. The results of this model are compared to
model C, unless otherwise specified.

Wheat production for domestic and export needs (1.3 billion bushels)
under this program requires 62.5 million acres of cropland (Table 2.23),
7 million fewer acres than under the free market model. This difference
occurs largely because of the elimination of wheat used for livestock
feed, a result of higher prices for wheat. The implementation of base
acreages for wheat reduces the acreage of wheat grown in the Southern
Plains and Mountain regions. The result is slightly higher average yields,
smaller acreages, and higher programmed prices for wheat.

Feed grains acreage changes in the opposite direction. Production
of feed grains for domestic and export needs (40.0 million tons) increases
8.2 million acres under this type of program as compared to the free
market model. Acreages of feed grains increase in the Pacific, Mountain,
and Southern Plains regions to replace livestock feed previously supplied
by wheat. When feed grains replace wheat as livestock feed, there is
a cost involved. An additional million acres of land are used to fill
the total demand for feed grains and wheat.

Soybean production requires 43.1 million acres of cropland. The
Corn Belt increases acreage significantly from 1965 levels to supply this
quantity of oilmeals.

Cotton acreage in most regions shows a decrease from 1965 levels;
total acreage for the United States declines by 2.6 million acres. The
Delta region shows a million-acre drop, and the Southeast makes up
the remainder of the reduction.

Excess capacity under this model shows approximately a 10-million-
acre decrease from levels of land retirement for 1965. As might be expected with similar programs, most of the regions show some of the
reduction in idle acres. Only the Appalachian and Southeast regions
show moderate increases. While total acres idled under this model are
not greatly different from the free market model with similar demand
levels, the implications are quite different for a large number of regions.
Under this model, most regions show a lower proportion of their cropland idled. The Northern Plains have only 2 regions, numbers 70 and

Table 2.23 ● Acreages of Major Crops and Unused Land by Regions, Actual 1965 and Projected 1980 Levels under Model E

Region	Wheat		Feed grains		Soybeans		Cotton		Converted land	
	1965	1980	1965	1980	1965	1980	1965	1980	1965	1980
					(thousand acres)					
United States	49,313	62,520	98,956	89,165	34,551	43,076	13,621	10,959	55,950	45,552
Northeast	786	1,460	3,267	2,512	443	1,347	0	0	1,334	390
Lake States	1,671	2,630	13,857	14,475	3,781	3,272	0	0	5,428	4,332
Corn Belt	5,181	6,543	35,027	31,017	19,024	25,478	336	320	10,820	6,949
Northern Plains	21,776	27,198	21,633	18,844	2,178	4,436	0	0	15,111	10,234
Appalachian	687	782	4,668	4,943	2,247	1,759	891	640	3,230	3,529
Southeast	200	302	3,883	4,110	1,314	2,394	1,898	46	4,257	4,632
Delta States	559	164	1,103	340	5,300	3,904	3,133	2,109	1,255	4,749
Southern Plains	7,975	9,539	8,304	7,108	264	486	6,120	6,517	8,146	7,062
Mountain	7,105	9,208	4,342	3,006	0	0	518	615	5,084	3,605
Pacific	3,373	4,694	2,872	2,810	0	0	725	712	1,285	70

71 in Figure 2.19, with over 75 percent of total cropland unused. Under
the free market model with the same level of demand, a number of
other regions in this area indicated as high a proportion of total cropland unused (or converted under competitive and free market assumptions). The Southeast also shows fewer regions with such a high proportion of cropland unused. Under the free market model, only 53
regions had idle acres. With this feed grain program, the number of
regions with idle acres increases to 86 out of a total of 144. A greater
distribution of the idle acres is evident; therefore the result is a wider
distribution of the excess crop acres under this type of farm program.

Programmed prices of major crops for this model and identical
levels of demand are higher than under a free market. The programmed
wheat price is $1.49 per bushel (Table 2.24), as compared to $1.27 under
a free market (Table 2.12). Feed grains remain almost constant, 78 cents
and 76 cents per bushel for the same models; soybeans also are relatively unaffected by the change in programs. Cotton price increases to
31.4 cents per pound with the added restraints of acreage control programs. In general it appears that continuation of this type of program
whereby soybeans are allowed complete freedom of production and

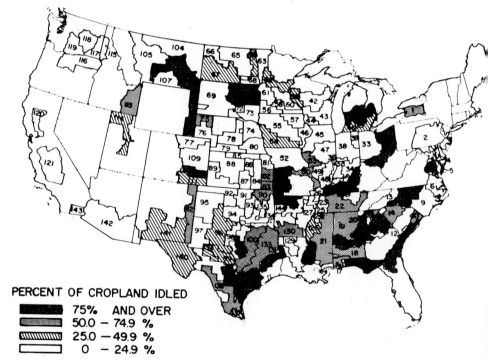

PERCENT OF CROPLAND IDLED

- 75% AND OVER
- 50.0 – 74.9 %
- 25.0 – 49.9 %
- 0 – 24.9 %

Fig. 2.19. Proportion of total cropland unused for major crops in
each of the 144 crop-producing regions under a feed grain program
with trend level exports in 1980.

Table 2.24 ● Programmed Prices of Major Crops and Programmed Rents Per Acre by Farm Production Region for Model E

Region	Wheat		Feed grains		Soybeans		Cotton[a]		Total crop rent	Source of rent	
	1965	1980	1965	1980	1965	1980	1965	1980		crop-land	acreage quotas
	($ per bu)		($ per bu)				(¢ per lb)		($ per acre)	($ per acre)	
United States	1.34	1.49	1.10	.78	2.49	1.28	28.0	31.4	...	...	...
Northeast	1.35	1.71	1.30	.95	2.43	1.44	...	...	12.04	7.74	4.30
Lake States	1.43	1.38	1.01	.63	2.49	1.21	...	...	5.52	4.29	1.23
Corn Belt	1.35	1.35	1.08	.54	2.50	1.11	...	...	9.76	8.62	1.14
Northern Plains	1.36	1.06	1.13	.62	2.35	1.18	...	...	7.33	3.17	4.16
Appalachian	1.38	1.73	1.24	.94	2.44	1.41	...	...	8.41	3.20	5.21
Southeast	1.42	1.83	1.24	.95	2.49	1.31	...	...	.28	0	.28
Delta States	1.29	1.79	1.27	.95	2.50	1.36	...	...	6.88	0	6.88
Southern Plains	1.34	1.66	1.25	.67	2.28	1.05	...	...	28.75	5.63	23.12
Mountain	1.26	1.15	1.23	1.08	...	1.44	...	...	8.93	2.74	6.19
Pacific	1.34	1.16	1.44	1.17	...	1.65	...	...	30.85	12.47	18.38

[a]Regional prices were not calculated.

other crops are controlled might result in continued slow decline in feed grains prices, a substantial decline in soybean prices over time, and a fairly stable price level for wheat and cotton.

Programmed rents for this model are slightly higher in most regions than for a free market with comparable levels of demand. Restraints placed on individual crops contribute substantially to the total value of rent. Cotton restrictions cause a sizeable part of the rent in the Appalachian, Delta, Southern Plains, and Pacific regions (Table 2.24). The wheat and feed grain programs are also of importance.

Labor requirements for the feed grain program are 32 percent lower than the man-hours used in 1965 (Table 2.25). The Delta region shows a 41 percent decrease, whereas the Northeast, Corn Belt, Appalachian, and Southeast regions all exceed a 30 percent decrease. Only the Pacific and Mountain regions requirements decrease by smaller amounts.

Capital requirements for this farm program increase 39 percent nationally between 1965 and 1980 (Table 2.26). The value of land and buildings rises from $159.4 billion to $210.5 billion—a 32 percent increase measured in constant dollars; machinery and equipment increase 75 percent in value over this period—from $25.2 billion in 1965 to an estimated $43.2 billion in 1980. Livestock inventories increase to produce the substantially higher quantities of meat required for domestic consumption. Livestock inventories for major animals are projected to rise from $14.4 billion in 1965 to $21.8 billion by 1980—a 51 percent increase.

MODEL F: ACREAGE QUOTAS AND TREND LEVEL EXPORTS IN 1980. Given a policy of minimum restraints on production, the feed grain program of the 1960s described under model E provides a means of controlling crop production. The government would continue a land diversion program which retires 45.6 million acres of cropland compared to the feed grain and wheat programs of 1965, which retired 42 million acres from production at a cost of $1.9 billion.[10] At this level of cost, continuing these programs would cost $30 billion over fifteen years. In general, increased demand for farm commodities may raise the level of commodity prices and increase the cost of retiring the same acreage of land. Consequently the cost of these programs is likely to rise during the next decade.

Faced with this knowledge, society might conclude that other means of controlling farm production are less demanding of public resources. Given this conclusion, two kinds of policies would be available: the first is a free market economy as described in earlier sections; the second is tighter acreage restraint which controls production without the need for costly land retirement programs. Acreage quota programs result in excess acres of land, but these acres lie idle, or are used for other minor crops or for hay and pasture land; the quota program could prevent

10. U.S. Dept. of Agriculture, *1965 Feed Grain and Wheat Programs: Statistical Summary* (Washington, D.C.: USDA ASCS, 1966).

Table 2.25 ● Labor Requirements by Regions, Actual 1965 and Projected 1980 Needs under Model E

Region	Percentage change all farm work 1965-80	All farm work (million man-hours)		All livestock		All crops	
		1965	1980	1965	1980	1965	1980
United States	-31.9	7,976	5,435	3,066	2,210	3,798	2,597
Northeast	-35.6	627	404	314	202	226	155
Lake States	-28.9	849	604	452	320	284	220
Corn Belt	-33.5	1,309	870	658	474	448	282
Northern Plains	-28.4	630	451	290	225	240	164
Appalachian	-38.1	1,157	716	341	226	658	408
Southeast	-39.6	801	484	219	169	484	267
Delta States	-40.7	594	352	179	135	340	182
Southern Plains	-29.6	709	499	247	156	353	278
Mountain	-20.0	470	376	174	143	230	190
Pacific	-18.2	830	679	192	160	535	451

Table 2.26 ● Capital Requirements in 1980 for Major Categories of Inputs under Model E

Region	Percentage change total capital 1965-80	Total capital		Projected 1980 value of		
		1965	1980	land and buildings	machinery and equipment	livestock inventories
				($ billion)		
United States	+38.5	198.9	275.5	210.5	43.2	21.8
Northeast	+20.8	10.9	13.2	8.2	3.8	1.2
Lake States	+47.5	16.1	23.7	14.7	6.7	2.2
Corn Belt	+36.6	45.0	61.6	46.1	10.6	4.9
Northern Plains	+46.3	23.0	33.7	22.4	7.7	3.6
Appalachian	+21.3	15.0	18.2	13.2	3.6	1.4
Southeast	+22.5	12.6	15.4	13.0	1.3	1.1
Delta States	+34.8	9.2	12.4	10.2	1.3	.9
Southern Plains	+43.3	24.2	34.6	29.5	2.9	2.2
Mountain	+45.5	17.0	24.7	19.7	2.5	2.5
Pacific	+47.1	25.9	38.0	33.5	2.8	1.8

excess acres from being planted to the major crops—wheat, feed grains, and cotton.

The acreage quota program analyzed in this section incorporates the trend level of exports with tight quotas on production of wheat, feed grains, and cotton. Soybeans are allowed on land restricted from other crops. The tight acreage quotas result in 37.9 million acres of idle cropland, the smallest surplus capacity of any model analyzed with trend level of exports (Table 2.27).

In addition to reducing the magnitude of surplus capacity, acreage quotas have the further effect of spreading the idle acres over more regions. Only three regions in Figure 2.20 indicate over 75 percent of total cropland unused. Most regions with idle acres show 25 percent or less of total cropland unused—a large reduction from the free market models analyzed. Had soybeans been restricted from acreages taken out of other crops, the idle acres would have been even more widespread. Under this program, 104 of the 144 regions have some unused land. The acreage quota program dispenses the gains and losses of land retirement programs over a greater number of regions than any other pro-

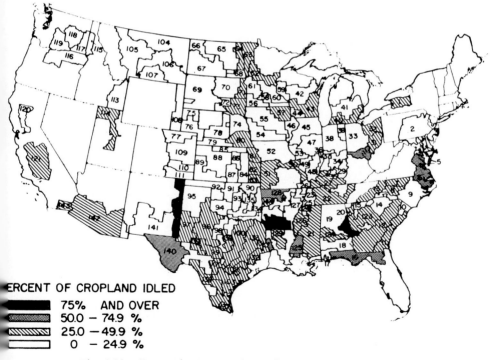

ERCENT OF CROPLAND IDLED

- 75%   AND OVER
- 50.0 – 74.9 %
- 25.0 – 49.9 %
- 0 – 24.9 %

Fig. 2.20. Proportion of total cropland unused for major crops in each of the 144 crop-producing regions under an acreage quota program with trend level exports in 1980.

Table 2.27 ● Acreages of Major Crops and Unused Land by Regions, Actual 1965 and Projected 1980 Levels under Model F

Region	Wheat 1965	Wheat 1980	Feed grains 1965	Feed grains 1980	Soybeans 1965	Soybeans 1980	Cotton 1965	Cotton 1980	Converted land 1965	Converted land 1980
					(thousand acres)					
United States	49,313	62,804	98,956	96,366	34,551	42,214	13,621	11,534	55,950	37,990
Northeast	786	1,454	3,267	3,004	443	966	0	0	1,334	286
Lake States	1,671	3,327	13,857	12,559	3,781	5,321	0	0	5,428	3,498
Corn Belt	5,181	6,477	35,027	31,544	19,024	27,286	336	261	10,820	4,751
Northern Plains	21,776	27,122	21,633	20,942	2,178	3,905	0	0	15,111	8,744
Appalachian	687	1,098	4,668	6,661	2,247	1,006	891	523	3,230	2,365
Southeast	200	278	3,883	5,060	1,314	1,115	1,898	1,712	4,257	3,319
Delta States	559	185	1,103	1,988	5,300	2,239	3,133	2,612	1,255	4,240
Southern Plains	7,975	8,370	8,304	7,882	264	376	6,120	5,344	8,146	8,370
Mountain	7,105	10,207	4,342	3,998	0	0	518	500	5,084	1,728
Pacific	3,373	4,286	2,872	2,728	0	0	725	582	1,285	689

gram analyzed; however it also requires the largest crop acreage of any model with trend level exports and higher total costs of production.

Programmed prices of commodities increase under this type of program. The programmed price of wheat is $1.92 per bushel nationally and programmed feed grains and cotton prices also increase above previous levels (Table 2.28). Soybean prices, by contrast, show some decline from the previous models, a result of this type of program. Tight acreage quotas reduce the acreage of feed grains in each producing region and allow soybeans to be grown on the restricted acreage. Soybean production increases in the more productive regions with lower per unit costs, and consequently the average programmed price of soybeans falls. However, restrictions on acreage of other crops forces production of these crops out of their most efficient areas of production, and consequently their programmed prices increase.

Programmed rents also increase with acreage quotas since the proportion of rent resulting from the quota increases substantially. This is caused when quotas become the limiting restraint on production. Therefore the average cropland rent is decreased (Table 2.28), but quota rents rise, and total rent is increased as well.

Labor requirements for this model total 5,524 million man-hours, 31 percent lower than 1965 man-hours used (Table 2.29); this level is equal to the needs for the maximum output model analyzed previously. Such results suggest that acreage quotas on crop production can slow the outflow of labor from agriculture; however, the magnitude of reduction at the national level is only 2 to 3 percent over the next fifteen years. Within individual regions, the difference is somewhat greater; the Delta States show a 36 percent decline with acreage quotas compared to their 54 percent decline with a free market (Table 2.17); the Southeast indicates a 30 percent decline compared to their previous 40 percent decline; and the Appalachian region reduces man-hours 38 percent compared to a 41 percent decrease under the competitive pressures of the marketplace. The Southern Plains, by contrast, show a greater decrease with acreage quotas—34 percent compared to 20 percent with a free market. The large shifts in acreage of cotton accounts for most of the differences, although decreased wheat acreage also uses less labor. Other regions do not show substantial changes in labor used between models B and F.

Capital values are higher with acreage quotas than with a free market or a feed grain program. This outcome is directly attributable to the increased rents resulting from the scarcity (reduced supply) of cropland under acreage quotas. The value of machinery and equipment for this model shows an increase over a free market of $1.5 billion (Table 2.30). The Northern Plains and Lake States account for most of this increase. Overall capital values increase 89.8 percent over 1965 capital values.

Termination of Export Subsidies ● In analyzing each of the previous

Table 2.28 ● Programmed Prices of Major Crops and Programmed Rents Per Acre by Farm Production Region under Model F

Region	Wheat 1965	Wheat 1980	Feed grains 1965	Feed grains 1980	Soybeans 1965	Soybeans 1980	Cotton[a] 1965	Cotton[a] 1980	Total crop rent	Source of rent crop-land	Source of rent acreage quotas
	($ per bu)						(¢ per lb)		($ per acre)		
United States	1.34	1.92	1.10	1.48	2.49	1.19	28.0	43.7	...	...	...
Northeast	1.35	2.13	1.30	1.63	2.43	1.31	...	...	28.32	2.08	26.24
Lake States	1.43	1.81	1.01	1.39	2.49	1.05	...	...	24.52	.92	23.60
Corn Belt	1.35	1.77	1.08	1.22	2.50	1.04	...	...	33.83	2.66	31.17
Northern Plains	1.36	1.49	1.13	1.29	2.35	1.07	...	...	22.22	1.70	20.52
Appalachian	1.38	2.16	1.24	1.60	2.44	1.28	...	...	28.62	2.80	25.82
Southeast	1.42	2.26	1.24	1.70	2.49	1.25	...	...	17.43	1.93	15.50
Delta States	1.29	2.22	1.27	1.66	2.50	1.23	...	...	25.77	.11	25.66
Southern Plains	1.34	2.08	1.25	1.34	2.28	.97	...	...	46.41	2.30	44.11
Mountain	1.26	1.57	1.23	1.77	...	1.37	...	...	23.98	.81	23.17
Pacific	1.34	1.59	1.44	1.86	...	1.54	...	...	57.63	17.86	39.77

[a]Regional prices were not calculated.

94

Table 2.29 ● Labor Requirements by Regions, Actual 1965 and Projected 1980 Needs under Model F

Region	Percentage change all farm work 1965-80	All farm work		All livestock		All crops	
		1965	1980	1965	1980	1965	1980
		(million man-hours)					
United States	-30.7	7,976	5,524	3,066	2,210	3,798	2,679
Northeast	-35.6	627	404	314	202	226	156
Lake States	-28.4	849	608	452	320	284	222
Corn Belt	-33.2	1,309	874	658	474	448	288
Northern Plains	-28.3	630	452	290	225	240	165
Appalachian	-37.8	1,157	720	341	226	658	412
Southeast	-30.0	801	561	219	169	484	336
Delta States	-36.2	594	379	179	135	340	206
Southern Plains	-33.6	709	471	247	156	353	253
Mountain	-19.1	470	380	174	143	230	193
Pacific	-18.7	830	675	192	160	535	448

Table 2.30 ● Capital Requirements in 1980 for Major Categories of Inputs under Model F

Region	Percentage change total capital 1965–80	Total capital		Projected 1980 value of		
		1965	1980	land and buildings	machinery and equipment	livestock inventories
				($ billion)		
United States	+ 89.8	198.9	375.4	311.4	44.4	21.8
Northeast	+ 30.0	10.9	14.2	9.2	3.8	1.2
Lake States	+140.1	16.1	38.6	29.4	7.0	2.2
Corn Belt	+146.0	45.0	110.8	94.9	11.0	4.9
Northern Plains	+ 91.4	23.0	44.1	32.7	7.8	3.6
Appalachian	+ 46.2	15.0	21.9	16.9	3.7	1.4
Southeast	+104.3	12.6	23.7	23.2	1.5	1.1
Delta States	+102.0	9.2	18.6	16.4	1.3	.9
Southern Plains	+ 52.1	24.2	36.7	31.6	2.9	2.2
Mountain	+ 54.6	17.0	26.3	21.1	2.7	2.5
Pacific	+ 56.6	25.9	40.5	36.0	2.7	1.8

models, it has been assumed that export subsidy programs are continued indefinitely. The magnitude of expenditures for these programs has been large. For the fiscal year ending in 1966, the value of exports under government programs totaled $1.6 billion.[11] Although some proportion of these expenditures is assumed to be recovered at a future date, the cost is still substantial. Remuneration for over half of these sales is made in foreign currency. Other programs including famine relief, foreign donations, barter, and long-term loans form a large part of these expenditures. International development programs comprise approximately 2.6 percent. In all probability, a substantial part of these exports in 1965–66 will end up as a cost of supporting farm incomes in the United States.

This final model assumes that government export subsidies for agriculture are terminated before 1980. Since 57 percent of wheat, 10 percent of feed grains, 21 percent of cotton, and a small amount of soybeans were exported under government subsidy programs in 1964,[12] a smaller quantity of each commodity would move without government subsidies; however, the exact amount of the decline is difficult to determine. As a result, the approach used in this study is to assume that the above proportions may continue into the future.

Estimates of commercial export possibilities for each crop are calculated from the trend export level and were presented previously in Table 2.6. The unsubsidized estimates (level 4 of Table 2.6) assume that exports in 1980 are the same proportion of total exports as in 1964. Multiplying these proportions by the 1980 trend export level gives an estimate of commercial exports in 1980. Using wheat as an example, commercial exports in 1964 were 43 percent of total exports. Assuming that 43 percent of the 1980 trend level of wheat exports move without subsidy (1,302 × .43 = 559.8), 560 million bushels are exported in 1980. Feed grains and oilmeals assume 90 percent of the trend level of exports and cotton 79 percent of the trend level of cotton lint exports. The following model incorporates acreage quotas and level four exports into the analysis.

MODEL G: ACREAGE QUOTAS WITH COMMERCIAL EXPORTS IN 1980. Under model G, exports are 560 million bushels of wheat, 36 million tons of feed grains, 17 million tons of oilmeals, and 4.7 million bales of cotton. Given these levels of export demand and the quantities required for domestic consumption, acreages of cropland required for crops in 1980 decrease from 1965 levels. Wheat acreage falls to 42.2 million acres, feed grains to 93.7 million acres, soybeans to 33.8 million acres, and cotton to 10.3 million acres (Table 2.31). Excess capacity is increased by the elimination of export subsidies. Cropland unused, a measure of

11. U.S. Dept. of Agriculture, Fact Book of U.S. Agriculture (Washington, D.C.: GPO, 1965), p. 76.

12. Ibid., pp. 77–78.

Table 2.31 ● Acreages of Major Crops and Unused Land by Regions of the United States, Actual 1965 and Projected 1980 Levels under Model G

Region	Wheat		Feed grains		Soybeans		Cotton		Converted land	
	1965	1980	1965	1980	1965	1980	1965	1980	1965	1980
					(thousand acres)					
United States	49,313	42,168	98,956	93,691	34,551	33,777	13,621	10,334	55,950	71,275
Northeast	786	1,419	3,267	3,004	443	595	0	0	1,334	693
Lake States	1,671	2,371	13,857	11,976	3,781	3,470	0	0	5,428	6,892
Corn Belt	5,181	4,081	35,027	30,184	19,024	22,088	336	261	10,820	13,693
Northern Plains	21,776	14,202	21,633	21,153	2,178	3,720	0	0	15,111	21,637
Appalachian	687	536	4,668	6,550	2,247	947	891	523	3,230	3,070
Southeast	200	231	3,883	5,061	1,314	522	1,898	512	4,257	5,159
Delta States	559	66	1,103	1,980	5,300	2,100	3,133	2,612	1,255	4,507
Southern Plains	7,975	8,115	8,304	7,185	264	335	6,120	5,344	8,146	9,733
Mountain	7,105	6,861	4,342	3,870	0	0	518	500	5,084	5,202
Pacific	3,373	4,286	2,872	2,728	0	0	725	582	1,285	689

excess capacity, totals 71.3 million acres. Unused cropland of this magnitude is similar to that projected under model A, which assumed 1965 level exports in 1980. On a regional basis, the Northern Plains idle an additional 6.6 million acres compared to 1965 idle acres; the Corn Belt also increases idle acres by almost 3 million from 1965 levels. The lower level of demand reduces the total number of acres required for production. As a result, the Northern Plains have 21.6 million acres of unused cropland, the Corn Belt has 13.7 million acres, and the Southern Plains have 9.7 million acres unused. Unsubsidized export levels significantly increase idle land.

Programmed wheat prices are substantially lower than those under the previous model (Table 2.32). A lower price results when the large decrease in wheat exports reduces acreage, and production is centered in regions with lower per unit costs of producing wheat. Feed grains, soybean, and cotton prices remain relatively similar to the previous model. Soybean prices are somewhat lower, a result of the 7-million-ton decrease in exports.

Programmed rents decline with the decline in prices. The effect of acreage quotas is still apparent. As the limiting factor controlling production, the quotas account for a large proportion of total rent; only the Pacific region shows a sizeable cropland rent.

Labor requirements of this level of demand are not significantly different from other models. Even though total acreage idled increases significantly, the quantity of labor required is similar to that needed for substantially higher levels of production. For this model, man-hours required are projected to decrease 32 percent for agriculture in 1980. The regional changes are shown in Table 2.33.

Capital values increase even under this lower level of demand, and the total capital values increase 72 percent for the United States over those of 1965. Regional changes for capital are shown in Table 2.34. Even with the elimination of export subsidies, acreage quotas could maintain and increase the value of fixed assets.

PROSPECTS IN CAPACITY ● The results in this chapter indicate that production capacity will remain large relative to demand in the 1970 decade. Under the free market model which assumes a trend level of exports, 48 million acres would be available to convert to other uses (Table 2.35). This quantity assumes that the discrete demand levels specified would be just met and the excess land would be converted to other uses. Of course the major use to which the converted land would go is to grass and beef production over a long period of time. As compared to crops, beef would be reduced in price under a free market program having this effect. Crop prices would decline sharply in the short run and a considerable amount of the land would be expected to remain in crops at lower prices. Under conditions of price flexibility, even more land would remain in grain at lower prices over a long term, with a

Table 2.32 ● Programmed Prices of Major Crops and Programmed Rents Per Acre by Farm Production Region under Model G

Region	Wheat		Feed grains		Soybeans		Cotton[a]		Total crop rent	Source of rent	
										cropland	acreage quotas
	1965	1980	1965	1980	1965	1980	1965	1980			
	($ per bu)		($ per bu)				(¢ per lb)		($ per acre)	($ per acre)	
United States	1.34	1.17	1.10	1.41	2.49	1.04	28.0	41.1	...	...	...
Northeast	1.35	1.47	1.30	1.57	2.43	1.21	...	...	19.93	.84	19.09
Lake States	1.43	1.16	1.01	1.33	2.49	0.93	...	...	20.02	.07	19.95
Corn Belt	1.35	1.06	1.08	1.16	2.50	0.90	...	...	28.08	.56	27.52
Northern Plains	1.36	.74	1.13	1.15	2.35	0.94	...	...	11.83	.52	11.29
Appalachian	1.38	1.45	1.24	1.55	2.44	1.18	...	...	23.75	1.18	22.57
Southeast	1.42	1.61	1.24	1.65	2.49	1.09	...	...	13.97	.76	13.21
Delta States	1.29	1.45	1.27	1.60	2.50	1.06	...	...	20.34	0	20.34
Southern Plains	1.34	1.30	1.25	1.24	2.28	0.81	...	...	35.98	.48	35.50
Mountain	1.26	.91	1.28	1.61	...	1.24	...	...	12.17	.07	12.10
Pacific	1.34	1.00	1.44	1.72	...	1.43	...	...	38.61	7.48	31.13

[a]Regional prices were not calculated.

Table 2.33 ● Labor Requirements by Regions, Actual 1965 and Projected 1980 Needs under Model G

Region	Percentage change all farm work 1965-80	All farm work		All livestock		All crops	
		1965	1980	1965	1980	1965	1980
		(million man-hours)					
United States	-32.4	7,976	5,391	3,066	2,210	3,798	2,558
Northeast	-35.7	627	403	314	202	226	154
Lake States	-29.6	849	598	452	320	284	214
Corn Belt	-35.1	1,309	850	658	474	448	265
Northern Plains	-31.4	630	432	290	225	240	147
Appalachian	-38.1	1,157	716	341	226	658	408
Southeast	-37.6	801	500	219	169	484	281
Delta States	-36.4	594	378	179	135	340	205
Southern Plains	-34.1	709	467	247	156	353	250
Mountain	-20.8	470	372	174	143	230	186
Pacific	-18.7	830	675	192	160	535	448

Table 2.34 ● Capital Requirements in 1980 for Major Categories of Inputs under Model G

Region	Percentage change total capital 1965-80	Total capital		Projected 1980 value of		
		1965	1980	land and buildings	machinery and equipment	livestock inventories
				($ billion)		
United States	+71.6	198.9	341.4	279.3	40.0	21.9
Northeast	+23.9	10.9	13.5	8.7	3.7	1.2
Lake States	+112.0	16.1	34.1	25.9	6.0	2.2
Corn Belt	+117.0	45.0	97.8	83.3	9.5	4.9
Northern Plains	+68.6	23.0	35.9	25.5	6.7	3.6
Appalachian	+40.1	15.0	21.1	16.0	3.6	1.4
Southeast	+83.8	12.6	23.1	20.8	1.2	1.1
Delta States	+82.7	9.2	16.8	14.6	1.3	.9
Southern Plains	+46.9	24.2	35.5	30.3	2.9	2.2
Mountain	+46.4	16.9	24.9	20.0	2.4	2.6
Pacific	+49.6	25.9	38.7	34.2	2.7	1.8

Table 2.35 ● Potential Converted or Retired Acres by Type of Program for 1980

Program	Model	Exports	Acreage
			(thousand acres)
Free market	A	1965 levels	78,448
Free market	B	trend levels	46,979
Free market	C	trend levels	48,219
Free market	D	use all capacity	0
1960s program	E	trend levels	45,552
Acreage quotas	F	trend levels	37,990
Acreage quotas	G	commercial levels	71,275

large acreage shifting to grass, and some shifting to trees. With export demand at levels just necessary to use up producing capacity on the present cropland base, there would be no surplus land. However under these conditions the United States would have 2.1 billion bushels of wheat for export. Similar increases would have to occur in exports of feed grains, cotton, and soybeans. Total world trade in wheat has been only around 2 billion bushels, hence the prospects of the United States exporting 2.1 billion bushels in ten years plus large amounts of other grains is unrealistic.

Under a 1960s type of farm program, with land retirement on a partial-farm basis and forced into all regions so that high-yield land also is removed from production, 46 million acres are posed to be retired if export demand is at trend levels. Under a mandatory acreage quota model similarly forcing land into retirement on a partial-farm, inter-regionally dispersed basis, 38 million acres are posed for retirement in 1980 under exports at trend levels.

These data are comparable to other results cited in Chapter 1 in supposing the continuation of a surplus capacity position to 1980. A great, unexpected development in exports and world food programs could absorb this capacity. However, such development is not now in sight, and U.S. exports of grains have fallen below the trend level assumptions in recent years as other countries have stepped up their food production and less has been invested in PL 480 food aid.

Regardless of the program in effect, labor employment is expected to drop considerably by 1980. On the basis of man-hours-used projections, the number of people employed is likely to drop in 1980 to around 60 percent of the 1965 level. In a similar vein, total capital used is projected to increase by 40 percent to 1980, measured in real terms. It appears that the capital-land and capital-labor substitution processes explained in Chapter 1 will be on hand during the 1970s to maintain respectively very large producing capacity and farm community adjustments related to larger farms and declining farm population.

CHAPTER THREE

Short and Intermediate Term Compensation Policies for Agriculture

THE PROJECTIONS of agricultural capacity and resource use in the previous chapter confirm that ongoing injections of capital into agriculture may cause the problems of overcapacity and structural adjustment to last at least another decade. Capital-land substitutions continue to increase the number of excess crop acres on which farmers can produce for domestic and export markets. Capital-labor substitutions continue to release additional labor from farming and result in outward migration from the rural areas of the nation. In combination, these substitutions continue the rapid rate of change which has affected the rural areas of the nation since the technological revolution in agriculture began in earnest in the 1930s. Undoubtedly, both the average farm family and its urban counterpart as well as their political leaders would wish that these trends were different—that the immense expenditure of public funds over the last 35 years on agricultural compensation programs could now end, and that public resources could be redirected toward other major problems which the nation has postponed examining and facing for a decade or more. But trends in farm production and food demand do not indicate any gentle or immediate solution to the problems of excess land acres or underemployed labor resources in agriculture.

The nation may find it necessary, based on the available evidence of potential farm production, to continue some type of government control and compensation program for the agricultural sector. While these programs do not reverse the outflow of labor from agriculture, they likely retard the rate at which farm families transfer to alternative employments. It is, in a very practical sense, this rate of transition and transformation of the farm sector which is the basic issue involved in the long discussions over farm program alternatives. There are alternatives which could "freeze" the pattern of farm production at some previous location and structure with changes in ownership and production combinations limited to changes growing out of the aging process. There are other program alternatives which would induce even more rapid changes in resource combinations to assure conformity with existing levels of technology and potential market-price relationships. Studies on this latter alternative have shown implications of immense structural change if instituted over a period as short as a decade. According to one analysis, farm numbers in the North Central region of the United States could be reduced to one-third their 1959 level by 1980, under an "income-efficient" resource reorganization.[1] The associated structural change implied in the supporting infrastructure of rural communities causes most policy makers to move slowly in removing the present production control programs. Resource and asset values have been established on expectations of gradual change or even a simple continuation of past and present relationships. To shift to a program with emphasis on market directed resource use would result in actual outcomes quite different from the set of expectations on which these investments were made and cause quite different levels of returns than anticipated. It is these potential losses from sharp shifts in farm programs which result in the gradual evolution of farm programs from one particular program to another. Most farm programs are initially tested on a limited basis, and if successful, are expanded to wider application. The annual diversion programs of the 1960s were initially placed on trial in the Acreage Reserve portion of the Soil Bank program in 1956. Found wanting in their initial trial as a result of a late start, they nevertheless were revived in the Emergency Feed Grains Act of 1961. Their success was almost unexpected, so much so that the Freeman administration proposed a substantially more restrictive control program in 1962. But the general public and farmers found the feed grain program to be a useful means of holding back aggregate supply while allowing those farmers not wanting to participate, to remain out of the programs. Its success with feed grains producers led to its extension to wheat producers in 1964 and to cotton producers in 1966.

The tendency for farm programs to evolve slowly has some important implications. It implies that any substantial change in programs will take a long period of time with each successive incremental change representing only a small difference from the past. Also, it suggests that the nation's agricultural leadership needs long-term planning to establish a step-by-step procedure for meshing the policy format with its long-term outlook. To do so will require that the leadership form some definite goals and objectives beyond immediate short-term plans.

1. Donald R. Kaldor and William Saupe, Estimates and Projections of an Income-Efficient Commercial Farm Industry in the North Central States, *Journal of Farm Economics* 48 (3, pt. 1): 578–96.

GOALS AND OBJECTIVES FOR FARM POLICY ● The overcapacity that characterizes the agricultural industry and the offsetting compensatory programs financed by the federal government are now thirty-five years old. These short-term programs have not brought agriculture to a point where the market alone is able to perform the function of allocating resources among the various crops and other lines of farm production. Also, it is fairly well agreed now that these programs do little to solve the problems of poverty caused by technological advances. These problems of low incomes and constant grinding poverty in agriculture provide a need for a substantial broadening of the focus of future farm policies. These policies need to recognize low incomes and ongoing poverty as side effects of the vast structural change occurring in rural America, change brought on by an influx of technology which economic development brought to the nation. Technological advances bring gains to some and losses to others. Compensation policies are a means of offsetting some of the losses if the appropriate recipients are reached. Past programs have not assured this outcome, since payments were proportional to production, and those suffering losses generally have little total production. Policies were designed more to reward those who were able through capital and knowledge to take wide advantage of this technical change than to compensate those who suffer losses. Unless future programs are revised, the upcoming structural changes in the industry will continue to result in losses to a great many families in agriculture. Future technical change will continue to remold the farm industry, even in the heavy commercial farm areas. There are substantial economies of size associated with present day farm technology, particularly in new equipment and machinery, which will cause further increases in average farm size and further reductions in farm numbers. In Iowa, for example, to use only four- and five-plow equipment combinations efficiently will require that average farm size increase from 150 crop acres to almost 300 crop acres. Average farm size including pasture, woodland, and hay land will also increase substantially. Implicit in this change is the fact that as few as one-half of the present farm operators will remain as commercial farmers. Many will initially shift to part-time jobs with farming as a supplementary occupation. Others will simply find it beneficial to move to a different occupation. Equity requires that those who must leave should be compensated for the losses they suffer.

Besides recognizing structural change and the resultant losses, a further improvement in policies for agriculture could result from a shift in outlook on the long-term capacity of the industry. Viewed in the perspective that grain production can exceed markets for at least a decade or more, the nation might better turn to policies which lead to improved resource combinations in agriculture—combinations where land, labor, and capital are more nearly in balance with existing levels of technology and relative prices. Such a change in emphasis might result in a shift to a policy format based on future technology rather than attempted return to conditions of the past. Four decades of temporary programs are convincing evidence that the nation has excess acres available for crop production, and constant improvement in farm technology almost guarantees that many of these acres may not be required for crop production again in the present century.

A policy that retires surplus acres on a year-to-year basis does not provide a permanent shift of cropland to other uses. Land diversion on a year-to-year and partial-farm basis seldom shifts cropland to noncrop uses. Expenditures are thus made over a period of time to restrain production, but at the end of the period the money has been paid out and the problems still remain. An extension of annual diversion programs over the next ten years would require direct payments of $30 billion or more. However with continuation of trends in technology and production, the problem of excess capacity will still be as large at the end of that period as the results in Chapter 2 made clear.

One alternative to annual diversion programs is to shift land from crop production in marginal areas on a long-run basis so that after the public expenditure has been made, a goal has been accomplished. Numerous means are available for attaining such long-run goals. Even if a long-run program of this nature ended with marginal land idle, it could still represent an improvement from an overall societal standpoint. There are, of course, important extensive uses for this land. The shift would, however, satisfy important policy needs to alleviate sacrifices and restore economic opportunity to large population groups in the communities affected. But transferring this land to permanent grass or trees should be placed on the policy agenda. The transfer will take at least a decade even after it is once started.

In addition to an improved resource mix for agriculture, government programs can continue to contribute over the long run to both farmer and consumer welfare through mechanisms to stabilize agricultural production and prices. Stability of farm income, a major objective of farm programs since the 1930s, is a relevant policy goal. While stability of retail food prices has not been stated as an objective of farm policy, it too is a relevant goal. The costs of farm programs are paid by society at large and especially by urban taxpayers. These groups have a basis for also expecting some gain from the programs in which they invest. Otherwise urban consumers may not continue to be willing to spend $3 billion annually on programs for controlling, storing, and disposing of farm surpluses, only to be faced with sharply higher food prices in years of reduced yields or increased foreign food needs.

Stability in producer and consumer food prices means adequate food reserves are necessary to insure the nation against food shortages both at home and abroad. Over the last decade, the United States has consistently exported over 20 percent of its total crop production. Under these circumstances, a domestic food shortage is not a major likelihood. However, the United States has developed a commitment in helping other nations prevent mass starvation or even severe food shortages. An appropriate or even necessary goal for future policy is maintenance of reserves of appropriate size for these purposes. We should not, however, use these reserves as a major means of supporting domestic prices or disposing of surplus production. Unselective use of this practice may have been beneficial to the United States in the short time span of the last decade. However, it is a very costly means for improving prices and handling domestic surplus stocks and capacity. Food aid should be viewed in a different context. Knowledge now available suggests that our food aid policies need to be carefully reconsidered and meshed with the goal of increasing agricultural production in underdeveloped countries. The present policy mix pays higher prices to farmers in developed countries so that they may increase production and ship the excess to less developed countries, thus dampening incentives of producers there. Future policies might recognize that agriculture in many underdeveloped countries represents a primary industry which can stimulate the process of economic development. Farm policies designed accordingly could encourage farmers in underdeveloped countries to expand production. The interrelationships between our domestic farm programs and international food aid need not retard or hamper this incentive.

To some extent, our present policies may prevail because we fail to understand the full interrelationships between economic development and agricultural problems. Just as we were unable to foresee technological developments over the last three decades, we may not now fully comprehend the importance of economic development in these countries to the long-run welfare of our domestic agriculture. This importance stems from the high-income elasticities of demand for food in underdeveloped countries. Consumers with high elasticities have a high propensity to consume additional food as their incomes rise. But a rise in income is dependent upon expansion of jobs in both agricultural and nonagricultural sectors. This process must start at the point where these nations already have resources or favorable natural endowments. And this situation is nearly always found in agriculture. Our domestic policies can contribute toward the goals of agricultural improvement and economic development in these countries through appropriate recognition of the detrimental effects of large shipments of food commodities into markets of other countries. These aspects of policy are discussed further in Chapter 7.

Several objectives for long-run farm policies have been reviewed. The development of future programs could be based on both our very large long-run capacity for grain production and the basic structural change occurring in the farm industry. Rapidly advancing farm technology not only extends our future capacity but also increases the cost of restraining it as the means of supporting prices. For a given level of prices, greater yields increase the opportunity costs of leaving land idle. Hence the payment per acre, especially if on the basis of year-to-year programs, requires increasingly large payments to encourage participation in land retirement. It is reasonable and logical that the nation attempt to develop a set of future programs which will hold capacity in check at lower government costs than are implied in year-to-year programs. Such programs might also ease the costs falling on communities which must undergo the major adjustments for more efficient long-run solutions to the problems of large supply capacity and farm structural changes.

PAST AND POTENTIAL POLICY ALTERNATIVES ● Recent policies and programs used to control farm production in the United States have both positive and negative aspects measured in terms of public outlays required and effects on farm income levels. On the positive side, annual diversion programs have raised and (or) supported income of producers, particularly those who operate economically viable units and produce larger than average quantities of output. They have provided means for bringing some equity in the distribution of gains from technological advances between consumers and commercial farmers. They have aided stability of farm commodity prices, especially grains and cotton. Also, these programs have more nearly assured the nation of an adequate supply of food for domestic and international uses, although not necessarily at minimum cost. They have had public acceptance, allowing "something to be done" for commercial agriculture. The rate of economic and social adjustment in rural areas may also have been slowed to rates which could more nearly be absorbed by rural communities and institutions. But these programs also have major limitations. The programs have high Treasury costs. They provide little compensation to those marginal farmers who sacrifice most from technological advances. They have little promise for rapidly moving the industry toward an improved resource combination which might allow a market-achieved balance between production and utilization.

Major weaknesses also revolve around the short-run, year-to-year nature of annual programs and insufficient provisions for improving economic opportunity for a large portion of the low-income sector of agriculture. This sector encompasses the major part of the 70 percent of all farms which have gross sales of less than $10,000. As Table 3.1 indicates, this group of farms contributes only a small part of total farm output, in fact, only 14.9 percent in 1967. These 2.2 million farms averaged only $1,717 of realized net farm income in 1967, including the value of farm-produced food and the rental value of the farm dwelling. These farms have a small share of farm sales and income, although they constitute a majority of farm families. They gain only a small share of the benefits resulting from price support levels generated by commodity loans, foreign aid programs, and direct payments provided for idling

Table 3.1 ● Selected Farm Characteristics According to Value of Sales Classes, 1961–69

Year	Farms with sales of					
	$20,000 and over		$10,000 to $19,999		less than $10,000	
	(thousand)	(%)	(thousand)	(%)	(thousand)	(%)
Number of farms						
1961	362	9.5	494	12.9	2,965	77.6
1963	411	11.5	491	13.8	2,359	74.7
1965	447	13.4	487	14.6	2,406	72.0
1967	501	15.9	492	15.6	2,153	68.5
1969	568	19.1	505	17.0	1,898	63.9
	($ million)	(%)	($ million)	(%)	($ million)	(%)
Cash receipts						
1961	19,778	54.1	7,497	20.5	9,307	25.4
1963	23,380	59.8	7,509	19.2	8,205	21.0
1965	26,547	63.5	7,678	18.4	7,588	18.1
1967	31,090	67.8	7,921	17.3	6,856	14.9
1969	36,977	72.6	8,167	16.0	5,879	11.4
	($ million)	(%)	($ million)	(%)	($ million)	(%)
Realized net income						
1961	4,842	38.3	2,835	22.4	4,969	39.3
1963	5,557	44.2	2,779	22.1	4,247	33.8
1965	6,879	49.2	3,037	21.7	4,077	29.1
1967	7,461	52.4	3,083	21.6	3,697	26.0
1969	9,539	59.0	3,273	20.3	3,342	20.7

Source: U. S. Dept. of Agriculture, Farm Income Situation, USDA ERS, July 1970.

land. These farms provide limited possibilities for any more effective use of labor and generally provide low returns to this resource.

Compensatory policies—the set of programs designed to bring equity in the distribution of gains from farm technical progress and large output capacity—also leave out that portion of the farm labor force annually displaced from agriculture and the rural merchants who suffer income declines with a thinning farm population. As mentioned previously, to contain a large producing capacity and provide long-run solutions for problems of farm structural change, lower-cost programs are unlikely to result until these groups are either brought into compensatory policies or provided improved economic opportunity in other pursuits.

At the other end of the income spectrum are the 30 percent of farms with sales of $10,000 or over which produce 85 percent of all farm commodities. Their average net income of $10,616 including perquisites exceeded the average income of $6,882 for all families in the United States in 1965.[2] Since present farm programs direct benefits to producers in proportion to the amount of their resources and production, farmers with sales of over $10,000 receive more than two-thirds of all government payments to farmers.[3] They stand to gain the major share of benefits directed to the farm sector as a result of our commodity programs.

A reexamination of the payment distribution under annual diversion is needed, especially in relation to those groups in the rural community who bear the costs of farm structural transformation and technological advance without any explicit compensation. The time has come in the evolution of American farm compensation policies when they should be oriented both to long-run solutions of the capacity problem and to a more complete spread of benefits to groups who bear costs of rapid technological transformations of agriculture. Given Treasury restraints on the amount of funds for compensation of agriculture, the latter may call for some diversion of benefits from larger farms to low income families of agriculture, laborers displaced without adequate skills for other employment, and other sacrificing groups of the rural community. One element of an overall mechanism to accomplish this end would be a limit to size of benefits to individual farmers. A reexamination of the structure of programs and the distribution of benefits does not, of course, imply the elimination of farm programs. It poses the need for their improvement. With or without payment limits, the need for long-run orientation of programs to move agriculture in a direction of self-effectuated balance between supply and demand is still necessary. Questions of the distribution of government payments and benefits should be solved independently from decisions of which programs are most effective for other purposes.

2. U.S. Dept. of Commerce, *Statistical Abstract of the United States,* 1967, p. 335.

3. Earl O. Heady, *A Primer on Food, Agriculture and Public Policy* (New York: Random House, 1967), p. 16.

ANALYSIS OF NEAR-TERM POLICY ALTERNATIVES ● Numerous policy alternatives exist for restraining the aggregate producing capacity of agriculture and providing a more equitable distribution of gains and costs of farm structural change: in this chapter, we explore four short- and intermediate-term alternatives for handling the overcapacity problems of the agricultural sector. Other alternatives could be examined and future chapters will be devoted to them.

One alternative evaluated incorporates the concept of bargaining power for agriculture. The analysis is based on the proposed government program introduced in the 90th Congress as Senate Bill 2973. That bill was designed to " . . . create a board, to be known as the National Agricultural Relations Board . . . (to) . . . initiate and conduct a referendum among producers of such agricultural commodity to determine whether or not said producers favor the establishment of a representative marketing committee. . . . For the purpose of negotiating with purchases of the commodity to determine a fair minimum price. . . ."[4] To provide for control over supply, the act provided that "whenever a marketing committee shall have established a minimum price for any commodity and thereafter shall also determine that the total supply of said commodity produced within the defined area will so substantially exceed the effective demand for said commodity during the marketing year as to nullify or defeat the purposes of this title, said marketing committee, in consultation with the Board and the Secretary of Agriculture, shall develop a plan or program of marketing allotment, with or without acreage or production limitations, and shall request the Board to submit said plan or program by referendum to the producers of said commodity within said defined area for the approval or rejection of said producers." Reduced to its basic form, the bill would have set up limitations on marketings through acreage or other production controls and then allowed for bargaining over the price level of the commodity. One analysis evaluates the production and utilization levels, prices, and incomes which might result under such a program.

A second type of program analyzed is multi-year land retirement. Envisioned in this program are five- or ten-year contracts which would remove land from production and return it to grass, trees, and other extensive (using few cultivation practices) uses. This proposal is evaluated for two alternative levels of cropland retirement, a 50-million-acre program and a 60-million-acre program. By removing less productive cropland on a bid basis, such a program could provide a means for an orderly transfer to a market oriented economy.[5]

4. U.S. Congress, Senate, Bill 2973, 90th Cong., 2nd sess., introduced February 15, 1968.

5. This type of change in farm policies has been recommended by many individuals and groups including the Presidential Advisory Commission of Food and Fiber. For background and viewpoints of the commission, see the *Report of the National Advisory Commission of Food and Fiber* (Washington, D.C.: GPO, July 1967), pp. 15–22, 66–72.

A third alternative examines the effects of continuing annual diversion programs of the kind employed during the 1960s. It evaluates the major outcomes which are likely if annual diversion programs for wheat, feed grains, and cotton continue. Effects on land use, domestic and export demand, commodity prices, farm income and expenses, government payments, and other variables are evaluated.

Finally, to provide a basemark against which other programs may be evaluated and compared, outcomes are estimated with a free market or market oriented farm economy. This type of market for agriculture would represent the largest change for the farm economy. For this reason, the effects of a free market are measured in terms of outcomes for the short run, a period of only one or two years, and outcomes for the longer run, a period at the end of three to five years or longer. The projected results differ, depending on whether the industry is in the initial stages of adjustment to unsupported market prices or whether adjustment to market prices has continued for several years.

Results for all alternative programs are specified in terms of 1970 levels of demand, both domestic and export, and in terms of available production capacity which takes into consideration the level of technology, costs of production, and the 1970 structure of agriculture. All prices are measured in terms of 1965–66 dollars and do not take into account effects of possible inflation.

In this chapter the primary objective is to analyze alternative farm programs which could be implemented and to provide estimates of production levels, price and income levels, and farm program costs for each alternative. Readers not interested in the detail of the methods used may turn to the sections on results.

METHODS AND PROCEDURES ● This study is based on a multiregional programming model similar in outline to that described in Equation (2.1) of the previous chapter. The time focus of this study is 1970 with all coefficients estimated to reflect the 1970 level of technology. Demand parameters reflect the projected 1970 size of population and income level. Since the development of a multi-regional programming model to simulate the total agricultural economy is an evolutionary process where each additional study adds understanding of essential economic relationships, further refinements are made in the basic model for this study. The model was expanded from 144 producing regions to 150 producing regions (Fig. 3.1). In opposite manner, the set of activities simulating a feed grains-soybean rotation was eliminated from the model. Many basic parameters were derived in a manner similar to the previous chapter; those given below are provided for greater depth and detail.

Crop Yield Projections ● Least-squares regression was used to estimate crop yields for 1970. Estimates were based on data for the period 1948–67

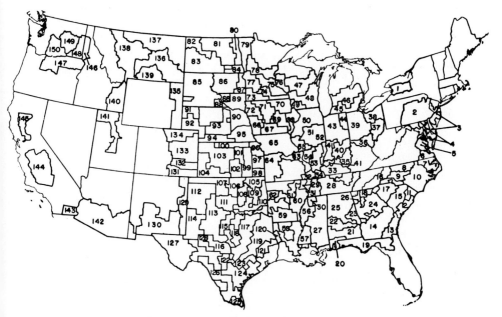

Fig. 3.1.   The 150 crop-producing regions.

using crop yields per harvested acre projected linearly by states. Table 3.2 shows the equation for the United States, R^2, and standard error for each crop for which yields were estimated. After deriving projected yields for each state, regional yields for each crop were estimated for each of the 150 production regions of the model. These estimates involved adjusting each state yield by the proportion each region yield was of the state yield as reported in the 1964 Census of Agriculture.

Land Restraints ● The cropland base for the crops in the model is the same as that from the previous model (see Table 2.1); maximum acreages are the sum of harvested and government retired acres in 1965. Since only seven crops are included in the model, acreage restraints are estimated only for those crops. Other crops, including fallow, are left a potential land base equal to that occupied in the past.

Costs of Production ● Production costs are the most difficult parameters to establish for the model. Data available to estimate a consistent set of cost estimates for the 150 individual regions are not available per se. Existing data also reflect wide variation in terms of specific costs included and in methods used to derive those costs. Since the basic cost data from the previous model were slowly becoming dated, all production costs were recalculated for this study. Labor costs were calculated for each of the seven crops by states with all producing regions within

Table 3.2 ● U.S. Crop Yield Equations

Equation	Years	Intercept	Time variable	Standard error of $\hat{Y}$	R^2
Wheat	1948-67	-14.808 (4.175)[a]	.634 (.072)	1.863	.81
Corn	1949-67	-79.592 (8.109)	2.288 (.139)	3.323	.94
Oats	1949-67	-14.253 (6.505)	.934 (.112)	2.666	.80
Barley	1949-67	-16.721 (5.312)	.834 (.091)	2.177	.83
Grain sorghum	1949-67	-92.465 (11.45)	2.168 (.196)	4.690	.88
Soybeans	1949-67	6.973 (3.286)	.271 (.056)	1.346	.58
Cotton[b]	1948-67	-50.425 (7.784)	1.592 (.137)	3.021	.89

[a] Standard errors of the coefficients are in parentheses.
[b] A dummy variable was included in the fitted equation for cotton to account for the change in the cotton program, support price level, and other effects which noticeably reduced cotton yield after 1966. This variable had a coefficient of -8.868 with a standard error of 6.637.

a state assumed to have the same labor costs per acre for each respective crop. To project labor costs per acre to 1970, data on man-hours per acre from a 1959 study[6] were adjusted by projecting trends in man-hours used per acre for feed grains, food grains, and oilmeals from the published data on efficiency of farm production.[7] These respective data were combined into the relationship,

$$LC_{ij}^{70} = \left[1 + \left(\frac{M_k^{66}}{59} \right) - 1 \left(\frac{t^{70} - t^{59}}{t^{66} - t^{59}} \right) \right] \left[m_{ijk} \, w_i \right] \qquad (3.1)$$

where the superscripts represent the respective years, and

LC_{ij} = projected labor costs per acre of the j-th crop in the i-th state
M_k = man-hours per harvested acre of feed grains, food grains, and oil crops in the k-th farm production region
m_{ijk} = man-hours per harvested acre of the j-th crop in the i-th state of the k-th farm production region for 1959
W_i = projected wage rate in the i-th crop for 1970
t = respective year

Power and machinery costs include fuel and lubrication, repairs, depreciation, insurance, and interest charges. Irrigation costs include charges for pump operation and repair and water costs. Power and machinery, irrigation, and fertilizer costs were obtained from Eyvindson.[8] Chemical costs including lime and pesticide costs and the cost of application are part of production costs. Data on application of lime are given only by state for all crops in a given state. Therefore it is assumed that lime costs are the same for each crop in a given state. Lime costs per acre are estimated by dividing total dollars spent on lime in a state by the total cropland harvested in a state.[9] Pesticide costs were obtained from unpublished U.S. Department of Agriculture data.

Estimates of average seeding rates and costs of farm seed are made by states. It was assumed that seeding rates and seed costs for a given crop are the same for all production regions within a state.

The final cost category is miscellaneous costs. Costs included under this heading are drying costs and interest on operating capital. Only

6. Robert C. McElroy, Reuben W. Hecht, and Earle E. Garrett, Labor Used to Produce Field Crops Estimates by States, USDA ERS *Statistical Bulletin* 346, 1964.

7. U.S. Dept. of Agriculture, Changes in Farm Production and Efficiency, USDA ERS *Statistical Bulletin* 233, supplement 4, 1968.

8. Roger Eyvindson, A Model of Interregional Competition in Agriculture Incorporating Consuming Regions, Producing Areas, Farm Size Groups and Land Classes. Ph.D. thesis, Iowa State Univ., Ames, 1970.

9. U.S. Dept. of Agriculture, *Agricultural Statistics*, 1966.

corn and grain sorghum were assumed to have drying costs. General
guidelines on amounts and charges for drying were obtained from U.S.
Department of Agriculture unpublished data. Interest on operating
capital was computed by assuming a 7 percent simple annual interest
charge over six months on the fixed and variable capital used in the
production process.

Domestic Demand Estimates ● To estimate the levels of demand in the
programming model, a procedure of estimating total population and
per capita consumption was used. Per capita consumption equations
were estimated for the following commodities: (1) beef and veal, (2) pork,
(3) lamb and mutton, (4) broilers and turkeys, (5) eggs, and (6) dairy
products. Table 3.3 gives the equations selected to project per capita
consumption for 1970, and Table 3.4 gives per capita and total consumption data.

   To convert the consumer demand for livestock products to demand
for the grain and oilmeal commodities included in the model, feed conversion rates explained in Chapter 2 were used. These rates were estimated for feed conversion efficiency expected for 1970, and the projected grain and oil demands for the several different livestock commodities were accumulated for the United States. These totals were
allocated among the thirty-one consuming regions of the model based
on past location of livestock production. In addition, final grain and
oilmeal demand includes estimates of demand for seed, industry, direct
human consumption, as well as feed for horses and mules and other
livestock. Formal models were not used to estimate these items but
levels for each were selected by using current data taking past trends into
account.

Government Program Costs ● Government program costs were estimated for two program alternatives—long-term land retirement and
the annual diversion programs. Under each program, costs were estimated for retiring adequate cropland to hold production in line with
the estimated level of demand. With the long-term land retirement program the cost for retiring an acre of cropland was estimated as the
difference between estimated gross returns per acre and estimated costs
of production for the highest revenue crop in each region. The formulation of gross returns is given as

$$P_{ij}Y_{ij} = GR_{ij} \qquad (3.2)$$

where

P_{ij} = price of i-th crop in the j-th producing region
Y_{ij} = yield of the i-th crop in the j-th producing region
GR_{ij} = gross returns per acre of the i-th crop in the j-th region

Costs of production are removed as in Equation (3.3):

$$GR_{ij} - (srvc_{ij} + lrvc_{ij}) = NR_{ij} \qquad (3.3)$$

where

$srvc_{ij}$ = short-run variable costs of production per acre of the i-th crop in the j-th region

$lrvc_{ij}$ = long-run variable costs of production per acre of the i-th crop in the j-th region

NR_{ij} = net revenue or return per acre of the i-th crop in the j-th region which includes a return to cover fixed costs per acre, mainly land taxes

Under annual diversion programs, costs of retirement per acre were estimated for each of three crops: wheat, feed grains, and cotton. These per acre retirement costs were derived from actual costs per acre of land retired under respective programs in the 1966 crop year.[10] Total payments under each program in each state were divided by total acres retired to give an actual payment received per crop acre. These payments include both the price support payment and the diversion payments under each program.

Generally costs of retirement per acre under the annual diversion programs are substantially higher than under the long-term land retirement program. The difference is explainable by the difference in production costs which a producer must cover if he participates in each type of program. Under a long-term program, fixed costs (fc_j) of production must still be covered, but other costs including both short-run and long-run variable costs may be removed: short-run costs by not purchasing the production inputs for crop production, and long-run costs of depreciation and operator labor by selling machinery and alternative employment. Under these circumstances the government payment (GP) per acre for a long-term program will be

$$GP_{ij} = NR_{ij} + fc_j \qquad (3.4)$$

While under the annual diversion program the government payment must also cover long-run variable costs as follows:

$$GP_{ap} = NR_{ij} + fc_j + lrvc_{ij} \qquad (3.5)$$

since in general it is not possible to sell machinery and find other employment for operator labor if the program terminates at the end of the

10. U.S. Dept. of Agriculture, 1966 Feed Grains and Wheat Programs and 1966 Upland Cotton Program, (Washington, D.C.: USDA ASCS, 1967).

Table 3.3 ● Equations Used to Project the Per Capita Demand of Meats, Dairy Products, Poultry, and Eggs

Equation[a] and commodity	Years	Intercept	X_1	X_2	X_3
Beef & veal	48-66	.78670 (.37885)	.42402 (.23055)	-.77355 (.06389)	.15696 (.08874)
Pork	48-66	3.00183 (.30724)	.47001 (.18697)	.25519 (.05181)	-.65281 (.07196)
Lamb & mutton	48-66	3.09387 (.88095)	...	.74857 (.27973)	.44317 (.27407)
Broilers	48-66	-1.39750 (.79268)	...	.30141 (.06969)	.31993 (.10176)
Turkeys	50-66	.21838 (.10705)	...	.00534 (.09051)	.36200 (.13750)
Eggs	48-66	3.29343 (.91105)	...	...	...
Dairy products	48-66	5.05854 (.38228)	...	...	...

NOTE: Standard errors are shown in parentheses. The independent variables are

X_1 = Real disposable personal income per capita.
X_2 = Deflated retail price index for beef and veal.
X_3 = Deflated retail price index for pork.
X_4 = Deflated retail price index for lamb and mutton.
X_5 = Deflated retail price index for poultry.

Table 3.3 ● (Continued)

X_4	X_5	X_6	X_7	X_8	T	R²
...	...	...	...	...	.57529 (.28213)	.98
...	...	...	...	...	-1.09962 (.22880)	.93
-2.05693 (.37297)	...	...	...	...	-.40084 (.21020)	.74
...	-.35827 (.12929)	...	...	...	1.30674 (.31856)	.99
...	-.60354 (.17333)	...	...	...	.83643 (.43908)	.98
...	...	...	-.18635 (.12180)	.69719 (.47525)	-1.00441 (.18583)	.94
...	...	-.48148 (.14956)	...	...	-.72046 (.00546)	.96

NOTE: Standard errors are shown in parentheses. The independent variables are
X_6 = Deflated retail price index for all dairy products.
X_7 = Deflated retail price index for eggs.
X_8 = Deflated retail price index for all foods.
T = Time variable 1948 = 48, 1949 = 49, ..., 1967 = 67.

aEquations are estimated in logarithms.

121

Table 3.4 ● Estimated 1970 and Actual 1966 Per Capita and Total Domestic Consumption of Specified Livestock Products

Item	Unit	Per capita consumption			Total consumption[a]		
		1966	1970[b]		1966	1970[b]	
			level 1	level 2		level 1	level 2
					(thousand)		
Beef & veal	Carcass wt (lb)	108.3	115.7	136.0	19,753	22,401	27,216
Pork (excl. lard)	Carcass wt (lb)	58.1	60.4	62.0	10,955	12,299	12,830
Lamb & mutton	Carcass wt (lb)	4.0	3.9	3.2	640	721	572
Broilers	Ready-to-cook (lb)	36.0	37.5	33.3	7,303	7,908	6,979
Turkeys	Ready-to-cook (lb)	7.8	8.1	7.6	1,560	1,726	1,615
Eggs	Number	313.0	302.0	302.0	5,070	5,210	5,210
Dairy products	Milk equivalent	616.0	595.0	595.0	116,728	121,945	121,945

NOTE: Consumption is estimated on a calendar year basis.

[a] Adjusted for imports and exports.
[b] Level 1 assumes government control programs continue. Level 2 assumes government control programs are terminated.

production year. Hence the payment under the annual diversion program will always exceed the payment per acre for a multi-period land retirement program. With a similar number of acres retired, a multi-period program can be expected to have considerably lower costs for the government.

ALTERNATIVE SUPPLY CONTROL, AND PRICE AND INCOME SUPPORT PROGRAMS ● To provide estimates of total government program costs we now examine several alternative supply control mechanisms for allocating resources among the various cropping activities in agriculture. Each mechanism represents a possible farm program or in the case of a free market, the pricing system, which could be used to (1) allocate and shift crop production among regions of the nation, and (2) shift cropland from one crop to another. Under a free market, market prices would allocate land among crops or cause it to lie idle if profit margins dictated that necessity. Free market prices also could shift crop production from regions with higher costs to regions of greatest competitive advantage. When a government farm program is used to allocate production, detailed administrative regulations are developed to allocate cropping "rights" among the many producing regions and areas. These regulations generally use government payments to induce a majority of farmers to cooperate with the program objectives and plant and harvest the required number of acres to satisfy potential demand. The possibility also exists of using mandatory quotas instead of government payments as a mechanism to allocate crop production. This alternative is examined under the concept of bargaining power.

A Free Market for Agriculture ● A free market would result for agriculture if the federal government (1) terminated voluntary production control programs for major crops and commodities, and (2) removed the offer to purchase and store quantities of agricultural commodities at some prespecified price level in order to support prices. The government could still purchase quantities of the crops at market prices and place them in storage so that reserves of food and other crops could be maintained. With the removal of production control and price support programs, farmers would base all decisions of what to produce, how much to produce, and how (what combination of resources to use) to produce it, on price signals from the market. Under this situation, price expectations (what the price will be at harvest time) become relatively more important. Since there is a considerable tendency among agricultural producers to use prices received in the past as estimates of what prices will be in the future, the shift from supply control programs to uncontrolled production will likely result in an increase in aggregate production for the following reason: Projecting past farm price levels to the end of the next production period, farmers expect gross value of sales to increase with larger acreages and quantities produced. But the past price level is a function of some particular quantity that moved through the market-place, and if the quantity brought to the marketplace is substantially increased, the price level declines. The decline in price will be sub-stantially greater than the increase in quantity, since demand for major grain crops is inelastic. (Price elasticity of demand is defined as the percentage change in quantity demanded associated with a percentage change in price. In algebraic form,

$$E_{dp} = [\% \; \triangle \; Q] \, / \, [\% \; \triangle \; P].$$

For feed grains the price elasticity has been estimated at —.25; or for each 1 percent increase [decrease] in market supply, price will decline [increase] by 4 percent. Any price elasticity of less than 1.0 is referred to as inelastic.) This set of circumstances would provide the following initial outcome under a free market: Farmers would individually increase production basing the expected price after harvest on past prices re-ceived. But the larger aggregate quantity when sold in the marketplace would necessarily force prices down to utilize the larger quantity. The drop in price would be greater than the increase in quantity sold and total returns would be reduced. Since costs of production would remain similar or even increase, net returns would decline.

In the initial production and marketing period, the price decline for crops would be considerable. However, livestock prices tend to lag one or more production periods behind changes in grain prices and hence livestock prices and incomes would be little affected during the initial production period. The numerical calculations for the initial period under a free market are shown below.

SHORT-TERM ADJUSTMENT TO A FREE MARKET. The initial response of farmers to removal of controls on crop acreages would be an increase in acreages planted to crops. The exact magnitude of this increase is diffi-cult to project since a large number of crop acres have remained idle under various government programs since 1956, and farmers have ad-justed both labor and capital inputs to mesh with the smaller cropland base. In the case of the crop acres in the Conservation Reserve Program, part of the 28 million acres remained seeded to grass or trees even when the program terminated. Taking into account that similar trends may occur with other programs as well as other uncertainties, acreages of crops are projected for a 1970 base crop year assuming that all govern-ment programs are terminated. The national estimates of crop acreages, yields, and production for a free market with short-term adjustment are shown in Table 3.5. These results are reported for the United States in aggregate although actual computations were completed for the 150 crop-producing regions in the United States.

With only prices from a free market to restrain total crop produc-tion, harvested acreages of both wheat and feed grains are projected

Table 3.5 ● **Projected 1970 Acreages, Yields, and Production under Alternative Farm Programs**

Crop	Actual 1961-65 average	Actual 1967	Free market short-term adjustment	Free market long-term adjustment	Land retirement 50 million acres	Land retirement 60 million acres	Annual land diversion	Rigid acreage quotas
Harvested acreages					(thousand acres)			
Wheat	48,017	59,004	65,830	64,231	55,233	53,800	53,279	50,602
Feed grains	101,086	100,654	101,204	88,924	85,533	83,123	87,158	87,009
Soybeans	29,694	39,742	40,940	39,592	36,907	37,179	37,515	33,148
Cotton	14,617	8,090	14,315	14,269	14,238	14,232	14,219	14,712
Yield per harvested acre								
Wheat (bu)	25.30	25.80	28.30	28.40	28.70	30.70	29.70	29.10
Feed grains (tons)	1.44	1.74	1.78	1.94	1.97	2.01	1.93	1.82
Soybeans (bu)	24.20	24.50	27.20	27.00	27.00	26.80	26.60	26.80
Cotton (lb)	491.00	452.00	506.00	508.00	509.00	509.00	510.00	493.00
Total production					(thousand)			
Wheat (bu)	1,214,024	1,524,349	1,804,707	1,824,160	1,584,314	1,652,985	1,580,377	1,471,961
Feed grains (tons)	145,383	175,054	180,328	172,891	168,105	166,751	168,343	158,684
Soybeans (bu)	718,687	972,701	1,113,157	1,068,869	996,374	996,322	997,864	888,291
Cotton (bales)	14,935	7,618	14,500	14,500	14,500	14,500	14,500	14,500

Source: U. S. Dept. of Agriculture, Crop Production 1967 Annual Summary, USDA ERS, December 1967.

above actual 1967 levels. With these levels of production for wheat and feed grains, stocks of wheat rise by an estimated 200 million bushels and feed grains by 12 million tons. Exports of major commodities with a free market are projected as follows: feed grains 32.0 million tons, wheat 925 million bushels, soybeans 500 million bushels, and cotton 5 million bales.

Such a large quantity of production has significant effects on prices of grain commodities in the time span of only one or two production periods. In Table 3.6 estimated prices for the initial production season with short-term adjustment to a free market are lower than any recently experienced. (See Equation [2.15] for an algebraic explanation of these prices.) Wheat, corn, and soybean prices decline substantially from 1967 levels.

The initial effect of removing all controls and price support is a sharp reduction in prices of major grains. Indeed these prices would not cover some major costs of producing these grains. In the short term, price levels are estimated to cover only out-of-pocket costs (seed, fertilizer, and other operating expenses) but not depreciation expense, return to operator labor, or other fixed expenses. This level of farm prices could only continue for a few production periods since many farmers with high per unit costs of production would find it uneconomical to continue production.

Even in the short run, these prices cause farm income to decline rapidly. Gross receipts from crops decline by one to two billion dollars (Table 3.7). Livestock receipts in the initial year are relatively unaffected since there is a lag of one or more production periods before livestock production expands to utilize the larger quantities of grain. Government payments also drop with only payments for soil conservation, wool, and sugar programs remaining. Cash receipts from farming total less than in recent years while production expenses continue upward, rising partly because of expanded crop acreage.[11] Net cash receipts are reduced considerably. Depreciation costs continue however and actual cash income would be cut in half. Even adding the value of farm perquisites and inventory changes, neither of which provide spendable income, net farm income in the initial period of production is below any recent level.

LONG-TERM ADJUSTMENT TO A FREE MARKET. Low prices and incomes resulting during the initial periods of adjustment to a free market would of necessity eventually reduce total production of agricultural commodities. While most producers would not reduce their rate of output, producers on cropland with marginal earning ability would find it necessary to completely cease production. Those ceasing production would be concentrated by communities, specifically in soil and climatic regions

11. Estimation of cash expenses was based on a method used in Luther G. Tweeten, Earl O. Heady, and Leo V. Mayer, Farm Program Alternatives, *CAED Report* 18, Iowa State Univ., May 1963.

Table 3.6 ● Projected 1970 Farm Level Prices under Alternative Farm Programs

Commodity and unit	Actual		Free market		Land retirement		Annual land diversion	Rigid acreage quotas
	1961-65 average	1967	short-term adj.	long-term adj.	50 million acres	60 million acres		
Crop prices (dollars)								
Wheat (bu)	1.67	1.39	.85	1.22	1.29	1.42	1.49	1.56
Corn (bu)	1.13	1.05	.70	.98	1.03	1.13	1.23	1.39
Soybeans (bu)	2.46	2.49	1.08	1.86	2.05	2.38	2.39	2.49
Cotton lint (lb)	.309	.256	.266	.232	.235	.238	.247	.254
Livestock prices (cents)								
Cattle and calves (lb)	19.8	22.6	22.0	17.6	22.0	22.0	22.0	27.0
Hogs (lb)	16.6	18.9	18.2	15.8	18.2	18.2	18.2	22.0
Sheep (lb)	16.8	18.9	19.5	19.1	19.5	19.5	19.5	20.5
Broilers (lb)	14.6	13.3	15.3	15.3	15.3	15.3	15.3	15.3
Turkeys (lb)	21.2	19.5	22.5	22.5	22.5	22.5	22.5	22.5
Eggs (doz)	37.1	31.2	35.4	35.4	35.4	35.4	35.4	35.4
Milk (cwt)	416.0	502.0	452.0	452.0	452.0	452.0	452.0	452.0

Source: U. S. Dept. of Agriculture, Agricultural Prices, 1967 Annual Summary, USDA SRS, June 1968; U. S. Dept. of Agriculture, Livestock and Meat Statistics, USDA ERS Statistical Bulletin 333, supplement, June 1968.

Table 3.7 ● Projected 1970 Farm Income by Source and Farm Production Expenses under Alternative Farm Programs

	Actual[a]		Free market		Land retirement		Annual land diversion	Rigid acreage quotas
	1961-65 average	1967	short-term adj.	long-term adj.	50 million acres	60 million acres		
	($ million)							
Crop receipts	16,832	18,383	15,522	17,453	17,693	18,412	18,906	19,011
Livestock receipts	20,254	24,405	23,016	21,984	23,016	23,016	23,016	24,386
Government payments	1,948	3,079	401	401	1,258	1,784	3,349	326
Wheat program	295	731	0	0	0	0	824	0
Feed grains	1,002	865	0	0	0	0	1,573	0
Cotton	54[b]	932	0	0	0	0	423	0
Other	597	550	401	401	1,258	1,784	529	326
Total cash receipts	39,034	45,867	38,939	39,838	41,967	43,212	45,271	43,723
Cash expenses[c]	24,629	29,079	27,467	27,074	27,248	27,403	27,880	27,783
Net cash receipts	14,405	16,788	11,472	12,764	14,719	15,809	17,391	15,940
Depreciation	4,544	5,741	5,500	5,200	5,500	5,500	5,500	5,500
Actual cash income	9,861	11,047	5,972	7,564	9,219	10,309	11,891	10,440
Farm perquisites[d]	3,157	3,194	3,350	3,350	3,350	3,350	3,350	3,350
Inventory change	347	403	593	350	350	350	350	350
Net farm income	13,365	14,643	9,915	11,264	12,919	14,009	15,591	14,140

[a]Data are from U. S. Dept. of Agriculture, Farm Income State Estimates 1949-66. supplement to Farm Income Situation, July 1967, August 1967; U.S. Dept. of Agriculture, Farm Income Situation, July 1968.

[b]1964-65 average.

[c]Current operating expenses plus taxes, interest, and landlord rent.

[d]Value of home consumption of farm products and gross rental value of farm dwelling.

where yields are relatively low and unstable. While a number of production periods would likely be required before production is stabilized in relation to demand, this state would eventually arrive. By then, producers on marginal cropland in regions with relatively high costs of production would have ceased production of major crops.

The second set of free market estimates presented assumes that these adjustments have occurred. Crop production is stabilized near potential demand, both domestic and export, at price levels which cover all major costs of production including family and hired labor. Labor is charged at a projected national farm wage rate of $1.50 per hour for 1970. Domestic demand levels are increased as a result of lower prices for livestock commodities. Harvested acreages, yields, and total production estimates for a free market economy in equilibrium at market derived prices are shown in Table 3.5. Major increases in utilization result during the period of adjustment. Wheat for feed increases to 320 million bushels, replacing feed grains in marginal feed grains production areas including some western areas of the United States. Feed grains acres are projected to decline partially for this reason, but also as production tends to concentrate on higher yielding acres in the Corn Belt. Total feed grains production is 173 million tons with an estimated 32 million tons being exported. The remainder is fed to livestock or used for seed, industrial, or food uses. Soybean acreage declines slightly, but total production still exceeds 1 billion bushels.

Prices for major grain crops rise above their initially depressed level after a period of a few years and are estimated to stabilize at the long-term level indicated in Table 3.6. There would then be no direct payment to supplement the market price. As livestock production expands to utilize the larger quantities of grain at lower prices, beef and pork prices slide downward. Other livestock prices are not projected to show any considerable change, although small differences would likely result. No attempt has been made to estimate the effects of a free market on poultry or egg prices. Production controls on milk are outside major government farm programs and are assumed to continue.

Farm income could improve once the farm industry had adjusted to a free market economy (Table 3.7). Crop receipts would increase, but aggregate livestock receipts would be somewhat lower as production remained expanded against an inelastic demand. Government payments would remain minimal, thus contributing little to total cash receipts. Cash expenses would drop slightly as acreages stabilized at a lower level. Depreciation also would be less because fewer farmers purchased additional capital inputs during the initial periods of adjustment. Both actual cash income and net farm income would increase over the short-term level with net farm income stabilizing near $11 billion. If, in the adjustment process, a fourth of the farm operators found it necessary to cease farming, net income per farm would return to near recent levels although aggregate farm income would remain reduced and income transactions in rural areas would continue depressed.

Longer-Term Land Retirement Programs ● Assuming that the results of a free market are unacceptable to a majority of the society in rural areas, some type of government program to restrain aggregate crop production is likely to continue. One type of program which could eventually result in transfers of cropland from crop production to other uses is a long-term land retirement program which removes all cropland from production on individual farms under a long-term contract. This program need not restrict individual crop production, but rather would reduce acreage of cropland available for planting crops. If combined with complementary programs, less productive cropland could be returned to grass, trees, or other natural states. Such a program would initiate a reversal of government policies and programs of the last century which continue to shift additional land from a state of low productivity to an advanced state of crop production.

Programs which continue to shift additional cropland into production compound the problem of excess production and raise the cost of controlling total farm output. Instead, programs are needed which return land from intensive crop production to extensive uses on a long-term basis. Such a program more nearly fills the present need for national farm policy. As explained in detail elsewhere, the nation's policy toward agriculture has changed as economic development occurred.[12] Initially the policy was of a developmental nature, geared to bring the vast open spaces of the nation under the plow. As additional land became more scarce, developmental policies shifted toward facilitating the use of other inputs—new knowledge through research and extension, capital through farm credit acts, electricity through REA, fertilizer through TVA, and several others. But these very inputs place the nation in a new stage of economic development. In this stage, food production expands because of the invention, mass production, rapid distribution, and application of technological innovations to existing acres of land, rather than as a result of increasing acres of cropland. Also in this stage, population growth provides the major source of domestic demand expansion. Income growth has little effect on the demand for food. As a result, increases in aggregate food demand can easily be supplied by the growth of output from a fixed land base, one which is considerably smaller than that available in the United States during the 1960s. Thus in this stage of economic development, a set of policies which permanently returns cropland to grass and trees is appropriate. The alternative products which this land could produce are now in high demand—recreation in national parks and wildlife reserves, golf courses and trails for hiking, biking, and horseback riding, lumber production to renew a century of accumulated slums, and even additional livestock production to substitute for imports. These are the kinds of new uses toward which our millions of surplus acres need to be reoriented. But only a con-

12. Earl O. Heady, *Agricultural Policy under Economic Development* (Ames: Iowa State Univ. Press, 1962).

siderable reorientation of agricultural programs will tend to bring about this outcome.

A long-term land retirement program would be one type of program which could start the process of returning land to grass, trees, and other uses. Such a program would not in itself provide large tracts of land for recreational uses or the necessary development costs but could provide a means to start toward this goal. The program we explore here is envisioned as follows: government contracts for the retirement of cropland would be offered on a bid basis with government payments per acre designed to equal net returns above total costs of production, plus an allowance for mowing or other weed control. In addition, a payment would be necessary for establishing grass or other vegetative cover in the initial year of each contract. Participation in the program would be limited to a maximum of 10 percent of all cropland in a region in any one year with a maximum of 50 percent of total cropland from a region being eligible for eventual entry into the program. The program is examined for two alternative levels: the first program retires 50 million acres of cropland from wheat, feed grains, soybeans, and cotton; the second retires 60 million acres of cropland from these same crops. Major aspects of the 50-million-acre program are discussed first. Both levels assume land retirement on a whole-farm basis.

LONG-TERM RETIREMENT OF 50 MILLION ACRES OF CROPLAND. Under a program of long-term retirement, the process of implementing an adequate-sized program will require a period of some years. We envision a program which would continue placing land under contract for a minimum of five years, at the end of which time the program would total 50 million acres and leave cropland available for the magnitude of major crops shown in Table 3.5.

Yields under this type of program would not differ greatly from those under a free market, since the distribution of production among states and regions would nearly approximate that of a free market with only the land base reduced by 50 million acres. Under these conditions national crop yields increase to the amounts indicated in Table 3.5.

A program of this kind would result in shifts of crop acreage toward locations of economic advantage. Feed grains and especially corn production would shift toward the Corn Belt, and wheat toward the Great Plains, especially Kansas and Nebraska. These shifts would occur as existing controls on production of individual crops were slowly removed over an initial five-year period while the long-term land retirement program built up to 50 million acres. In this manner, acreages of crops would slowly shift to areas of lowest production cost per unit, and acreage retired from production would slowly shift to the highest cost production areas of the nation.

With 50 million acres of cropland removed from potential production, prices of major commodities are only slightly above long-term free market levels (Table 3.6). (With continuation of farm programs lower exports are projected: wheat—850 million bushels, feed grains—28.0 million tons, soybeans—450 million bushels, and cotton—5.0 million bales.) The prices of wheat and corn (both near levels of recent years), are estimated as equilibrium prices, and cover all costs of production including depreciation and hired and operator labor. Prices of livestock are projected to continue near recent levels. Over time these prices generally reflect changes in the prices of inputs including grain. Since a majority of grain fed to livestock does not pass through the marketplace, a large part of livestock production is based on grain priced according to its cost of production. This cost would not change greatly under this type of government program, and livestock prices would tend to continue near present levels. Over a period of time, livestock prices would likely shift to reflect the opportunity costs of selling or feeding grain. No attempt has been made to determine what these changes would be for programs where the change in grain prices is relatively small.

Income levels are higher than free market levels with the continuation of farm programs, although the 50-million-acre land retirement program is estimated to provide less net farm income than in recent years. Our estimates project net farm income to stabilize near $12.6 billion with a long-term land retirement program of 50 million acres (Table 3.7). Crop receipts decline from 1967 levels because greater output fails to offset the lower prices which prevail. Livestock receipts increase from 1961–65 averages due mainly to an increase in quantities produced. Prices for livestock are projected to deviate little from recent past levels, and hence receipts are estimated to change approximately in proportion to quantities produced.

Government payments for all direct payment programs total $1.3 billion, with payments for the long-term land retirement program totaling $857 million. This cost of land retirement would provide payments on 50 million acres equal to present net returns per acre from crop production.

In Table 3.8 we provide a breakdown of the two long-term land retirement programs by regions of the United States. Location of acreage retired was derived through the principle that the least productive acres in each region would be retired under each program with a limit of 50 percent of total cropland retired in any region. (See Equation [3.4].) Using this principle for the 50-million-acre program, the largest acreage is located in the Northern Plains with the Southern Plains and Corn Belt also retiring a considerable number of acres. For the 50.2 million acres retired, the cost would total $857 million dollars annually. As is evident from Table 3.7 government payments for programs of land retirement in 1967 cost considerably more than this. The cost of this program would rise if acres are increased. The next alternative indicates the magnitude of increase for a 60-million-acre program.

Table 3.8 ● Land Retirement Costs and Acres Retired by the Ten Farm Production Regions of the United States for Two Alternative Levels of a Long-Term Land Retirement Program

Region	50 million acres			60 million acres		
	Acres retired	Annual cost per acre[a]	Annual total cost	Acres retired	Annual cost per acre[a]	Annual total cost
	(thousand)	($)	($ thousand)	(thousand)	($)	($ thousand)
United States	50,176	17.09	857,334	60,046	23.03	1,382,761
Northeast	2,312	14.11	32,622	2,447	19.25	47,105
Lake States	4,730	17.28	81,734	5,373	22.07	118,582
Corn Belt	6,702	22.37	149,924	10,048	33.89	340,527
Northern Plains	13,534	16.99	229,943	16,084	21.18	340,659
Appalachians	3,658	14.64	53,553	3,679	19.69	72,440
Southeast	4,487	15.13	67,888	4,818	19.63	94,577
Delta	2,432	17.04	41,441	2,870	25.37	72,812
Southern Plains	7,409	15.54	115,136	8,785	19.14	168,145
Mountain	3,809	15.50	59,040	4,424	19.33	85,516
Pacific	1,103	23.62	26,053	1,518	27.93	42,398

[a] Estimated annual net return per acre from crop production plus a $5 per acre allowance for mowing or other form of weed control. There would be an additional cost in the initial year of each contract for establishment of grass, trees, or other vegetative cover.

LONG-TERM RETIREMENT OF 60 MILLION ACRES OF CROPLAND. Enlarging the program by an additional 10 million acres has several effects: acreages of major crops are generally reduced; however, removal of additional marginal acreage causes yields to increase for some crops (Table 3.5). This is particularly true of wheat where removal of additional cropland in the Great Plains causes the average yield for the United States to rise. As the cropland base is reduced, prices of all commodities rise (Table 3.6).

With higher prices for crops, farm income also increases over the 50-million-acre retirement program. Crop receipts rise by nearly a billion dollars and government program payments increase with a larger program (Table 3.7). Total cash receipts rise by more than $1.2 billion with some small increase in cash expenses. Net farm income rises also under the larger land retirement program.

With higher crop prices, the average cost per acre retired, and annual program costs rise (Table 3.8). The increase in cost is due to increased net returns per crop acre which higher crop prices bring. As net returns from farming increase for each crop acre, the cost for bidding the land out of production and into retirement also increases. If the program was expanded to an even higher level, the cost could rise still further.

The 60-million-acre retirement plan would provide a net income for agriculture in aggregate at about the 1967 level. However, its cost would be less than half as much as the 1967 program. This type of program could be used to take net farm income to a higher level than the $14 billion indicated. However, the number of acres retired and the costs of the program also would increase.

Annual Land Diversion Programs ● With a four-year extension of the feed grain program in 1965, Congress set a precedent of extending what was initially termed emergency legislation into apparent long-term legislation. For reasons already explained, it would be preferable to shift to a longer-term program, which (1) is more appropriate to the present state of economic development and the technological structure of agriculture, and (2) moves the industry toward a self-initiating balance between production and utilization. However in the event that present programs do appeal to a majority of the members of Congress, we evaluate the potential effects of continuing these programs into the 1970s.

In an earlier chapter we traced the historical trends in acreages used for major crops. (See Table 1.2.) Generally, harvested acreage was shown to be declining. Wheat acreage harvested (except for 1967 when stocks were built up) has consistently been 5 to 6 million acres below the mid-1930s, and acreages in recent years have been 10 to 15 million acres below the early 1950s. Feed grains acreage harvested (except in the late 1950s when stocks were built up) has fallen 25 to 30 million acres since the mid-1930s, and cotton has declined some 15 to 18 million acres during this period. Only soybeans have increased acreage but even this crop now has a potential for building up surpluses.

As other crops preceded soybeans into a surplus market situation, acreage available for harvest was reduced through government programs. Acreage retired under government programs started in 1956, increased to 28.7 million acres in 1960, and rose to 63.3 million acres in 1966. (See Table 1.3.) Of this latter acreage, the wheat, feed grains, and cotton programs retired over 47 million acres. Total cost for these three programs was $2.7 billion in direct government payments. Actual government costs would be somewhat less than this amount, since under the wheat program, millers are required to purchase certificates from the government for that portion of wheat being sold into the domestic market.

The cost of these programs will increase if they are extended beyond 1970. For one reason, the Conservation Reserve Program with nearly 10 million acres out of production will terminate during this period. If at least half of this land returns to production, an additional 5 million acres will become available for crop production or retirement. For a second reason, our estimates suggest that fewer acres of cropland will be needed for crop production for major crops in the 1970s than in recent years, thus continuing the downtrend in cropland required for domestic and export uses.

In Table 3.5 we present estimates of cropland required for all major crops in 1970 with continuation of annual diversion programs. A major decrease occurs in acreage of cropland used for feed grains. Our results suggest that total acreage required to balance projected demand will decline by some 10 million acres compared to 1967. Wheat acreage should hold its own but soybeans and feed grains will taper off from 1967 highs. Cotton will apparently use more acres and approximate the 1961–65 average level. Export levels assumed were wheat—850 million bushels, feed grains—28.0 million tons, soybeans—450 million bushels, and cotton—5 million bales.

The above estimates assume that annual diversion programs continue to hold crop production near utilization. Given this assumption, crop prices continue near recent levels, except soybeans, which taper off slightly (Table 3.6). These are the market prices which are necessary if all costs of production are to be covered in marginal areas of production, including family and hired labor at $1.50 per hour. If producers accept the direct payment under this program to partially cover production costs, a greater quantity marketed may cause lower market prices to exist. With the continuation of annual diversion programs, livestock prices are projected to continue near present levels. With perquisites and changes in farm inventories added in, net farm income totals $15.6 billion (Table 3.7). With a continuing decline in the number of farms, average income per farm would improve.

Our estimates suggest that government costs for land retirement may continue to increase if annual diversion programs are extended. In Table 3.9 land retirement costs for the wheat, feed grain, and cotton programs are estimated for 1970. Costs per acre for land diversion rise as yields increase, assuming that price support payments in 1970 are at the same level as in 1966.

The acreage retired by the wheat, feed grain, and cotton programs is scattered over all producing regions on a partial-farm basis (as compared with the regional and whole-farm retirement schemes outlined for both 50 and 60 million acres). In addition, the current Cropland Adjustment Program which held 4.1 million acres out of production in 1967 was assumed to increase to 8.0 million acres by 1970. This additional cost causes total land retirement costs to exceed $3 billion. As a result of these programs, a total of 61.5 million acres of cropland is held out of production. Of this acreage only the 8 million acres under the Cropland Adjustment Program would likely remain out of production past the expiration date of the annual contract.

We conclude that continuing annual, short-term programs of land retirement provides no mechanisms nor means for reducing the program cost over time. Instead, as technology raises yields at faster rates than demand increases, total acres retired will have to increase. The cost of these temporary programs will continue to increase year after year unless there is a change to programs which permanently return land to other extensive uses. Such a change seems particularly appropriate for the 1970s in view of the small possibility that 50 million acres of currently retired cropland will be required for crop production in the next decade.

Bargaining Power Through Acreage Quotas ● The concept of farmers providing self-imposed programs to improve terms of trade with the rest of the economy has long appealed to many farm groups and farm leaders. The idea is quite simple: farmers would select a group of representative leaders who would then determine the appropriate quantities of agricultural commodities which can be offered for sale and still maintain "a fair and reasonable price to the producers thereof." The latest legislative proposal defined this price as including "(1) the direct cost of production including hired labor; (2) the reasonable value of the time, skill, and experience of the individual producing commodity or commodities; (3) a fair return upon essential invested capital; (4) continuation of the American family farm pattern of agricultural production; and (5) other appropriate factors including compensation comparable with that of other persons engaged in other means of earning a livelihood. . . ."[13] The proposal does not include a statement about the size of farm or quantity of output which a producer would have to

13. U.S. Congress, Senate, Bill 2973, 90th Cong., 2nd sess., introduced February 15, 1968.

Table 3.9 ● Acreages Diverted and Total Payments Required for Continuation of the Annual Wheat, Feed Grain, and Cotton Programs to 1970

Region	Wheat program diversion	Feed grain program diversion	Cotton program diversion	Total	Wheat program payments	Feed grain program payments	Cotton program payments	Total
	(thousand acres)				($ thousand)			
United States	10,134	40,641	2,750	53,525	823,942	1,572,728	423,200	2,819,870
Northeast	295	914	0	1,209	13,396	39,439	0	52,835
Lake States	379	3,876	0	4,255	26,860	172,831	0	199,691
Corn Belt	927	9,368	47	10,342	78,285	516,522	7,009	601,846
Northern Plains	3,789	9,413	0	13,202	352,453	314,018	0	666,471
Appalachians	436	3,387	163	3,986	12,666	146,047	20,012	178,725
Southeast	228	3,579	417	4,224	5,714	111,557	42,622	159,893
Delta	46	1,607	605	2,258	4,073	40,705	97,657	142,435
Southern Plains	2,052	6,091	1,339	9,482	136,930	175,177	197,593	509,700
Mountain	1,492	1,689	101	3,282	129,610	38,577	24,151	192,338
Pacific	490	717	78	1,285	63,955	17,825	34,156	115,936

NOTE: Under annual diversion programs total payments are comprised of price support (certificate) and diversion payments. The 1970 payments were calculated as follows: Wheat and feed grain programs - the certificate or price support payment per acre is assumed to equal 1966 payments. Diverted acre payments for 1970 are based on 1966 payments adjusted upward for projected yield increases between 1966 and 1970; Cotton program - payments under the cotton program were computed differently. The price support payment was calculated at $.060 per pound on the projected production from the price support acres. The diversion payment was computed at $.074 per pound on the projected production from the diverted acreage.

sell to earn this level of income although this is an essential component, since price alone provides no indication of income level. Size is important because, as illustrated from data on Iowa record-keeping farms, the cost of producing a dollar of output varied from $0.89 on 160-acre farms down to $0.59 on 600-acre farms in 1966. These costs do not include any return to management or to land; in the small farm case, $0.11 of each dollar of sales remains for this purpose while in the large farm case, $0.41 of each dollar of sales is available for this purpose. A "fair and reasonable price" for the small farm thus would be considerably higher than for a larger farm. These differences in costs among family farms provide a basis for debate over the level which reflects "a fair and reasonable price."

Setting aside some of the problems which will face any farmer committee authorized to conduct discussions on bargaining power, we analyze the effects of implementing acreage controls or production limitations on major agricultural commodities. The analysis includes livestock price levels similar to those which have been proposed as goals by farmer bargaining groups. A major step was to determine the effect which such prices would have on total utilization of major commodities. After determining the quantities of major crops which would be needed under the assumed price levels, we estimated the acreages of cropland required for each of the major crops. (Exports with the higher price levels of this alternative were assumed to be as follows: wheat—750 million bushels; feed grains—24.0 million tons; soybeans—400 million bushels; and cotton 5.0 million bales.) The estimates are based on projected 1970 yields which assume continued improvement in agricultural technology.

The results suggest that to satisfy the expected demand associated with the higher prices, acreages of wheat, feed grains, soybeans, and cotton would be as shown in Table 3.5. These are the levels at which acreage quotas would necessarily be set if production is to equal demand at the higher price levels. Two offsetting tendencies occur with implementation of acreage quotas and higher price levels. One tendency is for the quantity demanded both for domestic use in livestock production and in the export market to decline. This tendency reduces acreage needed to supply total demand. But offsetting this trend is the fact that as acreage quotas are imposed, production tends to be forced out of its optimum location and this causes less productive land to be used in production. Generally this land has lower yields. Lower yields create a tendency for more acres to be used to produce the quantity of grains demanded. Thus acreages decrease because a smaller quantity is demanded, but some of the decline in acreage is offset by a decline in average yields. In the course of these shifts, some inefficiency would be created when production was forced from cropland in regions with a comparative advantage into regions of lower productivity.

With reduced production of both crops and livestock, prices received by farmers increase (Table 3.6). These are equilibrium prices in the sense that quotas restrain production in regions which could produce at a lower cost. (While these are the prices used for the analysis of "bargaining power," they could also be attained by the programs analyzed earlier if acreage reduction or land retirement was extended to a sufficiently high level.) With higher levels of prices for major grain and oilseed crops, livestock prices are also higher. Quantities of livestock required would be somewhat smaller, but the increase in prices would more than offset the loss in sales.

Higher prices cause cash receipts from crops to increase over recent levels (Table 3.7). Crop receipts are above the 1967 level. Livestock receipts, while not exceeding those of 1967, would be above other recent years. Direct government payments would drop with the removal of programs to retire cropland. Payments remaining under the Sugar Act, Wool Act, and conservation programs would total $326 million. Total cash receipts add up to $43.7 billion.

Most cash farm expenses under a program of this kind are higher compared with alternative programs. Costs of feed purchases rise along with the cost of livestock purchases. Both these expenses are a function of price levels received by farmers. The increase in prices paid is somewhat offset by smaller quantities purchased, but higher prices received by farmers result in the higher expenses for these particular purchased inputs. Net cash receipts—total cash receipts less cash expenses—total $15.9 billion. Subtracting depreciation expense and adding in farm perquisites and changes in the value of farm inventories result in a net farm income slightly below the 1967 level.

The projected level of net farm income for this alternative falls between estimates for other farm programs. The results suggest that increases in farm prices would not offset the multi-billion-dollar drop in government payments which would result from termination of major government programs for agriculture. Even though increases in prices cause total cash receipts from both crops and livestock to approach recent highs, decreases in government payments as well as higher expenses associated with this production cause net farm income to be lower.

These results raise the question of whether farm commodity prices can be raised high enough through the means examined to offset decreases in cash receipts from government payments. Obviously, if prices could be raised high enough, the increase in cash receipts so resulting would more than cover the cessation of government payments. However raising farm prices very far above present levels poses several problems. One is a market obstacle. Purchases, both in domestic market and particularly in the export market, will decline as prices rise. Concurrently, a reduction in the quantity produced will be necessary to maintain the higher price level. But producers, realizing increased returns from the higher prices, will want to increase production—not decrease it—at the same time that quantities demanded and utilized are to be reduced. The underlying forces of imbalance could become even greater than at present and could cause the control of production to become increasingly difficult. To maintain higher prices, controls on production would have to be tightened beyond those established and used for voluntary programs; they would have to be mandatory if the bargaining power route is to work.

One means of holding higher prices would be for the government to continue its storage program: Raise the price floor, and then purchase that quantity of grain necessary to maintain this price in the marketplace. For this procedure to work without a sharp increase in stocks or a sharp drop in exports, the government would have to supply grain for export at world market prices. Assuming that domestic prices rose above present levels, the lower export price would result in the government subsidizing the export of grain. This same process used in the 1950s caused considerable consternation in international circles. Eventually the United States changed its farm programs and price support levels and finally switched to direct government payments to farmers as a means to lessen output, raise prices, and support farm income. The use of high price supports and heavily subsidized exports or a rapid buildup of domestic stocks may not be practical options for the future, not necessarily because farmers are unsatisfied with these programs, but mainly as a result of international policy considerations and the unwillingness of the public to bear large storage costs. It seems unlikely that these means of raising farm prices will be available to farmers in the near future unless we choose to ignore the export market which, as we pointed out earlier, now accounts for approximately 20 percent of all farm production.

What then is the outlook for farmer bargaining power as the sole means for increasing prices and income? It is evident that these means can be effective only if mandatory acreage or marketing quotas are imposed. Used alone, price increases resulting from bargaining-power-imposed marketing reductions would be offset over a considerable range of increase by cessation of direct government payments under present voluntary control programs. A further increment in prices and a further reduction in output would be necessary to offset the loss of income from government payments. But the question remains: How far could prices be raised against restraints in export demand and farmer willingness to accept self-imposed production restraints if the government were not engaged in commodity storage, export subsidies, and payments for reducing acreage and production? The answer to this question is crucial and poses the possibility that farmer bargaining power cannot function effectively for the large complex of agriculture represented by feed grains and livestock without government programs and monetary payment.

THE OUTLOOK FOR INTERMEDIATE TERM PROGRAMS ●
Several specific program alternatives have been analyzed. Many more could be examined. However, those investigated have received special attention or discussion recently.

Any one of the alternative government programs analyzed here could be used to attain higher prices and incomes than those projected. In each case, the amount of land removed from production would have to be greater than the amounts indicated. For this reason, the government costs of each program also would be higher, but the relative position of each program with respect to government costs would be maintained. In the case of bargaining power without government payments, self-imposed restrictions on land use and production would need to be stricter to attain higher prices and incomes. Of course, any substantial upward alteration in domestic price levels would reduce the prospects for commercial exports. Hence production would have to be reduced further or the government would have to invest more in storage and international food aid.

It should also be recognized that because of the stage of economic development, relative prices of resources, and the new capital technologies being applied by farmers, none of the programs which are designed to restrict output and attain higher commodity prices would solve the farm and rural-community problems which revolve around structural transformation of agriculture. This structural transformation which brings a greater use of capital equipment, larger farms, and the replacement of labor will continue under any of these program alternatives, just as it has been proceeding under the programs of the last decade. It is indeed time for programs to include elements to alleviate the sacrifices falling on many farm families, laborers, and rural communities as a result of this transformation process. It is necessary, for programs which will help alleviate these costs which fall on some rural communities and farm families, to give proper emphasis to retraining, job placements, vocational training, community planning and guidance, and investment generally in economic opportunity and public services.

It is also possible in actual policy formulation to combine aspects of various programs analyzed in this chapter. One possibility as the main means of bringing agriculture into a self-sustaining balance with respect to market supplies and demand would be emphasis on long-term land retirement supplemented by programs to alleviate broad adjustment problems of the rural community. Combined with this main program could be a smaller program fashioned after annual wheat and feed grain programs to handle variability in production and export demand resulting from weather or other emergency and unforeseen contingencies. However, a storage program properly designed to encourage stability in market supplies and prices, involving either purchases or sales from government stocks at appropriate times and prices, could also serve the latter purposes. The actual combination of programs to be adopted is left to the arena of the policy makers. But this analysis clearly points out that a shift to programs with a set of goals revolving around long-term resource adjustment is necessary to meet the need of a society living in a very advanced industrial and technological environment.

CHAPTER FOUR

Long Term
Land Retirement Programs

IN THE PREVIOUS CHAPTER we looked at a number of different land retirement programs—of both short and intermediate term. In this chapter we extend the analysis to several long-term farm programs. For over three decades the problem of overcapacity to produce grain commodities has been approached through the mechanism of land retirement. One permanent approach to solving the problem would be to permanently remove unrequired crop acres from crop production. This approach could use one of several different mechanisms. One means would be for the government to purchase the land from farmers and return it to grass or trees. Another means would be for the government to use an easement approach where the rights to crop production would be purchased from the farmer for the time until additional cropland might be needed for crop production. A third means of permanent removal of land from crop production would be to use an easement approach to set up a program of encouraging farmers to convert cropland back to grass and graze it.

This chapter focuses on these three major long-run alternatives and evaluates each under two levels of participation. One level of participation would allow all land in a region to be removed from production and placed in the program. A second level of participation would restrict cropland entering the program to one-half the cropland in any region. In addition, under the grazing program the effect of expanding beef production is evaluated, assuming (1) one-half the excess cropland is grazed, and (2) all excess cropland is grazed (except that required for additional grain production for increased beef feeding). The effects on prices of livestock commodities are evaluated under the grazing alternatives, and under all alternatives the estimates are carried through to effects on farm income and government costs for each program.

OBJECTIVES AND ALTERNATIVES ● This chapter is directed, as previous chapters, toward quantifying the effects of alternative land retirement programs. These quantitative estimates as well as those in previous chapters are presented to provide an improved basis for public administrators, farm leaders, and the public at large to make decisions on farm policies. In providing estimates for specific farm program alternatives, we do not propose to examine all important possibilities. Neither do we suppose that all those examined are readily acceptable to the public. The estimates for the alternatives are provided to allow greater knowledge particularly of the income and cost effects of the programs examined.

As with the previous chapters, this analysis relates mainly to commercial agriculture. Problems of commercial farms are of course intertwined with those of rural communities. If farm enlargement and the decline in the farm labor force occur rapidly, the effects spread throughout the entire rural community. Gross receipts of local businesses decline and capital losses fall on those whose facilities become redundant. Local governments and other institutions face similar problems as their costs continue but demand for their services decline. Studies and policy evaluations are needed of the broader adjustment problems and costs which face the rural community under alternate government farm programs. Public policy decisions require knowledge of the potential effects of selected long-term program alternatives on farm income, government costs, amount and location of land adjustments, crop and livestock production, and related items.

In this chapter comparisons of program alternatives are made for the year 1975, based on projections of yields, demand, and other basic variables to this date. Three specific program alternatives relating to variations in regional concentration of cropland adjustment are evaluated. These include—

1. A government land purchase program under which cropland would be purchased by the federal government and withheld from crop production. With this program, adequate cropland would be purchased on a regional least-cost basis to maintain a specific set of farm prices. Such a program is evaluated when all cropland in production regions is eligible to participate and when only one-half the cropland is allowed in the program.
2. A government program of permanent land rental or easement purchase under which land would be rented by the government on a long-term basis, or the government would use easements to transfer all "rights" to produce specified crops (wheat, feed grains, cotton, and soybeans) to itself. Land rental or easement purchase is similarly evaluated under two alternative levels of participation. In the discussion which follows, we use the term *easement* with a meaning

paralleling long-term rental. The farmer would "sell" his rights to produce all crops during the specified period; or he would "sell" his rights to produce any crop except trees, grass, and pasture.

3. A government program of land easement designed to remove cropland from crop production, transfer it to grass, and encourage grazing. This program is evaluated under the same two levels of participation of any production area with, in addition (a) grazing limited to one-half the cropland under one alternative, and (b) all excess cropland being grazed under the other alternative.

The method used in this chapter is to determine the location and amount of land taken out of production in a spatially least-cost manner which would allow the output of commodities to attain specific prices and minimize the cost of retiring or shifting cropland to other uses.

The least-cost regional pattern of land retirement with no restrictions on acres retired in any region is termed *unrestricted* participation. Acreages under this alternative are the same in amount and location for the land purchase program, diversion under long-term rental or easement purchase, and under increased grazing. Similarly the alternatives with a restraint that no more than 50 percent of the land in one region can be withdrawn is termed *restricted* participation. The amount and location of cropland removed from production is the same under land purchase, long-term rental or easement purchase, or under the program of increased grazing.

PRICE ASSUMPTIONS AND RELATED PARAMETERS ● All three alternative land-use programs are analyzed with respect to the same basic assumptions for farm prices, population, per capita income and consumption, exports, and similar items. In Table 4.1, parameters used for all nongrazing land-use alternatives are projected for 1975. Farm level prices of major commodities are set near 1967 levels. Production of grains under each program meets prespecified levels of domestic and export demand. In addition, carry-over stocks of the major commodities are assumed constant for all models. The analysis also assumes the land base will remain constant between 1965 and 1975.

METHOD AND TERMINOLOGY ● The analysis which follows is based on results from a 150 region linear programming model similar in basic outline to the model of Chapter 3. (See Fig. 3.1.) However, to provide a mechanism to allow prespecified price levels for grain commodities, the model was changed to contain an objective function with profit maximization as its decision criterion. The basic change was addition of commodity-selling activities for each consuming region. The model is specified as follows:

Table 4.1 ● Parameters Used for Nongrazing, Land-Use Alternatives, Past Levels and Projected 1975

Item and unit	Actual		Projected[a]
	1965	1967	1975
Population (thousand)	192,838	196,830	221,653
Disposable income per capita ($)	2,427	2,736	3,000
Per capita consumption levels		(lb carcass wt)	
Beef and veal	104.5	109.7	127.0
Pork	58.5	63.9	60.0
Lamb and mutton	3.7	3.9	3.8
Prices received by farmers		($ per bu)	
Wheat	1.35	1.39	1.25
Corn	1.16	1.05	1.05
Soybeans	2.54	2.49	2.25
		($ per lb)	
Cotton lint	0.281	0.256	0.260
Cattle and calves	0.200	0.226	0.220
Hogs	0.206	0.189	0.182
Sheep	0.200	0.189	0.195
Projected exports of major commodities		(million)	
Wheat (bu)	867.4	761.1	900.0
Feed grains (tons)	29.1	22.6	31.0
Soybeans (bu)[b]	366.9	391.9	514.3
Cotton lint (bales)	2.9	4.7	5.0

[a] All prices and incomes for 1975 are in 1966 equivalent dollars and do not take into account inflation from 1966 to 1975.

[b] Quantities measured in bushels of soybean equivalent.

$$\text{Maximize } f(r) = \sum_{k=1}^{31} \sum_{j=1}^{4} P_{jk} Q_{jk} - \sum_{i=1}^{150} \sum_{j=1}^{4} c_{ij} X_{ij}$$

$$- \sum_{k=1}^{31} s_k w_k - \sum_{g=1}^{31} \sum_{k=1}^{31} \sum_{k'=1}^{31} z_{gkk'} T_{gkk'} \quad (4.1)$$

subject to

$$D_{1k} \geq \sum_{i=1}^{n_k} y_{i1} X_{i1} - g_k w_k \pm \sum_{k=1}^{31} \sum_{k'=1}^{31} b_{1kk'} T_{1kk'} \quad (4.2)$$

$$D_{2k} \geq \sum_{i=1}^{n_k} y_{12} X_{12} + g_k w_k \pm \sum_{k=1}^{31} \sum_{k'=1}^{31} b_{2kk'} T_{2kk'} \quad (4.3)$$

$$D_{3k} \geq \sum_{i=1}^{n_k} y_{i3} X_{i3} + \sum_{i=1}^{n_k} y_{i3} X_{i4}$$

$$\pm \sum_{k=1}^{31} \sum_{k'=1}^{31} b_{3kk'} T_{3kk'} \quad (4.4)$$

$$D_4 \geq \sum_{i=1}^{150} y_{i4} X_{i4} \quad (4.5)$$

where

P_{jk} = per unit selling price of j-th commodity in the k-th consuming region, $k = 1, 2, \ldots, 31$ to represent the thirty-one consuming regions and j to represent the four commodity-producing activities:

$$j = 1 = \text{wheat}$$
$$j = 2 = \text{feed grains}$$
$$j = 3 = \text{soybeans}$$
$$j = 4 = \text{cotton}$$

Q_{jk} = quantity of the j-th crop sold in the k-th consuming region where $Q_{jk} \leq D_{jk}$. All other restraints on land use and conditions to prevent negative production, transfer, and transportation are identical to those for the cost minimization model of Chapter 3.

For the specified price level studied, a set of projected per acre yields and costs was computed for each crop in each producing region. Total demand levels for wheat, feed grains, oilmeals, and cotton were projected for thirty-one consuming regions of the nation. In short, Equation (4.1) maximizes the net return from production of wheat, feed grains, soybeans, and cotton, given the costs of producing these crops, their selling prices, and the costs of transportation between the various consuming regions.

ANALYSIS OF SPECIFIC LONG-TERM LAND CONVERSION AL-TERNATIVES ● With four decades of farm price and income problems growing out of an overabundance of crop production capacity, and the trends for the future previously established, substantial evidence suggests that a more permanent type of land retirement program is suitable for adjusting the levels of output from the agricultural industry. Many different programs could be established ranging from the free market approach to the acreage quota approach, both examined in the last chapter. In between these two points on the spectrum of farm programs, both similar in terms of the mandatory aspects of adjustment, there are several more voluntary types of programs such as the annual diversion programs used for wheat, feed grains, and cotton during the 1960s. A second type would be a multi-year program which retired cropland from production for several annual production periods. It is this kind of program that we first examine below.

LAND RENTAL PROGRAMS ● The land rental program envisioned is examined in the context of a decade possibly not being long enough to remove the overcapacity problem of agriculture, and hence this program would need to continue to an indefinite date. An annual cost is estimated for the program under two levels of participation in any region. Under one level of participation all cropland in a region could participate in the program; under a more restricted program only one-half the cropland in any region could enter the program.

Long-Term Land Rental with Unrestricted Participation ● With unrestricted government land rental programs in 1975, all excess cropland in a region can be rented by the government on a whole-farm basis. These programs, paralleling somewhat the Soil Bank Program of the 1950s, would hold land completely out of production with no grazing allowed. Crop production would be located on the most efficient acres in regions of greatest comparative advantage. With crop production optimally located in regions of lowest resource cost, and demand requirements met for projected 1975 levels, wheat acreage is near the 1968 level but the national wheat yield is higher (Table 4.2). Feed grains production with optimal location and a long-term land rental program requires 10.1 million acres less than in 1968. The national average corn yield in 1975 is projected at 13 bushels per acre above the 1968 national average.

With an unrestricted land rental program, national soybean acreage is below the 1968 level but 1975 average yield of soybeans is projected at 2.5 bushels per acre above the 1968 yield. Total cotton acreage is estimated at 2.7 million acres more than in 1968, and national yield of cotton lint is estimated at 72 pounds per acre more than in 1968. The location of cropland retired with an unrestricted government program in 1975 is shown in Figure 4.1. Areas of heaviest concentration include the Northern Plains, an area extending from the Panhandle of Oklahoma through eastern Kansas to western Missouri and a belt running through the Southeast. With no restrictions on the amount of land retired in a given area, government costs are minimized through concentration of land retirement in those areas which have the lowest comparative advantage in production of major crops.

Under a program of government land rental on a whole-farm basis, total retired acres will include land from major crops and other cropland in farms. Given the excess cropland from major crops (57.5 million acres) and using experiences of the Conservation Reserve Program of 1960, the additional acres (i.e., flax, some tame hay land, etc.) are estimated to total 16.1 million acres (Table 4.3). Adding together land from major crops and minor crops, acres under the program total 73.6 million. The total annual cost is estimated at $1.2 billion, an average rent of $16.10 per acre for the 73.6 million acres retired.

The $1.2 billion for land retirement for 1975 is less than one-half the annual estimated costs ($2.8 billion) of annual land diversion programs continued beyond 1970. (See Ch. 3.) The annual cost is less under the long-term rental program because land retirement is allowed to concentrate in regions of lowest comparative advantage (most marginal land) for the major crops. The cost of a given amount of crop production supply control is less on land of lower productivity because costs absorb a greater proportion of the yield or gross revenue per acre. Hence a program which retires cropland based on its expected net revenue per acre will optimally retire low yielding acres which generally also have the lowest retirement cost per acre.

These estimates suggest a substantial saving in program costs for long-term land rental on a regional and whole-farm basis as compared to annual land diversion programs which extend supply control over all regions on a fractional basis. Even if a premium of 25 percent above estimated normal net returns per acre (or if normal profit margins were underestimated to this extent) were necessary to get sufficient land retired to meet the production and price goals specified earlier, the estimated

Table 4.2 ● Acreages, Yields, and Production of Major Crops with Unrestricted and Restricted Government Programs of Retiring Cropland in 1975

Crop	Actual		Projected 1975	
	1965-67 average	1968	Unrestricted	Restricted
Harvested acreages	(thousand acres)			
Wheat	52,282	56,039	4,819	56,584
Feed grains	97,168	97,847	88,722	89,045
Soybeans	36,543	40,949	38,192	38,523
Cotton	10,419	10,318	13,089	12,797
Yield	(per harvested acre)			
Wheat (bu)	26.20	28.50	32.00	31.00
Feed grains (tons)	1.66	1.74	2.12	2.11
Soybeans (bu)	24.80	26.40	28.90	28.60
Cotton (lb)	509.00	508.00	581.00	595.00
Total production	(thousand)			
Wheat (bu)	1,370,049	1,597,858	1,734,048	1,754,104
Feed grains (tons)	161,733	170,596	187,773	188,073
Soybeans (bu)	906,344	1,079,490	1,103,749	1,101,758
Cotton (bales)	10,609	10,912	15,209	15,228

Source: U. S. Dept. of Agriculture, Crop Production 1968 Annual Summary, USDA ERS, December 1968.

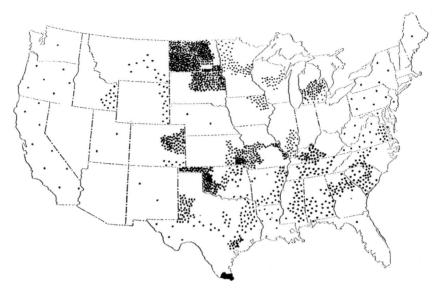

Fig. 4.1. Unrestricted government farm programs. Each dot represents 35,000 acres. U.S. total is 57,461,000 acres.

costs of long-term rental would still be less than one-half of that projected under annual land diversion programs extended beyond 1970.

While government costs under this alternative would be substantially lower, major adjustments would face rural communities where land diversion would concentrate. Further depopulation of farms would occur, as occurred under programs of the 1960s. Farm families could be left as well off as previously in the sense that they are given the same return per acre through a long-term rental or easement purchase program and are free to follow other employment or economic opportunity. However, costs would fall on local merchants, and fewer families would have to pay for public service and other institutional costs as the farm population and business volumes in rural areas declined. These costs or burdens which fall on the nonfarm sector of rural communities were present even under the dispersed supply control programs of the 1960s. Few rural farm communities did not have rapid population declines over the period 1950–70. In some communities a third or more of the population migrated out in ten years. Even under annual land diversion programs, these adjustments occur and their associated costs fall on rural communities lacking an important industrial base. In many communities during the 1960s, wheat, feed grain, and cotton programs may have accentuated the trend, as a premium toward fewer and larger farms was encouraged under the certainty of prices and lack of limitation on payments to an individual farmer.

Hence, with the ongoing rush of new technology toward larger and

Table 4.3 ● Cropland Retired or Purchased and Government Costs for an Unrestricted Program (Whole-Farm Basis) in 1975

Region	Major crop acres rented or purchased[a] (thousand acres)	Other cropland rented[b] (thousand acres)	Total acres rented (thousand acres)	Average annual payment per acre[c] ($)	Total annual rental cost ($ million)	Other cropland and pasture purchased (thousand acres)	Total acres on farms purchased[d] (thousand acres)	Average cost per acre[e] ($)	Total purchase cost ($ million)
United States	57,461	16,090	73,551	16.10	1,184	45,090	102,551	187	19,182
Northeast	510	143	653	11.99	8	275	785	428	336
Lake States	5,634	1,578	7,212	12.86	93	2,415	8,049	276	2,224
Corn Belt	5,433	1,521	6,954	20.63	143	2,630	8,063	320	2,577
Northern Plains	20,334	5,694	26,028	15.00	390	11,842	32,176	103	3,303
Appalachians	4,271	1,196	5,467	15.51	85	4,785	9,056	291	2,639
Southeast	3,438	963	4,401	15.83	70	4,998	8,436	221	1,865
Delta	2,617	733	3,350	25.63	86	3,265	5,882	269	1,580
Southern Plains	10,130	2,836	12,966	17.10	222	6,721	16,851	165	2,788
Mountain	4,428	1,240	5,668	11.29	64	6,160	10,588	84	887
Pacific	666	186	852	26.78	23	1,999	2,665	369	983

[a] Land released from the production of wheat, feed grains, soybeans or cotton.

[b] If acreages released from production from the major crops are idled under a whole-farm cropland retirement program, additional acreages of other crops (i.e., rye, some tame hay land, etc.) would also be eligible for the program. Estimates of other cropland retired are made by multiplying major crop acres idle, by a correction factor, 1.28, calculated from acres under contract in the 1960 Conservation Reserve.

[c] Annual cost per acre is the estimated annual net return per acre from crop production plus a $5 per acre allowance for weed control.

[d] Total acres on farms purchased is estimated by adjusting total major cropland acres purchased (57.5 million acres) by a ratio of cropland to total land in farms. Other cropland and pasture purchased is equal to total acres on farms purchased minus crop acres purchased.

[e] Average cost per acre is for land and buildings. Costs in 1975 are estimated by assuming a 3 percent per year increase in land prices from 1966 to 1975 due to productivity advances. No adjustment is made for inflation between 1966 and 1975.

fewer farms, a long-term land program to retire marginal acres, if spread over a sufficiently long time, might have only slightly greater consequences to rural communities than annual land diversion programs. Estimated costs to the government for long-term rental would be $1.2 billion, or even $1.5 billion if a 25 percent increase above normal net returns per acre were necessary to get sufficient participation or offset unrecognized costs. The difference between $2.8 billion for present programs and the cost for long-term rental would provide a large fund for developing programs to compensate or provide greater economic opportunity for the nonfarm sector of rural communities. A program for these purposes is needed just as much as one is needed to compensate farmers under rapidly advancing agricultural technologies and inelastic demands. Both are economically justifiable if they accomplish their objectives in terms of economic growth and technological advances which otherwise have a distribution of benefits bringing gains to some and costs, reduced incomes, and capital losses to others.

Estimates of net farm incomes for this program are given in Table 4.4. With the whole-farm cropland retirement program, net farm income is higher than actual income in 1967. Although government payments are less under the 1975 program than in 1967, cash receipts from larger farm marketings increase more than enough to offset this decrease.

Long-Term Land Rental with Restricted Participation ● With a government land rental program with restricted participation, up to one-half of the total cropland of any region can be taken out of production on a whole-farm basis. With a program that limits the acres retired in any particular region to 50 percent of total crop acres, crop production generally requires more acres per crop. Wheat requires 1.8 million more acres of cropland than under the previous program and 0.8 million more than in 1968 (Table 4.2). Feed grains require 0.3 million more acres as compared to the unrestricted program and 8.8 million fewer acres than harvested in 1968. The national yield of corn is projected at 13.1 bushels above the 1968 average. Soybean acreage is estimated at 0.3 million more acres than for the unrestricted program and 2.4 million acres down from 40.9 million in 1968, while the average yield of soybeans is estimated to increase 2.2 bushels over 1968. With these major crop acreages, 55.3 million acres of cropland remain unused. For the specified prices to be achieved, this cropland must be retired from production.

Under a long-term rental program where cropland is retired on a whole-farm basis, 70.8 million acres (55.3 million acres of major crops and 15.5 million acres of minor crops) enter the program at an annual total cost of $1.4 billion (Table 4.5). The average rental cost per acre rises to $20.45 with the restricted program, as compared to $16.10 under the unrestricted program. Land rents rise because land in more productive regions is idled under the restricted program.

Figure 4.2 shows the location of retired major crop acres for the

Table 4.4 ● Farm Income and Government Payments with Unrestricted and Restricted Government Rental Programs in 1975

Income & expenses	Actual			Projected 1975[a]	
	1961-65 average	1965	1967	Unrestricted	Restricted
	($ million)				
Farming operations					
Cash receipts from farm marketings	37,086	39,350	42,788	48,010	48,025
Cash expenses incurred in production	24,629	25,951	29,079	31,400	31,400
Net receipts from farm marketings	12,457	13,399	13,709	16,610	16,625
Depreciation expenses	4,544	4,982	5,741	6,321	6,321
Actual receipts from farm marketings	7,913	8,417	7,968	10,289	10,304
Nonmoney income[b]	3,157	3,113	3,194	3,295	3,295
Inventory change	347	994	403	350	350
Net returns from farming	11,417	12,524	11,565	13,934	13,949
Government sources					
Feed grain program	1,002	1,391	865	0	0
Wheat program	295[c]	525	731	0	0
Cotton program	54	70	932	0	0
Total major program payments	1,351	1,986	2,528	0	0
Cropland adjustment and soil bank	260	160	214	1,184[e]	1,447[e]
Other government payment programs[d]	337	317	336	365	365
Total direct program payments	1,948	2,463	3,078	1,549	1,812
Total net farm income	13,365	14,987	14,643	15,483	15,761

[a]All values are measured in 1966 equivalent dollars with no adjustment for inflation to 1975.
[b]Includes the value of home consumption of farm products and the rental value of farm dwelling.
[c]1964-65 average.
[d]Includes ACP, Great Plains Conservation, Sugar Act, and Wool Act payments.
[e]Annual value of land rental or easement purchase.

Table 4.5 ● Cropland Retired or Purchased and Government Costs for a Restricted Government Program (Whole-Farm Basis) in 1975

Region	Major crop acres rented or purchased[a] (thousand acres)	Other cropland rented[b] (thousand acres)	Total acres rented (thousand acres)	Average annual rent per acre[c] ($)	Total annual rental cost ($ million)	Other cropland and pasture purchased (thousand acres)	Total acres on farms purchased[d] (thousand acres)	Average cost per acre[e] ($)	Total purchase cost ($ million)
United States	55,333	15,491	70,824	20.45	1,447	49,520	104,853	208	21,793
Northeast	936	262	1,198	11.99	14	827	1,763	415	732
Lake States	4,929	1,380	6,309	16.81	106	2,063	6,992	266	1,860
Corn Belt	8,248	2,309	10,557	31.87	336	2,989	11,237	397	4,463
Northern Plains	16,500	4,620	21,120	18.48	390	9,813	26,313	116	3,064
Appalachians	3,641	1,019	4,660	17.22	80	4,016	7,657	298	2,279
Southeast	4,144	1,160	5,304	17.96	95	6,117	10,261	224	2,298
Delta	2,691	753	3,444	26.14	90	3,374	6,065	266	1,613
Southern Plains	9,196	2,575	11,771	18.44	217	5,998	15,194	163	2,470
Mountain	3,882	1,985	4,969	15.81	79	10,440	14,322	81	1,163
Pacific	1,166	326	1,492	26.78	40	3,883	5,049	367	1,851

[a]Land released from the production of wheat, feed grains, soybeans, or cotton.

[b]If acreages released from production from the major crops are idled under a whole-farm cropland retirement program, additional acreages of other crops (i.e., rye, some tame hay land, etc.) would also be eligible for the program. Estimates of other cropland retired are made by multiplying major crop-acres idle, by a correction factor, 1.28, calculated from acres under contract in the 1960 Conservation Reserve.

[c]Annual cost per acre is the estimated annual net return per acre from crop production plus a $5 per acre allowance for weed control.

[d]Total acres on farms purchased is estimated by adjusting total major cropland acres purchased (55.3 million acres) by a ratio of cropland to total land in farms. Other cropland and pasture purchased is equal to total acres on farms purchased minus crop-acres purchased.

[e]Average cost per acre is for land and buildings. Costs in 1975 are estimated by assuming a 3 percent per year increase in land prices from 1966 to 1975 due to productivity advances. No adjustment is made for inflation between 1966 and 1975.

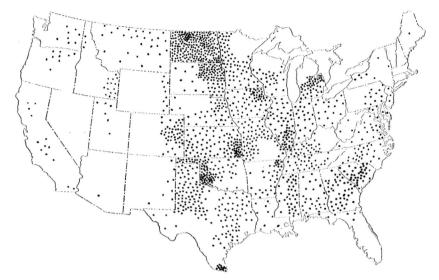

Fig. 4.2. Restricted government farm programs. (Maximum of 50% of a region can be bought or rented.) Each dot represents 35,000 acres. The U.S. total is 55,334,000 acres.

restricted program alternatives. Land shifted from crop production under the 50 percent restriction is spread over more regions than under the unrestricted programs shown in Figure 4.1. Land withdrawal still falls heavily in the same areas with a heavy concentration of land designated for retirement in the Northern Plains, an area starting in the Panhandle of Oklahoma and running through eastern Kansas to western Missouri and some areas in the Southeast.

For comparison, land under contract in the Conservation Reserve as of 1960 is shown in Figure 4.3. Areas of heaviest concentration follow the same general pattern indicated in Figures 4.1 and 4.2. Total acres shown are less because the Conservation Reserve Program was not large enough to attain the production and price goals implied in this study. Had the acreage been as large, the location and amount of land withdrawn by regions under the Conservation Reserve Program would have been highly parallel to the pattern of programs in this chapter.

Projected net farm incomes for the restricted programs are reported in Table 4.4. With the whole-farm land rental program and retirement restricted to 50 percent of the land in a region, total net farm income for 1975 is above both the unrestricted program and 1967 levels. Although the government payment portion of farm income decreases from 1967 levels, cash receipts rise more than enough to offset decreased payments as well as increased costs. As a result, net income is more than a billion dollars higher than under 1967 farm programs.

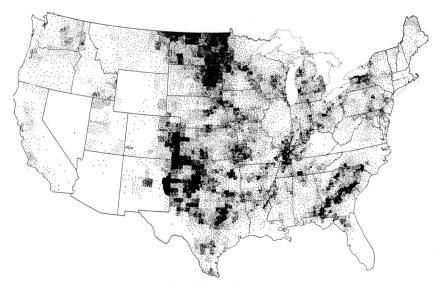

Fig. 4.3. Conservation Reserve Program acreage under contract as of July 15, 1960. Each dot represents 1,000 acres. Data entered on a county unit basis. U.S. total is 28,659,973 acres.

LAND PURCHASE PROGRAMS ● A second kind of program which could permanently remove cropland from production would be government purchase of the acres of cropland which are no longer required for crop production. This program could be carried on over a period of time in order to minimize the undesirable effects on agriculture and rural areas. For the government to purchase cropland, a program of whole-farm purchases would be required with some additional acres of minor crop and pasture entering the program. While the program as analyzed here does not provide for grazing, once the government owned the land, it could be managed similarly to the public land in western states where grazing at controlled levels is allowed at specified grazing fees.

Land Purchase with Unrestricted Participation ● A land purchase program is examined below in which all farmland in a region is eligible for purchase so long as some acreage of major crops is grown. Farms entering the program are brought in on a bid basis with the result that acres of marginal cropland would be purchased. These acreages are derived from the same model used under the land rental program with unrestricted participation. The objective here is to estimate the cost of purchasing the cropland from the farm owner rather than renting it from year to year or even for a decade or more. Net farm income would total $14.3 billion compared to $15.5 billion with the unrestricted rental program. The $14.3 billion does not include any payment for land purchase (which would be $1.9 billion per year over ten years, interest excluded) while the $15.5 billion includes $1.2 billion for land rental payments (Table 4.4).

Total acreage of farms to be purchased is estimated by adjusting the acres of cropland which are no longer required for production of major crops, by a ratio of cropland to total land in farms estimated from the 1964 Census of Agriculture. For 1975 demand levels, major crop requirements leave 57 million acres of cropland unused. To purchase 57 million acres formerly used for wheat, feed grains, soybeans, and cotton with land purchases restricted to whole farms requires a total purchase of 102.6 million acres of land (Table 4.3). Under this program whole farms are bought out of production with land from major crops, minor crops, pasture, and grass purchased by the government. An additional 45 million acres of other land would have to be purchased.

To estimate the costs of land per acre, 1966 land prices[1] are adjusted upward for estimated productivity changes between 1966 and 1975. No allowance is included for any additional price changes due to inflationary factors. With the increased level of land prices, the total cost of purchasing 102.6 million acres of farmland is estimated at $19 billion.

The average cost per acre for the program is estimated at $187 with a range of $428 in the Northeast to $84 in the Mountain region. In terms of regional location of land placed under government ownership, the Northern Plains, Southern Plains, and Mountain states place large amounts of cropland under the program. Only the Northeast and Pacific regions would be relatively unaffected by the program.

The magnitude of cropland which would be removed from crop production under a program of this kind would have significant effect on some particular regions and communities. Allowing all cropland in any region to participate in the program increases the magnitude of burden that would fall on particular communities.

Land Purchase with Restricted Participation ● The government would purchase cropland under this program in similar fashion to the previous program except that each region would be limited in amount to one-half the major crop acres in any region. The major crop acreages which would be purchased parallel those under the land rental program with restricted participation and these same acres would be purchased by the government and permanently removed from crop production.

Under this program, there are 55.3 million acres of cropland which are unused after demand levels for wheat, feed grains, and cotton are filled. Net farm income is $14.3 billion compared to $15.8 billion with

1. U.S. Dept. of Agriculture, *Farm Real Estate Developments* (Washington, D.C.: USDA ERS, April 1968).

the restricted rental program. The $14.3 does not include any payment for land purchase (which would be $2.2 billion per year over ten years, interest excluded), whereas the $15.8 billion includes $1.5 billion for land rental payments (Table 4.4). The purchase of these acres on a whole-farm basis would require purchase of an additional 49.5 million acres of other cropland and pasture. In total, 104.9 million acres of farmland would be removed from agriculture and turned over to government ownership (Table 4.5). With a limit on the proportion retired in any region, the program spreads into more regions, and a higher cost per acre results from the better quality of land purchased. The per acre cost is $208 under this program compared to $187 under the previous program. With the higher cost per acre the total dollar cost rises some $2.6 billion higher.

Compared to the unrestricted program the degree of concentration is considerably less under this program. The Northern Plains have 26.3 million acres purchased compared to 32.3 million acres under the program in the previous section. The regions showing sizeable increases are the Mountain, Pacific, Southeast, and Corn Belt.

The costs for the land purchase programs appear high in total when compared to annual programs which cost only $2.0 to $3.0 billion annually; yet the potential cost is considerably lower when placed in the context of the next decade. Spread over a ten-year period, the annual cost of land purchase would amount to $1.9 to $2.2 billion per year (assuming land values remained at the specified levels). To this amount would have to be added any annual interest payments involved for purchase, with payments spread over ten years, and costs of administering such a program. Of course under the expectation of continued inflation of land prices the purchase price would likely exceed the projected amounts. Further, land purchase of this magnitude would likely increase the price of land to the government. However, the annual diversion program of the 1960s cost the government over $2.5 billion annually, but had no effect in reducing the long-term capacity problem. Under a land purchase program, the government could eventually own the land without the further requirement that it continue outlays after ten years. Even if we boosted the amount to $2.5 billion per year, or $25 billion over ten years (assuming the added amount was necessary to cover interest payments, inflation, and rising demand prices), the purchase program would have a much lower cost over twenty years than continuation of annual diversion programs for the same period of time. In ten years, under a land purchase program, the public would own the excess land and would not need to make further annual payments to hold it from production. Under continued annual diversion programs, the capacity problem could still exist in ten years and public outlays continue. While complete implementation of a government land purchase program would probably raise the supply price of land to the government somewhat above the $19 to $22 billion projected cost, the cost would still be less than implied with continuation of annual diversion programs over a ten-year period and even long-term rental programs over two or three decades.

ALTERNATIVE USES FOR EXCESS CROPLAND ● The two program alternatives examined previously, long-term land rental and permanent land purchase by the government, were examined under the expectation that no use would be made of the idled cropland for agricultural purposes. But there are many economic uses which could be made of this land for both farming and nonfarming enterprises. For farming, one use would be to allow grazing of the cropland. Use of land for this purpose would cause less economic disturbance in rural areas than completely idling cropland from all production. We thus examine below whether using excess acres of cropland for grazing would have positive or negative effects on farm income, as compared to complete withholding of land from production.

The program examined here assumes the government would enter into easement contracts with farm operators whereby an easement of cropping rights on land in the program would be purchased from the farmer but he would retain the right to raise livestock on the land. Two levels of grazing are examined. Under one program grazing is limited to one-half the total crop acres, and under a second program, all cropland is allowed to be grazed. The restricted and unrestricted limitations on participation in the program are also maintained in this analysis.

The alternatives examined include—

1. An easement program with unrestricted participation where idled cropland is converted to pasture and hay with (a) grazing allowed on 50 percent of the land, and (b) grazing allowed on all idled acres.
2. An easement program with restricted participation where idled cropland is converted to pasture and hay, and (a) grazing is allowed on 50 percent of the land, and (b) grazing is allowed on all idled acres.

New equilibrium quantities and prices are estimated for each alternative level of beef production based on available supply and demand equations.[2]

Under the program alternatives for 1975 examined previously in this chapter, it was assumed that an equilibrium existed between forage demand (i.e., pasture and hay) and forage supply. Thus any addition of hay and pasture acres is assumed to add a net quantity to total production of livestock. Acreages of additional pasture, hay, feed grains, and soybeans for each specific program are given in Table 4.6. Under

2. Supply equations used are from Alvin C. Egbert and Shlomo Reutlinger, A Dynamic Long-Run Model of the Livestock-Feed Sector, *Journal of Economics* 47 (December 1965): 5, 1288–1305. Demand equations used are from the multiple regression analysis of per capita consumption of red meats and poultry explained in Chapter 3.

Table 4.6 ● Use of Cropland Released from Production of the Major Crops under a Government Easement Program with Grazing

Use of cropland	Unrestricted programs		Restricted programs	
	50 percent grazing	100 percent grazing	50 percent grazing	100 percent grazing
		(thousand acres)		
Pasture	28,277	56,652	27,108	54,297
Hay	5,375	10,733	5,116	10,242
Feed grains	2,225	4,407	2,268	4,485
Soybeans	898	1,759	920	1,800
Total	36,775	73,551	35,412	70,824

the various programs, each ten acres used for additional pasture and hay requires about one additional acre of cropland for feed grains and oilmeal production for use in feeding and finishing cattle for slaughter.

The largest demand for additional feed grains and oilmeal production is with a restricted land conversion program where all land is used for beef production. While total acres released from production of the major and minor crops are lower under the restricted easement program, less marginal land is included, which raises the average pounds of beef produced per acre. As a result, total pounds of beef produced are slightly higher under the restricted land conversion programs than under the unrestricted programs.

An Unrestricted Easement Purchase Program with Grazing Allowed ●
Under this set of programs all restriction on participation by regions is removed and any proportion of cropland in a given region may enter the program. The grazing possibilities are again examined under two levels—grazing of one-half the cropland and grazing of all cropland—as indicated in Table 4.10. In Table 4.7, one-half the excess crop acres are assumed to be converted to grazing. With 33.7 million more acres of grazing land, an additional 6.4 billion pounds of beef are produced. The average cost of production is estimated at 15.7 cents per pound. Given this level of increase in production, the projected price for cattle and calves is 19.0 cents, and seven of ten farm production regions are estimated to cover costs of production. The average easement payment to make farmers as well off as with "no grazing" is estimated at $10.43 per acre, and the total cost of the program for the government is $943 million.

In contrast, if all the additional cropland is grazed, total beef is projected to increase by 12.8 billion pounds (Table 4.8). Since beef price declines to an average of 16.3 cents per pound for cattle and calves, only four farm production regions cover the costs of producing the additional beef. As a result, the average easement payment per acre rises to $15.42, and the total cost for the program is estimated at $1.0 billion.

Assuming one-half of all excess cropland is used for additional beef production, per capita consumption of beef and veal is projected to increase 17 pounds over the no-grazing program (Table 4.9). To increase consumption this amount, the market clearing price for cattle and calves is 3 cents per pound less than under a program of no grazing of idle acres, with unrestricted land rental.

Assuming all excess cropland acres are used for additional beef production, per capita consumption of beef and veal increases 33.4 pounds over the no-grazing program. To gain this level of consumption, the average farm level (market clearing) price for all cattle and calves is 5.7 cents below the no-grazing price level.

New equilibrium prices and quantities for pork show smaller changes than those described for beef. The largest change occurs under

Table 4.7 ● Returns from Grazing and Government Costs for an Unrestricted Government Easement Program with 50 Percent of Retired Cropland Used for Beef Production

Region	Cropland converted to grazing[a] (thousand acres)	Beef produced per acre[b] (lb)	Total additional beef produced (million lb)	Average cost of production per pound[c] (¢)	Net revenue from grazing[d] ($ per acre)	Program payment no grazing[e] ($ per acre)	Easement payment[f]	Annual government program cost ($ million)
United States	33,652	190.7	6,417	15.67	5.67	16.10	10.43	943
Northeast	298	201.1	60	19.33	-6.31	11.99	18.30	9
Lake States	3,184	264.1	841	16.27	1.98	12.86	10.88	81
Corn Belt	3,101	242.8	753	15.65	9.88	20.63	10.75	105
Northern Plains	12,075	162.6	1,963	14.45	9.07	15.00	5.93	268
Appalachian	2,537	161.5	410	17.08	-.55	15.51	16.06	83
Southeast	1,963	242.5	476	15.45	3.59	15.83	12.24	83
Delta	1,547	173.4	268	16.89	-.78	25.63	26.41	59
Southern Plains	5,993	170.4	1,021	16.34	2.83	17.10	14.27	84
Mountain	2,575	206.5	532	15.60	9.38	11.29	1.91	197
Pacific	379	245.2	93	18.35	3.72	26.78	23.06	37

a One-half the acres released from production of the major crops (Table 4.3) adjusted downward to reflect additional acres of feed grains and oilmeals needed with the other one-half of excess acres retired under a long-term, no-grazing land retirement program.

b Beef production per acre is computed by multiplying projected cropland pasture and hay yields by the projected feed conversion rate for pasture and hay.

c Costs per pound of beef are based on data from R. F. Brokken, Interregional Competition in Livestock and Crop Production in the United States: An Application of Spatial Linear Programming, Ph.D. thesis, Iowa State Univ., Ames, 1965.

d Net revenue per acre from beef is the difference obtained by multiplying the respective selling price and average production cost of beef by the quantity of beef produced per acre.

e Estimated retirement payment per acre is the net revenue for net returns from crop production plus a $5 per acre allowance for mowing and other forms of weed control.

f The easement payment is the difference between the retirement payment with no grazing and the net revenue from beef when grazing is allowed.

Table 4.8 ● Returns from Grazing and Government Costs for an Unrestricted Government Easement Program with Grazing Allowed on All Retired Cropland

Region	Cropland converted to grazing[a] (thousand acres)	Beef produced per acre[b] (lb)	Total additional beef produced (million lb)	Average cost of production per pound[c] (¢)	Net revenue from grazing[d] ($ per acre)	Program payment no grazing[e] ($ per acre)	Easement payment[f] ($ per acre)	Annual government program cost ($ million)
United States	67,385	190.7	12,850	15.67	.68	16.10	15.42	1,039
Northeast	598	201.1	120	19.33	-10.94	11.99	22.93	14
Lake States	6,380	264.1	1,685	16.27	-4.41	12.86	17.27	110
Corn Belt	6,124	242.8	1,509	15.65	3.08	20.63	17.55	107
Northern Plains	24,171	162.5	3,929	14.45	4.44	15.00	10.56	255
Appalachians	5,079	161.6	821	17.08	-4.40	15.51	19.91	101
Southeast	3,932	242.5	954	15.45	-2.26	15.83	18.09	71
Delta	3,097	173.4	537	16.89	-4.84	25.63	30.47	94
Southern Plains	11,998	170.4	2,044	15.34	-1.57	17.10	18.67	224
Mountain	5,156	206.5	1,065	15.60	-3.47	11.29	7.82	40
Pacific	760	245.2	186	18.35	-3.12	26.78	29.97	23

[a] One-half the acres released from production of the major crops (Table 4.3) adjusted downward to reflect additional acres of feed grains and oilmeals needed with the other one-half of excess acres retired under a long-term, no-grazing land retirement program.

[b] Beef production per acre is computed by multiplying projected cropland pasture and hay yields by the projected feed conversion rate for pasture and hay.

[c] Costs per pound of beef are based on data from R. F. Brokken, Interregional Competition in Livestock and Crop Production in the United States: An Application of Spatial Linear Programming, Ph.D. thesis, Iowa State Univ., Ames, 1965.

[d] Net revenue per acre from beef is the difference obtained by multiplying the respective selling price and average production cost of beef by the quantity of beef produced per acre.

[e] Estimated retirement payment per acre is the net revenue for net returns from crop production plus a $5 per acre allowance for mowing and other forms of weed control.

[f] The easement payment is the difference between the retirement payment with no grazing and the net revenue from beef when grazing is allowed.

163

Table 4.9 ● Estimated Effects on Consumption and Prices in 1975 of Alternative Levels of Grazing with Unrestricted and Restricted Government Crop Easement Programs

Commodity	1967 actual	1975 Unrestricted			1975 Restricted	
		no grazing[a]	50% grazing	100% grazing	50% grazing	100% grazing
Per capita consumption				(lb)[b]		
Beef & veal	109.7	127.0	143.7	160.4	144.2	161.3
Pork	63.9	60.0	59.1	58.4	59.0	58.3
Lamb & mutton[c]	3.9	3.8	3.8	3.8	3.8	3.8
Broilers	37.1	41.0	40.9	40.8	40.9	40.8
Turkey	8.6	9.0	9.0	9.0	9.0	9.0
Total consumption				(million lb)		
Beef & veal	21,472	28,150	31,825	35,553	31,962	35,753
Pork	12,506	13,299	13,100	12,945	13,078	12,922
Lamb & mutton	759	842	842	842	842	842
Broilers	7,258	9,088	9,066	9,043	9,066	9,043
Turkey	1,681	1,955	1,955	1,955	1,955	1,955
Estimated prices				(¢ per lb)		
Beef & veal	22.6	22.0	19.0	16.3	18.9	16.2
Pork	18.9	18.2	17.3	16.5	17.2	16.4
Lamb & mutton	18.9	19.5	18.2	17.0	18.1	17.0
Broilers	13.3	15.3[d]	12.8[d]	10.8[d]	12.7[d]	10.8[d]
Turkey	19.5	...[d]	...[d]	...[d]	...[d]	...[d]

aResults of this alternative were provided previously (Tables 4.3 and 4.5) and are given here only for comparison.
bQuantities are pounds of carcass weight for red meats and pounds of ready-to-cook for poultry.
cConsumption of lamb and mutton was assumed to be unaffected by changes in beef consumption.
dTurkey prices are held constant under all alternatives.

the 100 percent grazing program under which per capita consumption of pork is 1.6 pounds less than under the level for no grazing in 1975. The national average farm level price for hogs then falls to 16.5 cents, or 1.7 cents less.

Per capita consumption of broilers varies only slightly between the various unrestricted programs. With the 100 percent grazing program in 1975, per capita consumption of broilers is only 0.2 pounds below that for the no-grazing beef level. On the other hand, farm prices of broilers fall considerably as compared to the no-grazing beef level in 1975.

Net farm incomes for the unrestricted grazing programs are given in Table 4.10. The relative positions of the programs are as follows: 50 percent grazing has a net farm income of $16.0 billion estimated for 1975; the no-grazing alternative, $15.5 billion; and grazing of all idle acres, $14.9 billion. But the distribution of net income among producers would not be the same for all three programs. Livestock producers who did not receive the easement payments would have lower incomes under the grazing alternatives. Consumers would benefit from lower beef prices and expanded levels of consumption. These are but a few of the gains and losses that are implied by such a program.

Considering regional groups of farm producers, the decline in beef prices under programs of expanded beef production could transfer certain costs of advancing technology, farm structural adjustments, and program changes from crop farms in crop-producing regions to cattle producers in range and grassland regions. Crop farmers, even in concentrated land retirement regions, could be paid enough to leave them as well or better off under expanded beef production programs, thus encouraging their participation. Crop farmers in the central corn and wheat areas could increase production as land retirement was concentrated elsewhere to make up partly or entirely for cessation of government diversion payments. But if diverted cropland is used for grazing and cattle production, specialized cattle producers in regions of grass and range would suffer a large reduction in income with reduced beef prices. Hence unless ways were found to nullify this indirect transfer of farm adjustment costs from crop farmers to cattle producers, grassland and range producers may exert pressure to prohibit grazing on land diverted from crop production. It is quite likely that society does not prefer transfer of costs among major producer groups.

A Restricted Easement Purchase Program with Grazing Allowed ●
Under this program, acreages of cropland are removed from crop production in similar fashion and location as under the land rental program (Table 4.6). A total of 70.8 million acres of cropland is available for conversion to grass and other crops necessary to provide feed for expanded livestock production. As specified in Table 4.6, two levels of grazing are allowed. Under the first, one-half the excess acres (32.2 mil-

Table 4.10 ● Projected Net Farm Income and Government Payments for Unrestricted and Restricted Government Easement Programs with Alternative Levels of Grazing in 1975

Income & expenses	1967 actual	Unrestricted 1975			Restricted 1975		
		no grazing	50% grazing	100% grazing	no grazing	50% grazing	100% grazing
		($ million)					
Farming operations							
Cash receipts from crops	18,383	19,832	19,947	20,093	19,847	19,960	20,110
Cash receipts from livestock	24,405	28,178	28,225	27,386	28,178	28,168	27,359
Cattle & calves	10,551	12,655	13,193	12,891	12,655	13,177	12,891
Hogs	3,780	3,877	3,637	3,429	3,877	3,611	3,402
Sheep & lambs	299	375	355	338	375	353	338
Poultry & eggs	3,559	4,128	3,897	3,585	4,128	3,884	3,585
Dairy	5,770	6,693	6,693	6,693	6,693	6,693	6,693
Other	446	450	450	450	450	450	450
Cash expenses from production	29,079	31,400	30,729	31,090	31,400	30,713	31,090
Net receipts from farm mkt.	13,709	16,610	17,443	16,389	16,625	17,415	16,379
Depreciation expenses	5,741	6,321	6,425	6,525	6,321	6,425	6,525
Actual receipts from farm mkt.	7,968	10,289	11,018	9,864	10,304	10,990	9,854
Nonmoney income[a]	3,194	3,295	3,295	3,295	3,295	3,295	3,295
Inventory change	403	350	350	350	350	350	350
Net returns from farming	11,565	13,934	14,663	13,509	13,949	14,635	13,499
Government sources							
Feed grains, wheat, and cotton programs	2,528	0	0	0	0	0	0
Soil Bank or easement purchase programs	214	1,184	943	1,039	1,447	1,195	1,296
Other[b]	336	365	365	365	365	365	365
Total program payments	3,078	1,549	1,308	1,404	1,812	1,560	1,661
Total net farm income	14,643	15,483	15,971	14,913	15,761	16,195	15,160

[a]Includes the value of home consumption of farm products and the rental value of farm dwelling.
[b]Includes ACP, Great Plains Conservation, Sugar Act, and Wool Act payments.

lion acres), are converted to hay and pasture and grazed, and under the second, 64.5 million acres are converted to hay and pasture.

With the restricted easement program, participation is limited to 50 percent of the total cropland base of any region. Less marginal land thus enters the program with more land located in higher yielding regions. Although fewer total acres are diverted from production of major and minor crops, this land has a greater productivity in hay and pasture. Using approximately one-half of the excess cropland under the restricted program for additional pasture and hay would add 6.6 billion pounds of beef on the market (Table 4.11). With a United States average production cost of 15.8 cents per pound, all but three of the ten farm production regions could cover costs of production. The average easement payment to farmers is $14.62 per acre compared to an average of $20.45 per acre when grazing is not allowed (Table 4.5). The payment per acre for the land rental program is reduced by the value of the beef produced ($5.83 per acre) and total government payments decline from $1.4 billion to $1.2 billion.

A second possibility would be to allow all land in the easement program to be grazed. Under this type of program (Table 4.12) more than 13 billion pounds of beef and veal would be added on the market. With an estimated production cost of 15.8 cents per pound of beef and a U.S. farm price of 16.2 cents, only three farm production regions cover costs of production. (No charge for land was included in the costs of production figures.) The average easement payment is $20.08 per acre when grazing is allowed, compared to an average payment of $20.45 (Table 4.5) when grazing is prohibited. The total cost of the program to the government is $1.3 billion with grazing and $1.4 billion without grazing.

Some major differences arise however in terms of consumption of beef, prices paid by consumers, and levels of farm income. With a restricted land conversion program with 50 percent grazing allowed, consumption of beef and veal is estimated to increase 17.2 pounds over the no-grazing program (Table 4.9). To gain this increase, market clearing farm prices for cattle and calves decline to 3.1 cents per pound below the level when no grazing is allowed. Under the program when all acres are grazed, per capita consumption of beef and veal would increase 34.3 pounds over the level for the no-grazing program. The farm price (market clearing) of cattle and calves then is 5.8 cents lower than when no grazing is allowed on retired acres.

Equilibrium prices and quantities for pork with a restricted land conversion are also shown in Table 4.9. The market clearing price for hogs is estimated at 16.4 cents with all land grazed for additional beef production. The price of hogs with 50 percent grazing is one cent per pound below the estimate for the no-grazing program.

Estimates of resulting net farm incomes under the various restricted easement programs are given in Table 4.10. Projected net farm income

Table 4.11 ● Returns from Grazing and Government Costs for a Restricted Government Easement Program with 50 Percent of Retired Cropland Used for Beef Production

Region	Cropland converted to grazing[a] (thousand acres)	Beef produced per acre[b] (lb)	Total additional beef produced (million lb)	Average cost of production per pound[c] (¢)	Net revenue from grazing[d] ($ per acre)	Program payment no grazing[e] ($ per acre)	Easement payment[f] ($ per acre)	Annual government program cost ($ million)
United States	32,224	205.4	6,618	15.80	5.83	20.45	14.62	1,195
Northeast	548	190.1	104	20.03	-7.47	11.99	19.46	18
Lake States	2,778	273.8	761	15.97	2.63	16.81	14.18	92
Corn Belt	4,631	281.7	1,305	15.55	11.47	31.87	20.40	263
Northern Plains	9,784	168.9	1,653	14.55	9.07	18.48	9.41	287
Appalachian	2,164	163.8	354	17.08	-.70	17.22	17.92	79
Southeast	2,368	245.3	581	15.55	3.16	17.96	14.80	83
Delta	1,588	176.3	280	16.89	-.95	26.14	27.09	88
Southern Plains	5,449	176.2	927	16.34	3.01	18.44	15.43	193
Mountain	2,251	214.8	484	16.40	7.80	15.81	8.01	57
Pacific	663	254.9	169	18.35	3.62	26.78	23.16	35

[a]One-half the acres released from production of the major crops (Table 4.5) adjusted downward to reflect additional acres of feed grains and oilmeals needed with the other one-half of excess acres retired under a long-term, no-grazing land retirement program.

[b]Beef production per acre is computed by multiplying projected cropland pasture and hay yields by the projected feed conversion rate for pasture and hay.

[c]Costs per pound of beef are based on data from R. F. Brokken, Interregional Competition in Livestock and Crop Production in the United States: An Application of Spatial Linear Programming, Ph. D. thesis, Iowa State Univ., Ames, 1965.

[d]Net revenue per acre from beef is the difference obtained by multiplying the respective selling price and average production cost of beef by the quantity of beef produced per acre.

[e]Estimated retirement payment per acre is the net revenue for net returns from crop production plus a $5 per acre allowance for mowing and other forms of weed control.

[f]The easement payment is the difference between the retirement payment with no grazing and the net revenue from beef when grazing is allowed.

168

Table 4.12 ● Returns from Grazing and Government Costs for a Restricted Government Easement Program, with Grazing Allowed on all Retired Cropland

Region	Cropland converted to grazing[a] (thousand acres)	Beef produced per acre[b] (lb)	Total additional beef produced (million lb)	Average cost of production per pound[c] (¢)	Net revenue from grazing[d]	Program payment no grazing[e] ($ per acre)	Easement payment[f]	Annual government program cost ($ million)
United States	64,539	205.4	13,256	15.80	-.37	20.45	20.08	1,296
Northeast	1,097	190.1	209	20.03	-11.84	11.99	23.83	26
Lake States	5,567	273.8	1,524	15.97	-3.97	16.81	20.78	116
Corn Belt	9,281	281.7	2,614	15.55	3.58	31.87	28.29	263
Northern Plains	19,587	168.9	3,309	14.55	4.26	18.48	14.22	279
Appalachian	4,333	163.8	710	17.08	-4.60	17.22	21.82	95
Southeast	4,745	245.3	1,164	14.44	-2.75	17.96	20.71	98
Delta	3,180	176.3	561	16.89	-5.08	26.14	31.22	99
Southern Plains	10,910	170.2	1,857	16.34	-1.40	18.44	19.84	216
Mountain	4,510	214.8	969	19.40	1.65	15.81	14.16	64
Pacific	1,329	254.9	339	18.35	-3.57	26.78	30.35	40

[a]One-half the acres released from production of the major crops (Table 4.5) adjusted downward to reflect additional acres of feed grains and oilmeals needed with the other one-half of excess acres retired under a long-term, no-grazing land retirement program.

[b]Beef production per acre is computed by multiplying projected cropland pasture and hay yields by the projected feed conversion rate for pasture and hay.

[c]Costs per pound of beef are based on data from R. F. Brokken, Interregional Competition in Livestock and Crop Production in the United States: An Application of Spatial Linear Programming, Ph.D. thesis, Iowa State Univ., Ames, 1965.

[d]Net revenue per acre from beef is the difference obtained by multiplying the respective selling price and average production cost of beef by the quantity of beef produced per acre.

[e]Estimated retirement payment per acre is the net revenue for net returns from crop production plus a $5 per acre allowance for mowing and other forms of weed control.

[f]The easement payment is the difference between the retirement payment with no grazing and the net revenue from beef when grazing is allowed.

169

with a restricted land conversion program and 50 percent grazing is estimated at $16.2 billion in 1975 compared to $15.8 billion if the idle cropland is not used for beef production. On the other hand, estimated net income when all cropland is grazed is lower than other 1975 estimates. With maximum beef production, increased government payments do not offset lower livestock revenues, and estimated net farm income declines.

Net farm income levels are somewhat lower under the unrestricted grazing programs compared to the restricted grazing alternatives (Table 4.10). Under all three unrestricted programs government payments are lower, and net farm income is lower as a result.

POLICY IMPLICATIONS ● Several alternative long-term land-use programs have been analyzed in this chapter. All have used data for 1975, with estimates of production, government costs, net farm income, and the amount and location of land diversion or conversion. All alternatives suppose some type of land withdrawal or conversion program to hold production of crops at a level to attain the level of crop prices indicated in Table 4.1. One alternative examined would involve government purchase of enough land to control farm production and attain the specified level of prices. The government would purchase land in regions of lowest government cost on a whole-farm basis. Under an unrestricted program in which entire regions could be withdrawn from production, an estimated 103 million acres of land are purchased at a cost of $19 billion at estimated 1975 land prices. If spread over ten years, the annual purchase cost would be $1.9 billion. Annual net farm income under this program is estimated at $14.3 billion. (If the $1.9 billion were added, the annual "cash flow" of income and principal would be $16.2 billion.) If payments were spread over ten years and 6 percent interest paid on the remaining principal (interest payments of around $680 million), the annual cost would be increased to $2.7 billion per year. The government would then own the land and would not need to make annual payments in subsequent years to control production and support prices and income. The government could simply withhold from production the land that it then owns. Under annual land diversion programs at the 1970 cost level for ten years (Chapter 3) the government would pay out $2.8 billion per year, or $28 billion in ten years; but at the end of the period the government would not own the cropland. Assuming the continuance of surplus capacity, cessation of the program in ten years would allow prices to decline or require reinitiation of the program with continued government costs in subsequent years.

As has been outlined elsewhere, outright purchase of land would appear to have less public acceptability than other programs which divert

an equal amount of production from the market.[3] Accordingly analysis
was made of long-term land rental programs with land diverted in the
same amount and locations. Under the rental program, the government
would simply pay farmers an annual rent to hold their land out of production. Under an unrestricted program allowing land to be diverted
in the program on a whole-farm basis without alternative uses for any
production, the annual government cost estimated for 1975 would be
$1.2 billion and net farm income would be $15.5 billion. Under a third
set of programs examined, called an easement program with grazing,
farmers would sell their rights to produce crops. If the easement programs were adjusted to allow all of the land under an unrestricted
program to be used for hay and pasture for additional beef production,
government costs would be $1.0 billion and net farm income $14.3 billion in 1975. If all land diverted under a restricted easement program
were used for beef production, annual government costs would be $1.3
billion and net farm income would be $14.3 billion. However if the
rental program were restricted so that no more than half the land in
any region could go into diversion and could not be used for additional
beef production, annual government payments (at 1975 rates) would be
$1.4 billion. Net farm income would be $15.8 billion as compared to a
net farm income of $14.6 billion including government payments in
1967.

These data show a wide range of government costs to attain goals of
price support for U.S. agriculture in 1975. They have however quite
different effects in permanence of solution of capacity problems and the
distribution of the burden of agricultural adjustment to new technologies
which substitute for land and labor. Annual land diversion programs of
the 1960s spread their benefit widely over all major farming regions.
However they had high Treasury costs and provided no prospects of
permanently solving the capacity problem. Neither did they arrest the
rapid depopulation of the rural countryside stemming from farm technological change. They did little or nothing for low-income farms, for
those replaced from agriculture by new technology, or for that portion
of the rural nonfarm population which experienced income or capital
losses as the farm population declined. A government land purchase
program could provide a long-term solution to the capacity problem in
ten years or less. However if interest and administrative costs are added,
a purchase program would initially leave funds low for offseting losses
to rural communities as the adjustment process is concentrated in regions of lowest comparative advantage—generally the same regions which
would bear the same type and extent of adjustment under a free market
system.

3. Earl O. Heady and Alvin C. Egbert, Programming Regional Adjustments in Grain
Production to Eliminate Surpluses, *Journal of Farm Economics* 51 (November 1959):
718.

The long-term land rental or easement programs analyzed in this chapter would also concentrate cropland diversion on a regional basis. Those regions with lowest comparative advantage would have large acreages of cropland diverted from production. If however the land could be used for beef, some employment (in addition to that already generated from beef production and other noncrop activities) would be restored. Agriculture would be less intensive than it is presently, and farms would be larger and fewer—a continuation of the current trend under existing programs. However a long-term rental or easement program could readily free upwards of $1.5 billion to help rural communities adjust to the ongoing and prospective reduction in farm numbers and employment as farms become larger and more capital intensive.

The public acceptability of unrestricted land conversion programs on either a rental or easement basis would depend on the extent to which all sectors of rural communities could be adequately compensated and provided economic opportunities which are equitable in comparison with the opportunities available under national economic growth in urban or industrial centers. The nation badly needs an economic and social policy for the entire rural community—farm as well as nonfarm. Annual land diversion programs in force during the 1960s provide means of income support and compensation for farmers, especially on larger farms, who would otherwise suffer under the ongoing rush of capital technology. They do not provide means of compensation or of generating economic opportunity however for nonfarm persons who may suffer restraints or reduction in income as the same farm technology replaces workers and reduces nonfarm business and employment volume in the rural community. Even if costs were underestimated by 20 percent for the alternative programs such as long-term land rental or easement purchase, the difference in government costs between these programs and past annual land diversion programs would still be large. It would free enough funds to go a long way in solving the widespread problems of rural communities and bring greater equity to those who now bear the major uncompensated costs of rapid farm structural adjustment. Perhaps to the funds saved from the alternative programs could be added public funds for formulation of a complete economic policy for rural communities.

The adjustments, which continue even under annual land diversion programs, should not be speeded up to the point that rural communities cannot absorb them, or have extremely heavy indirect costs attached. Instead, shifts should be phased over a sufficiently long time and meshed with an overall economic and social policy for rural communities so that equity is generally guaranteed for both farm and nonfarm people of rural areas. Modification of farm programs to allow savings in costs, supplemented by other public allocations, would allow diversion of national resources for this purpose. Only when equity is guaranteed throughout the entire rural community will it be possible to modify farm programs so that they have prospects of bringing long-run solutions to the farm capacity problem. The savings implied here provide one potential resource in this direction. Some of the freed funds could be used for improved education, vocational training, and occupational guidance in rural areas. Funds could also be used for retraining facilities, retraining grants, and minimum income assistance to displaced persons while in training or relocating. In addition, transfer payments could be given to individuals who suffer severe drops in asset values in the rural communities, such as store owners. Also programs could be implemented at the national level to establish area development districts. For older persons nearing retirement age, social security payments could be started at an earlier age with eventual graduation to the conventional age for all persons. Finally some funds could be used for research to determine the most desirable structure for the rural community in the future.

PUBLIC DECISIONS ● The several alternatives outlined in this chapter all represent types of land retirement or diversion directed toward restraints on supply and attainment of specified price levels. The data generated in the analysis show the level of production, net farm income, government costs, and amount and location of land retired. Obviously, differences between short-term or other programs are not "black and white." There are many different combinations of amount, location, and part- or whole-farm participation in which land can be retired.

At one extreme, land retirement can be scattered over the entire nation on a partial-farm basis as it is under annual land diversion programs. For reasons already explained this alternative has high costs. One step away from this alternative, land retirement could be spread regionally as it is under annual land diversion programs, but on a whole-farm basis. Costs would decline somewhat under this arrangement. As a further step away, land retirement can be partially concentrated (e.g., a 25, 50, or 75 percent limit) on a regional and whole-farm basis. We study these alternatives in Chapter 5. Or it can be concentrated at another extreme on a regional and whole-farm basis. Each step away from one extreme toward the other involves also a change in (1) government costs for participation, and (2) the distribution of the costs of adjustment. Under annual land diversion programs, government costs are high but the indirect costs to communities are spread over wide areas geographically. If retirement is allowed to concentrate up to 25 percent of each region on a whole-farm basis, program costs could decline still further but the indirect burden or costs of adjustment would concentrate more in some regions than others. The indirect costs are represented in further population decline and the associated reduction in business volume and employment in the rural sector. If land retirement is concentrated entirely in terms of marginal areas and comparative advantage, government costs are lowest, but the indirect costs of adjustment are probably highest.

It is the trade-off among government costs, amount and location of land retirement, and indirect social costs which should be weighed as the public representatives select from land diversion and supply restraint programs. The choice is not one of "either, or." Rather, a combination or mix of programs can be selected depending on the value or weight which is attached to government costs, farm income, rural community costs, and consumer food bills.

It is from alternatives and consequences such as these that the public must decide. The advantages of the various programs might be melded in various ways. For example, rather than to use a sudden break from annual diversion programs to long-term regional land retirement, the shift might be phased over ten years. Change then would not be thrust so rapidly on the regions where diversion is concentrated. Then too, the savings in government costs might be supplemented by other public appropriations to compensate and aid both farm and nonfarm persons affected adversely through reductions in farm numbers and the farm population. The quantities presented illustrate the gain in one direction and costs in another as programs are shifted from one extreme to another. It is these quantities and trade-offs that the public and administrators concerned must use in selecting improved or optimal farm programs for the future.

CHAPTER FIVE

Land Retirement and Alternative Levels of Farm Product Prices

THE PREVIOUS CHAPTERS have examined the effects on farm income and related variables of several alternative farm programs when placed in operation over a given period of time. Each was examined as a complete program with no modifications of the control elements being possible if the results (level of price, farm income, or government cost) were unacceptable. But in practice, policy makers do not approach program formulation in this manner. Programs are established with specific price and income levels as stated goals, and control mechanisms are adjusted to achieve these prespecified objectives. Government costs of the program are open-ended in that provision is made to finance whatever degree of participation is necessary to hold prices to the specified support level. If participation in the control program falls short of that needed to adjust supply to demand, government storage programs absorb excess quantities of production, and prices are maintained at the specified level.

The following study approaches formulation of farm programs from this realistic point of view. It assumes that alternative price levels could be established for agriculture ranging from those shown previously for a free market to some level above recent support prices. The major question is: What degree or magnitude of supply control (land retirement) is necessary to achieve each specified level of prices? In addition, each price level is examined under alternative distributions of idled acres among regions. Since land quality varies among regions, restricting the proportion of a region which can be retired affects the total acreage which must be retired to achieve a given level of price. A change in total acres retired changes government costs of retirement as well as the distribution of government payments for land retirement and the burden of rural adjustment growing out of reduced input purchases in local communities and reduced numbers of farm families.

The objective of this chapter is to estimate the trade-offs between prices, net farm income, government costs, amount and distribution of land retired, and regional distributions of government payments and adjustments under several alternative land retirement programs. These trade-offs are analyzed for the year 1975 based on projection of yields, demands, and other basic variables to that date.

PARAMETERS OF THE STUDY ● The study has two basic sets of parameters, the levels of farm prices or policy objective to be achieved, and the degree of regional concentration of idled land allowed. The year 1975 is used as the time reference of the study. Given that date and projected population and income levels, each farm price level has a set of per capita consumption estimates associated with it, and corresponding total quantities of wheat, feed grains, and oilmeals required for direct consumption and feed for livestock production. In addition, export market demand is estimated for wheat, feed grains, soybeans, and cotton. Production of crops meets these prespecified levels of domestic and export demand for each price level. Carry-over stocks of major commodities are held constant for all price levels. Also the cropland base is assumed to remain constant between 1965 and 1975.

Price Levels and Land Retirement Alternatives ● Three projected price levels—the lower, medium, and higher levels—are examined in this analysis. The alternative crop prices, along with the corresponding livestock prices, are presented in Table 5.1.

The following government land retirement programs are analyzed for each level of farm product prices:

1. A land rental program with no restrictions on the concentration of land diversion (unlimited diversion) in farm production regions.
2. A rental program with a restriction that no more than 75 percent of the cropland in any region can be retired by government programs.
3. A rental program with a restriction that no more than 50 percent of the cropland in any region can be retired by government programs.
4. A rental program with a restriction that no more than 25 percent of the cropland in any region can be retired by government programs.

Per Capita Consumption and Export Levels ● Figure 5.1 summarizes per capita consumption estimates for beef and veal, pork, and broilers for each price level studied. With the lower set of farm prices in 1975, per capita consumption of beef and veal is projected at 30 pounds more than actual in 1968. Consumption of pork is projected to be slightly lower and consumption of broilers slightly higher than the 1968 level.

For the medium set of farm prices in 1975, per capita consumption

Table 5.1 ● Prices Received by Farmers for Major Commodities, Past and Projected 1975

Item and unit	Actual prices		Projected prices 1975[a]		
	1967	1968	Lower (L)	Medium (M)	Higher (H)
Crop prices			($)		
Corn (bu)	1.03	1.06	.85	1.05	1.25
Wheat (bu)	1.39	1.24	1.00	1.25	1.50
Soybeans (bu)	2.49	2.42	1.50	2.15	2.75
Cotton (lb)	0.25	0.22	0.26	0.26	0.26
Livestock prices			(¢)		
Cattle and calves (lb)	22.3	23.4	18.5	22.5	27.0
Hogs (lb)	18.9	18.6	15.0	18.2	21.0
Broilers (lb)	13.3	14.3	13.5	15.3	17.0

Source: U. S. Dept. of Agriculture, Agricultural Prices 1968 Annual Summary, USDA SRS, June 1969.

[a] All prices for 1975 are measured in 1966 equivalent dollars and do not take into account inflation from 1966 to 1975.

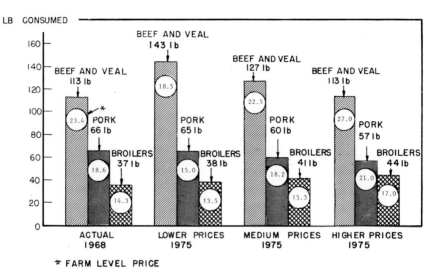

Fig. 5.1. Per capita consumption: projected for 1975 and actual figures for 1968.

of beef and veal is estimated at 14 pounds above the 1968 level. Pork consumption is estimated at 6 pounds per person less than 1968 and broiler consumption at 4 pounds more than 1968.

With the higher set of crop and livestock prices in 1975, per capita consumption of beef and veal is projected at the same as 1968. Pork consumption is projected at 9 pounds per person less than actual consumption in 1968. Broiler consumption is estimated to increase to 7 pounds per person more than actual consumption in 1968. With higher prices for beef and pork, consumers shift toward consumption of broilers.

Figures 5.2, 5.3, and 5.4 summarize export levels of wheat, feed grains, and oilmeals for each price level included in the study. Wheat exports are assumed to be the same, 700 million bushels, for all three price levels. With the International Wheat Agreement, wheat exports are restricted by intercountry agreements, and the price of wheat is not the primary determinant of exports. Actual wheat exports were 542 million bushels in 1968.

Exports of both feed grains and oilmeals are assumed to be more responsive to price changes. Feed grains exports range between 28.5 million tons (corn equivalent) under lower prices ($0.85 corn) and 21.1 million tons under higher prices ($1.25 corn). Actual feed grains exports were 17 million tons in 1968. Soybean exports are highest (514 million bushels soybean equivalent) under lower prices ($1.50 soybeans), and lowest (360 million bushels) with higher prices ($2.75 soybeans) in 1975. Cotton lint exports are estimated at 5 million bales for all price

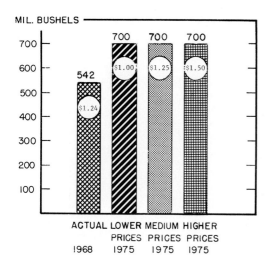

Fig. 5.2. Wheat exports.

levels studied since the price of cotton lint is held constant throughout this analysis.

The three price levels and four land retirement alternatives result in twelve different combinations of price levels and programs. For each of these combinations, we estimate the level of farm income, amount of treasury costs, number of acres of land retired, location of diverted land, and the regional distribution of government payments to farmers. These quantities show the amount of change or sacrifice in one item (e.g., the

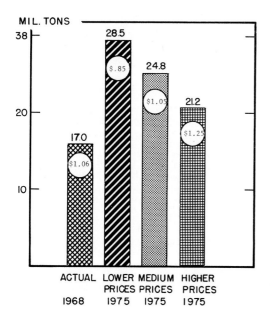

Fig. 5.3. Feed grains exports (corn equivalent).

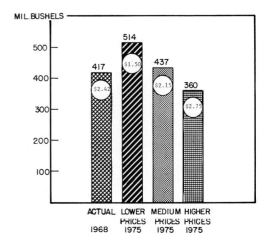

Fig. 5.4. Oilmeal exports (soybean equivalent).

total cost of programs) while another item (e.g., the price level or regional concentration of land retirement) is changed or achieved.

METHOD AND TERMINOLOGY ● The analysis which follows is based on results from a 150-region (Fig. 3.1) linear programming model. (For a detailed description of the basic linear programming model used in the analysis see Chapter 4.) For each price level studied, a set of projected per acre yields and production costs was computed for each crop in each producing region. Total demand levels for wheat, feed grains, oilmeals, and cotton were projected for 31 consuming regions of the nation. The programming model was applied within the land restraints and demand levels specified for each region. The model then maximized the net return from production of wheat, feed grains, soybeans, and cotton, given the costs of producing these crops, their selling prices, and the cost of transportation between the various producing and consuming regions.

The following terms are used throughout the analysis:

Major crops are wheat, feed grains, soybeans, and cotton.

Minor crops include flax, rye, buckwheat, and tame hay.

Unlimited diversion allows entire regions to be retired from crop production in a voluntary (bid) rental program on a long-term whole-farm basis. Lower prices with unlimited diversion are designated by L_u and medium and higher prices both with unlimited diversion are designated by M_u and H_u respectively.

Seventy-five percent maximum diversion allows a maximum of 75 percent of the cropland in any region to be retired from crop production under a voluntary (bid) rental program. The three price levels are designated by L_{75}, M_{75}, and H_{75}.

Fifty percent maximum diversion allows a maximum of one-half of any region to be retired from crop production under a voluntary (bid) rental program. The three price levels are designated by L_{50}, M_{50}, and H_{50}.

Twenty-five percent maximum diversion allows a maximum of one-fourth of any region to be retired from crop production under a voluntary (bid) rental program. The three price levels are designated by L_{25}, M_{25}, and H_{25}.

Payment Levels for Land Retirement Programs ● The payment necessary for farmers to participate in each of the specified programs is assumed to equal the estimated net return per acre for major crops considering all costs (except land). In other words, the farmer could simply "rent" his land to the government and make the same return as now realized. Actually he could receive a higher return, since through whole-farm participation he could eliminate certain overhead costs such as those related to machinery and equipment, and investment in these capital items would be freed for use elsewhere. Also his labor would be freed for employment in other alternatives. The payment levels are also a function of each price level since the expected net return from farming is a function of the expected price. See Chapter 3, Equations (3.2) through (3.5), for a more detailed explanation of payment levels.

This method of payment calculation assumes that farmers are willing to rent land to the government and earn a return equal to the expected return from farming. In the short run some farmers would not want to stop farming at the computed level of payment. On the other hand, some farmers would participate even at a lower payment rate, since this level of compensation plus employment of labor and capital elsewhere would give them a greater net income. Many farmers approaching or reaching retirement age might participate at a payment rate lower than one made competitive under actual farm operation, since their alternative would be to rent the farm.

Under each of the price levels analyzed, a minimum per acre payment is provided and a payment of $5 per acre is added for weed control and related costs. The computed payments are estimated to achieve farmer participation for land retirement only. They do not include additional income supplements as in the case of wheat, feed grain, and cotton programs used in the 1960s.

RESULTS OF THE ANALYSIS ● The analysis in this chapter initially focuses on the level of land retirement necessary to achieve the previously specified price levels. Next the per acre payment and total government costs of each program are provided. Additional sections of the study evaluate the effect of alternative price levels and land retirement programs on aggregate production, net farm income, and location and distribution of (1) government payments to farmers and (2) acres retired with each program.

For each level of farm prices specified, there is some magnitude of land retirement or supply control which could hold that level of price, given the concurrent objective that stocks of grain remain constant. Even under lower prices, the removal of all supply control programs would undoubtedly result in production levels in excess of demand in the initial production periods. Consequently, stocks would rise with a fixed level of support prices; or if supports were removed completely, prices would drop to even lower levels.

This analysis assumes that a land retirement program is used to mesh production with each level of demand and price. A specific number of crop acres must be retired under these circumstances, given the specified price level to be achieved and the specified proportion of a region's cropland which is allowed in the program. These combinations of price levels and levels of participation and the resulting total amounts of cropland retired are summarized in Figure 5.5. Each of the twelve alternatives is based on projected demand and supply conditions for 1975.

The type of retirement program used is a significant factor in

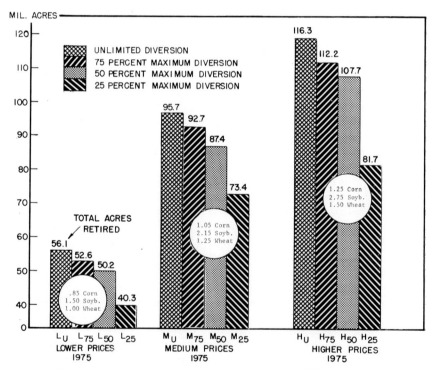

Fig. 5.5.   Total crop acres retired by program, 1975.

determining the extent of adjustments necessary in rural communities. A land retirement program with unlimited diversion in any region would have a different effect on a rural community than would a program limiting diversion to 25 percent. For rural communities located in largely marginal areas of production (resulting perhaps from climate, soil fertility, weather variability, or other natural factors), the effect of unlimited retirement would be a large reduction in economic activity. Some rural communities would find their economic base wiped out as farms and farmers retired and farmers perhaps moved to other locations. Programs limiting land retirement to a maximum of 75 percent, 50 percent, or perhaps only 25 percent in each region would have less negative effect on rural communities.

The Soil Bank Program of the 1950s was not popular because it allowed fairly high levels of concentration in land retirement in rural communities. It provided measures for income improvement only for farmers and neglected to offset the effects of such programs on local businesses and institutions.

A land retirement program with unlimited regional concentration would have even more severe effects than those of the 1950s Soil Bank Program, with farm communities in marginal areas of production absorbing the major portion of the adjustment effects created. However when land retirement is limited to a maximum of 25 percent of the cropland in a given region, all areas of the country must absorb some of the adjustment effects.

Alternative Price and Land Retirement Levels ● With lower prices for the agricultural sector in 1975, total retired acres vary from 40.3 to 56.1 million depending on the type of program selected. With unlimited diversion, 56.1 million acres must be retired to balance supply and demand. With a program allowing a maximum of 25 percent diversion (L_{25}), the total number of diverted acres declines to 40.3 million.

The variation in total acres retired for a given price level is a result of the variation in quality of land between regions. With an unlimited diversion program, acres retired tend to come from regions with lowest net returns—and lowest yields per acre. When production is allowed to concentrate in the most productive regions, land retirement concentrates in marginal, lower yielding regions; fewer acres are needed for a given level of ouput and more acres must be retired. To the extent that land retirement is allowed to concentrate in low yielding regions, the program must retire a larger total number of crop acres to balance supply and demand. A comparison can also be made between alternative programs for the medium and higher price levels. With the medium set of prices, unlimited diversion requires retirement of 95.7 million acres while a program of 25 percent maximum diversion results in 73.4 million acres diverted. With the higher set of prices, acres retired vary from a high of 116.3 million with unlimited diversion to a low of 81.7 million under 25 percent maximum diversion.

The relationship between the number of acres retired and the national price level works out as follows for the unlimited diversion program: To raise the corn price from $0.85 to $1.05 per bushel requires, on the average, that an additional 37.6 million acres be retired from production, a ratio of just under 2 million retired acres for each increase of one cent per bushel in the corn price. From $1.05 to $1.25 per bushel of corn, an average of 20.6 million more acres must be retired, a ratio of just under 1 million acres per one cent increase in the price of corn. The latter ratio is smaller since higher yielding acres are removed from production as the price level and the total number of acres retired increase. The higher yielding acres reduce total production by a larger amount for each acre retired and the price level rises—or to say it another way, the acreage reduction necessary to achieve a given increase in the price level is relatively less as more and more acres are retired from production.

Alternative Price Levels and Payment Rates Per Acre ● Average payment rates per acre for the various programs and price levels are pre-

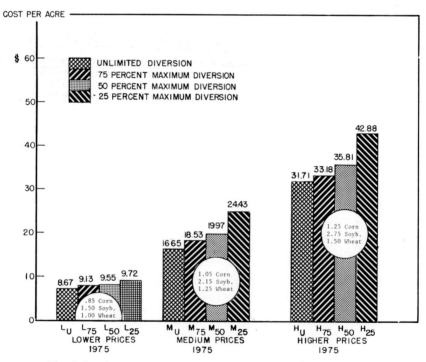

Fig. 5.6.   Average government cost per acre retired by program, 1975.

sented in Figure 5.6. Payments per acre are a function of the price level since payments are determined by the expected net return from cropping in each region. With the lower set of prices, and average payment rates per acre varying from $8.67 to $9.72, many regions would not cover all costs of production for wheat, feed grains, and soybeans; others would have only a small positive return. Since the payment rate would be zero under these circumstances, a minimum payment of $1.50 per acre was assumed necessary to achieve participation and to cover land taxes and other fixed costs. An additional $5.00 was added for weed control, giving the minimum per acre payment for the lower price program of $6.50. The minimum payment is $11.00 per acre for medium prices and $15.00 per acre for higher price programs. With lower prices, a large part of the cropland in the program is retired at minimum payment rates and the resulting average payment rates are relatively similar. As the price level increases, the return on cropland rises, and the payment rate necessary to enroll adequate cropland to balance supply and demand is also larger.

With medium prices, the rise in per acre cost becomes more pronounced as more restraints are placed on the proportion of land diverted in each region, and retired acres are spread over more and more regions. The payment rate rises even faster with the higher set of prices. The average payment rate per acre with higher prices and unlimited diversion is almost twice as high as for the medium price program of the same type.

Alternative Price Levels and Total Government Cost ● Total government costs for the various programs and price levels studied are presented in Figure 5.7. Each of the program costs include $365 million for operation of the Sugar Act, Wool Act, and other minor programs. These costs vary because (1) the number of acres retired increases as we move from the lower price level to the higher price level, and (2) the price level itself increases the total cost of retirement, since expected net returns become larger as the higher price levels are assumed. Higher prices mean both more acres retired and a higher payment per acre, resulting in a rapid rise in total government costs for land retirement. For the three price levels analyzed total annual government costs vary from a low of $0.8 billion up to $4.2 billion.

With the lower set of prices, total government costs for diversion are highest with unlimited diversion and lowest with 25 percent maximum retirement. With the latter program the average cost per acre retired is higher than for other lower price programs (Fig. 5.6), but fewer acres are retired as the 25 percent restriction forces more land from higher yielding regions into the program. As a result, total government costs are lower with the 25 percent restriction than for any other lower price program.

With the medium set of prices, total farm program costs range from

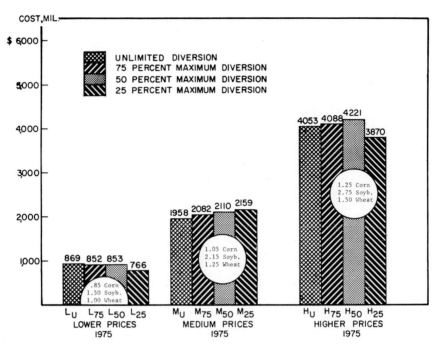

Fig. 5.7. *Total government costs by program, 1975.*

$2.0 billion with unlimited retirement up to $2.2 billion under the 25 percent restriction.

With the higher set of prices and unlimited diversion, total government costs are $4.1 billion, while under program H_{50} total costs rise to $4.2 billion. With program H_{25} government costs fall to $3.9 billion as a larger amount of higher yielding land is brought into the program and a much greater amount of less productive land is used for crop production. As a result total government costs are lower for program H_{25} than for any other higher price programs (even though average cost per acre is higher). These data point up a rather interesting aspect about the relationship between the aggregate cost of land retirement and the percentage of any region which can be retired. The aggregate cost is very similar regardless of which type of restriction is placed on the number of acres retired in a region as long as we compare within a specified price level. If we compare alternative price levels, there is substantial difference between the total costs of land retirement.

These trade-offs emphasize that a number of goals and criteria must be considered before a particular farm policy or farm policy combination is selected. Especially important is the level of income and the optimum distribution of payments and retired cropland across the United States. We discuss these aspects of land retirement programs in the following sections of this chapter.

Alternative Price Levels and Net Farm Incomes ● The level of farm income and farm program cost associated with each program and price level is given in Figure 5.8. Net farm income ranges from $12.2 billion to $18.5 billion. In general, net farm income increases with the amount of land retired and the level of prices attained under the various programs. In other words, the more acres that are retired the higher is the price level and the higher is net farm income.

With the lower set of prices and unlimited retirement, net farm income is estimated at $13.3 billion in 1975. As more restrictions are placed on retirement in each region, net farm income declines. The lowest net income, $12.2 billion under L_{25}, is mainly a result of higher cash expenses associated with this program.

The medium price programs follow a similar pattern. Net farm income is $16.6 billion with unlimited diversion, but is only $14.6 billion when retirement is restricted to a maximum of 25 percent of a region. The lower farm income under program M_{25} is mainly a result of higher cash expenses with this pattern of production.

For the higher price level, net farm income is lowest under program H_{25} ($16 billion) and highest with program H_u ($18.5 billion). With the price level constant, all programs analyzed have essentially the same

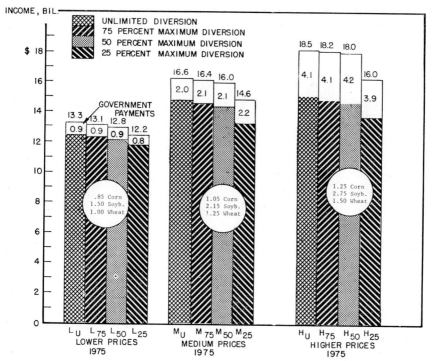

Fig. 5.8. Net farm income by program, 1975.

cash receipts from farm marketings. Differences in net farm incomes are a result of regional changes in the distribution of production and corresponding changes in expenses and government payments. Changes in expenses cause most of the variations in net farm incomes when government payments are relatively constant. Under a given set of prices, these changes reflect the cost of inefficiency associated with more restrictive programs as production is allocated to different regions and soils.

LOCATIONAL AND DISTRIBUTIONAL EFFECTS OF ALTERNATIVE LAND RETIREMENT PROGRAMS ● The various programs examined have both national and regional implications for the farm sector and rural communities. In the aggregate, each program affects the level of total farm income and government payments. At the regional level, the restrictions placed on retirement of cropland in each region affect the location of diverted cropland and the distribution of government payments. These latter aspects are examined below for the programs previously outlined.

Location of Retired Cropland with Lower Prices ● The regional distribution of diverted acres for each farm production region under the lower price level is specified in Table 5.2. With the lower set of prices and unlimited diversion in 1975, a total of 57 million acres is retired for the United States. The rank of regions retiring land is Northern Plains, Southern Plains, Mountain, and the Corn Belt.

With 75 and 50 percent maximum diversion the major regions retiring land are still the Northern Plains, Southern Plains, Mountain, and the Corn Belt. Under program L_{25} a total of 41.2 million acres is retired. The Northern Plains again have the highest proportion of acres retired. The Southern Plains region is second but the Corn Belt moves into third. In general, the Northern Plains and Southeast and Mountain states decrease the amount of cropland diverted as a tighter restriction is placed on the regional concentration of retired cropland. In contrast, the amount of cropland diverted in the Corn Belt and Appalachian and Delta states increases as the program becomes more restrictive.

Distribution of Government Payments with Lower Prices ● The distribution of government payments for programs under the lower price level is given in Table 5.3. The payment distributions follow a pattern similar to the land retirement patterns described. With unlimited diversion and lower prices in 1975, government payments for land retirement total $494 million. The payment pattern compares in rank of regions with the land retirement pattern for the same program: Northern Plains, Southern Plains, and Mountain regions. The Delta region is fourth.

Table 5.2 ● Distribution of Acres Diverted by Program for the Ten Farm Production Regions under the Lower Price Level in 1975

Region	Unlimited diversion		75 % maximum diversion		50 % maximum diversion		25 % maximum diversion	
	Total acres diverted (thousand)	Percentage of total	Total acres diverted (thousand)	Percentage of total	Total acres diverted (thousand)	Percentage of total	Total acres diverted (thousand)	Percentage of total
United States	56,992	100.0	53,406	100.0	51,057	100.0	41,197	100.0
Northeast	652	1.1	893	1.7	893	1.7	1,029	2.5
Lake States	3,470	6.1	2,646	5.0	3,527	6.9	2,776	6.7
Corn Belt	4,421	7.8	4,317	8.1	3,921	7.7	4,682	11.4
Northern Plains	24,185	42.5	21,297	39.8	17,535	34.4	14,256	34.5
Appalachians	2,185	3.8	2,074	3.9	2,383	4.7	2,452	6.0
Southeast	2,594	4.5	2,432	4.6	2,271	4.4	1,411	3.4
Delta	2,881	5.1	2,881	5.4	3,596	7.0	2,304	5.6
Southern Plains	10,483	18.4	11,020	20.6	11,483	22.5	7,973	19.4
Mountain	5,268	9.2	4,993	9.3	4,595	9.0	3,461	8.4
Pacific	853	1.5	853	1.6	853	1.7	853	2.1

Table 5.3 ● Distribution of Government Payments by Program for the Ten Farm Production Regions under the Lower Price Level in 1975

Region	Unlimited diversion		75 % maximum diversion		50 % maximum diversion		25 % maximum diversion	
	Total annual payments	Percentage of total	Total annual payments	Percentage of total	Total annual payments	Percentage of total	Total annual payments	Percentage of total
	(thousand)		(thousand)		(thousand)		(thousand)	
United States	493,986	100.0	487,478	100.0	487,668	100.0	400,543	100.0
Northeast	4,239	0.9	5,802	1.2	5,802	1.2	6,687	1.7
Lake States	22,557	4.6	17,197	3.5	22,927	4.7	18,046	4.5
Corn Belt	28,736	5.8	28,058	5.8	32,820	6.7	47,901	12.0
Northern Plains	161,074	32.5	151,210	31.0	122,920	25.2	108,631	27.0
Appalachians	15,800	3.2	14,997	3.1	16,871	3.5	16,842	4.2
Southeast	18,233	3.7	17,196	3.5	16,148	3.3	10,369	2.6
Delta	55,577	11.3	55,577	11.4	71,998	14.8	54,357	13.6
Southern Plains	112,482	22.8	124,744	25.6	131,024	26.9	92,645	23.1
Mountain	69,745	14.1	67,154	13.8	61,615	12.6	39,522	9.9
Pacific	5,543	1.1	5,543	1.1	5,543	1.1	5,543	1.4

With both the 75 and 50 percent maximum diversion programs, these four regions maintain their relative positions. But with a limit of 25 percent maximum diversion the Delta region is third and the Corn Belt is fourth. Estimated payments to farmers are lower under program L_{25} than for other alternatives. Although the average payment per acre is highest for L_{25} (see Fig. 5.6), the total number of acres retired is less (Fig. 5.5) and total payments are also lower. Net farm income under program L_{25} is lower than for any other program (Fig. 5.8).

Location of Retired Cropland with Medium Prices ● The largest amount of retired cropland with unlimited diversion and medium price levels is in the Northern Plains (Table 5.4). The Southern Plains rank second and the Southeast is third. A total of 95.7 million acres is retired under program M_u for the United States.

With medium prices and 75 percent maximum diversion, the Northern Plains and the Southern Plains rank numbers one and two. But the Lake States move into third position and the Corn Belt ranks fourth. With a limit of 50 percent maximum diversion, the Corn Belt moves into third position and the Lake States are fourth, a reversal from the 75 percent maximum diversion program.

With program M_{25} a total of 73.4 million acres is retired. Only the Northern Plains maintains its relative position as the Corn Belt moves into second position and the Southern Plains fall to third. Of all medium price programs, this program has the lowest net farm income—$14.6 billion (Fig. 5.8). In general, as the retirement program becomes more restrictive, the more productive regions retire more cropland and the marginal regions retire less. Since production costs are higher in marginal regions, net farm income falls.

Distribution of Government Payments with Medium Prices ● The regional distributions of government payments for the medium price programs are summarized in Table 5.5. The payment distributions follow a pattern similar to the acreage distributions for this set of prices.

Total government payments are $1.6 billion under medium prices and unlimited diversion. The rank of regions in payment receipts is as follows: Northern Plains, Southern Plains, Southeast, Corn Belt, Lake States, Mountain, Delta, Pacific, and Northeast regions. A considerable shift takes place however as concentration is restricted to 25 percent. With medium prices and 25 percent maximum diversion, government payments total $1.8 billion. The Corn Belt receives 31.4 percent and the Northern Plains receive 20.4 percent of the total payments. The share of payments to the Southeast declines from 11.9 percent under M_u to 4.1 percent under M_{25}. Although total government payments under M_{25} are highest of all programs under medium prices, net farm income is the lowest—$14.6 billion. The more inefficient interregional pattern of production associated with this program causes farm expenses

Table 5.4 ● Distribution of Acres Diverted by Program for the Ten Farm Production Regions under the Medium Price Level in 1975

Region	Unlimited diversion		75 % maximum diversion		50 % maximum diversion		25 % maximum diversion	
	Total acres diverted (thousand)	Percentage of total	Total acres diverted (thousand)	Percentage of total	Total acres diverted (thousand)	Percentage of total	Total acres diverted (thousand)	Percentage of total
United States	95,668	100.0	92,650	100.0	87,380	100.0	73,440	100.0
Northeast	4,757	5.0	3,791	4.1	3,274	3.7	1,963	2.7
Lake States	10,248	10.7	9,938	10.7	10,211	11.7	7,642	10.4
Corn Belt	7,656	8.0	9,575	10.3	13,594	15.6	16,977	23.1
Northern Plains	29,241	30.4	26,788	28.9	20,873	23.9	18,910	25.8
Appalachians	7,590	7.9	6,140	6.6	5,340	6.1	4,301	5.9
Southeast	10,677	11.2	8,876	9.6	7,260	8.3	3,765	5.1
Delta	3,978	4.2	4,524	4.9	3,644	4.2	3,713	5.1
Southern Plains	12,402	13.0	13,125	14.2	15,380	17.6	9,948	13.5
Mountain	7,827	8.2	7,293	7.9	5,762	6.6	4,658	6.3
Pacific	1,292	1.4	2,600	2.8	2,042	2.3	1,563	2.1

Table 5.5 ● Distribution of Government Payments by Program for the Ten Farm Production Regions under the Medium Price Level in 1975

Region	Unlimited diversion		75 % maximum diversion		50 % maximum diversion		25 % maximum diversion	
	Total annual payments (thousand)	Percentage of total	Total annual payments (thousand)	Percentage of total	Total annual payments (thousand)	Percentage of total	Total annual payments (thousand)	Percentage of total
United States	1,592,583	100.0	1,716,753	100.0	1,745,172	100.0	1,794,335	100.0
Northeast	71,840	4.5	58,037	3.4	51,481	2.9	30,869	1.7
Lake States	131,550	8.3	141,516	8.2	166,427	9.5	153,684	8.6
Corn Belt	148,744	9.3	211,530	12.3	333,028	19.2	563,763	31.4
Northern Plains	385,307	24.2	376,174	21.9	306,237	17.6	366,846	20.4
Appalachians	118,937	7.5	97,689	5.7	105,556	6.0	101,188	5.6
Southeast	189,918	11.9	158,866	9.3	139,462	8.0	72,841	4.1
Delta	113,305	7.1	125,077	7.3	105,573	6.0	132,281	7.4
Southern Plains	208,148	13.1	228,892	13.3	274,605	15.7	178,823	10.0
Mountain	127,912	8.0	123,919	7.2	109,625	6.3	89,238	5.0
Pacific	96,922	6.1	195,053	11.4	153,178	8.8	104,802	5.8

to be considerably higher than for other programs. However, the smaller income is distributed more evenly among all regions.

Location of Retired Cropland with Higher Prices ● The distribution of diverted acres for programs under the higher price level is summarized in Table 5.6. Under higher prices and unlimited diversion in 1975, retired cropland totals 116.3 million acres, highest of any of the programs analyzed. With the higher price level, two shifts take place: demand is reduced somewhat in response to the higher price levels, and retirement programs must be larger to balance production with the smaller demand. The result is a larger total acreage retired under the programs.

With unlimited diversion, the Northern Plains rank first, the Southern Plains are second, the Lake States third, and the Corn Belt fourth. With both programs H_{75} and H_{50}, the Northern Plains rank first in retired cropland, but the Corn Belt moves into second position. The Lake States are third and the Southern Plains fourth with program H_{75} while with H_{50}, the Southern Plains are third and the Lake States fourth. Program H_{25} retires the least cropland of all programs under the higher price level. As retirement is spread over all regions, the number of acres required to balance supply and demand declines.

Distribution of Government Payments with Higher Prices ● The distributions of government payments for the higher price level are given in Table 5.7. These distributions are different than the cropland retirement patterns for higher prices. Under program H_u the Northern Plains rank first, but the Corn Belt is second, the Southeast is third, and the Southern Plains rank fourth.

Under higher prices and 75 percent maximum diversion, the Northern Plains and Corn Belt each receive about 20 percent of the government payments. The Southern Plains rank third. Under program H_{50}, payments to farmers are $3.9 billion, and the Corn Belt ranks first, the Northern Plains are second, and the Southern Plains third. The Corn Belt also ranks first under program H_{25} which has total government payments of $3.5 billion. The Northern Plains are second and the Southern Plains third, the same rank as under program H_{50}. Under H_{25}, as compared to H_u, the Corn Belt moves up sharply in percentage of payments while the Southeast declines by a relatively large amount. For the higher price levels, H_{25} has the lowest net farm income.

AGGREGATE PRODUCTION EFFECTS OF ALTERNATIVE PROGRAM RESTRICTIONS AND PRICE LEVELS ● As the final set of data, we provide the estimated effects on total acreages, production, and yields, of shifting from one level of restriction on land retirement to another within a given price level and between price levels. Within a price level, total demand remains constant, hence any change in acreage

Table 5.6 ● Distribution of Acres Diverted by Program for the Ten Farm Production Regions under the Higher Price Level in 1975

Region	Unlimited diversion		75 % maximum diversion		50 % maximum diversion		25 % maximum diversion	
	Total acres diverted (thousand)	Percentage of total	Total acres diverted (thousand)	Percentage of total	Total acres diverted (thousand)	Percentage of total	Total acres diverted (thousand)	Percentage of total
United States	116,332	100.0	112,207	100.0	107,683	100.0	81,731	100.0
Northeast	4,757	4.1	3,912	3.5	3,155	2.9	1,963	2.4
Lake States	13,433	11.5	14,334	12.8	11,555	10.7	7,837	9.6
Corn Belt	13,045	11.2	16,941	15.1	20,483	19.0	22,610	27.7
Northern Plains	33,104	28.5	31,331	27.9	25,312	23.6	19,468	23.8
Appalachians	7,591	6.5	6,174	5.5	6,861	6.4	4,645	5.7
Southeast	12,524	10.8	9,961	8.9	7,301	6.8	3,765	4.6
Delta	6,306	5.4	5,192	4.6	5,633	5.2	3,732	4.6
Southern Plains	14,271	12.3	14,134	12.6	18,140	16.8	9,988	12.2
Mountain	8,188	7.0	7,628	6.8	7,202	6.7	4,850	5.9
Pacific	3,113	2.7	2,600	2.3	2,042	1.9	2,873	3.5

Table 5.7 ● Distribution of Government Payments by Program for the Ten Farm Production Regions under the Higher Price Level in 1975

Region	Unlimited diversion		75 % maximum diversion		50 % maximum diversion		25 % maximum diversion	
	Total annual payments (thousand)	Percentage of total	Total annual payments (thousand)	Percentage of total	Total annual payments (thousand)	Percentage of total	Total annual payments (thousand)	Percentage of total
United States	3,688,340	100.0	3,723,107	100.0	3,855,831	100.0	3,504,598	100.0
Northeast	171,247	4.6	143,593	3.9	114,049	3.0	70,618	2.0
Lake States	359,890	9.8	419,133	11.3	361,867	9.4	280,781	8.0
Corn Belt	488,884	13.3	708,724	19.0	942,703	24.3	1,360,679	38.8
Northern Plains	749,065	20.3	767,595	20.6	701,323	18.2	639,751	18.3
Appalachians	269,306	7.3	220,168	5.9	293,223	7.6	218,560	6.2
Southeast	457,528	12.4	371,130	10.0	279,830	7.3	144,600	4.1
Delta	259,892	7.0	217,062	5.8	245,619	6.4	175,275	5.0
Southern Plains	423,299	11.5	424,316	11.4	518,769	13.5	293,677	8.4
Mountain	198,023	5.4	191,392	5.1	194,211	5.0	143,350	4.1
Pacific	311,269	8.4	259,994	7.0	204,237	5.3	177,307	5.1

reflects a shift of production among regions. One qualification of this statement must be made. There is provision made to allow wheat to substitute for feed grains in feeding rations. However, this kind of shift is also determined by restrictions placed on retirement in any one region. To be more specific, an increase in total acreages reflects the degree of inefficiency in crop production caused by the restriction on location of retired cropland.

Production Effects with Lower Prices ● With the lower set of prices, in 1975 total wheat acres vary from 48.2 million with 75 percent maximum diversion up to 57.4 million with 25 percent maximum diversion in a region (Table 5.8). Wheat yield is estimated at 40.7 bushels per acre with program L_u, and 29.6 bushels per acre under L_{25}. Wheat production varies from a low of 1.5 billion bushels with 75 percent maximum diversion to a high of 1.7 billion bushels under program L_{25}. More wheat is used for feed purposes under program L_{25}, and consequently total wheat production is higher. With lower prices and 25 percent maximum diversion in any given region, more marginal land is brought into production and the resulting yield is lower while total acreage is higher.

Total feed grains acres are lowest (96.2 million) with unlimited diversion and reach a high of 99.5 million acres with program L_{75}. Feed grains yields follow a pattern similar to wheat. Fewer acres of feed grains are required with unlimited diversion, since feed grains become concentrated in areas with the highest yields. Yields are highest (1.90 tons of corn equivalent per acre) with program L_u and lowest (1.78 tons) with program L_{25} as more marginal land is farmed. Total feed grains production is also highest (184 million tons) under program L_{75} but lowest (177 million tons) with program L_{25}. As is the case with wheat, variation in feed grains production can be explained by the amount of wheat used for feed (i.e., wheat is a substitute for feed grains).

Acreages and production of soybeans and cotton are essentially constant for all programs with lower prices in 1975. Yields of soybeans and cotton follow the same pattern as wheat and feed grains. Yields are highest with unlimited diversion (L_u) and lowest under program L_{25}. In general as restrictions are placed on the location of retired cropland, more marginal land is farmed, acres of crops harvested increase, and yields decrease.

Production Effects with Medium Prices ● With the medium set of prices, acreages, production, and yields of the major crops follow a pattern similar to lower prices (Table 5.9). The magnitude of the variables differs, since to attain medium prices requires a corresponding reduction in total supply, and the amount of production cleared through the market would be less than under lower prices.

Total wheat acres range from 43 million with 75 percent maximum

Table 5.8 ● Estimated Acreages, Yields, and Production for the Lower Price Level in 1975 with Prior Years for Comparison

Crop	Actual		Projected 1975 by program			
	1967	1968	Unlimited diversion (L_u)	75% maximum diversion (L_{75})	50% maximum diversion (L_{50})	25% maximum diversion (L_{25})
Harvested acreages			(thousand acres)			
Wheat	58,771	55,309	48,722	48,212	50,576	57,413
Feed grains	100,750	96,602	96,218	99,504	98,898	99,327
Soybeans	39,757	40,659	43,584	43,610	43,687	44,092
Cotton	7,997	10,175	12,799	12,799	12,799	12,831
Yield per harvested acre						
Wheat (bu)	25.80	28.40	30.70	30.40	30.00	29.60
Feed grains (ton)[a]	1.72	1.70	1.90	1.85	1.85	1.78
Soybeans (bu)	24.50	26.60	26.00	25.90	25.90	25.70
Cotton (lb)	452.00	532.00	529.00	529.00	529.00	527.00
Total production			(thousand)			
Wheat (bu)	1,522,382	1,570,433	1,496,760	1,466,760	1,515,522	1,698,951
Feed grains (ton)[a]	172,809	164,557	183,055	184,003	182,464	176,688
Soybeans (bu)	976,060	1,079,662	1,131,365	1,131,365	1,131,365	1,131,365
Cotton (bales)	7,458	10,822	13,531	13,531	13,531	13,531

Source: U. S. Dept. of Agriculture, Crop Production 1968 Annual Summary, USDA ERS, December 1968.

NOTE: Corn at $0.85 per bushel, wheat at $1.00 per bushel, soybeans at $1.50 per bushel, and cotton at $0.26 per pound in 1975.

[a]Feed grains are reported in tons of corn equivalent.

Table 5.9 ● Estimated Acreages, Yields, and Production for the Medium Price Level in 1975 with Prior Years for Comparison

Crop	Actual		Projected 1975 by program			
	1967	1968	Unlimited diversion (M_U)	75% maximum diversion (M_{75})	50% maximum diversion (M_{50})	25% maximum diversion (M_{25})
Harvested acreages			(thousand acres)			
Wheat	58,771	55,309	43,573	42,986	46,008	56,207
Feed grains	100,750	96,602	79,138	81,712	82,666	82,657
Soybeans	39,767	40,659	35,705	35,651	35,713	36,271
Cotton	7,997	10,175	12,691	13,083	13,195	13,337
Yield per harvested acre						
Wheat (bu)	25.80	28.40	32.80	31.80	30.90	30.40
Feed grains (ton)[a]	1.72	1.70	2.17	2.13	2.08	1.97
Soybeans (bu)	24.50	26.60	28.80	28.80	28.80	28.30
Cotton (lb)	452.00	532.00	533.00	517.00	513.00	507.00
Total production			(thousand)			
Wheat (bu)	1,522,382	1,570,433	1,425,871	1,367,110	1,421,903	1,709,998
Feed grains (ton)[a]	172,809	164,557	171,990	173,842	172,115	163,041
Soybeans (bu)	976,060	1,079,662	1,026,889	1,026,889	1,026,889	1,026,889
Cotton (bales)	7,458	10,822	13,531	13,531	13,531	13,531

Source: U. S. Dept. of Agriculture, Crop Production 1968 Annual Summary.

NOTE: Corn at $1.05 per bushel, wheat at $1.25 per bushel, soybeans at $2.15 per bushel, and cotton at $0.26 per pound in 1975.

[a]Feed grains are reported in tons of corn equivalent.

diversion to 56.2 million with 25 percent maximum diversion in a region. With unlimited diversion, the national wheat yield is estimated at 32.8 bushels per acre versus 30.4 bushels per acre under program M_{25}. With program M_{25} more marginal land is farmed and the resulting wheat yield is lower. Wheat production ranges between 1.4 billion bushels under program M_{75} and 1.7 billion bushels with program M_{25}. Again this variation is due to the increased use of wheat for feed purposes under program M_{25}.

Total feed grains acres vary from 79.1 million under program M_u up to 82.7 million with 50 percent maximum diversion. The lowest yield of feed grains is 1.97 tons per acre under program M_{25} and highest (2.17 tons) with program M_u. Feed grains production is highest (174 million tons) with program M_{75} and reaches a low of 163 million tons under program M_{25}. This variation in feed grains production is a result of the use of wheat for feed purposes. As feed grains production declines under a particular program, wheat production rises accordingly.

Acreages and production of soybeans and cotton with medium prices in 1975 are essentially constant for all programs studied. Yields of soybeans and cotton follow the same pattern as wheat and feed grains yields. Yields of both crops are highest with unlimited diversion (M_u) and lowest with the most restrictive diversion program M_{25}. As under lower prices when restrictions are placed on the location of retired cropland, more marginal land is farmed, acres of crops harvested increase, and yields decrease.

Production Effects with Higher Prices ● Acreages of major crops are significantly reduced with the higher price level (Table 5.10). Total wheat acres are 40.2 million with unlimited diversion and 56.0 million with 25 percent maximum diversion. Yields of wheat are estimated at 34.5 bushels per acre with program H_u versus 31.2 bushels under program H_{25}. Wheat production varies from a low of 1.4 billion bushels under program H_{75} to a high of 1.7 billion bushels under program H_{25}. This difference in total wheat production is again a result of variations in the amounts of wheat used for feed purposes.

Total feed grains acreages vary from a low of 72.1 million with program H_u to a high of 80.5 million acres under program H_{25}. Feed grains production is lowest (152 million tons) with program H_{25} and highest (164 million tons) under program H_{75}. Variations in total feed grains production also result from the use of different quantities of wheat for feed purposes under the various programs and price levels.

Soybean acres show greater variation under higher prices than under the other two price levels. Total soybean acres vary from a low of 29.7 million with program H_u to a high of 31.9 million under program H_{25}. Soybean production is constant for all programs with higher prices, but yields range from 31.3 bushels per acre with program H_u down to 29.3 bushels under program H_{25}. Cotton production is constant under

Table 5.10 ● Estimated Acreages, Yields, and Production, under the Higher Price Level in 1975 with Prior Years for Comparison

Crop	Actual 1967	Actual 1968	Projected 1975 by program — Unlimited diversion (H_u)	75% maximum diversion (H_{75})	50% maximum diversion (H_{50})	25% maximum diversion (H_{25})
Harvested acreages			(thousand acres)			
Wheat	58,771	55,309	40,212	41,330	43,408	55,971
Feed grains	100,750	96,602	72,083	73,885	74,717	80,479
Soybeans	39,767	40,659	29,736	29,858	30,238	31,879
Cotton	7,997	10,175	12,934	13,113	13,263	13,667
Yield per harvested acre						
Wheat (bu)	25.80	28.40	34.50	33.20	32.90	31.20
Feed grains (ton)[a]	1.72	1.70	2.27	2.22	2.17	2.05
Soybeans (bu)	24.50	26.60	31.30	31.20	30.80	29.30
Cotton (lb)	452.00	532.00	523.00	516.00	510.00	495.00
Total production			(thousand)			
Wheat (bu)	1,522,382	1,570,433	1,385,681	1,371,967	1,426,951	1,747,253
Feed grains (ton)[a]	172,809	164,557	163,489	163,922	162,190	152,100
Soybeans (bu)	976,060	1,079,662	931,130	931,130	931,130	931,130
Cotton (bales)	7,458	10,822	13,531	13,531	13,531	13,531

Source: U. S. Dept. of Agriculture, Crop Production 1968 Annual Summary.

NOTE: Corn at $1.25 per bushel, wheat at $1.50 per bushel, soybeans at $2.75 per bushel, and cotton at $0.26 per pound in 1975.

[a] Feed grains are reported in tons of corn equivalent.

all programs and price levels, and acreage varies only slightly. Cotton yields are highest (523 pounds of lint per acre) under program H_u and lowest (495 pounds) with program H_{25}. Once again as locational restrictions are placed on retired cropland, more marginal land is farmed, acres of cropland harvested increase, and yields decrease.

Price Levels and Acreage Levels ● From this set of data, several obvious conclusions emerge. One conclusion is that the price level attained is clearly a major factor determining the size of the "farm plant" necessary to satisfy food needs. Allowing prices to drop to the lower price level means expanded production with acreages of most major crops at higher levels. Farmers who desire expanded levels of production might find this alternative quite promising. For those farmers desiring higher prices, the associated reduction in acreage is substantial. Their acceptance of the lower acreages necessary to hold these price levels is less assured, and the potential for a large increase in carry-over stocks is evident. Farmers feel direct conflicts between the desire to expand total production on the thousands of individual farms in the nation and the desire for higher farm incomes growing out of higher farm prices. These conflicts are presently resolved through the political processes of government although the uninhibited marketplace could also resolve these conflicts. The above data provide at least one set of estimates of the effects of each change in prices and the corresponding shifts which are necessary in production.

SUMMARY OF POLICY CONSIDERATIONS ● Several land retirement alternatives directed toward controlling supply to attain a specified price level have been analyzed in this chapter. Any of the alternative land retirement programs allow attainment of the three price levels considered. Several different land retirement programs would also allow attainment of a given price level. However, each alternative program differs in the amount of land retired to attain the price level, the location of land retired, total government costs and net farm income, the geographic distribution of payments, and the regional location of agricultural adjustments. The data for each program studied in this chapter can be used to determine the trade-offs among these items—the amount of one item which must be sacrificed to attain more of another item.

It is our hope that this information will be useful to farm groups, the general public, and policy administrators in decisions relating to future farm policies. Of course, the set of policy alternatives analyzed in this study involves only a few of the many possible. Other possibilities include marketing quotas, free market prices, direct payments without production controls, or subsidization of inputs and outputs. This chapter has been concerned only with some alternatives in land retirement as a means of attaining given levels of supply control and prices.

The many alternatives in land retirement as a mechanism of supply

control can be combined in various manners. Under annual land diversion programs of the 1960s, retirement was on a partial-farm basis
dispersed over all major producing regions. Programs limited to partial-
farm land retirement are more beneficial to tenant farmers since the
unit is not withdrawn from the rental market. At the other extreme,
land retirement could be on a whole-farm basis concentrated in marginal
crop-producing regions as we have seen under some alternatives of this
chapter. Each type of program has particular advantages and disad-
vantages. Programs vary in success of their long-term solutions to overcapacity problems. They vary in their costs of attaining a given level
of supply control and price supports; annual programs based on partial-
farm retirement over more regions have higher costs than long-term programs on a whole-farm basis concentrated in marginal producing regions.
The programs have differential impacts on the interregional distribution of government payments and the social costs of adjustment.

Public policy decisions and selection are responsibilities of the
appropriate groups who must decide the relative importance or weights
to be attached to various degrees of regional concentration of retirement,
distribution of government payments, and secondary or social costs of
adjustment. An optimal policy can be prescribed or selected only in
light of these weights and trade-offs—the amount of one item gained or
sacrificed (long-term solution, government costs, farm income, secondary
social or adjustment costs, regional distribution of retirement or payments, etc.) for a sacrifice or gain of another item in the same set. Different land retirement schemes are not "black or white" or "either, or"
choices. It is possible to combine them in many ways. A partial-farm
method spread over regions can be combined with another program
such as whole-farm retirement on a regional and long-term basis. For
example, the Feed Grain Program was carried on simultaneously with
the Conservation Reserve and Cropland Adjustment programs during
the 1960s. This arrangement represented a combination of annual and
long-term programs, whole-farm and partial-farm participation, and
interregional dispersion with regional concentration characteristics. Also
the most desired type of program could be phased in as the primary
mechanism over a five-, ten-, or twenty-year time span. The variety of
combinations of time periods covered, magnitude of program, price and
income level, and location alternatives is nearly limitless for farm programs. The job of the policy maker is large and time consuming under
these circumstances. But eventually these decisions must be made unless agriculture is again to return solely to the marketplace for its di-
rectives in production and marketing decisions.

CHAPTER SIX

Resource Adjustment in Rural Areas

PAST CHAPTERS have dealt at length with alternative ways of managing the overabundant capacity of the U.S. agricultural industry. The many alternatives examined and quantified focused primarily on price and income problems and the related government costs for stabilizing and supporting the farm economy. Several of these alternatives implied serious structural change for the agricultural industry as well as for rural communities. While these implied changes were pointed out, no attempt was made to explain the many economic forces which underlie the structural change occurring in agriculture. In this chapter we draw together several pieces of evidence which measure and explain the ongoing structural change in agriculture. We begin by looking at the changing number of farms in the industry, the trends from the last two decades, and the projections to 1980. Later sections look at various explanatory variables related to structural change in agriculture and rural communities. We end with a discussion of the effects that shifting large amounts of land back to grass or trees would have on particular regions and areas of agriculture.

STRUCTURAL ADJUSTMENT ● The process of changing the structure of agriculture has many different aspects. One type of ongoing change affects resource combinations on individual farms of the nation. Farm operators continuously reorganize combinations of capital and land—using more or less machinery, seed, or fertilizer per acre—and combinations of capital and labor—substituting machines to do jobs which labor previously carried out. These kinds of changes improve the efficiency of farm production and generally lead the individual farmer to expand his land base. With the land base for all farms fixed, a reduction in total farm numbers must take place. This is the second aspect of structural change, a change in the total number of farms, number of farm families, number of persons in rural communities, and eventually number of farm towns and communities.

These ongoing changes in structure have been looked upon with considerable pessimism over the last several decades. As Edward Higbee has so lucidly stated, "It is hard for the nation to face up to the fact that throughout the economy, it is more profitable to employ capital than to employ people. A new technology and modern tax policy have made it smart business to use machines rather than men wherever possible. Machines can be depreciated through the fast write-off—a gain. Men must be pensioned—a loss. When capital and men compete for employment, the shrewd entrepreneur will hire capital because he can predict more accurately what it will do and what it will cost. On the farm this means that a family which is long on labor but short on capital has become obsolete as a production unit."[1] As some production units become obsolete, others with stronger capital positions take over the land and raise output per acre to profitable levels. The end result is fewer farms and fewer farmers.

Projection of Farm Numbers ● As structural change has proceeded, farm numbers, acres per farm, technological inputs per farm, total investment per farm, taxes paid per farm, location and quality of rural schools, sources of production inputs, and even rural church viability have been affected. One indicator of structural change is the declining number of farms. Between 1954 and 1964 farm numbers decreased by 34 percent in the United States. Although part of this decline resulted from a change in definition of what constitutes a farm, the reduction in farm numbers was nevertheless sizeable.

As farm numbers decline, the number of people directly involved in the production process also declines. The result is that changes in farm numbers have broad implications for the whole rural area. There are fewer people to attend and support rural churches as well as fewer children to attend rural schools; the costs of supporting churches and schools fall on fewer individuals, with sizeable increases per household (although not necessarily per dollar of farm production). Farm families find an increasing sparseness of population in rural areas which provides less social interaction and involvement.

Decline in farm numbers has been a general phenomenon for every region of the United States, but some regions have changed at a substantially faster rate. Between 1959 and 1964, the Northeast, Appalachian, Southeast, and Delta regions lost farms at a faster rate than other regions (Table 6.1). The Pacific, Mountain, and Southern Plains lost farms at a slower rate, as did the Northern Plains and Lake States.

The implications of further reduction in farm numbers over the next ten years are very broad for rural areas of the nation. As suggested

1. Edward Higbee, *Farms and Farmers in an Urban Age* (New York: Twentieth, 1963), pp. 4–5.

Table 6.1 • Farm Numbers by Regions and U.S. Total with Percentage Decrease Between Census Years, 1949–64

Region	All farms 1964	Percentage change 1959–64	All farms 1959	Percentage change 1954–59	All farms 1954	Percentage change 1949–54	All farms 1949
United States	3,152,513	14.9	3,703,894	22.6	4,782,416	11.1	5,382,162
Northeast	227,370	20.2	285,064	24.6	377,951	14.8	443,510
Lake States	343,383	11.7	388,694	15.1	457,705	9.1	503,251
Corn Belt	662,761	13.5	766,536	14.9	900,757	9.4	994,458
Northern Plains	271,140	11.2	305,477	11.6	345,476	6.7	370,430
Appalachian	529,543	17.4	640,875	26.3	869,541	10.5	971,046
Southeast	272,685	22.1	345,410	34.1	524,225	13.5	605,988
Delta States	251,505	18.2	307,587	34.8	472,118	15.4	557,993
Southern Plains	293,835	8.7	321,747	21.9	411,926	13.1	473,813
Mountain	134,114	10.0	149,080	17.2	180,026	7.6	194,858
Pacific	166,177	14.1	193,424	20.4	242,691	8.9	266,815

Source: U. S. Dept. of Commerce, U. S. Census of Agriculture, 1949, 1959, and 1964, Bureau of the Census.

before, schools and churches are directly affected but other groups and organizations also have a stake in such change. Local government, input suppliers, purchasers, and processors of farm commodities are all affected by the changing economic base in rural areas. To such groups, changing farm numbers and sizes have implications for planning future organizations and enterprises.

To provide some indication of future structural change, numbers of farms were projected to 1980 using a logarithmic equation applied to 160 regions of the United States. The equation was

$$F = ae^{bT + cD} \qquad (6.1)$$

where F is farm numbers, T is time, and D is a dummy variable which measures the definitional change in farms between the Agricultural Census of 1954 and 1959. This functional form was used to project both the total number of farms and the number of commercial farms.

ALL FARM NUMBERS. The numbers of farms estimated for future time periods are shown in Table 6.2. For the United States the number of farms is projected to decline from 3.2 million in 1964 to 2.2 million in 1980 or by nearly a third. The largest change is expected in the Northeast where farm numbers are projected to decrease 44 percent. Various forces including technical change in farming and transportation as well as the relocation of production to areas of greatest comparative advantage account for differential changes among regions. Relatively large declines in farm numbers are indicated for the Southeast and Delta regions as cotton acreage is reduced, livestock enterprises increase and cause extensification, and farms become more highly mechanized. Regions showing the least change include the Lake States, Corn Belt, Northern Plains, Mountain, and Pacific regions. These regions each show from 20 to 25 percent decrease in total numbers of farms. The continued reduction of farm numbers and increase in size indicate that the social and economic problems of rural areas are not going to disappear readily. In general, increased farm size and fewer numbers will also require an expansion of the area base for social services provided to rural communities.

COMMERCIAL FARM NUMBERS. Estimates of commercial farm numbers are based on the same method as were all farm numbers. Numbers of commercial farms (those with sales over $2,500) are projected to decline by 15 percent by 1980 (Table 6.3). The smaller decline in commercial farms results from consolidation of some farms into larger, more efficient units. As farms are consolidated and increase in size, a larger proportion have sales above $2,500 (the level used by the U.S. Department of Agriculture as denoting commercial farms). If the definition of a commercial farm is changed to $5,000 (or even $10,000) in gross sales by

Table 6.2 ● Number of All Farms by Regions, Actual 1964 and Projected for 1970, 1975, and 1980

Region	Percentage change 1964-80	Actual[a] 1964	1970	Projected 1975	Projected 1980
United States	-28.7	3,152,513	2,768,295	2,492,982	2,248,027
Northeast	-44.4	227,370	182,142	151,522	126,317
Lake States	-24.0	343,383	309,395	283,883	260,840
Corn Belt	-25.0	662,761	594,778	543,756	497,317
Northern Plains	-20.6	271,140	248,724	231,316	215,255
Appalachian	-32.6	529,543	455,673	402,714	356,874
Southeast	-34.8	272,685	231,844	202,794	177,829
Delta States	-32.7	251,505	216,623	191,276	169,155
Southern Plains	-27.1	293,835	256,679	235,381	214,062
Mountain	-22.4	134,114	122,616	112,936	104,136
Pacific	-24.0	166,177	149,821	137,404	126,242

[a]U. S. Dept. of Commerce, Census of Agriculture for 1964.

Table 6.3 ● Numbers of Commercial Farms by Regions, Actual 1964 and Projected for 1970, 1975, and 1980

Region	Percentage change 1964-80	Actual[a] 1964	1970	Projected 1975	1980
United States	-15.2	2,162,693	2,034,791	1,931,822	1,836,690
Northeast	-26.7	155,854	138,578	125,765	114,219
Lake States	-13.9	265,835	251,243	239,760	228,856
Corn Belt	-10.0	497,426	477,733	462,293	447,680
Northern Plains	-8.7	235,892	223,152	213,196	203,805
Appalachian	-19.4	325,183	303,680	283,119	262,181
Southeast	-15.4	161,792	151,616	143,673	136,905
Delta States	-17.1	140,944	129,886	122,576	116,852
Southern Plains	-14.8	174,030	164,789	155,875	148,238
Mountain	-13.2	100,553	95,291	91,167	87,259
Pacific	-13.8	105,184	98,823	94,398	90,695

NOTE: Commercial farms are defined as farms with over $2,500 gross sales per year.

[a]U. S. Dept. of Commerce, Census of Agriculture for 1964.

1980, even fewer farms will be classified as commercial units. However, using the present definition, 1.8 million commercial farms are projected for 1980. With 2.2 million total farms and 1.8 commercial farms, 0.4 million part-time farms are indicated for 1980—a decline of one-third. This decline will result particularly through the increase in farm size and the attraction of many part-time farmers to other occupational opportunities.

Projected Capital Needs per Farm ● While farm numbers will decline by 1980, the farmers who remain will use more total capital than at present. To gain some idea of what the individual farm capital needs will be, average farm capital requirements for 1980 are estimated in each of the farm production regions of the United States. For this purpose, total capital requirements are taken from Table 2.26. Those estimates assume the continuation of a 1960s type of farm program through 1980. Total capital needs in each region are then divided by projected farm numbers, thereby giving estimates of average capital needs per farm. These estimates, shown in Table 6.4, indicate capital invested in land and buildings, machinery and equipment, and livestock inventories will increase by 94 percent per farm between 1965 and 1980.

Regional differences in capital needs are apparent. The Northeast, Delta States, and Southern Plains more than double total capital requirements. All other regions, except the Appalachian, would nearly double capital values per farm. Even the Appalachian region increases capital per farm by 70 percent. These large increases in capital per farm will continue the trend of replacing labor resources in agriculture with capital. As a result, food production in the United States will depend to an even greater extent on capital inputs by 1980.

Judging from the large increases projected in capital needs per farm, many farm firms of 1980 may face real challenges in gaining control over the large quantities of capital necessary for operation. In addition to capital needed for land and buildings, machinery and equipment, and livestock inventories, farm operators will use increasing quantities of purchased inputs. Additional problems may arise in intergenerational transfers of these large quantities of capital. The result may be a substantial change in the institutional form of farm ownership and operation.

Forces Changing Farm Size ● The forces bringing a reduction in farm numbers to the nation are part and parcel of the whole process of economic development. As development proceeds, technology causes a complete shift from an agrarian structure built on labor inputs to an industrial structure using huge quantities of capital. In the latter type of economy, the substitution of capital for labor becomes a means toward increasing the efficiency and reducing the cost of production in almost all sectors. Agriculture joins in this process by substituting machines

Table 6.4 ● Capital Investment Per Farm, Actual 1965 and Estimated 1980

Region	Percentage change total capital 1965-80	Total capital per farm 1965ª	Total capital per farm 1980	Projected 1980 capital per farm for Land and buildings	Projected 1980 capital per farm for Machinery and equipment	Projected 1980 capital per farm for Livestock inventories
				($)		
United States	+94.3	63,089	122,576	93,647	19,268	9,661
Northeast	+117.4	48,045	104,444	64,987	30,028	9,429
Lake States	+94.1	46,784	90,822	56,533	25,870	8,419
Corn Belt	+82.1	67,964	123,744	92,679	22,246	9,819
Northern Plains	+84.2	84,986	146,583	104,045	35,823	16,715
Appalachian	+69.5	28,522	48,353	35,078	9,653	3,622
Southeast	+87.9	46,196	86,780	72,986	7,462	5,114
Delta States	+100.4	36,544	73,235	60,388	7,733	5,114
Southern Plains	+117.0	82,203	178,402	151,962	14,975	11,456
Mountain	+87.3	126,676	237,315	189,070	24,065	24,180
Pacific	+93.7	155,629	301,397	265,252	22,267	13,878

ªU. S. Dept. of Agriculture, Agriculture Finance Review, Vol. 26, supplement 1-79, USDA ERS, 1966.

for labor and animal power. This substitution process is encouraged in two ways: one is that the process of development raises wages for labor; the second is that development reduces the cost of capital. The shift in the relative prices of labor and capital causes farmers to increase their use of machines and decrease their use of labor. While the initial result is a reduction in the drudgery and monotony of farm work, the ultimate outcome is less labor required to produce the food and fiber needs of the nation.

Mechanization and Farm Size ● One of the major sources of increased capital in agriculture has been machinery and equipment. As machines became readily available in sizes fitted to large as well as small farming operations, farmers responded by continuously substituting machines for labor. Machines were desirable because they generally lowered production costs, but their work-reducing nature was also highly satisfying to farmers faced with the heavy tasks of agriculture. As machines replaced labor on farms, the optimum combination of land and machinery also changed. The inherent efficiencies of larger machines required a larger acreage of cropland if fixed costs were to be held to a minimum. Some measure of the implied change in farm size as machinery size increased is given in Figure 6.1. Explained simply, Figure 6.1 suggests that each addition of one plow in machinery size on an average farm in southern Iowa should result in the number of acres of cropland increasing by 80—if per acre machine costs are to remain near a minimum. If a larger machinery combination is used on a smaller acreage, costs per acre and per bushel rise rapidly, reducing the net return to land and management.

One measure of how well farms have adapted to changing machinery sizes is shown in Figure 6.2. In 1950 commercial farms in Iowa averaged 124 crop acres per farm. Although no data are available on the average size of machinery combinations used, farmers generally used two-plow and three-plow machinery combinations during this period, combina-

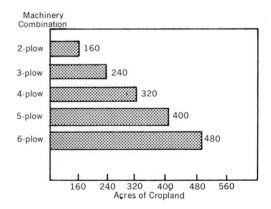

Fig. 6.1. Optimum land-machinery combinations for southern Iowa.

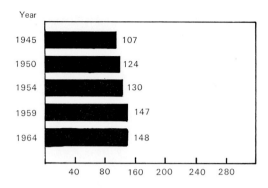

Fig. 6.2. *Average crop acres harvested on all commercial farms in Iowa.*

tions optimally used on 160 to 240 crop acres. By 1964 machinery size had generally increased to four-, five-, or six-plow and even larger combinations. These machinery combinations would optimally have been used on 320, 400, or 480 acres of cropland. But acres of cropland per farm had not generally increased by similar amounts. Commercial farms increased to 148 acres per farm, still far below the suggested least-cost land-machinery combination for larger equipment. While acres per machinery combination can always be expected to be below optimum as farmers attempt to improve timeliness and ease of operation, these data suggest that technological advancement in farm machinery has far outpaced changes in farm size.

Mechanization and Labor Requirements ● The process by which capital is substituted for labor is subtle and ofttimes unapparent. In agriculture, the substitution process does not mean the replacement of a given number of men on a particular farm by a new machine. Instead, the usual type of situation is a temporary underemployment of labor on the farm as the operator uses a new and larger machine to speed up a given work activity. One example of a machine which replaced labor on farms and increased the optimum size of farms is the corn picker. During the 1930s an average Corn Belt farmer with a team of horses and a wagon could pick 80 bushels of corn per day. In an average picking season of perhaps twenty rain-free days, he could harvest 1,600 bushels of corn. With corn averaging 40 bushels per acre, the average farm operator was limited to forty acres of corn. While some farmers hired labor to pick corn, the tendency toward owner-operator farming discouraged this practice. Thus farm size tended to be small with an average of twenty-two acres of corn per farm in the 1930s. (See Table 6.5.)

In the 1930s and 1940s farmers shifted from hand picking to mechanical harvesting equipment. The one-row mechanical picker allowed one man to pick over 200 bushels of corn per day and with twenty rain-free days, total bushels picked in a season increased from 1,600 to 4,000. Even with a higher average yield of 50 bushels per acre,

Table 6.5 ● Changes in Acres of Corn Harvested Per Man in the Corn Belt with Different Types of Equipment

Item	1930s hand pick with team & wagon	1940s one-row mechanical picker	1950s two-row mechanical picker	1960s four-row corn combine
		Illustrative data		
Bushels picked per day	80	200	450	1,200
Average days per season	20	20	20	20
Total bushels picked per season	1,600	4,000	9,000	24,000
Corn yield per acre (bu)	40	50	60	80
Total corn acres one man can handle	40	80	150	300
		Actual data		
Corn acres per farm[a]	22	44	49	69
Average Corn Belt farm size[b]	76	140	182	240

NOTE: The Corn Belt includes Iowa, Illinois, Indiana, Missouri, and Ohio.

[a] Actual acres of corn per Corn Belt farm for 1935, 1945, 1954, and 1964 from the U. S. Dept. of Commerce, U. S. Census of Agriculture.

[b] Actual acres per commercial Corn Belt farm for 1935, 1945, 1954, and 1964 from the U. S. Dept. of Commerce, Census of Agriculture.

one man could harvest eighty acres of corn. With similar changes occurring in other activities (plowing, planting, etc.), average farm size could double if the farm operator had access to adequate capital. Initially, the change was a large reduction in the hours of labor an individual operator had to spend in corn harvest. But as mechanical harvest became dependable and assured rapid completion of corn harvest, farm operators substituted more acres of corn production for the leisure time allowed by the one-row corn harvester.

But the one-row corn picker was not the final improvement in corn picking. The two-row picker was in wide use by the 1950s and the four-row corn combine was introduced in the 1960s. A farm operator with adequate capital to purchase a four-row outfit could harvest and store an average of 300 acres of corn in a season. With total acreage of corn actually declining between 1945 and 1964, the number of men required for corn harvest dropped sharply. Some farmers increased production of livestock. But many found themselves underemployed as machines speeded work. For those unable to gain access to more land, it was often necessary to leave farming for other jobs. Mechanization reduced labor requirements for farming, allowed increases in farm size, and eventually reduced the number of farming units required to produce total food needs in the United States.

Economic Pressures on Farm Size ● Mechanization is not alone as a cause of structural change in farming. Other inputs like fertilizer, insecticides, and biological innovations raised yields per acre and reduced total acres in production. These various inputs all worked through the marketplace to lower the farm price of food. Lower prices meant lower returns for farmers unless output could be increased by more than price declined. The process meant that small farmers found it difficult to remain in operation. These realities are evident in recent data from cost and return records for Iowa farmers who participate in Farm Records Associations. While not representative of all Iowa farmers, these data do indicate a clear relationship between farm size and net returns.

In Figure 6.3, 1966 cost and return data are summarized for participating Iowa farms of 160–600 acres. The value of crops and livestock produced per acre, a farmer's gross return, was higher for small farms. But costs per acre were also higher and net returns per acre were under $15 on 160-acre farms. As farm size increased, gross return per acre declined, but so did costs per acre. A large part of the lower production costs was explained by lower machine costs which varied from $29 per acre on 160-acre farms to $18 per acre on 600-acre farms. Other categories of costs per acre for taxes, fertilizer, and similar materials varied little. The one additional category which did vary was operator and family labor cost per acre. As farm size increased, the charge or allowance for family and operator labor fell from $19 to $7 per acre. Operator and

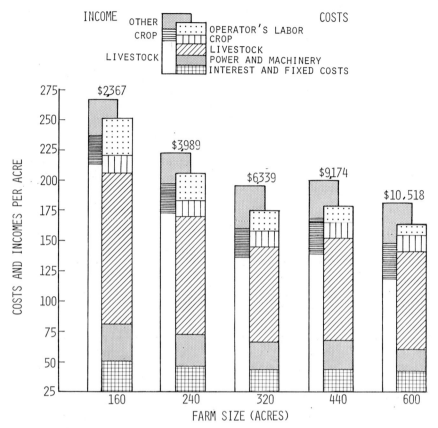

Fig. 6.3. Costs and incomes on Iowa farms in 1966, based on Iowa farm records summary (1966).

family labor was spread over more acres on the larger farm, and labor costs per acre dropped accordingly.

These differences in cost between large and small farms cause a large difference in net returns to land, capital, and management. On 160-acre farms, net returns of $15 per acre resulted in a per farm income of $2,367. But on 600-acre farms, a net return of just over $17 per acre when combined with the larger number of acres gave a return of $10,518 per farm.

These data for 1966 indicate that there was little difference in net returns per acre for different-sized farms in Iowa. The large difference in income per farm was explained by the size of the farm. However, the 1966 production year was unusual in terms of the set of prices that existed for crops and livestock. Small farms tended to gain from higher livestock prices, since livestock makes up a higher proportion of income per acre on the smaller farm. This same trend is not as evident in the

data for 1968 which are shown in Figure 6.4. Gross returns per acre
for 1968 are much lower and more nearly constant for varying farm sizes.
This small variation in gross income per acre, combined with higher
production costs per acre on the smaller farms, results in net losses to
capital, land, and management. Lower production costs on the larger
farms results in positive incomes to farms of 320 acres and larger. The
lower level of farm prices in 1968 gives lower net incomes for all sizes
of farms, but the larger farms have a significant income advantage.

Given the incentives of larger incomes associated with larger farms,
farm operators will continue to expand farm size. Small farm operators
with less than optimum combinations of land, labor, and capital will
find it increasingly difficult to compete as real prices of farm commodities slowly trend downward to reflect the growing production capacity
and output resulting from modern technology and lower costs of pro-

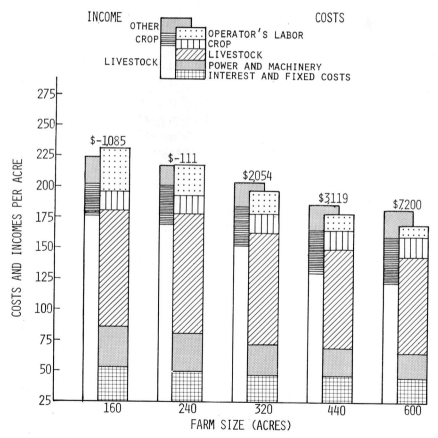

Fig. 6.4. Costs and incomes on Iowa farms in 1968, based on Iowa
farm records summary (1968).

ducing crops on larger farms. As previously noted, machine costs per acre are significantly lower on larger farms, indicating the need to spread large depreciation costs of modern machines over a larger number of acres. Labor costs also decline with increased farm size which indicates the tendency for labor to be more fully employed on larger farms. Both of these forces as well as the prospects of larger machines of the future will cause future increases in farm size, decrease in farm numbers, and fewer people on farms by 1980.

STRUCTURAL CHANGE AND RURAL COMMUNITIES ● The full effects of structural change in agriculture do not end at the farm gate but rather extend into the main streets of rural communities. As farm numbers decline and farm family customers leave the area, a whole set of service businesses in rural towns feel a decline in sales. Such secondary effects growing out of the structural transformation of agriculture have led to widespread support in small towns and communities for farm programs which reduce the economic pressure on less efficient farms to terminate farming operations. Programs of price support have kept market prices of major commodities above market clearing levels, thus keeping marginal farms and marginal farming areas in crop production. In turn, farm programs removed a substitute set of acres located on almost all farms and in almost all regions of the nation from crop production. In this way the full effects of capital-land and capital-labor substitutions were spread over all farming regions and diminished the intensity for any one particular region. While some amount of production efficiency was given up, a great deal of economic and social welfare was gained for the farm and nonfarm rural families involved.

Programs to spread effects of structural change across all farming regions have not removed all effects on small communities. Even farming states with highly fertile and productive cropland where only a minimum number of acres were diverted from production still felt the effects of structural change in rural towns. While little research has focused on the full effects of these changes (especially compared with the amounts spent on analyzing structural change in farming), aggregate data indicate how changes in the structure of agriculture reflect throughout rural towns. Figure 6.5 summarizes data on changes in the number of retail stores in Iowa for the period 1958–67. The total number of retail stores declined by 7 percent with the number of certain businesses declining even more rapidly. Nearly one-fourth of all food stores, building material and hardware stores, and farm equipment dealers went out of business during this one decade. Partially offsetting this decline was a large increase in stores selling feed, grain, and farm supplies. But the gains to owners of feed stores are independent of the losses to other businesses which discontinued operation.

Some indication of the economic forces contributing toward a reduction or expansion in store numbers is given in Figure 6.6. Total sales

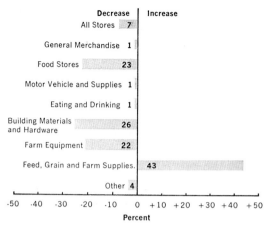

Fig. 6.5. Percentage change in number of retail stores by commodity groups, Iowa, 1958–67. (Excludes stores operated exclusively by the proprietor and/or unpaid family labor.) Source: Census of Business, 1958 and 1967, U.S. Dept. of Commerce. Reprinted from Eber Eldridge, C. Phillip Baumel, and Don Nelson, One Stop Agribusiness Centers: What Impact on Iowa Communities, Iowa Farm Science, April 1970, pp. 3–7.

of all retail stores in Iowa increased by 50 percent between 1958 and 1967. Some stores, most notably building materials and hardware, experienced a much smaller increase. If one takes account of the impact of inflation over this period, the value of sales in these stores actually declined. In fact, all stores had to increase sales by an average of 15.7 percent just to keep ahead of the effects of inflation. With a tendency toward declining profit margins in most retail businesses, just keeping up with inflation probably meant that a business could not maintain its net income position. Families dependent on income from such businesses found a slowly declining standard of living. Some found it neces-

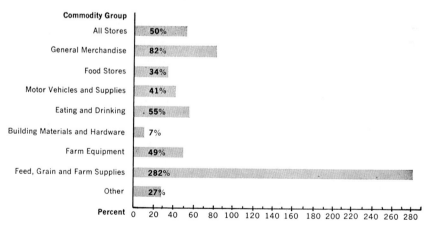

Fig. 6.6. Percentage increase in sales of retail stores by commodity groups, Iowa, 1958–67. (Excludes stores operated exclusively by the proprietor and/or unpaid family labor.) Sources: Census of Business, 1958 and 1967, U.S. Dept. of Commerce. Reprinted from Eldridge, Baumel, and Nelson, One Stop Agribusiness Centers, Iowa Farm Science, April 1970, pp. 3–7.

sary to terminate their businesses and move to other areas where expanding production levels brought rising employment and income levels. Rural areas dependent on agriculture for major production enterprises found the opposite trend as technology increased output per man at a rapid rate and total man-hours required for agriculture declined. In addition, total acres of cropland needed also declined, speeding up the decline in labor requirements.

FARM PROGRAMS AND STRUCTURAL CHANGE ● The reduction in land area needed for crop production has sizeable implications for marginal farming regions of the United States. Given a farm program to encourage retirement of marginal areas of production, these areas would transfer large acreages from intensive farming activities to extensive farming activities. For some regions transferring from intensive (cropping) to extensive (grassland) farming would mean a vast change in the structure of rural communities. To illustrate the magnitude of this change, we selected two farming areas in the Great Plains, one extensive and one intensive, and made a comparison of the structures of each. An eleven-county area located in Nebraska is representative of extensive farming with livestock on pasture and range as the major farming activity. This region, largely restrained by soil and climatic conditions, already has a community and farming structure based on extensive farm operations. A second thirteen-county area, located in South Dakota, is a more general farming area with both crop and livestock production. This area has considerable marginal land which, if given the opportunity to enter government programs, would do so. A large portion of the cropland in this particular region was retired on a voluntary bid basis under the Conservation Reserve Program of the 1950s. If a similar program was again set up, or if agriculture were to depend on market prices to allocate production among regions, this particular region would be under considerable economic pressure to transfer land from crop production to other uses. Eventually, the structure of the marginal farming area might approach that of the grassland farming area. While this shift would be slow and require at least a decade, the changes implied are considerable. In Table 6.6, data for the two areas indicate that in terms of land area the two are of similar size, and total land in farms is nearly equal. But here the similarities of the two regions end. The marginal farming area has about three times as much of its farmland in crops as the grassland area has. The grassland farming area has over 7 million acres of its farmland in pasture; the marginal farming area has only about 3 million acres in pasture. These differences in land use cause a sharp difference in numbers of farms; the marginal farming area had 8,602 in 1964, and the grassland farming area had 3,448.

Further differences are also evident. Less than one-fourth as many people live in the extensive farming area as in the general farming area.

Table 6.6 ● Major Characteristics of a Marginal Farming Community and of a Grassland Farming Community in the Great Plains

Area characteristics	Units	Marginal crop farming area	Grassland farming area
Total land area	acres	8,576,640	9,011,840
Land in farms	acres	8,238,881	8,583,681
In crops	%	45.7	15.3
In pasture	%	38.0	81.7
Farms	number	8,602	3,448
Average size	acres	958	3,506
Total population	number	108,782	23,795
On farms	%	31.6	36.9
Towns	number	81	41
Under 1,000 pop.	number	71	38
1,000 to 2,500 pop.	number	7	2
Over 2,500 pop.	number	3	1
Total cash receipts	$	115,025,330	50,886,412
From crops	$	35,584,189	1,374,186
From livestock	$	79,379,837	49,504,186
Total cash expenses	$	52,579,292	24,675,393
For livestock	$	18,528,518	8,945,002
For feed	$	11,149,385	7,774,235
For fuel	$	10,842,236	2,999,350
For seed	$	2,806,097	230,085
For fertilizer	$	1,300,987	329,215
Machinery inventory			
Automobiles	number	11,609	3,505
Motor trucks	number	12,611	3,767
Tractors	number	23,432	8,500

Source: U. S. Dept. of Commerce, Population Census for 1960, Bureau of the Census; U. S. Dept. of Commerce, Census of Agriculture for 1964.

NOTE: With a government program to retire less productive acres, the marginal farming area would tend to shift toward a structure like the grassland farming area. While the shift would be very slow, the results in terms of number of farms, towns, people, and sales of local businesses would be substantial.

Of these, about the same proportion of people live on farms, about 35 percent in both regions. There is also a large difference in the number of towns and communities which each farming base supports. The grassland farming area has forty-one towns with two towns over 1,000 population and one town over 2,500 population. The marginal farming area has eighty-one towns with seven towns over 1,000 population and three towns above 2,500 population.

The explanation for the different structures is found in the cash flows from farming operations in each area. Cash receipts in the grassland farming areas were $50.9 million in 1964, the latest data available for these regions. The marginal farming area receipts were twice as large, $115.0 million. Cash expenditures by farmers were also twice as great in the marginal farming area. The machinery inventory, indicating past expenditures for large capital items, shows a large difference in the two areas. The grassland area had 8,500 tractors on hand while the marginal farming area had 23,432. Automobiles and motor trucks were in a similar ratio for the two areas.

The evidence presented above, while representing different communities because of natural endowments of soils and climate, helps to explain the changes which occur when land is shifted from crop production to idleness or grassland. As total acres of cropland used for crop production have trended downward, the changes in purchase of farm inputs have affected local towns and communities. To reduce the effect on any particular location, programs have taken a few acres out of production on each farm in all production areas.

These programs have received wide support by the nonfarm public in rural areas. These groups tend to lose less economically under such programs than under programs which remove whole farms. Under a whole-farm retirement program, landowners or operators receive an equivalent net return on each acre of cropland. Closing down their farming operations, with compensation for doing so, they can migrate occupationally and geographically to employment opportunities which provide a supplemental source of income. Older operators can simply retire. But with the land out of production the picture differs for local businesses. Purchases of machines, gasoline, seed, and fertilizer decline. Local communities feel a sharp drop in farm input sales as well as consumer expenditures. These result in a decline in employment opportunities, an increase in the rate of business terminations, and dislocation of proprietors and their families.

But it should not be forgotten that these same trends and outcomes have also occurred under past government programs where only a few acres of land on each farm were removed from production. The process of farm structural change has been going on for some time. Government programs had a tendency only to slow the rate of change.

GAINS AND LOSSES FROM TECHNOLOGICAL TRANSFORMA-
TION ● Regarded in retrospect, the capitalization and industrializa-
tion of agriculture has released a large amount of manpower from food
production. For the nation as a whole, the result was that fewer labor
resources were required to produce the food and fiber needs of the nation. For the family leaving farming, the outcome may or may not have
represented an improvement in economic and social conditions. Given
the appropriate set of skills, families transferring to nonfarm occupations
could improve their earning ability. But such a transfer requires different
skills, education, or training in general. These additions may have costs
attached to them. In terms of social conditions, the transfer may have
little effect if rural living is continued, even at the same annual income.
If the transfer is to a larger-sized city, however, social standings and real
income may suffer considerably. Higbee has pointed out that "since
agriculture has developed a highly effective production machine and
its unneeded human resources have been shifted to the city, America
has been confronted with two kinds of surpluses. In the country there is
a surplus of food. In the city there is a surplus of labor. To relieve
these twin problems, two forms of public subsidy have been required—
one to compensate farmers for food they cannot sell, the other to compensate the unemployed for labor they cannot expend. Thus far the
federal budget to relieve the problem of farm surpluses has been more
generous than the federal budget to relieve the urban problem of surplus people. This in part is due to the influence of rural spokesmen
who contend that the problem of human surpluses is one for local
governments to resolve with local tax funds while the problem of farm
surpluses is one for the national treasury."[2]

The rapid adoption of farm capital technologies brings gain to the
urban or town industry which produces the new inputs. It brings gain
to leading farmers with the capital to adopt them rapidly enough to
increase profits. It brings gains to the workers who are employed to
fabricate them. Unfortunately, however, the persons added to the pay-
roll of fabricating plants are seldom those displaced from farming
through the same capital technologies. Sacrifice, either in the short run
or the long run, is often the reward of those who must leave farming.
The sacrifices spread to the small towns of the rural community as the
farm population thins through the process of technological improvement
and farm consolidation. A reduced volume of business has a multiplier
effect as it reduces retail volume for many establishments, reduces or
lowers the income from employment in village businesses, and provides
lowered support generally for rural institutions.

On the gain side, rapid technological advances bring gains to consumers in the form of lower real prices for food. They can even bring

2. Higbee, *Farms and Farmers*, p. 5.

reduced absolute prices if the resulting larger output or supply potential is not offset by price supports or other policy measures. They also bring gains to consumers as workers are reduced in agriculture, and more labor is available to produce other goods and services. In this context, farmers with enough capital to push rapidly forward in farm size and advanced technology can increase profits if they increase output by a greater proportion than prices decline. But farmers who are unable to do so bear a cost of structural change as their incomes decline. Falling particularly in this category are older farm persons, young farm families with insufficient capital, and others out of reach of new technical knowledge and its implementation at the farm level.

CHAPTER SEVEN

Net Cost of Demand Expansion under Public Law 480

THE OVERCAPACITY of U.S. agriculture has been underscored in almost every chapter of this book. More importantly, its effects have been evident to agricultural interests for several decades. In the recent past any relaxation of supply control programs has resulted in a sizeable jump in output of basic crops and eventually in livestock commodities. These "facts of life" are well known to the nearly 3 million farmers who make up the farm sector.

Efforts to remove the persistent overcapacity problem of U.S. agriculture have focused on two alternative types of programs. One set of programs attempted to shift the aggregate supply curve of farm commodities to the left through restricting the land input on thousands of individual farms. The second set of programs focused on shifting the aggregate demand curve to the right through programs to increase the quantities of food utilized by millions of individual consumers, both at home and abroad. These two sets of programs have been carried forward together as a means of relieving the pressures on U.S. farming to adapt the resource base to the new technological plateau on which farming operations rest. Programs of supply control have received the most attention in recent years (and the greatest amounts of public funds). But large amounts of public funds have also been expended on food distribution and disposal programs as well. Consequently, given the long-term outlook for supply capacity and world food requirements, some additional analysis of the net cost of demand expansion programs seems justified. This chapter analyzes the role of food aid in reducing the overcapacity problem and estimates the net government cost of shipments of major commodities under food aid programs.

BACKGROUND OF FOOD AID AND LAND RETIREMENT ●
The twin government programs of retiring cropland from production
with federal payments and the exportation of major crops under government programs with special conditions of financing are both a legacy
of the high price supports and expanded production levels established
during World War II. Programs of enlarging exports of major crops
under special kinds of financing were officially initiated in 1954 under
the Agricultural Trade Development and Assistance Act (PL 480, 83rd
Congress). Retirement of large acreages of cropland under government
programs began in 1956 with the inauguration of the Soil Bank Program. Public Law 480 programs provided that surpluses of farm commodities could be sold under special terms, or in some cases, simply
donated to foreign countries. Under the special terms provision, commodities were provided to countries in return for their own currency,
and this currency was placed in U.S. bank accounts in the recipient
country. Under the donation provision, supplies of food commodities
could be given to victims of disaster. Provision was also made for food
supplies to move through welfare organizations to persons otherwise
unable to fill their need for food. A later addition to the program allowed
sale of commodities for long-term credit at low interest rates but with
eventual payment in dollars.

The introduction of both land retirement and export promotion
programs in the 1950s was not coincidental. Both programs grew out
of difficulties of overproduction and low prices in the agricultural sector.
The overproduction problems were partly a carry-over of the enlarged
production base of the World War II period and partly a result of the
sharp decline in export markets after the Korean conflict. Farmers
achieved a rapid growth in farm productivity after 1950. Yields of all
major crops increased in excess of 3 percent annually. (See Table 1.1.)
By 1959, few disagreed with Willard W. Cochrane when he pointed
out that ". . . the aggregate output of agriculture is outdistancing a
very rapid rate of population growth in the United States by more than
one-half of one percent per year. And where the income elasticity of
raw farm products approaches zero, as in the United States, this imbalance . . . properly measures the additional pressure of supply on
demand each year, hence measures the increased downward pressure on
farm prices (or, under price supports, the widening of annual rate of
surplus)."[1] The downward pressures on farm prices resulted in a major
emphasis on two policy alternatives: reduced acreages of land for major
crops and increased shipments of farm commodities to foreign markets.
Land retirement was instituted to slow growth in output; demand expansion was initiated to increase exports to nations recuperating from
the effects of World War II and the Korean conflict.

1. Willard W. Cochrane, Farm Technology, Foreign Surplus Disposal and Domestic
Supply Control, *Journal of Farm Economics* 41, no. 5 (December 1959): 886.

Long-Term Trends in Agricultural Trade ● United States exports of agricultural commodities have increased considerably since PL 480 programs were started. Between 1952–56 and 1962–66, world trade in wheat doubled and the proportion of world wheat exports supplied by the United States increased from 33.5 to 38.5 percent (Table 7.1). Feed grains (corn, barley, and oats) also followed a similar trend; world trade more than doubled over the period and the proportion shipped by the United States rose from 30.3 percent to 47.5 percent. In the case of wheat, Canada was the main country affected by the increased U.S. shipments. However while Canada's proportion of wheat exports declined, the large increase in total world wheat trade still allowed Canada larger total exports in 1962–66 than a decade earlier. In the case of feed grains, the reduction of shipments from Canada resulted primarily from increased demand for domestic utilization. As more feed grains were used domestically, smaller quantities were available for export.

The last century of world trade in agricultural commodities indicates some substantial shifts in the food situations in individual countries. At one period in history, India exported 10 percent of the total world trade in wheat. This has dwindled until today that nation is a large importer of wheat. Another historical feature of agricultural trade has been a change in exports of wheat from Russia. During the late stages of the Czarist era, that country exported nearly one-fourth of all wheat moving in world trade. After 1917, exports of wheat nearly ended and only recently have they shown a tendency to increase. A similar trend is evident with feed grains. Before 1917, Russia exported over one-third of the corn, oats, and barley in world trade. After 1917, those exports dropped sharply, and only in recent years has Russia increased its share of feed grains exports. A downward trend is also evident in farm exports from the Danube countries (which include most of Western and Eastern Europe). Exports of both wheat and feed grains from these countries have dropped during the last century.

Besides the United States, two remaining nations, Argentina and Australia, export sizeable quantities of wheat and feed grains. Argentina at one period was a major exporter of wheat and feed grains. Australia has more recently become a major wheat exporter, and in recent years has ranked third in the world. The United States provided one-fourth of world wheat exports and one-fifth of world feed grains exports as early as 1885. Only during 1934–38 did U.S. wheat shipments fall below 10 percent of total world trade. Total wheat shipments fell during this period, indicating the effect of severe economic conditions on trade between nations. However, world feed grains trade during this period remained fairly stable.

Crop Production and Land Use ● The favorable record of exports from the United States indicates that total agricultural production has far

Table 7.1 ● Percentage Distribution of Annual World Exports (Gross) of Wheat and Feed Grains from 1854-58 to 1962-66

	1854-58	1884-88	1909-13	1924-28	1934-38	1952-56	1962-66
				Wheat (%)			
United States	24.9	35.8	14.5	22.1	8.0	33.5	38.5
Canada	6.4	1.2	12.6	35.2	27.9	31.3	23.4
Russia	12.0	25.3	22.3	2.1	4.2	2.6	6.4
Danube countries	9.8	18.6	15.8	4.2	7.6	1.1	2.2
Argentina	...	1.4	13.2	16.8	19.3	8.8	7.4
Australia	...	2.4	6.9	10.6	16.4	9.8	11.4
India	3.2	10.1	7.1	2.1	1.6	...	...
Other	43.7	5.2	7.6	6.9	15.0	12.9	10.7
Total	100.0	100.0	100.0	100.0	100.0	100.0	100.0
				(thousand metric tons)			
Total	2,544	9,500	19,696	23,852	17,332	27,142	55,489
				Feed grains (%)			
United States	16.8	20.3	9.2	10.0	7.8	30.	47.5
Canada	2.6	4.0	1.9	7.9	3.2	20.2	2.9
Russia	16.8	36.4	36.2	3.7	3.1	2.6	4.8
Danube countries	26.9	24.4	17.3	15.8	11.1	3.2	4.4
Argentina	...	3.7	23.2	44.9	53.3	14.2	11.4
Australia	...	...	...	0.2	0.6	5.0	2.3
Other	36.9	11.2	12.2	17.5	20.9	24.5	26.7
Total	100.0	100.0	100.0	100.0	100.0	100.0	100.0
				(thousand metric tons)			
Corn	535	2,590	6,800	8,452	10,049	5,386	22,745
Barley	350	1,910	5,536	3,541	2,655	5,900	6,933
Oats	272	1,414	3,041	1,658	878	1,511	1,429
Total	1,157	5,914	15,377	13,651	13,582	12,797	31,107

Sources: Data for 1854-58 to 1952-56 are from Robert M. Stern, A century of food exports, pp. 127-42, in Robert L. Tontz (ed), Foreign Agricultural Trade: Selected Readings (Ames: Iowa State Univ. Press, 1966); data for 1962-66 are from FAO, Trade Yearbook, Rome, 1967.

exceeded domestic needs. That favorable record has largely resulted from two factors: a supply of land resources which have been relatively elastic even at constant commodity prices, and the continuous introduction of various kinds of yield-increasing technologies which doubled production per crop acre between 1910 and 1960. Over the decade between 1952–56 and 1962–66, production increased so rapidly that government programs were initiated and reduced major crop acreages by 43 million acres (Table 7.2). Even with reduced acreages, total farm production rose 15 percent, a result of a 28 percent increase in production per acre.

The required reduction in harvested crop acreage resulted largely from overproduction of a few specific crops. Wheat acreage in the early 1950s totaled over 70 million acres as high prices held over from World War II induced increased plantings. By 1962–66, acreage quotas had reduced harvested wheat acreage by some 10 million acres although total production continued to climb, the result of an upturn in yields. Between 1884–88 and 1934–38 wheat production per acre did not increase at all, and yields were actually lower in the latter period. But by the mid-1950s, wheat production per acre was up nearly 50 percent and a decade later had doubled the 1934–38 average. Total production rose greatly between the 1880s and 1962–66, and the sharp changes in production were reflected in large fluctuations in export levels (Table 7.1) particularly during the two periods, 1934–38 and 1962–66.

While wheat acres first increased after 1880 and then declined, feed grains acreage continually declined. In 1884–88, the three feed grains—corn, oats, and barley—were harvested from a total of 168.6 million acres of cropland. Grain sorghum was not included since it only recently became a major crop in the United States. Also, it was not included in Table 7.2 and to provide comparability was left out of Table 7.3. But yields of feed grains started increasing early in the 1900s and rose consistently after the 1934–38 period. By 1962–66, feed grains yields were nearly four times the 1884–88 average. Acreage was reduced almost by half between 1884–88 and 1962–66. Some of the freed acres were shifted first into wheat production, but later many were removed from all production under government programs of land retirement.

Cotton acreage in the United States has also gone through a cycle of expansion and contraction. Between 1884–88 and 1924–28, harvested cotton acreage more than doubled. But acreage tapered off after that and during the 1930s averaged below 30 million acres annually. Even during World War II, cotton acreage continued to decline, and two decades later, 1962–66, cotton acreage harvested was less than one-half of the 1930s average in the United States. Production of cotton has remained relatively constant since 1903–13. Cotton prices have trended upward for most of this period. In recent years, a government program has reduced the market price and substituted direct government payments to maintain total revenue per bale of cotton.

As these data show, total crop acreage in the United States has

Table 7.2 ● Acreages, Yields, and Production of Major Crops in United States with Export Acreages and Prices Received by Producers

	1854–58	1884–88	1909–13	1924–28	1934–38	1952–56	1962–66
All crops							
Harvested acreage	…	…	329	359	334	341	298
Export acreage	…	…	36	50	22	42	72
Crop failure acreage	…	…	10	14	33	15	8
Production (per acre)[a]	…	…	69	69	64	90	118
Total production	…	…	64	72	68	95	110
Wheat							
Harvested acreage	…	36.30	48.10	56.10	55.40	58.10	47.50
Export acreage	…	5.80	3.70	8.90	2.20	15.40	27.10
Yield (per acre)	…	13.20	14.20	14.70	12.90	18.60	25.90
Total production	…	479.90	681.70	826.40	715.60	1,080.40	1,231.00
Price (per bu)[b]	…	.73	.87	1.20	.65	2.04	1.63
Cotton							
Harvested acreage	…	18.30	33.00	41.80	28.40	20.40	13.40
Export acreage	…	5.70	11.20	12.20	6.70	2.70	4.00
Yield (per acre)	…	.36	.39	.36	.45	.72	1.04
Total production	3.1	6.60	13.00	15.00	12.70	14.70	14.00
Price (per lb)	…	8.52	12.01	18.29	10.26	32.91	29.14
Feed grains[c]							
Harvested acreage	…	168.60	145.40	150.90	140.80	128.50	88.40
Yield (per acre)	…	.40	.65	.52	.54	.93	1.53
Total production	…	66.80	94.90	77.90	75.40	119.40	135.60
Price (per ton)	…	13.68	22.24	36.16	23.72	48.93	40.83

Sources: U. S. Dept. of Commerce, Historical Statistics of the United States, Colonial Times to 1957, Statistical Abstract of the United States Supplement, Bureau of the Census, 1960; and Statistical Abstract of the United States, 1964–68.

NOTE: Acreages are million acres; yields per acre are bushels for wheat, pounds for cotton, and tons for feed grains; total production is million bushels for wheat, million bales for cotton, and million tons for feed grains.

[a]Simple 5-year average of published production index, 1957–59 = 100.
[b]Weighted 5-year average.
[c]Corn, oats, and barley; grain sorghum is not included.

trended downward over the last several decades. Harvested acreage of all crops reached a high in the period 1924–28, with production from 50 million acres entering export markets. Total acres of harvested crops tapered off during the 1934–38 period primarily as a result of weather, although severe economic conditions also caused some reduction. But the decline in the total number of harvested acres of crops in the 1934–38 period was only temporary; large increases took place during World War II. Crop acreages remained large through 1954 primarily because the Korean conflict provided a demand for most commodities. Export acreage totaled 42 million acres between 1952–56 with prices for major commodities at record levels.

The decade after the Korean conflict saw a rapid decline in acreages harvested. Total crop acreage harvested fell to twentieth century lows. Wheat, feed grains (not including grain sorghum), and cotton acreages totaled 149 million acres in the period 1962–66. These crops used nearly a hundred million acres less cropland in 1962–66 than in 1924–28, falling from 248.8 million acres. Fortunately for entrepreneurs with large investments in farmland, other crops expanded somewhat, notably soybeans and grain sorghum, and government programs removed large acreages of cropland from potential production. Instead of a large reduction in land prices as might have occurred, land prices continued to climb throughout most of this period.

Land Diversion and Government Export Programs ● Several types of government programs have been utilized in removing acres of cropland from production since 1956. Total diverted acres increased from 13.6 million to 63.3 million between 1956 and 1966 (Table 1.3). The Feed Grain Program removed a large number of acres from production and facilitated a further reduction in feed grains acreage. The Conservation Reserve Program initially played a major role in removing cropland from production.

Although land diversion programs prevented a large amount of potential production, a significant part of what was produced still found no commercial market. To keep grain stocks from accumulating to unacceptable levels, a part of this production was moved into markets where nutritional demand existed but economic demand did not. Some of this production went into domestic programs to supplement the diet of low-income families. But a much larger portion was shipped into foreign markets under PL 480.

Wheat was the major crop exported under specially financed government programs (Table 7.3). In several years after the inception of the program, over 40 percent of U.S. wheat production moved into world markets under its provisions. A much smaller proportion of feed grains, less than 3 percent in most years, moved under government programs. Primarily this small proportion is a result of the domestic use of most feed grains; less than 15 percent of feed grains production

Table 7.3 ● Exports of Major Cereals under PL 480 Programs, 1954-67

Year beginning July	Sales for foreign currency or long-term dollar credit	Disaster relief, foreign donations and other assistance	Barter	Total PL 480 shipments	Total production[a]	Percentage PL 480 exports of production
			Wheat (thousand bu)			
1954	23,802	16,954	46,459	87,215	983,900	8.86
1955	94,347	14,652	66,716	175,715	937,094	18.75
1956	200,536	23,924	87,086	311,546	1,005,397	30.99
1957	179,023	31,688	9,807	220,518	955,740	23.07
1958	227,914	31,732	20,062	279,708	1,457,435	19.19
1959	300,648	32,827	25,662	359,137	1,117,735	32.13
1960	327,214	61,499	34,090	422,803	1,354,709	31.21
1961	386,396	63,316	41,337	491,049	1,232,359	39.85
1962	413,065	58,721	6,493	478,279	1,091,958	43.80
1963	400,102	69,076	35,167	504,345	1,146,821	43.98
1964	500,633	55,932	12,441	569,006	1,283,371	44.34
1965	459,675	65,957	45,522	571,154	1,315,613	43.41
1966	253,535	51,739	67,351	372,625	1,311,702	28.41
1967	331,534	13,828	80,352	425,714	1,522,382	27.96
			Feed grains[b] (thousand tons)			
1954	153	8	529	769	114,073	0.67
1955	551	46	3,493	4,090	120,846	3.38
1956	805	295	2,318	3,418	119,308	2.86
1957	1,110	434	359	1,903	132,424	1.44
1958	1,401	362	590	2,353	144,121	1.63
1959	1,375	373	1,101	2,849	149,605	1.90
1960	1,031	578	957	2,566	155,618	1.65
1961	1,038	840	1,193	3,071	140,626	2.18
1962	840	451	741	2,032	142,899	1.42
1963	995	501	277	1,773	156,432	1.13
1964	861	451	385	1,697	134,200	1.26
1965	1,659	452	236	2,347	157,400	1.49

Table 7.3 ● *(Continued)*

Year beginning July	Sales for foreign currency or long-term dollar credit	Disaster relief, foreign donations and other assistance	Barter	Total P L 480 shipments	Total production[a]	Percentage P L 480 exports of production
1966	3,500	412	426	4,338	157,600	2.64
1967	1,758.	485	659	2,902	175,100	1.66

Source: U. S. Congress, House, <u>1968 Annual Report on Public Law 480</u>, 91st Cong., 1st sess., H. Doc. 104 (1969).

[a]Calendar year.
[b]Includes corn, oats, barley, and grain sorghum.

233

is exported. Over 50 percent of the wheat crop has been exported under PL 480 in some recent years.

The history of land diversion and export programs points out that supply reduction and demand expansion represent alternative methods of handling excess production capacity of U.S. agriculture. The United States has developed two specific sets of programs, one to provide its agricultural sector with a market for its excess land resources, and a second to absorb excess commodities above domestic and commercial export demand. Together, these two sets of programs have slowed the outflow of resources from the agricultural industry.

Costs for Supply Control and Demand Expansion ● Costs of programs to restrain production or increase demand have increased substantially since their inception. Land-use and price support programs had a total cost of $257 million in 1954 with the majority being spent on conservation programs (Table 7.4). After 1956, costs for these programs doubled as the Soil Bank Program was initiated to restrain crop production. As the number of acres retired increased in 1957, total costs again doubled, reaching over $1 billion. While this trend was temporarily reversed in 1959 and 1960, it started again after 1961 and reached $2 billion by 1964 and $3.5 billion by 1968. For this level of expenditure, several things were accomplished. Some 50 million acres of cropland were held out of production, other acres of cropland were improved through conservation practices, and farmers received price support payments on portions of the remaining production. These various government programs resulted in direct income transfers to farm owners and tenants from the remainder of society.

A second set of transfer payments to farmers occurred less directly. These payments were made through government purchase of quantities of agricultural commodities through the CCC. Commodity Credit Corporation purchases allowed farmers to maintain a level of production above that dictated by domestic and commercial export demand. The majority of these commodities were eventually shipped to other countries under financing terms which allowed payment in their local currency. Most of these currencies were not convertible to major world currencies and hence could only be used for purchases within the recipient country.

The costs of PL 480 programs also increased after their inception in 1954. In the first full year of operation, these programs had a total cost of $430.9 million for purchase, shipment, and distribution of commodities in recipient countries (Table 7.5). This cost doubled in the second year of operation and again the next year. It reached a high in 1962 when total outlays were $2.4 billion but tapered off after that.

Together, programs of price support, supply control, and export expansion totaled nearly $50 billion during the period 1954–68. On the benefit side these programs assisted U.S. agriculture in the structural

Table 7.4 ● Government Payments to Farmers under Various Land-Use and Price Support Programs, 1954–68

Calendar year	Conservation Program	Sugar Act	Wool Program	Soil Bank Program	Feed Grain Program	Wheat Program	Cotton	Total[a]
				($ millions)				
1954	217	40	...	...	...	...	...	257
1955	188	41	...	...	...	...	...	229
1956	220	37	54	243	...	...	...	554
1957	230	32	53	700	...	...	...	1,016
1958	214	44	14	815	...	...	...	1,089
1959	228	44	82	323	...	...	...	682
1960	217	59	51	370	...	...	...	693
1961	230	53	56	334	772	42	...	1,484
1962	224	64	54	304[b]	841	253	...	1,736
1963	222	67	37	304[b]	843	215	...	1,686
1964	227	79	25	199	1,163	483	39	2,169
1965	215	75	18	160	1,391	525	70	2,452
1966	220	71	34	145	1,293	679	773	3,266[c]
1967	226	70	29	129	865	731	932	3,071[c]
1968	215	75	66	114	1,366	747	787	3,452[c]

Source: U.S. Dept. of Agriculture, Farm Income Situation, USDA ERS, July 1969.

[a] Includes Great Plains conservation payments since 1958.
[b] Includes land-use adjustment program and cropland conversion and Appalachia programs.
[c] Includes cropland adjustment program.

Table 7.5 ● Gross Cost of Financing Programs Carried Out under the Agricultural Trade Development and Assistance Aid of 1954

Year beginning July 1	Title I Sales for foreign currencies	Title I Long-term credit sales for dollars	Title II - donations Famine and other emergency relief	Title II - donations Voluntary agency programs	Title III Bartered materials for supplemental stockpile	Total
			($ millions)			
1954	129.5	...	86.9	214.5	...	430.9
1955	624.2	...	93.6	271.2	...	989.0
1956	1,396.4	...	124.9	234.1	217.3	1,972.7
1957	1,144.7	...	121.4	254.3	83.9	1,604.3
1958	1,113.3	...	97.9	178.7	314.7	1,704.6
1959	1,308.0	...	95.5	130.8	192.4	1,726.7
1960	1,557.3	...	198.6	169.3	200.5	2,125.7
1961	1,606.1	29.0	241.9	191.7	193.3	2,262.0
1962	1,739.4	80.3	215.6	238.8	99.7	2,373.8
1963	1,636.2	65.1	228.2	341.6	37.7	2,308.8
1964	1,505.8	211.0	147.2	174.6	40.6	2,079.2
1965	1,287.8	274.6	222.5	148.3	25.8	1,959.0
1966	1,067.8	221.7	335.9	34.2	32.5	1,692.1
1967	784.8	350.0	344.6	...	25.9	1,505.3

Source: U. S. Congress, House, 1968 Annual Report on Public Law 480.

adjustment problems growing out of the introduction of labor-saving output-increasing innovations. These innovations reduced labor and other resources needed per unit of food and thereby reduced food cost to society. Society in turn, through various government programs, placed limits on the amount and rate of structural adjustment required of the agricultural sector. The combination of programs used indicates that both supply reduction and demand expansion are feasible alternatives for handling and maintaining the food-producing capacity of the agricultural sector.

ESTIMATING THE NET COST OF U.S. FOOD AID ● As we have already noted, the United States has for some years given sizeable amounts of aid to other nations, both in the form of monetary resources and aid-in-kind. In 1966, 30.7 percent of U.S. aid consisted of shipments of food commodities under PL 480 programs (Table 7.6). Technically, these shipments were sold in return for local currency or long-term credit, but the preponderance of evidence is that a sizeable portion of such shipments will eventually turn out to be a form of economic aid, or in some instances, a simple grant. Even for that portion for which repayment is likely, the pricing policy should reflect the long-term ability of nations to repay and the realistic U.S. Government cost of such aid.

At least in the near future, the agricultural policy alternatives open to the U.S. Government are limited. Through a long series of public decisions, this nation has specified a set of public programs to maintain the social welfare of our agricultural sector and assure the nation of an abundant supply of food. To achieve this purpose, a large acreage of land is annually retired under government programs. Two possible alternatives exist regarding this land: It can be used to produce for noncommercial export markets, or it can be continually retired from production under government programs. In the past, the combination of these programs was determined partly by available government revenue and partly by the magnitude of food needs in other countries.

Supply reduction and demand expansion are complementary methods of handling excess production capacity of U.S. agriculture. A specific set of programs provides the agricultural sector with a market for excess land resources in one instance, and in another instance a market for price-supported commodities produced in excess of domestic and commercial export demand. These two programs have jointly managed to slow the structural reorganization of the agricultural industry and the outflow of resources.

To measure the net cost of food shipments under the two alternative uses of land (retirement or subsidized exports), a linear programming model was developed to simulate resource use in the agricultural sector. The major resource considered was cropland, since this resource forms a basic input in the crop production process and has been used as the major mechanism for controlling the aggregate supply of com-

Table 7.6 ● U.S. Economic Assistance to Other Regions of the World, by Kinds, during Fiscal Year 1966

Region	Total economic assistance	Kind of economic assistance ($ million)				Region share of total assistance (%)	PL 480 share of region's total assistance (%)
		Loans	Grants	PL 480	Other[a]		
Near East-South Asia	1,474.5	548.2	74.2	823.9	28.2	26.4	55.9
Latin America	1,387.7	505.4	142.0	202.2	538.1	24.7	14.6
East Asia[b]	1,264.9	76.6	761.5	292.6	134.2	22.5	23.1
Africa	388.3	88.9	80.6	141.8	77.0	6.9	36.5
Europe	468.0	-.3	-.2	205.4	263.1	8.3	43.9
Other	631.8	0	266.2	60.1	305.5	11.2	9.5
Total	5,615.2	1,218.8	1,324.3	1,726.0	1,346.1	100.0	30.7

Source: Agency for International Development, Proposed Foreign Aid Program FY 1968, (Washington D.C.: U. S. GPO, May 1967). Tables 1 and 2.

NOTE: Does not include military aid which totaled $1,046 million in 1966 (Statistical Abstract of the United States, 89th edition, 1968).

[a]Includes Export-Import Bank long-term loans; Peace Corps, supplementary contribution to the Inter-American Development Bank and the International Development Association; and other miscellaneous programs.
[b]Includes Vietnam.

modities. Through government programs the available supply of cropland has been institutionalized; that is, production units have been given specific allotments for production of certain crops. When the national base or allotment has resulted in overproduction at supported price levels, the government has retired excess acres of land from the producer to reduce aggregate production.

Supply control or land retirement programs have in effect placed a two-way restraint on the total land resources available for major crops. One restraint arises because total cropland available is limited for any given level of technology. This restraint takes the form

$$x_1 + x_2 + \ldots + x_n \leq L \qquad (7.1)$$

where x_i represents the amount of land used in the production of crop i; $(i = 1, \ldots, n)$. Thus land use in the production of crops cannot exceed total available cropland L. Under conditions where land resources required for crop production are less than total land available, the inequality of this restraint holds, and excess land resources remain idle.

But with supply control programs in use in the United States, excess land resources are no longer forced by the market to lie idle when removed from production under government programs. To account for this new type of relationship in a model for evaluating land resource use, an additional land-using activity must be defined so that

$$x_1 + x_2 + \ldots + x_n + R = L \qquad (7.2)$$

where $x_1, x_2, \ldots, x_n$ denotes acres of crops, and R is retirement of acres of cropland under government programs. These two kinds of activities must use all available cropland. If all land is required for production to meet potential demand, then retirement activities remain at zero level. However if potential production exceeds demand, then retirement activities absorb the excess cropland.

Whether cropland is used for production of a crop or is retired under a government program, there are costs associated with its use. These costs may be expressed in a cost function,

$$C = \Sigma c_i x_i + c_r R \qquad (7.3)$$

which specifies that retiring each unit of cropland costs c_r, and each unit used for crop production costs c_i. To derive a net cost of using cropland for production of the i-th crop, Equation (7.2) can be solved for R and substituted into Equation (7.3) giving

$$C = \Sigma c_i x_i + c_r(L - \Sigma x_i) \qquad (7.4)$$

and total cost becomes a function of the total supply of land and total acres of crop production. Equation (7.4) can be rearranged as

$$C = \Sigma(c_i - c_r)x_i + c_rL \tag{7.5}$$

which denotes that the cost of each unit of x_i is the cost of crop production c_i less the cost of retiring the same cropland c_r. Thus the net cost of producing an acre of crop is

$$NC = c_i - c_r \tag{7.6}$$

The net cost per unit of production may be found by dividing Equation (7.6) by the yield per acre of the i-th crop.

The concept of net cost outlined above is an integral part of the linear programming model for this study. As used, it represents a means of estimating the net cost of using marginal units of cropland for supplying food to other nations or of retiring the cropland from production under government programs. It provides estimates of the net government cost of food shipments provided to other nations under PL 480 programs and provides a basis for developing pricing policies for future sales under these programs.

A Model to Measure Net Cost of Food Aid Shipments ● The model used for this chapter is similar to Chapter 3 in that the United States is divided into 150 crop-producing areas and 31 demand regions for the analysis. Each demand region includes one or more production areas. The following activities are defined for the model:

1. Crop production activities are defined for production of wheat, feed grains, soybeans, and cotton in each production area to satisfy domestic and commercial export demand in the 31 demand regions; a separate set of activities is defined for production of wheat, feed grains, and cotton for export under PL 480 programs.
2. Land retirement activities are defined for retiring from production cropland in each of the 150 crop production areas not required to satisfy domestic demand, commercial export demand, or shipments of wheat, feed grains, or cotton under PL 480 programs.
3. Transportation activities are defined for inland transportation of wheat, feed grains, and soybeans from points of production to point of domestic utilization in each of the 31 demand regions or the port of commercial export.
4. Shifting activities are defined for shifting wheat from food use to feed use within each of the 31 demand regions.
5. Shipping activities are defined for shipment of each commodity— wheat, feed grains, and cotton—from the United States to each recipient country under PL 480 programs.

For each of the activities in the model an associated cost is estimated. Together these costs form the total cost function C where

$$
C = \sum_{i=1}^{150} \sum_{j=1}^{4} c_{ij} X_{ij} + \sum_{i=1}^{150} \sum_{j=1}^{3} c_{ij} Z_{ij}
$$

$$
+ \sum_{i=1}^{150} \sum_{k=1}^{3} c_{ik} R_{ik} + \sum_{n=1}^{31} \sum_{n'=1}^{31} \sum_{j=1}^{3} c_{nn'j} T_{nn'j}
$$

$$
+ \sum_{n=1}^{31} c_n S_n + \sum_{r=1}^{7} \sum_{j=1}^{3} c_{rj} U_{rj} \qquad (7.7)
$$

and

    X is crop production for domestic and commercial export
    Z is crop production for shipment under PL 480 programs
    R is land retirement under government programs
    T is inland transportation of commodities between the n-th and n'-th demand regions (n $\neq$ n')
    S is shifting of wheat from food use to feed use, and
    U is international shipping of food aid commodities

The subscripts define the

    i-th crop production area
    j-th crop produced within each crop production area
    k-th government program for retiring cropland
    n-th and n'-th demand regions in the United States and
    r-th recipient country which receives food aid

Domestic and commercial export demand is included in the models as a set of restraints which must be satisfied by the production activities. Demand for wheat, feed grains, and soybeans is specified for the thirty-one demand regions defined for the United States. Demand for cotton is specified as an aggregate for the United States. These demands form a set of restraints requiring that—

$$
\sum_{i=1}^{m} a_{ij} X_{ij} - q_n S_n \pm \sum_{n=1}^{31} \sum_{n'=1}^{31} s_{nn'j} T_{nn'j} \geq D_{nj} \qquad (7.8)
$$

$$
\sum_{i=1}^{m} a_{ij} X_{ij} + q_{nj} S_{nj} \pm \sum_{n=1}^{31} \sum_{n'=1}^{31} s_{nn'j} T_{nn'j} \geq D_{nj} \qquad (7.9)
$$

$$\sum_{i=1}^{m} a_{ij}X_{ij} + \sum_{i=1}^{m} a_{ij}X_{ij}$$

$$\pm \sum_{n=1}^{31} \sum_{n'=1}^{31} S_{nn'j}T_{nn'j} \geq D_{nj} \tag{7.10}$$

$$\sum_{i=1}^{m} a_{ij}X_{ij} \geq D_{j} \tag{7.11}$$

where Equation (7.8) expresses the demand for wheat for the n-th demand region; Equation (7.9) expresses the demand for feed grains in the n-th demand region; Equation (7.10) expresses the demand for oil-meals (supplied by both soybeans and cottonseed) for the n-th demand region; Equation (7.11) expresses the demand restraint for cotton lint for the United States; and m is the number of crop production areas within the n-th demand region.

A second set of demand restraints is defined for shipments of commodities under PL 480 programs. In the model, demand for PL 480 shipments is expressed in two parts: one is an intermediate demand for major commodities prior to shipment to overseas destinations, and the second is the final demand of particular recipient countries. The intermediate demand restraints require that

$$\sum_{i=1}^{150} a_{ij}Z_{ij} \geq 0 \tag{7.12}$$

where Z_{ij} is production of the j-th commodity in the i-th production area where

$$j = 1 \text{ is wheat}$$
$$j = 2 \text{ is feed grains}$$
$$j = 3 \text{ is cotton lint}$$

These intermediate demands for food aid commodities simulate the storage of commodities by the government. In the model, these demand restraints remain at zero level which in actuality indicates maintenance of some level of carry-over stocks—i.e., inflows equal outflows. The final demand for commodities shipped under PL 480 programs is in food deficit countries. These final demands are defined as

$$\sum_{r=1}^{7} \sum_{j=1}^{3} a_{rj}U_{rj} \geq D_{rj} \tag{7.13}$$

where D_{rj} is demand for the j-th commodity in the r-th recipient countries. U_{ij} is international shipment of the j-th commodity from the United States to recipient countries under PL 480 programs. These demand levels are initially set at zero levels for each respective crop under consideration and demand is expanded by discrete quantities in the model. Together with domestic and commercial export demand, this completes the set of demands for agricultural commodities in the model.

The remaining restraints in the model are associated with cropland. The basic activities in the model, crop production and land retirement, each use acres of cropland. In each of the 150 production areas, a restraint exists on the total acres of cropland available for production of major crops or for retirement under government programs. This restraint provides that

$$a_{ij}X_{ij} + a_{ij}Z_{ij} + a_{ik}R_{ik} \leq L_i \qquad (7.14)$$

where all activities are defined above, and the a_{ij} are coefficients expressing the amount of resource L_i required in the i-th region per unit of each crop production process and a_{ik} is similarly the amount required per unit of the k-th land retirement process. There are three types of land retirement processes analyzed in the study. Each is designed to simulate a realistic type of government land retirement program:

1. Annual land retirement—this set of programs simulates programs of land retirement for each of the major crops: wheat, feed grains, and cotton. The distribution of land retired and the cost per acre was based on recent patterns and costs.
2. Long-range land retirement—this program assumes that all cropland in a production area is eligible for retirement under a single government program. Costs per acre for retiring cropland are the estimated net revenue over cost of production for crops included in each production area.
3. Long-range land retirement with restrictions—this program assumes that retirement programs are limited to one-half of all cropland in any production area. Costs per acre are estimated as above.

Each of these land retirement programs forms a set of restraints on crop production for the particular model in which it is used. In the model specifying a retirement program for each of the crops—wheat, feed grains, and cotton—the restraints in the model restrict crop production in each production area by retiring a prespecified quantity of cropland for each crop. These programs require that

$$a_{ik}R_{ik} \geq K_{ik} \qquad (7.15)$$

where K is land removed from production in the i-th region under the k-th government program.

The second type of program, long-range land retirement, forms two types of restraints in the model in which it is used. When no limitation is placed on the amount of land retired in any production area, the restraint is of the form

$$a_{ik}R_{ik} \leq L_i \qquad (7.16)$$

whereas in the model in which a restraint of one-half of any production area could be retired, the restraint is

$$a_{ik}R_{ik} \leq .5L_i \qquad (7.17)$$

One final restraint was added to the model which is unique. That restraint was formed to express the relationship whereby all cropland must either be used for crop production or retired under government programs. This restraint replaced Equation (7.14) and requires that

$$a_{ij}X_{ij} + a_{ij}Z_{ij} + a_{ik}R_{ik} = L_i \qquad (7.18)$$

thereby causing all cropland in each region to be used by one of the production or nonproduction activities. The decision as to which process will use the supply of cropland is based on the associated costs specified in Equation (7.7). As costs change for the alternative types of land retirement programs R_{ik}, the optimal combination of activities will also change. But one set of optimal activities is infeasible because of the restraint formed by Equation (7.18). That set of activities would exist when the demand for crop production uses less than the available supply of cropland. Under these conditions the optimal and perhaps "first-best" outcome would be for the model to specify this excess cropland to remain unused. But Equation (7.18) will not allow this outcome. Rather the model simulates present political realities whereby land not required for crop production does not return to grass or trees but is held in nonuse under government programs. Within these constraints farmers still attempt to form efficient production units to minimize total production costs for the agricultural sector. Similarly the objective of the model is to find an optimum set of activities which will minimize the total cost of producing, transporting, shifting, and shipping commodities to satisfy specified levels of domestic and international demand. The constraint specified in Equation (7.18) prevents the attainment of the optimum set of activities, and through the use of shadow prices generated by the model, provides a measure of the net opportunity costs of commodities produced and shipped under PL 480.

Model Parameters ● Several sets of parameters are required for the model. These include (1) output coefficients for each crop production activity for each of the 150 production areas, (2) costs for each activity in the model including crop production activities, land retirement activities, commodity shifting activities, inland transportation activities, and international shipping activities, (3) cropland restraints for each crop included in the analysis, and (4) domestic and export demand levels for each commodity. Only commodity demands differ significantly from parameters of the model explained in Chapter 3.

Total demand for the specified commodities includes domestic demand, commercial export demand, and noncommercial export demand or shipments under government programs. Domestic demand is estimated for 1970 based on domestic population size and average per capita consumption levels for direct consumption. For feed grains and oilmeals, a derived demand is estimated based on demand for livestock products and historical trends in feed conversion rates. Demand for domestic consumption of each commodity is constant throughout the analysis.

Commercial export demand is estimated for 1970 based on trends of recent years. Commercial exports are defined as unassisted sales as well as those with government assistance in the form of (1) extension of credit and credit guarantees for relatively short periods, (2) sales of government-owned commodities at less than domestic market prices, and (3) export payments in cash or in kind.

Noncommercial export demand includes PL 480 programs. These demands include wheat, feed grains, and cotton and represent the major variables in the model. Noncommercial demand for each commodity is varied from zero level of shipments to a level in excess of past or expected levels of shipments. Each commodity is separately considered and demand levels for the other two commodities are set near recent levels. For example, as noncommercial demand for wheat is varied from zero to 525 million bushels, demand for feed grains under these programs is set at 3.0 million tons and cotton at 2.0 million bales.

Demand levels for each of the commodities included in the model are specified in Table 7.7. Actual commodity utilization levels are provided for 1966–68 marketing years and projected for the 1970 marketing year.

Analytical Procedure ● In this model, parametric programming is used, after a set of optimal activities and their levels are derived, to vary both demand levels and activity costs. In this manner the model is a means of estimating the net cost of supplying alternative levels of food aid because it simultaneously simulates the government programs of price support and commodity purchase.

To estimate the net cost of providing varying levels of agricultural commodities to recipient nations under PL 480, the model includes a

Table 7.7 ● Demand Levels Specified for Domestic Use, Commercial Export, and Varying Levels of Exports under PL 480

Commodity	1966-68 marketing years			Estimated 1970 marketing year									
	Domestic use	Commercial exports	Other exports[a]	Domestic use	Commercial exports	Alternative levels of P L 480 exports							
						0	1	2	3	4	5	6	7
						(million)							
Wheat (bu)	585.0[b]	301.0	433.0	591.0[b]	300.0	0	75.0	150.0	225.0	300.0	375.0	450.0	525.0
Feed grains (tons)	144.6	19.2	2.1	145.4	22.0	0	1.5	3.0	4.5	6.0	7.5	9.0	10.5
Cotton (bales)	8.9	1.6	2.3	9.1	1.5	0	1.0	2.0	3.0	4.0	5.0	6.0	7.0
Oilmeals[c] (tons)	22.8	10.0	...	24.1	12.2	...	...	...	...	...	...	...	...

[a] Includes exports under P L 480, programs for barter, and other exports financed by the U. S. Government.
[b] Does not include feed for wheat.
[c] Includes both soybeans and cottonseed. Oilmeals exports under P L 480 are included with commercial exports.

full set of activities which simulate the processes of crop production, government purchase, and storage and shipment of commodities under PL 480 programs. A considerable number of governmental decisions are required before the eventual shipment of commodities to recipient countries under PL 480 programs. (See Fig. 7.1.) In the model, decisions in steps 1 through 3 of Figure 7.1 are prespecified while steps 4 through 6 are internal to the model. In step 6, sales for domestic utilization are assumed to be zero while shipments under PL 480 programs are specified for discrete intervals.

Initially PL 480 demands are set at zero level for each specified commodity. After finding the optimal combination of activities for that shipment level, the PL 480 demand vector for the specified commodity is increased by discrete intervals. At each specified increase, estimates are derived of the per unit net cost of providing the marginal unit of the commodity to the recipient country. This per unit cost measures

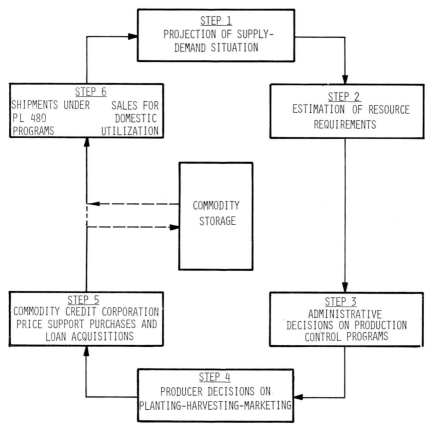

Fig. 7.1. Public policy processes for food and fiber. Broken lines indicate optional path.

the net opportunity cost of using cropland and other resources to produce the commodity for the market established by PL 480 programs, as
compared to retiring the cropland (with other resources remaining idle)
under government programs. Per unit costs for wheat, feed grains,
and cotton are estimated over a wide range of shipment levels.

One of the major difficulties encountered with the model was to
simulate the purchase of commodities by the government at support
prices (step 5 in Fig. 7.1). The usual minimum cost linear programming
model selects activities to satisfy a given level of demand based on the
criterion of least cost. As demand is increased, more costly units of
production are required and costs for providing the marginal unit also
increase. Costs for supplying an increasing amount of a commodity for
export would normally rise as more marginal production areas provide
the additional units of production.

But the process by which commodities become available for shipment under PL 480 programs provides that costs for marginal and average units are equal. The price support mechanism which results in
commodities becoming available through the CCC for food aid programs sets a constant price for all units, 1, 2, . . . , n. To simulate
this constant purchase price in the model, parametric cost programming
was used to vary cost elements on shipping activities as the quantity
of commodities shipped under PL 480 programs increased. This process
is shown in Figure 7.2 where the total cost (tc) of procurement and
shipment of commodities under PL 480 programs is broken down into
variable costs for producing each unit, a return to fixed factors used in
production, and costs for transportation, storage, and shipping. The
dotted line defines the support price (sp) for each commodity. In the
model, the cost coefficient on the shipping activity (U_{rj}) includes the
difference between production costs (pc) and tc. In this manner, a
constant cost is simulated for producing, storing, and shipping a unit
of the j-th commodity as follows:

$$c_j Z_j + c_{rj} U_{rj} = \overline{tc}_{rj} \qquad (7.19)$$

where tc is the total cost for all activities required to produce (Z_j) and
deliver (U_{rj}), a unit of the j-th commodity to the r-th recipient country.
As the element c_j increases, the cost element c_{rj} is reduced in magnitude,
thus holding tc_{rj} constant. Total costs are taken from actual costs of
operating PL 480 programs in the 1966–68 period. These data are given
in Table 7.8 along with quantities shipped under PL 480 programs for
1966–68.

As described above, the parametric programming techniques used
in conjunction with the model provide two types of simultaneous variation: one variation allows a discrete change in the quantities of the
food aid demand vector; the second variation allows for a discrete change

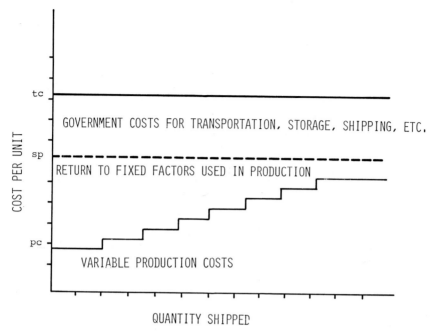

Fig. 7.2.   *Simulated cost structure of PL 480 shipments.*

in the shipping cost vector. The practical significance is that this combination of changes in the model allows simulation of actual world conditions for production, government purchase, and eventual shipment of commodities to overseas destinations under PL 480 programs.

Recipient Countries ● Countries included in the study were chosen based on past records of receiving food aid under PL 480 programs and on their location throughout the world. An effort was made to establish a recipient country in each of the major areas of the world. (See Fig. 7.3.) The analysis assumes that as food shipments are expanded, each of the countries in the study receives a fixed proportion of each increment of aid. These proportions are based on the programmed quantities of wheat, feed grains, and cotton under agreements signed with these countries in the period 1966–68.

An average of 323 million bushels of wheat per year was programmed for shipment under Title I of PL 480 during 1966–68 (Table 7.9). India was scheduled to receive 52.6 percent, and Pakistan 10.6 percent. India and Pakistan were also scheduled to receive the largest proportion of feed grains shipments, 62.0 and 6.4 percent respectively. Cotton programmed for shipment under Title I of PL 480 was distributed somewhat differently. Korea was scheduled to receive 30.0 percent with India receiving 24.0 percent. Taiwan received 6.6 percent

Table 7.8 ● Quantities and Costs Incurred for Purchase and Shipment of Commodities under PL 480 Programs for Fiscal Years 1966–68

Commodity and fiscal year	Total quantity shipped[a]	Costs incurred for				Total costs
		Commodity purchase	Ocean transportation	Export payment	Other costs	
Wheat	(thousand bu)			($ thousand)		
1968	362,987	597,202	83,885	16,611	...	697,698
1967	273,269	511,525	8,392	43,181	48,016	611,114
1966	485,075	803,714	99,847	214,694	150,166	1,268,421
3-year average	373,403	636,843	63,977	91,404	65,995	858,219
Average cost	...	1.71	.17	.24	.18	2.30
				($ per bu)		
Feed grains	(thousand tons)			($ thousand)		
1968	1,952	95,758	8,607	...	...	104,365
1967	3,844	195,715	29,579	...	91,168	316,462
1966	2,007	101,910	11,723	...	4,803	118,436
3-year average	2,598	130,997	16,620	...	31,958	179,575
Average cost	...	1.41	.18	...	.34	1.93
				($ per bu[b])		
Cotton	(bales)			($ thousand)		
1968	955,212	119,591	980	...	...	120,571
1967	1,189,482	142,774	1,618	2,153	759	147,304
1966	625,745	78,283	553	13,940	10,422	103,198
3-year average	922,556	113,436	1,049	5,359	3,723	123,567
Average cost	...	0.246	0.002	0.012	0.008	0.268
				($ per lb)		

Source: Commodity Credit Corporation, Report on Financial Conditions and Operations, June 30 Quarterly Report, issued in September 1966, 1967, and 1968.

[a]Includes sales for foreign currency, sales for dollars on credit terms and disposition under Title II except commodities in prepared form (rolled oats, rolled wheat, etc.).
[b]In corn equivalent.

Fig. 7.3.   Major recipient countries under PL 480.

of these shipments. Altogether an average of 91.8 million bushels of feed grains and 1.0 million bales of cotton were programmed under PL 480 programs each year between 1966 and 1968.

One country, Mexico, was included in the analysis to provide an estimate of the price differential resulting from international shipping costs for feed grains, even though no commodities were programmed during the period 1966–68. Mexico has received a small amount of feed grains under PL 480 programs since their inception in 1954.[2]

ESTIMATED NET COST OF FOOD AID SHIPMENTS WITH ALTERNATIVE LAND RETIREMENT PROGRAMS ● The cost of providing quantities of wheat, feed grains, and cotton to each specified country is estimated in the following sections of this chapter. These estimated net costs take into account the "savings" from no longer retiring cropland which is used to produce for shipment under PL 480 programs and are based on the concept of net opportunity cost.[3] Included in these costs are all activities necessary to provide a unit of each commodity to the countries specified. Per unit costs are derived for the marginal unit of production—that unit which is produced after domestic and commercial export demand is satisfied. Each set of costs is based on the assumption that a particular type of land retirement program is used to control aggregate production. The land retirement program is of importance because of differences in cost of retiring

2. For quantities shipped to each country, see *Report on Public Law 480* published annually by the U.S. Congress, House, since 1964 and semi-annually between 1954 and 1964.

3. For an explanation of the concept of opportunity cost in the linear programming framework, see Earl O. Heady and Wilfred Chandler, *Linear Programming Methods* (Ames: Iowa State Univ. Press, 1958), pp. 21–26.

Table 7.9 ● Average Yearly Quantities of Commodities and Percentage Received by the Specified Countries under Title I, PL 480 for the Years 1966–68

Country	Wheat		Feed grains[a]		Cotton	
	Average	Percentage	Average	Percentage	Average	Percentage
	(thousand bu)		(thousand bu)		(thousand bu)	
All countries	323,149	100.0	91,752	100.0	1,012.3	100.0
Congo	1,498	0.5	341	0.4	22.3	2.2
Morocco	8,308	2.6	...	...	12.9	1.3
Sudan	3,488	1.1	...	...	...	...
Tunisia	2,204	0.7	1,583	1.7	7.7	0.8
India	170,075	52.6	56,907	62.0	243.3	24.0
Pakistan	34,405	10.6	5,905	6.4	7.7	0.8
Korea	11,204	3.5	1,088	1.2	303.3	30.0
Taiwan	...	...	...	...	66.7	6.6
Brazil	24,496	7.6	...	...	...	...
Chile	1,470	0.5	984	1.1	30.0	3.0
Mexico	...	...	...	...	...	...
Others	66,002	20.4	24,945	27.2	318.4	31.4

Source: U. S. Congress, House, Annual Report on Public Law 480, 1966, 1967, and 1968, H. Doc. 179 (1968), 296 (1968), and 104 (1969).

NOTE: Includes Title I and Title IV shipments for 1966.

[a]The feed grains total of 91,752 thousand bushels includes the following quantities (all in thousands of bu): corn - 22,933; barley - 1,239; oats - 23; and grain sórghum - 67, 557.

an acre of cropland under alternative programs. As explained previously, under present political realities the net cost of crop production per acre is the total cost less the cost of retiring the acre under a government program. As the cost of retiring cropland increases, the net cost of producing the commodity decreases if production costs are stable. Three types of land retirement programs are evaluated.

Net Costs with Long-Range Land Retirement, No Restrictions ● The per unit cost of wheat, feed grains, and cotton for PL 480 programs is estimated first for a food aid program under which wheat shipments vary from zero to 525 million bushels, and cropland is retired from production for an extended period of time with the location of acres retired based on comparative advantage; no restriction is placed on the number or proportion of acres retired in any production region.[4] Acres in the most marginal areas of production would be retired with the program payment based on the net return above all costs of crop production except land taxes.

Net costs per unit of each commodity under this type of land retirement program are specified in Table 7.10. At the initial level, 75 million bushels of wheat are shipped under PL 480 programs with an estimated net cost of $1.40 per bushel. As shipments expand, the cost per bushel rises. The cause of this increase is somewhat complex. As we pointed out earlier, the total government cost of purchase and shipment of a unit of a commodity is maintained at a constant level by the model. To hold this cost constant, the differential between the support price and production costs is reduced as the cost of producing a unit increases. (See Fig. 7.3.) Since this cost is constant, the only variable becomes the cost per acre of land retirement. As an additional acre is returned to production for PL 480 programs, the number of acres of cropland retired decreases. But of greater importance, as acreage brought back into production comes from increasingly marginal land, the net cost per unit of food increases. Consequently retirement costs for the land become lower. Hence the increasing cost of each unit shipped under PL 480 implies that as production is expanded, the savings from not retiring this cropland diminish. As this value declines, the net cost of each unit shipped increases.

The net cost of providing wheat in this economic environment rises to $2.01 when 525 million bushels of wheat are shipped compared to a gross CCC cost of $2.30 per bushel for the wheat shipped under

---

4. Limitations on the amount of land retirement in any production area have considerable effect both on the total cost of retiring cropland and on the rural communities affected by the program. The latter grows out of the tendency for marginal cropland to be concentrated in particular areas, i.e., the Great Plains and the Southeastern states. For an analysis of this effect, see Earl O. Heady and Norman K. Whittlesey, A Programming Analysis of Interregional Competition and Surplus Capacity of American Agriculture in the United States in 1980, *Research Bulletin* 538, Iowa State Univ., Ames, July 1965.

Table 7.10 ● Net Cost for Food Aid, Assuming the United States Employs a Long-Range Land Retirement Program with No Limits on Retirement in Any Producing Area

Recipient country or area	Level of P L 480 shipments[a]							
	0	1	2	3	4	5	6	7
	Wheat ($ per bu)							
Weighted average	0	1.40	1.60	1.71	1.74	1.80	1.89	2.01
Brazil	0	1.33	1.53	1.64	1.67	1.73	1.82	1.96
Morocco	0	1.35	1.55	1.66	1.69	1.75	1.84	1.98
India–Pakistan	0	1.41	1.61	1.72	1.75	1.81	1.90	2.04
Turkey	0	1.40	1.60	1.70	1.73	1.79	1.88	2.03
Korea	0	1.38	1.58	1.69	1.72	1.78	1.87	2.01
	Feed grains ($ per bu)[b]							
Average	0	1.57	1.58	1.59	1.61	1.67	1.68	1.68
Mexico	0	1.42	1.44	1.44	1.46	1.52	1.53	1.53
Chile	0	1.58	1.59	1.60	1.62	1.68	1.69	1.69
Tunisia	0	1.51	1.53	1.53	1.55	1.61	1.62	1.62
Sudan	0	1.61	1.63	1.63	1.66	1.72	1.72	1.73
India–Pakistan	0	1.58	1.59	1.60	1.62	1.68	1.69	1.69
Israel	0	1.52	1.54	1.54	1.57	1.63	1.64	1.64
Korea	0	1.54	1.56	1.56	1.58	1.64	1.65	1.65
	Cotton (¢ per lb of lint)							
Average	0	20.0	20.6	20.6	21.5	22.2	22.8	25.5
Chile	0	20.1	20.6	20.6	21.5	22.2	22.8	25.5
Congo	0	20.1	20.7	20.7	21.6	22.3	22.9	25.6
India–Pakistan	0	20.1	20.6	20.7	21.5	22.2	22.8	25.6
Korea–Taiwan	0	20.0	20.6	20.6	21.5	22.2	22.8	25.5

[a]Quantities are: (million bu of wheat; million tons of feed grains; million bales of cotton):

Wheat	0	75.0	150.0	225.0	300.0	375.0	425.0	525.0
Feed grains	0	1.5	3.0	4.5	6.0	7.5	9.0	10.5
Cotton	0	1.0	2.0	3.0	4.0	5.0	6.0	7.0

[b]Feed grains price is per bushel of corn or equivalent nutritive value of other feed grain.

PL 480 programs during 1966–68 (Table 7.8). The increase from $1.40 at 75 million bushels of wheat to $2.01 at 525 million bushels indicates the magnitude of decrease in land retirement costs as shipments of wheat are increased. The differential of $0.90 per bushel between gross and net costs at the low level of shipments indicates that for each bushel of wheat not produced as a result of retiring cropland, government costs are this amount. For the average acre with a projected yield of 30 bushels, this implies that retiring an acre of cropland would cost $27.00. At the maximum level of wheat shipments, the differential is $0.29 per bushel. Assuming the same level of yield, the estimated cost of land retirement is only $8.70 per acre.

The net cost of feed grains is estimated at $1.57 per bushel of corn when 1.5 million tons are shipped, and rises to $1.68 when a total of 10.5 million tons are shipped. (Feed grains prices are measured in terms of corn although other kinds of feed grains are also shipped.) This cost compares to an average gross CCC cost of $1.93 per bushel incurred for feed grains shipped for the years 1966–68. The small change in net cost per bushel of feed grains implies that the cost of land retirement remains relatively constant over this magnitude of change in number of acres harvested. One reason for this is the relatively small size of feed grains shipments. Even at the maximum level, 10.5 million tons, less than 6 percent of total feed grains production would be exported under PL 480 programs. This amount of feed grains would use only slightly more than 5 million acres of cropland if the average yield is 2.0 tons per acre.

The net cost of cotton ranges from $0.200 per pound for 1.0 million bales to $0.255 per pound for 7.0 million bales. This compares with an average cost of $0.268 per pound for shipments from 1966 through 1968. The greater rise in cost per pound of cotton than for feed grains indicates that the cost of land retirement in cotton areas fluctuates more than it does in feed grains areas. Also, the 7.0 million bales level of cotton shipments represents 40 percent of total production. This level is well in excess of recent levels of cotton exports under PL 480 programs, and would require that nearly all land available for cotton be returned to production. At that point, almost no savings would occur from reduced land retirement and hence the cost of cotton per pound of lint approaches the gross cost of these shipments.

Net Costs with Long-Range Land Retirement with Restrictions ● A second type of government program examined would ship the same quantities of wheat, feed grains, and cotton lint with a limitation placed on the land retirement program. Under this program, land retirement in any production region is restricted to no more than 50 percent of total cropland. Retired acres would be spread over more production area, and land with a higher net return from crop production (and a higher cost for retirement) would be retired. Consequently the cost of retirement increases but this results in a decrease (compared to the previous program) in cost for commodities for PL 480 programs.

Estimates of net cost per unit of wheat, feed grains, and cotton are specified in Table 7.11 for this type of land retirement program. These estimates indicate the net cost of wheat is $1.29 per bushel with shipments of 75 million bushels. As shipments expand, the cost per bushel increases and reaches $1.71 at 525 million bushels. The individual country estimates point up the location aspect of cost; shipments to Brazil have an estimated cost of $1.22 per bushel when total shipments are 75 million bushels and increase to $1.63 at the maximum level considered. Shipments to India-Pakistan are the most costly, ranging from $1.30 to $1.72 per bushel. These differences are a result of the estimated transportation cost differentials of shipping to alternative countries.

Feed grains costs are lower than in the previous model, varying on an average from $1.43 per bushel to $1.57 per bushel. Feed grains shipments vary from 1.5 to 10.5 million tons. Mexico has the lowest cost for shipments while Sudan has the highest cost per bushel provided. Again these cost differences result from international transportation.

Costs for cotton for this type of program rise from $0.189 per pound to $0.234 per pound. Cotton costs are somewhat different from either wheat or feed grains in that transportation and other costs are a smaller proportion of total costs. Wheat costs under PL 480 programs in 1966–68 were broken down into 74.3 percent commodity purchase and 25.7 percent transportation and other costs. Feed grains costs were similar with commodity purchase accounting for 73.1 percent of total costs per unit. For cotton, 91.8 percent of all costs in 1966–68 were for commodity purchase with only 8.2 percent for transportation, export payments, and other costs. The lower costs for cotton for these other items primarily result because support prices for cotton are competitive with world market prices and hence only minor export payments are required.

Costs for transportation for all commodities have been reduced because "an amendment to Public Law 480 signed October 8, 1964, included a provision eliminating local currency financing of ocean transportation in U.S. flag vessels. Now only the differential between U.S. and foreign flag rates is paid by CCC where commodities are required to be transported in U.S. vessels."[5] As a result of these changes there is only a small differential in prices among different countries receiving cotton under PL 480 programs.

Net Costs with Annual Land Retirement—Direct Payment Programs ●
A final food aid program considered is one with a land retirement program which individually retires wheat, feed grains, and cotton cropland

5. U.S. Congress, House, *1964 Annual Report on Public Law 480*, 89th Cong., 1st sess.. H. Doc. 130.

Table 7.11 ● Net Cost for Food Aid, Assuming the United States Employs a Long-Range Land Retirement Program with a 50 Percent Limit on Retirement in Any Producing Area

Recipient country or area	Level of P L 480 shipments[a]							
	0	1	2	3	4	5	6	7
Wheat ($ per bu)								
Weighted average	0	1.29	1.34	1.47	1.59	1.59	1.61	1.71
Brazil	0	1.22	1.27	1.40	1.52	1.52	1.54	1.63
Morocco	0	1.24	1.29	1.42	1.54	1.54	1.56	1.66
India–Pakistan	0	1.30	1.35	1.48	1.60	1.60	1.62	1.72
Turkey	0	1.29	1.34	1.47	1.59	1.59	1.61	1.70
Korea	0	1.28	1.32	1.45	1.57	1.57	1.59	1.69
Feed grains ($ per bu)[b]								
Average	0	1.43	1.46	1.48	1.49	1.56	1.56	1.57
Mexico	0	1.28	1.32	1.33	1.34	1.41	1.41	1.42
Chile	0	1.44	1.47	1.49	1.50	1.57	1.57	1.58
Tunisia	0	1.37	1.40	1.42	1.43	1.50	1.50	1.51
Sudan	0	1.48	1.51	1.52	1.53	1.61	1.61	1.61
India–Pakistan	0	1.44	1.47	1.49	1.50	1.57	1.57	1.58
Israel	0	1.39	1.42	1.44	1.44	1.52	1.52	1.52
Korea	0	1.40	1.43	1.45	1.46	1.53	1.53	1.54
Cotton (¢ per lb of lint)								
Average	0	18.9	20.0	20.0	20.6	20.6	21.4	23.4
Chile	0	18.9	20.1	20.1	20.7	20.7	21.4	23.5
Congo	0	19.0	20.1	20.1	20.7	20.7	21.5	23.5
India–Pakistan	0	18.9	20.1	20.1	20.7	20.7	21.4	23.5
Korea–Taiwan	0	18.9	20.0	20.0	20.6	20.6	21.4	23.4

[a]Quantities are (million bu of wheat; million tons of feed grains; million bales of cotton):

Wheat	0	75.0	150.0	225.0	300.0	375.0	425.0	525.0
Feed grains	0	1.5	3.0	4.5	6.0	7.5	9.0	10.5
Cotton	0	1.0	2.0	3.0	4.0	5.0	6.0	7.0

[b]Feed grains price is per bushel of corn or equivalent nutritive value of other feed grain.

on an annual basis with direct payments to producers on a proportion of production as an incentive to participate. Costs per acre for retirement of cropland under these programs are higher than for previous programs. These higher costs result primarily because, under an annual program, producers still retain all factors of production necessary to operate their firm at full capacity. Retaining these factors of production in case the program should cease the following year results in producers incurring costs for depreciation and underemployed labor. Payments for land retirement must cover these costs to gain participation of producers. Hence the payment per acre for a program of this kind will be larger than for the long-range program where excess factors of production can be sold and excess labor employed in other pursuits.

Costs for shipping wheat and other commodities to recipient countries under PL 480 programs with this type of provision are given in Table 7.12. The initial 75 million bushels of wheat are estimated to cost $0.08 per bushel. Costs rise with shipments between 75 and 150 million bushels, reaching $0.50 per bushel. At the maximum level considered, 525 million bushels, the net cost per bushel is $1.31. These data indicate that the net cost of wheat shipments under PL 480 programs is relatively low when measured against the high cost of retiring land under those programs used in recent years to control production and maintain returns to wheat producers. Moreover, these costs indicate that shipments of wheat have a much lower net cost than gross costs incurred by CCC would suggest. While the gross cost for each bushel of wheat shipped under PL 480 in 1966–68 was $2.30, there is a clear indication that retiring these same acres would have cost nearly as much had these shipments not been made, particularly for the initial 100 million bushels shipped. At the average level of shipment for 1966–68, 375 million bushels, the average net cost is estimated at $1.13 per bushel, approximately 49 percent of the gross cost of shipments.

Estimated costs for feed grains shipments with annual land retirement programs are lower than either program previously considered, although not as significantly as wheat. At an initial level of 1.5 million tons, the cost is estimated at $1.08 per bushel, approximately 75 percent of the previous program. As shipments increase, costs per bushel increase, reaching $1.34 per bushel at 10.5 million tons of feed grains.

The net cost of cotton shipped under PL 480 programs is also lower for this program. Cotton costs at 1.0 million bales are estimated to be 13.8 cents per pound of cotton lint, which is 73 percent of the previous program cost. As shipments expand, costs increase and reach 19.2 cents per pound of lint at 7.0 million bales.

The estimated costs for all commodities considered with this land retirement program are considerably lower than for the previous programs, a result of the higher costs for retiring land with annual retirement programs.

Table 7.12 ● Net Cost for Food Aid, Assuming the United States Employs Annual Land Retirement, Direct-Payment Programs for Wheat, Feed Grains, and Cotton

Recipient country or area	Level of P L 480 shipments[a]							
	0	1	2	3	4	5	6	7
	Wheat ($ per bu)							
Weighted average	0	.08	.50	.87	1.05	1.13	1.27	1.31
Brazil	0	.00	.42	.79	.97	1.05	1.19	1.23
Morocco	0	.02	.44	.81	.99	1.07	1.21	1.25
India–Pakistan	0	.09	.51	.89	1.06	1.14	1.28	1.32
Turkey	0	.05	.54	.84	1.02	1.10	1.24	1.28
Korea	0	.05	.57	.84	1.02	1.10	1.24	1.28
	Feed grains ($ per bu)[b]							
Average	0	1.08	1.10	1.15	1.17	1.32	1.34	1.34
Mexico	0	.93	.95	1.01	1.03	1.17	1.19	1.19
Chile	0	1.09	1.10	1.16	1.18	1.32	1.34	1.34
Tunisia	0	1.02	1.04	1.10	1.12	1.26	1.28	1.28
Sudan	0	1.13	1.14	1.20	1.22	1.36	1.38	1.38
India–Pakistan	0	1.09	1.11	1.16	1.18	1.33	1.35	1.35
Israel	0	1.04	1.05	1.11	1.13	1.27	1.29	1.29
Korea	0	1.05	1.07	1.12	1.14	1.29	1.31	1.31
	Cotton (¢ per lb of lint)							
Average	0	13.8	1.68	17.2	17.2	17.7	18.2	19.2
Chile	0	13.8	16.8	17.2	17.2	17.7	18.2	19.2
Congo	0	13.8	16.8	17.2	17.3	17.8	18.2	19.2
India–Pakistan	0	13.8	16.8	17.2	17.2	17.7	18.2	19.2
Korea–Taiwan	0	13.7	16.7	17.1	17.2	17.7	18.2	19.1
[a]Quantities are (million bu of wheat; million tons of feed grains; million bales of cotton):								
Wheat	0	75.0	150.0	225.0	300.0	375.0	425.0	525.0
Feed grains	0	1.5	3.0	4.5	6.0	7.5	9.0	10.5
Cotton	0	1.0	2.0	3.0	4.0	5.0	6.0	7.0

[b]Feed grains price is per bushel of corn or equivalent nutritive value of other feed grains.

GUIDELINES FOR PRICING PL 480 COMMODITIES ● The estimated per unit cost of PL 480 shipments specified above for each of the alternative land retirement programs is based on actual costs incurred under these programs during 1966–68. These costs are subject to change over time because of changes in price support levels, proportion of international transportation costs borne by the CCC, and world prices of commodities. The latter prices determine to a large extent the level of export subsidy necessary to make these commodities competitive in world markets. Since the costs are specific to a past period, an attempt is made to make estimated costs more applicable to future pricing of PL 480 commodities.

To develop this type of guideline for pricing of future shipments, the estimated net average cost for commodities for each alternative land retirement program is compared with the gross CCC costs for the period 1966–68. The equation

$$\frac{\text{Estimated Net Opportunity Cost}}{\text{Gross CCC Cost for Commodities}} = \text{Pricing Coefficient} \quad (7.20)$$

provides an estimate of the appropriate price to be charged for PL 480 shipments, given (1) the type of land retirement program actually in use at a particular time, and (2) the actual CCC costs of food aid commodities.

In Table 7.13, we have summarized the Pricing Coefficient (PC) for all the various land retirement programs examined in this study. The PCs vary according to the level of shipment, the particular commodity shipped, and the land retirement program. For wheat, the PC varies from 3.5 with an annual land retirement program and a shipment of 75 million bushels of wheat, to 87.4 with a long-range retirement program and 525 million bushels. The PCs for annual programs are considerably lower for all levels of wheat shipments than for other programs. This result is expected, given the estimated costs from Table 7.12.

The PCs for feed grains and cotton are generally higher than for wheat for a similar shipment level and land retirement program. These data suggest that shipments of feed grains are optimally priced if the return is 81.3 percent of the CCC cost when 1.5 million tons are shipped and a long-range land retirement program is used to control aggregate production. For the same level of shipment, feed grains shipments priced at 56.0 percent of their CCC cost are optimal if annual programs with direct payments are used to control production. For these respective programs, percentages rise to 87.0 and 69.4 at the maximum level of shipments.

The PC for cotton with a 1.0 million bale shipment varies from 74.6 with a long-range land retirement program to 51.5 with an annual land retirement program. These coefficients increase to 95.1 with the long-

Table 7.13 ● Ratio in Percent of Net Cost to Gross CCC Costs for Shipments of Wheat, Feed Grains, and Cotton during 1966–68 under Alternative Supply Control Programs

Type of land retirement program	Level of PL 480 shipments[a]						
	1	2	3	4	5	6	7
	(%)						
Wheat							
Long-range retirement No restrictions	60.9	69.6	74.3	75.7	78.3	82.2	87.4
Long-range retirement 50% restrictions	56.1	58.3	63.9	69.1	69.1	70.0	74.3
Annual land retirement Direct payments	3.5	21.7	37.8	45.7	49.1	55.2	57.0
Feed grains							
Long-range retirement No restrictions	81.3	81.9	82.4	83.4	86.5	87.0	87.0
Long-range retirement 50% restrictions	74.1	75.6	76.7	77.2	80.8	80.8	81.3
Annual land retirement Direct payments	56.0	57.0	59.6	60.6	68.4	69.4	69.4
Cotton							
Long-range retirement No restrictions	74.6	76.9	76.9	80.2	82.8	85.1	95.1
Long-range retirement 50% restrictions	70.5	74.6	74.6	76.9	76.9	79.8	87.3
Annual land retirement Direct payments	51.5	62.7	64.2	64.2	66.0	67.9	71.6

NOTE: Gross CCC costs in 1966–68 are $2.30 per bushel of wheat, $1.93 per bushel of feed grains, and 26.8 cents per pound of cotton (Table 7.8).

[a]Quantities are (million bu of wheat; million tons of feed grains; million bales of cotton):

Wheat	75.0	150.0	225.0	300.0	375.0	425.0	525.0
Feed	1.5	3.0	4.5	6.0	7.5	9.0	10.5
Cotton	1.0	2.0	3.0	4.0	5.0	6.0	7.0

range program when 7.0 million bales are shipped and 71.6 when annual programs are used with this level of shipment. During this period 1966–68, an average of 1.0 million bales of cotton was programmed for shipment to recipient countries under PL 480.

To conclude this discussion on pricing levels and provide comparisons with actual data, we have calculated the actual cost recovery coefficients for commodities annually programmed for shipment between 1966 and 1968. While data are not available for the individual commodities, they are available on the proportion of gross CCC costs recovered in the contracts signed between 1966 and 1968. To calculate these proportions, export market values of PL 480 shipments are compared with the CCC costs of these shipments. For the period 1966–68, this proportion rose sharply. From a level of 60.0 percent in 1965, the level of cost recovery rose to 69.5 in 1966, to 80.9 in 1967, and 84.7 in 1968. To test these recovery rates against those which would exist if the pricing levels of this study were used, we calculated the level of recovery for wheat, feed grains, and cotton which would have been experienced if the concept of net cost had been applied to pricing. To provide an estimate of these levels of pricing, PCs from Table 7.13 for the level of shipments corresponding to 1966–68 averages were weighted with the proportion of wheat, feed grains, and cotton actually programmed for shipment in each year between 1966 and 1968.[6]

These weighted pricing coefficients are given below for the period 1966–68:

	Estimated	Actual
1966	54.9	69.5
1967	50.0	80.9
1968	39.4	84.7

In all cases the proportions derived using the results of this study are well below the actual levels of cost recovery. Furthermore, as costs for land retirement rose in 1967 and 1968, the net costs for food shipments declined. Actual recovery rates went up however. These data indicate that in the years specified, the level of pricing was substantially above levels indicated from the analysis in this study.

6. The procedure was as follows:

$$\sum_{i=1}^{3} P_{ikt} PC_{ikn} = PC_t$$

where P_{ikt} is the proportion that the i-th crop is of the total value of wheat, feed grains, and cotton shipped in the t-th year when k-th government program is used to control aggregate production; PC_{ikn} is the estimated Pricing Coefficient for the i-th crop, assuming the k-th government program is used and the n-th level of commodity is shipped; and PC_t is the estimated average pricing coefficient that would have optimized the pricing of commodities in the t-th year.

EFFECTS ON CROP PRODUCTION AND LAND RETIREMENT

● Several additional aspects of food aid shipments are analyzed in this chapter. The effect on land retirement of increasing food aid shipments is evaluated. Further, the interregional nature of the model provides a means of measuring the regional effects of changing shipment levels under PL 480 programs. Finally, the magnitude of crop acreages required for different levels of PL 480 shipments is also derived. Each of these aspects is discussed below for the different farm programs analyzed.

Production Effects with Unlimited Long-Range Land Retirement ●
During the period 1966–68 an average of 373 million bushels of wheat was annually exported under PL 480 programs. According to data shown in Table 7.14, if we adopt the 1970 level yields, this quantity of wheat (level 5 = 375 million bushels) would require 14.1 million acres of cropland for production. Given the level of domestic demand postulated (591 million bushels) plus 300 million bushels of commercial export demand, total wheat acreage is estimated at 56.1 million acres. Of the acreage producing under PL 480 programs, over 60 percent is located in the Northern Plains. Other major areas include the Southern Plains (1.8 million acres) and the Mountain States (1.5 million acres).

Elimination of PL 480 shipments would cause total wheat acreage to decline to 43.0 million acres. Other alternative levels of shipments would have less severe effects. But all reductions in wheat shipments have a positive effect on total land retirement. These estimates suggest that for 1970 technology, shipping 375 million bushels of wheat under PL 480 programs would leave some 53.0 million acres for retirement under government programs. Reducing PL 480 shipments to 225 million bushels (level 3) would increase land retirement to 58.7 million acres, and complete elimination of these shipments leaves a total of 66.6 million acres unused. These figures are based on the assumption that 3.0 million tons of feed grains and 2.0 million bales of cotton are still shipped under these programs. Eliminating all PL 480 shipments would increase retired acres still further.

Shipments of feed grains under government sponsored programs are considerably smaller than wheat. In 1966–68 an average of 2.6 million tons of feed grains was shipped into export market under these programs (Table 7.8). This level of shipment is estimated to require nearly 2.5 million acres and, combined with domestic and commercial export demand, requires a total of 89.6 million acres of feed grains for the yield levels postulated. Acreages of feed grains totaled 95.4 million acres in 1969, wheat—47.6 million acres, and cotton—11.1 million acres. As might be expected the Corn Belt is the major producer for PL 480 programs, with nearly 70 percent of the acreage located in this region. The comparative advantage of production in this region combined with low cost water transportation to the Gulf ports gives the Corn Belt an advantage in supplying feed grains to the export market.

Table 7.14 ● Allocation of Cropland, Assuming the United States Employs a Long-Range Land Retirement Program with No Limits on Retirement in Any Production Area

Crop and region[b]	Level of P L 480 shipment[a] (thousand acres)							
	0	1	2	3	4	5	6	7
Wheat								
Acres harvested	42,992	46,016	48,511	50,303	53,256	56,143	58,169	59,766
For P L 480	0	3,080	5,828	8,463	11,397	14,096	16,214	18,578
Northeast	0	0	0	0	72	72	117	345
Lake States	0	0	24	82	236	518	518	520
Corn Belt	0	0	0	0	64	464	1,727	2,360
Northern Plains	0	2,860	4,474	5,667	7,723	9,009	9,009	9,009
Appalachian	0	0	0	43	43	63	63	142
Southeast	0	0	0	0	15	15	29	41
Delta	0	0	100	265	270	270	274	306
Southern Plains	0	81	90	627	1,181	1,806	1,912	2,439
Mountain	0	95	843	1,459	1,473	1,473	1,738	2,304
Pacific	0	44	297	320	320	406	827	1,112
Acres retired	66,625	63,699	60,907	58,718	55,799	52,965	50,481	48,416
Feed grains								
Acres harvested	87,169	88,093	88,927	89,597	90,287	91,095	91,907	92,612
For P L 480	0	883	1,696	2,366	3,086	3,933	4,745	5,431
Northeast	0	0	0	0	0	0	0	0
Lake States	0	0	0	0	137	433	808	924
Corn Belt	0	504	1,169	1,625	1,969	2,055	2,329	2,794
Northern Plains	0	322	398	459	615	1,021	1,103	1,103
Appalachian	0	0	0	0	0	0	17	17
Southeast	0	0	0	0	0	1	11	13
Delta	0	11	19	19	19	19	19	21
Southern Plains	0	7	71	152	152	188	188	334
Mountain	0	16	16	88	171	171	199	199
Pacific	0	23	23	23	23	45	71	71
Acres retired	60,494	59,579	58,718	57,843	57,018	55,974	55,170	54,468

Table 7.14 ● *(Continued)*

Crop and region[b]	Level of P L 480 shipment[a]							
	0	1	2	3	4	5	6	7
				(thousand acres)				
Cotton								
Acres harvested	11,149	12,274	13,579	14,387	15,323	16,296	17,051	17,734
For P L 480	0	1,125	2,430	3,238	4,174	5,147	5,903	6,586
Corn Belt	0	0	173	173	173	173	173	173
Appalachian	0	0	0	173	19	386	423	452
Southeast	0	50	329	329	338	383	610	857
Delta	0	396	398	642	718	1,227	1,330	1,399
Southern Plains	0	656	1,507	2,071	2,903	2,928	3,169	3,169
Mountain	0	23	23	23	23	23	171	171
Pacific	0	0	0	0	0	27	27	365
Acres retired	60,205	59,365	58,345	57,781	57,227	56,340	55,868	55,545

[a] Quantities are (million bu of wheat; million tons of feed grains; million bales of cotton):

	0	1	2	3	4	5	6	7
Wheat	0	75.0	150.0	225.0	300.0	375.0	425.0	525.0
Feed grains	0	1.5	3.0	4.5	6.0	7.5	9.0	10.5
Cotton	0	1.0	2.0	3.0	4.0	5.0	6.0	7.0

[b] Acreages are for each crop as shipments under P L 480 programs are expanded for that particular crop. Exports of all other crops are held constant under that model. The retired acres are also specifically related to the level of exports of that crop under P L 480 programs but are total acreages retired from all crops.

Shipments of cotton under PL 480 programs averaged nearly 1.0 million bales in the 1966–68 period. This level of shipment is estimated to require 1.1 million acres of cotton with approximately 65 percent located in the Southern Plains under this type of land retirement program. Eliminating cotton exports under PL 480 programs drops total acreage to 11.1 million acres. Retired acres of major cropland total 60.2 million, but this assumes shipments of 3 million tons of feed grains and 225 million bushels of wheat remain.

Production Effects with Limitations on Long-Range Land Retirement ● One consistent conclusion throughout the previous chapters on farm programs has been that unlimited land retirement would have severe effects on those rural communities surrounded by large amounts of low productivity land. Given the opportunity to retire cropland under the cost-income squeeze of present day agriculture, producers on this land would likely find it advantageous to participate heavily in programs. This participation could leave the rural community with a weakened economic base, and business, schools, churches, and the social structure would take on an "air of depression." For these reasons, we have included a program with limited long-range land retirement to estimate the resource cost of reducing the rural community costs associated with removing excess capacity from agriculture.

The general outcome of placing a limitation on land retirement is an increase in the acreage required to produce a given level of crop output. The change in wheat acreages is not very significant however, showing an increase of approximately one-half million acres for the same level of demand and the limitation on retirement. For example, shipment of 150 million bushels (level 2) with a 50 percent limitation on retirement requires 49.0 million acres (Table 7.15) while the unlimited retirement program requires 48.5 million acres (Table 7.14). The resource cost in this instance includes the production costs and use of an additional half million acres of cropland for wheat production. If each acre had production costs of $20 per acre, this additional cost would total $10.0 million for this program.

The increase necessary for feed grains acreage is somewhat greater, averaging over 3 million acres. The larger change in feed grains indicates the greater difference in crop yields between areas of differing productivities. As a limit is placed on the retirement of cropland, production is required on acres in less productive areas. Some land must also be retired from production in highly productive areas if supply is not to exceed aggregate demand. Consequently production is shifted from highly productive areas to less productive areas with the result that lower yielding acres are used and a larger number of acres are required to produce the same level of output. This shift is more significant for feed grains (corn especially) than for wheat, since there is a greater difference in yields between regions for corn.

The effect on cotton acreage is insignificant. Cotton uses a relatively minor acreage of cropland and hence is only slightly affected by a change in the land retirement program. Also, for areas where cotton is grown, its competitive position is relatively great and almost no other use of this cropland can remove it from cotton production. Thus, placing a limitation on retirement of marginal cropland does not cause a shift in production, and total acreage of cotton remains independent of the program.

One effect that does show clearly under the cotton program analysis is the difference in the total number of acres retired under the two programs. As a limitation is placed on the proportion of cropland which is retired in each region, the total number of acres retired declines. This result is consistent with the previously explained effect on production. As retirement is restricted more acres are required to produce a given level of output; fewer acres remain idle and eligible for retirement under a government program. The total cost of crop production rises as more acres are farmed, but the cost of land retirement may decline with fewer acres retired if a similar price level is established (Ch. 5).

Production Effects with Annual Land Retirement ● Annual programs of the type used during the 1960s for major crops represent a further step toward limiting the proportion of any region which can be retired. These programs generally limit any farmer to retiring 20 to 50 percent of his farm. Payment levels are adjusted to encourage land of all levels of productivity to enter the program. Thus retirement is spread widely over all crop-producing regions with few regions retiring more than the minimum amount, since some farmers do not participate in the programs.

The result of further spreading retired acres over more regions is a substantially enlarged wheat acreage. The major explanation is that as crop acres are restricted in each region, some additional price pressure causes a shift in demand for feed grains and wheat. With enlarged demand for wheat, the number of acres of wheat produced increases. This effect clearly shows up in these data; wheat acreage increases over 8 million acres while feed grains remain about constant (Table 7.16). Output of feed grains declines and output of wheat rises; feed grains acreage remains relatively constant as more marginal acres are placed in production and average yields decline. Wheat acreage rises to offset the decline in feed grains production and thus the total feed unit output of wheat and feed grains is maintained. In this way livestock production would remain unchanged under the various land retirement programs.

As with the previous program changes analyzed, the shift to an even more restricted program causes almost no change in cotton acreage. But a sizeable effect does show up on total land retirement. As land in all regions is placed in land retirement programs fewer total acres are

Table 7.15 ● Allocation of Cropland, Assuming the United States Employs a Long-Range Land Retirement Program with a 50 percent Limit on Retirement in Any Production Area

Crop and region[b]	Level of P L 480 shipment[a] (thousand acres)							
	1	2	3	4	5	6	7	8
Wheat								
Acres harvested	43,308	46,430	48,995	49,937	52,526	55,199	57,958	60,430
For P L 480	0	3,142	6,251	8,752	11,170	13,915	16,564	18,959
Northeast	0	0	0	0	235	318	345	345
Lake States	0	0	0	54	236	236	490	563
Corn Belt	0	0	0	11	462	720	1,151	2,415
Northern Plains	0	2,799	5,229	6,758	7,073	8,672	9,920	9,920
Appalachian	0	0	21	64	75	75	75	150
Southeast	0	0	1	1	14	27	30	53
Delta	0	18	22	163	306	306	306	307
Southern Plains	0	81	81	99	805	1,217	1,860	2,077
Mountain	0	179	745	1,282	1,558	1,558	1,558	2,300
Pacific	0	65	152	320	406	786	829	829
Acres retired	63,260	60,628	57,903	56,270	53,411	50,720	47,786	45,299
Feed grains								
Acres harvested	90,226	91,012	91,653	92,533	93,275	94,226	95,042	95,817
For P L 480	0	793	1,588	2,428	3,082	4,009	4,825	5,713
Northeast	0	0	0	0	0	0	0	0
Lake States	0	0	0	0	0	342	808	1,000
Corn Belt	0	546	1,250	1,625	1,971	2,056	2,289	2,610
Northern Plains	0	126	217	501	706	1,094	1,195	1,550
Appalachian	0	0	0	0	0	17	17	17
Southeast	0	0	0	0	0	0	0	17
Delta	0	10	10	10	10	24	24	27
Southern Plains	0	7	7	73	176	203	209	209
Mountain	0	81	81	174	174	202	212	212
Pacific	0	23	23	45	45	71	71	71
Acres retired	57,740	56,882	56,270	55,120	54,187	53,125	52,253	51,302

Table 7.15 ● *(Continued)*

Crop and region[b]	Level of P L 480 shipments[a]							
	0	1	2	3	4	5	6	7
	(thousand acres)							
Cotton								
Acres harvested	11,186	12,375	13,598	14,411	15,465	16,458	17,336	18,095
For P L 480	0	1,189	2,412	3,225	4,279	5,240	6,034	6,761
Corn Belt	0	0	0	83	173	173	173	173
Appalachian	0	5	34	143	452	509	509	509
Southeast	0	140	338	347	357	364	706	1,108
Delta	0	399	458	732	913	1,261	1,331	1,331
Southern Plains	0	622	1,559	1,897	2,361	2,910	3,096	3,168
Mountain	0	23	23	23	23	23	192	248
Pacific	0	0	0	0	0	0	27	224
Acres retired	54,792	54,000	52,781	51,974	51,461	50,933	50,422	49,976

[a]Quantities are (million bu of wheat; million tons of feed grains; million bales of cotton):

Wheat	0	75.0	150.0	225.0	300.0	375.0	425.0	525.0
Feed grains	0	1.5	3.0	4.5	6.0	7.5	9.0	10.5
Cotton	0	1.0	2.0	3.0	4.0	5.0	6.0	7.0

[b]Acreages are for each crop as shipments under P L 480 programs are expanded for that particular crop. Exports of all other crops are held constant under that model. The retired acres are also specifically related to the level of exports of that crop under P L 480 programs but are total acreages retired from all crops.

Table 7.16 ● Allocation of Cropland, Assuming the United States Employs Annual Land Retirement–Direct Payment Type Programs for Wheat, Feed Grains, and Cotton

Crop and region[b]	Level of P L 480 shipment[a] (thousand acres)							
	0	1	2	3	4	5	6	7
Wheat								
Acres harvested	51,486	54,624	57,799	60,223	62,329	63,806	65,675	67,266
For P L 480	0	3,138	6,313	9,095	11,768	14,302	16,409	18,706
Northeast	0	0	0	27	71	99	345	343
Lake States	0	0	0	0	59	104	345	220
Corn Belt	0	0	0	407	601	709	1,844	2,477
Northern Plains	0	1,799	3,867	5,780	7,260	9,284	9,487	9,921
Appalachian	0	0	0	0	100	109	167	167
Southeast	0	0	0	4	17	29	58	58
Delta	0	2	3	224	271	311	311	311
Southern Plains	0	496	505	580	677	677	751	1,527
Mountain	0	1,559	1,723	1,847	2,415	2,430	2,522	2,555
Pacific	0	198	215	226	297	550	704	1,125
Acres retired	53,596	50,458	48,108	46,365	44,687	43,357	41,558	39,625
Feed grains								
Acres harvested	89,352	90,739	91,437	92,177	92,881	94,038	94,906	95,700
For P L 480	0	1,445	2,167	2,917	3,481	4,628	5,505	6,360
Northeast	0	26	26	26	26	26	26	26
Lake States	0	36	113	152	152	252	587	900
Corn Belt	0	161	798	1,425	1,968	2,292	2,365	2,458
Northern Plains	0	454	454	504	504	1,056	1,367	1,809
Appalachian	0	0	0	0	15	0	36	36
Southeast	0	0	0	0	30	30	46	46
Delta	0	25	25	30	30	105	105	105
Southern Plains	0	116	124	153	153	176	282	282
Mountain	0	377	377	377	382	441	441	441
Pacific	0	250	250	250	250	250	250	257
Acres retired	47,493	46,365	45,501	44,777	44,081	43,304	42,515	41,821

Table 7.16 ● (Continued)

Crop and region[b]	Level of P L 480 shipments[a]							
	0	1	2	3	4	5	6	7
				(thousand acres)				
Cotton								
Acres harvested	10,596	11,875	12,850	13,882	14,985	15,972	17,021	17,839
For P L 480	0	1,282	2,266	3,312	4,179	4,937	5,927	6,676
Corn Belt	0	107	173	173	173	173	173	173
Appalachian	0	188	191	509	509	509	509	509
Southeast	0	20	366	378	378	436	867	943
Delta	0	316	694	1,029	1,294	1,294	1,330	1,334
Southern Plains	0	619	740	1,121	1,507	1,964	2,485	3,105
Mountain	0	32	72	72	225	225	225	248
Pacific	0	0	30	30	93	336	338	365
Acres retired	47,475	46,772	46,365	45,614	44,999	44,392	43,877	43,382

[a]Quantities are (million bu of wheat; million tons of feed grains; million bales of cotton):

Wheat	0	75.0	150.0	225.0	300.0	375.0	425.0	525.0
Feed grains	0	1.5	3.0	4.5	6.0	7.5	9.0	10.5
Cotton	0	1.0	2.0	3.0	4.0	5.0	6.0	7.0

[b]Acreages are for each crop as shipments under P L 480 programs are expanded for that particular crop. Exports of all other crops are held constant under that model. The retired acres are also specifically related to the level of exports of that crop under P L 480 programs but are total acreages retired from all crops.

271

retired to reduce output by a given amount. This reduction varies
from 6 to 10 million acres under the various commodities and levels of
PL 480 shipments considered.

Generalizing, the major effects associated with the more restricted
programs include the following: (1) a larger acreage of cropland is
required for major crop production as land retirement programs are
restricted in each region; (2) fewer total acres have to be retired to reduce
output by a given amount; and (3) cotton production is nearly unaffected
by the shift in land retirement programs. On a regional basis, enlarged
shipments of wheat under PL 480 programs causes a major increase in
wheat acreage in the Northern Plains. Enlarged shipments of feed
grains show major effects on Corn Belt acreage, and the major effects
of enlarged cotton shipments accrue to the Delta and Southern Plains
regions. For the maximum shipment levels analyzed, total crop acres for
the major crops shown require over 30 million acres of cropland, some
10 percent of total land used for crops in recent years.

ROLE OF PL 480 PROGRAMS IN FARM POLICY ● Demand expansion programs have filled an important role in U.S. domestic farm
policy for the last several years. A sizeable amount of several major
commodities has been removed from the domestic market to government
storage and later provided to other nations under favorable financing.
Through these programs, the U.S. farm sector has produced larger levels
of output than would have existed in the absence of these programs.
This action has been consistent with one of the original thoughts in
PL 480 programs. "Many farmers," it was suggested in 1954, "would
prefer raising their normal acreage of wheat, cotton, or other crops instead of reducing acreage under quota restriction if some method could
be found for needy people to use the products from the 'excess acres'."[7]

This tendency for U.S. farmers to prefer to maintain existing levels
of crop acreages in the face of declining export demand levels caused some
major conflicts in farm policy during the early years of PL 480 programs. Commodity price support programs resulted in large amounts
of major commodities flowing into government storage bins as demand
slackened. As stocks continued to increase even after PL 480 programs
were instituted, government costs for commodity storage climbed year
after year. Between 1954 and 1955 stock levels climbed 16.2 percent
and rose again in 1956 (Table 7.17). With the help of drought in
1956 and PL 480 shipments, stock levels declined in 1957 but rose consistently after that up to 1961. As stocks continued to increase, considerable pressure developed to move these stocks into world markets
under nearly any conditions of sale. This pressure was noted by John H.
Davis in reviewing the use of food as a tool in world development in

7. Statement of Clyde N. Rogers, Director, Town and Country Department, Ohio
Council of Churches, testifying before the U.S. Congress, House Committee on Agriculture, 83rd Cong. 2nd sess., February 2, 1954.

Table 7.17 ● Carryover Stocks and CCC Costs Recovered in Programmed Shipments under PL 480 Programs, 1950–68

End of crop year	Index of carry-over stocks[a] (1954=100)	Expected cost recovery[b] (%)	End of crop year	Index of carry-over stocks[a] (1954=100)	Expected cost recovery[b] (%)
1950	68.7	...	1960	150.1	59.7
1951	51.3	...	1961	162.8	58.7
1952	38.9	...	1962	148.8	63.5
1953	68.8	...	1963	147.0	56.6
1954	100.0	...	1964	143.7	66.2
1955	116.2	70.1	1965	132.4	60.0
1956	130.7	59.7	1966	117.1	69.5
1957	120.7	60.1	1967	93.5	80.9
1958	121.0	65.0	1968	89.9	84.7
1959	146.7	65.1			

Sources: U. S. Congress, House, Semiannual Report on Public Law 480, 1954–63; Annual Report on Public Law 480, 1964–68.

[a]The index of carry-over stocks of wheat, feed grains, and cotton is calculated as $(P_{i54}Q_{ij}/P_{i54}Q_{i54})$ (100) where i = crops, j = year with 54 = 1954. The price weights (P_{ij}) are average prices received by farmers in 1954.

[b]Calculated as $\dfrac{\text{Export market value of P L 480 shipments}}{\text{Estimated CCC costs for commodities}}$

1958, "the objective most emphasized by the proponents of Public Law 480 in 1954 was the disposal of United States farm surpluses, which at the time were accumulating in the hands of Commodity Credit Corporation at the rate of almost $3 billion per year."[8]

Over the decade after 1954, considerable debate ranged on whether this in fact was the major function of PL 480 programs and whether excess production was being programmed in a manner to maximize its developmental effects in recipient nations. This question was again raised after passage of the Food Aid Act of 1966, which placed major emphasis on assuring ". . . a progressive transition from sales for foreign currencies to sales for dollars (or to the extent that transition to sales for dollars under the terms applicable to such sales is not possible, transition to sales for foreign currencies on credit terms no less favorable to the United States than those for development loans under section 201 of the Foreign Assistance Act of 1961, as amended, and on terms which permit conversion to dollars at the exchange rate applicable to the sales agreement) at a rate whereby the transition can be completed by December 31, 1971."[9] For most if not all countries, this change represented a hardening of terms under which PL 480 shipments were received.

As one measure of how stock levels and food aid shipments are related, a simple correlation test was run on the relationship between carry-over stocks and the price charged recipient countries for these commodities for the period 1950–68. This test showed the expected inverse relationship existed; as grain stocks increased, the recovery rate decreased and as grain stocks decreased, the recovery rate increased. The correlation coefficient had a value of —.66 which is significant at the .99 probability level. This simple test would seem to confirm that the major emphasis over this period was in using food aid programs as a means of reducing levels of carry-over stocks.

One should point out however that this relationship between stock levels and PL 480 programs was consistent with the purpose for which the program was established. It was set up to assist U.S. agriculture with the difficult problems of structural adjustment brought on by advancing technology. These problems appeared in the form of low prices and low incomes. But basic resource problems underlay these more visible problems. Looking back on fifteen years of change in the industry, there is little doubt of the usefulness of programs which maintained output, price, and income levels while labor resources transferred to other occupations. Perhaps another decade will result in a further movement toward an optimum combination of resources in agriculture. It will be at least 1980 before this transition is completed however and may take even longer.

8. John H. Davis, Surplus Disposal as a Tool for World Development—Objectives and Accomplishments, *Journal of Farm Economics,* 40:1484.

9. Public Law 480, 83rd Congress, *Agricultural Trade Development and Assistance Act of 1954* (68 Stat 454), as amended through July 29, 1968. Enacted July 10, 1954.

CHAPTER EIGHT

A Simulation Model
for Agricultural Policy

This chapter describes a simulation model applied to the basic land diversion program popularly called the "Feed Grain Program." It is concerned with the methods by which certain policy goals can be attained. When initiated in the 1960s, policy goals of the Feed Grain Program included the following and related items: participation of farmers in land diversion to lessen market supply, improvement of farm prices and income, reduction of government stocks, reasonable Treasury costs, and a competitive export position. Variables which could be manipulated to achieve these goals included payment rates for idling land, price support, direct payment levels, and amount of land withdrawal allowed per farm. This chapter examines methods for determining how the "input" or "control" variable might be manipulated to attain various levels of the "output" variables or policy goals. It also examines response surfaces or substitution rates for achieving these goals. The incentive for land diversion under the Feed Grain Program included direct payments and eligibility for price support loans. Hence payment and loan rates become part of the set of variables to be examined in relation to farmer participation in the land idling program as a means to attain goals of lower grain supplies, reduced commodity stocks, higher prices, and improved farm income.

One function of social science is to provide policy makers with feasible policy alternatives and the consequences of each. The aim of a policy is to bring about a given change in the behavior of the socio-economic system to attain specified goals. Different routes to a given policy target or objective usually exist. Accordingly, tools are needed which assist in predicting the impact of alternative policies on a socio-economic system. A suitable model of the economy would enable the social scientist to substitute experiments on models for experiments on the real system. Experiments with the real system, as in physical or biological sciences, are prohibitively expensive or politically impossible.

275

Nevertheless the scientist can construct a model of the socioeconomic system to approximate the real system in various degrees. A properly formulated model should respond to different policy alternatives in a manner which parallels the response of the real socioeconomic system. The purpose of the experiment is to provide alternative predictive information about the probable behavior of the real system.

Simulation is a numerical technique for solving complex socioeconomic models. The analytic technique of model solution attempts to deduce general relationships that express endogenous variables in terms of the given parameters and exogenous variables. It usually involves models composed of sets of mathematical and logical statements describing the behavior of a system over an extended time. However, more complex and realistic models of the economic system usually cannot be solved analytically but necessitate the use of the simulation approach. In this approach, specific numerical solutions are first obtained. The general solutions are derived by induction from these specific numerical solutions. A set of specific numerical solutions constitutes an experiment. A model solved by the simulation technique is termed a *simulation model*.

The need for simulation models arises from the inherent complexity of economic systems and the need for a comprehensive method to study such systems. On both the micro or firm level and macro or aggregate level, economic processes are interwoven with noneconomic processes. They create a highly interrelated system of physical and information flows among many components and involve a large number of relationships. Economic structures have usually been treated as systems in the macroscopic, aggregative sense. This approach has proved useful in predicting the behavior of the economic system as a basis for policy formulations. However it does not allow analysis of either intermediate results or the impact of alternative courses of action on the individual components which make up the system. Conversely, the macro approach does not allow analysis of individual actions in the overall performance of the total economic system. Models which relate to the behavioral relationship of the individual components of a system and the use of this knowledge in predicting the behavior of the system can prove very useful in policy analysis. The problems involved in constructing such models were very great until the advent of sophisticated computers which have made it possible to employ simulation as one of the major tools in the analysis of complex socioeconomic systems.

PURPOSE OF THE STUDY ● The overall purpose of the study in this chapter is to develop and apply a method for designing optimal decision rules for implementing a specific agricultural policy. The optimal rules are derived via experimentation and hence are termed empirical rules. The method is applied to the land diversion program known as the Feed Grain Program. This program was designed to encourage voluntary participation of producers to restrain output and stop or reduce the buildup of feed grains surpluses. Hence the methodological nature of this study is designed to analyze producer response to different aspects of input variables represented in the Feed Grain Program. As an element of this objective, we are also interested in prescribing the program conditions which allow attainment of the specified policy ends with an efficient combination of government costs, production or surplus control, and net farm income.

The analysis is based on data gathered from a sample of Iowa farms. Illustration is then made of the application of the model to the entire feed grains—livestock sector, and the determination of the substitutability of goals and goal attainment in farm policy formulation. In this sense, the investigation should be viewed as a pilot project. It demonstrates how the problem of deriving optimal, empirical decision rules can be approached.

LAND DIVERSION UNDER THE FEED GRAIN PROGRAM ●

The main instruments for the control of feed grains production have been acreage allotments or land diversion programs. Major incentives to participate in these programs were supported prices for grain and payments to participants who idled their land. Noncompliers have not generally been entitled to such support prices and payments, except in 1956, 1957, and 1958, when price support was in effect for noncompliers too, but at a lower level than for compliers. Land diversion payments are a form of direct compensation to producers who voluntarily withdraw land from production. Such were the payments for idling land under the Acreage Reserve and the Conservation Reserve Programs, as well as the Feed Grain Program.

Attempts to control feed grains output had been unsuccessful, judging by the mounting surpluses during the period from post–World War II up to the 1960s. With the exception of the years 1950–52 and a short period in the mid 1960s, the market price for corn was below the support level. This difference motivated producers to deliver feed grains to the Commodity Credit Corporation (CCC) to receive the price support nonrecourse loan. In 1961, when the Emergency Feed Grain Program went into effect, feed grains stocks carried over under the price support plan totaled about 75 million tons, and about 10 percent of all corn production was being delivered to the CCC. By 1961, government investment in price support loan programs amounted to more than $9 billion.[1]

Several features of previous programs were combined into the Feed Grain Program. The program, to be politically feasible, was based on voluntary participation. The compensation plan included both a price incentive scheme from the previous acreage allotment program

1. Geoffrey Shepherd, Appraisal of the Federal Feed Grains Programs, *Iowa Agriculture and Home Economics Experiment Station Research Bulletin* 501, 1962.

and the direct payment method of the Soil Bank Program. Direct compensation included payments for land retired from production and, after 1963, a price support payment per bushel of feed grains produced on the permitted acreage, over and above the price support loan rate. An indirect benefit for participants was provided by infrequent government sales of surplus grain at a relatively low price, which helped to maintain a price margin between the support rate and market price.

Provisions for Land Retirement under the Feed Grain Program ● The producers of corn and grain sorghum were eligible to take part in the Feed Grain Program under which acreages of land devoted to corn and grain sorghum were diverted from crops. The program was voluntary but participation by farmers producing corn and grain sorghum was required for eligibility for price support on corn, grain sorghum, barley, oats, and rye. To qualify as a cooperator and to be eligible for price support, a minimum reduction of 20 percent of the established base of a farm was required. The farm base was established by the Agricultural Stabilization and Conservation Service (ASCS) county committee from the acreage of these crops grown on each farm in 1959 and 1960. The maximum acreage that could be idled and receive a diversion payment varied from year to year, ranging from 20 percent to 100 percent of the base, the higher figure applying only to farms with a base of 25 acres or less. Land diverted from crops and devoted to conservation under the Feed Grain Program was in addition to the farm's average acreage devoted to conservation uses in 1959 and 1960. Each farm had a *permitted acreage* for corn after the operator decided how many acres of land to divert from crop production. The permitted acreage was figured by subtracting the diverted acreage from the farm's base acreage. Thus the permitted acreage became the largest acreage of any feed grain crop that could be produced if the farm was to continue as a cooperating farm.

Year-to-year alterations in the provisions of the Feed Grain Program have involved changes in the price support loan rate, kinds and amounts of production eligible for price support loans and for income support payments, the upper limit on diversion, and payment rates for different levels of acreage diversion. These changes provide the basis for experimentation in the policy model. They are the input variables manipulated to attain certain goals or levels of output variables for the Feed Grain Program.

SOURCE OF DATA ● The basic data for this analysis were obtained from a survey conducted by the U.S. Department of Agriculture in cooperation with the Iowa Agricultural and Home Economics Experiment Station. The survey, based on a questionnaire, covered six counties in the north central cash-grain area and six counties in the southern pasture area of Iowa. The purpose of the survey was to appraise the

Feed Grain Program in selected producing areas. The two study areas have quite different characteristics.

For the survey, a random sample of participant and nonparticipant farms in the 1961 Feed Grain Program was drawn from records maintained in the county ASCS offices. The final sample consisted of 78 participants and 72 nonparticipants in the north central Iowa counties, and 82 participants and 67 nonparticipants in the south central Iowa counties. Descriptive information on cropping practices, land ownership, and participation in the Feed Grain Program was obtained from ASCS records for the sample farms. Each sample farm was then contacted in a field survey to obtain additional information regarding the organization of farms and their response to the Feed Grain Program. The 299 sample farms constituted the basic decision units of the simulation model. For the purposes of methods of the study, it was assumed that the sample served as a reasonable representation of the Corn Belt region.

THE MODEL ● The basic units of the model are agricultural firms (farms) engaged in the production of grain, livestock, and other agricultural products. The economic environment provides these units with limited information concerning prices and yields of major crops and livestock. Then, based on this information and on its own experience, each firm makes certain allocations and production decisions. In the model this farm management process is termed the *micro-simulator*. Each farm evaluates its own economic performance relative to that of other farms in the same county. The farms interact through the market where their products are sold.

At the end of each decision period the output variables of all farms included in the model are aggregated and sample estimates of the corresponding regional quantities are derived. These estimates are aggregated into a system referred to as the *macro-simulator*. The aggregated system represented by the market determines prices, given the total level of output. In addition, government intervention, in the form of the variables of the Feed Grain Program, regulates or modifies the market mechanism. Experiments are conducted on different variants of this program. Each variant is applied to the same system under identical conditions.

Figure 8.1 provides an overall view of the system. It starts with reading the initial conditions and parameters for one complete computer run of the simulation model. Each run tests a different policy variant (decision rule) and consists of one or more sequences. A sequence is a fixed number of calendar years. Each sequence starts with the same initial conditions and parameters. However, each sequence involves a different series of random inputs: yields and random variables from a standard normal distribution. Prices are also random because corn supplies, which depend on total production and thus on yields, are random too. Thus, in terms of experimental design, a run is a treat-

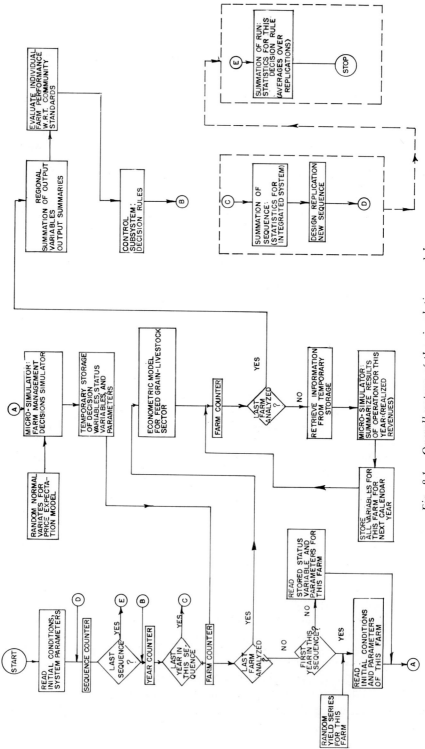

Fig. 8.1. Overall nature of the simulation model.

ment combination and a sequence is a replicate. In all runs, all similarly indexed sequences are subject to the same series of random inputs. The operation of the simulated system in each sequence is summarized in relevant statistics. After the last sequence ends, relevant statistics are obtained for the whole run. A different program variant is next analyzed, requiring another simulation run.

Figure 8.2 illustrates the interdependence between the farm decision model (micro-simulator) and the market equilibrium model and government control (macro-simulator). It emphasizes the manner in which production decisions are made. The farm decision model at period t is independent of market processes at period t, since decisions are based on past prices and yields. Actual production and profits are realized only after the production of period t has been marketed.

The Micro-Simulator ● The agricultural firm is the basic component of the simulation model. In the real system, this elemental unit (the family farm) is both a producing firm and a consuming household. In this analysis, attention is focused on the family farm as a producing firm. The simulation model attempts to represent the decision-making process of the firm and the ensuing decisions. In many cases such processes are characterized by situations in which a decision maker resorts

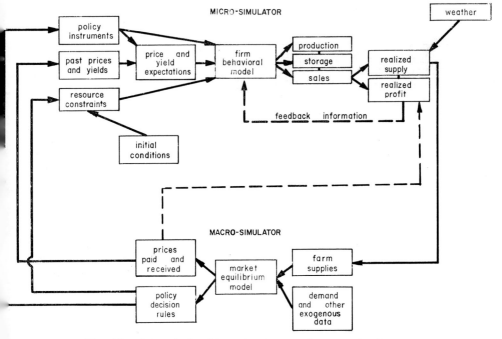

Fig. 8.2. Interrelationships of micro- and macro-simulators.

to a "rule of thumb." This does not guarantee a correct or optimally accurate solution of the problem facing him but, as noted elsewhere, facilitates a quick solution.[2]

As an example of a heuristic procedure, suppose a farm manager must make a decision concerning the purchase of steer calves for feeding and marketing a year hence. Assume further that he makes the decision on the basis of break-even price (BEP) calculations. This is a form of partial budgeting and is not uncommon among farmers. The farmer will buy if

$$\left(\frac{AB}{BEP} - DES \right) \geq 0, \ AB > 0 \tag{8.1}$$

where $AB =$ (expected price $-$ BEP), and $DES =$ a decision parameter, let us say, a margin of 5 or 10 percent, as determined by the operator. This inequality is a decision rule. The sensitivity of some output variables such as per farm income may be tested for various stipulated levels of the parameter.

Generally, such an approach is adopted in this model whenever rules of thumb seem to prevail among farmers. When these are not known or are not available, past behavioral relationships are extended via regression analysis. Both procedures could be considered positive or descriptive approaches in terms of method. (In addition to the farm management simulator a linear programming model was constructed to compare the results of a model based on an explicitly normative behavior with one which did not assume perfect rationality in the attainment of goals, and which did not necessarily involve profit maximization as a unique rational objective. Unfortunately, time and budget considerations made it impossible to complete this analysis.) Only those decision processes directly associated with the Feed Grain Program are discussed here.

The Participation Decision ● In a voluntary program such as the Feed Grain Program a farmer may choose to participate or stay out. If he decides to participate, he must comply with certain provisions which restrict his freedom of action. If he stays out he is not bound by any of the restrictions but he is not entitled to the direct benefits of the program. It is conceivable to consider the universe of farmers in a given region as being subdivided into two major sub-populations: participants and nonparticipants. The status of an individual farmer is characterized by a set of variables from a multivariate density function. The task is to find an efficient method of classifying him into either one of the populations. The situation is complicated by the dynamic prop-

2. J. C. Headley, and A. B. Carlson, Problem Solving—The Decision Process and Management Behavior, *Journal of Farm Economics* 45 (1963): 1219–25.

erties of this problem. A given farmer with a certain set of values (measurements) of status variables at period t, might take on a different set at $t + 1$, $t + 2$, etc. He might then be represented by a different point in the probability space, requiring a periodic reclassification of each farm. To accomplish this, a standard classification procedure of multivariate analysis, the *discriminant function*, was employed. For a given collection of sample units which belong to either one of two populations, and a given set of common measurements on each of these units, the discriminant function is a linear combination of the measurements best discriminating between the two groups. It is an optimal method in terms of some a priori criteria. Its application to the participant decision is discussed below. Let

b_i = the coefficients in the discriminant function, $i = 1, \ldots, k$
X_{ij} = the i-th status variable on unit j (at a given time), $j = 1, \ldots, n$
$X'_{i,s}$ = the mean of the i-th variable for all units belonging to group s, $s = 1, 2$
X''_i = the grand mean for the i-th variable over all units

The linear combination of the X_{ij}'s

$$Z_j = b_1 X_{1j} + b_2 X_{2j} + \ldots + b_k X_{kj} \qquad (8.2)$$

is the discriminant function. Further, define the discriminant functions for the means

$$Z'_s = \Sigma_i b_i X'_{i,s} \qquad (8.2a)$$
$$Z'' = \Sigma_i b_i X''_i \qquad (8.2b)$$

For any given period, Z_j was computed on the basis of the values of the status variables of any given individual in that period. However, Z'' and Z'_s were computed for the original sample values and remained fixed over the period of analysis. The j-th individual was classified as belonging to either group 1 or group 2 accordingly as $Z_j \gtrless Z''$. Thus, for example, if $Z_j > Z''$, and also $Z'_1 > Z''$,[3] the individual would be classified in group 1. Except for a constant term the estimated discriminant function[4] was

$$Z = -0.001123X_1 - 0.005807X_2 + 0.002401X_3 + 0.02901X_4$$
$$+ 0.05467X_5 - 0.00011X_6 - 0.02182X_7 - 0.02139X_8 \qquad (8.3)$$

---

3. It should be noted that for any effective discriminant function $Z'_1 > Z''$, $Z'_2 < Z''$.

4. The variance ratio test yields $F = 53.7$ which is significant at 0.001 level, i.e., highly significant.

where

X_1 = operator's age
X_2 = animal units per acre of cropland lagged one year
X_3 = hay base in percent of cropland

$$X_4 = \frac{\text{total acreage on farm}}{\text{sample average acreage per farm}}$$

X_5 = past participation in government land retirement programs

$$X_5 = \begin{cases} 0 \text{ if no participation} \\ 1 \text{ if he participated in at least one of these programs} \end{cases}$$

X_6 = index of diversion payment level
X_7 = index of price support level
X_8 = index of minimum diversion level

Measurements X_6 to X_8 were dummy variables indicating the operator's probable reaction to changes in the Feed Grain Program. The information was obtained from responses to a number of questions in the survey questionnaire. The postulated changes were (1) increasing or decreasing diversion payment per acre by $\pm$ 10, $\pm$ 20, and ± 30 percent of the 1961 level, (2) increasing corn price support from \$1.20 to \$1.35, and (3) reducing the required minimum diversion rate from 20 to 15 percent of the feed grains base. The manner in which these dummy measurements were used in the discriminatory analysis is discussed by Orcutt.[5] Equation (8.3) yields the following values for Z'_p, Z'_{np}, and Z'':

$$Z'_p = 0.2777$$
$$Z'_{np} = -0.3197$$
$$Z'' = 0.0$$

where p = participants, np = nonparticipants. Accordingly, an individual with a $Z_j = 0.4$ would be classified as a participant.

There existed noticeable differences between the groups which did and did not participate in the 1961 program. Table 8.1 lists these differences for variables X'_1 to X'_5. The participants were younger, raised less livestock (usually cash-grain farmers), had a smaller hay base (which is associated with a smaller livestock operation, especially cattle feeding and beef cows), had larger farms on the average, and participated more often in other government programs in the past. These differences support the conceptual division of these farm producers into two populations.

5. Guy H. Orcutt, Simulation of Economic Systems: Model Description and Solution, *Proceedings of the American Statistical Association,* Business and Economic Statistics Section, Chicago, 1964.

Table 8.1 ● Measurement Means for Two Groups in the Discriminatory Analysis

	Measurement	Group means	
		Participants	Nonparticipants
X_1	Age	46.00	50.00
X_2	Animal units/cropland	0.60	1.10
X_3	Hay base/cropland	0.23	0.28
X_4	Total acres/sample mean	1.05	0.94
X_5	Past participation	0.44	0.27

Diverted Acreage Decision ● A participating operator under the Feed
Grain Program diverted a minimum portion of his feed grains base to
qualify for price support loans and income payments. He could also
divert acreage in excess of the mandatory minimum up to an upper
limit specified in the program, for which he received diversion payments. Farms with a feed grains base of less than twenty-five acres
formed a separate category with respect to the upper limit on diversion.
They could divert the whole base if they so chose. They are handled
as a separate group in the regression equation by employing a dummy
variable for base size. Equation (8.4) represents the diversion decision:

$$DIV_t = 95.645 - 42.231FGB - 0.145RL + 0.159HL_{t-1}$$
$$- 1.285AC_{t-1} + 0.0002RL^2 + 0.012AC_{t-1}^2 \qquad (8.4)$$
$$\quad (0.425) \qquad\quad (0.00004) \qquad\quad (0.0048)$$
$$R^2 = 0.50$$

where

DIV_t = diverted acres above the minimum diversion, in percentage of cropland acreage
FGB = a dummy variable for base size,
$$FGB = \begin{cases} 0 \text{ if base} \le 25 \text{ acres} \\ 1 \text{ if base} > 25 \text{ acres} \end{cases}$$
RL = rented land in percent of total acreage, base year
HL_t = hired labor in hours per acre of feed grains base, period t
AC_t = corn acreage in percent of cropland acreage, period t

The regression coefficients are significant at the 5 percent level.
(Standard errors are in parentheses under the conforming coefficient.)
The negative coefficient for FGB indicates that farms with a base smaller
than twenty-five acres diverted more than the obligatory minimum (since
then FGB = 0). The sign of RL implies that tenant operators tend to
divert the minimum while owner-operators divert, on the average, more
than the minimum.

Loan and Delivery Decision ● A farmer complying with land diversion
requirements could obtain a price support, nonrecourse loan at an established rate per bushel. His year's total corn production on land remaining in production serves as collateral, and the loan issued by the CCC
within one-half year after harvest could be as large as the value of the
crop. The quantity of corn placed under loan is determined mainly by
the relative levels of the government loan rate and the November–May
market price for corn. With the loan maturing in July, the farmer decides whether to repay the loan plus interest and sell on the open market,
or deliver to CCC. The relationship between June–August prices and
the loan rate thus affect the quantity of corn delivered to CCC from that

under support. (See Table 8.2.) The decisions of whether to put corn under loan and to deliver to CCC differ, however, to a significant extent. The delivery decision should be obvious unless the price difference is negligible: Sell to the higher bidder—the market or the government. The decision to place corn under loan is influenced not only by the price spread, but also by *expected* differences between later market prices and the current loan level. Also, in some cases the need for short-term working capital to finance the purchase of fertilizer, feed, etc., rather than price differentials, influences the decision. In placing corn under loan, an element of hedging exists.

Two regression equations were estimated to express these relationships from past farmer behavior. Equation (8.5) is the loan decision function and Equation (8.6) is the delivery decision function.

$$C_t = -1.886 + 4.768(P_{1t}/L_t) - 2.801(P_{1t}/L_t)^2 + 0.044T \quad (8.5)$$
$$ (1.359) (0.73) \phantom{- 2.801(P_{1t}/L_t)^2} (0.0126)$$

$$R^2 = 0.85$$

$$C_{dt} = 3.888 - 3.357(P_{2t}/L_t) \quad (8.6)$$
$$\phantom{C_{dt} = 3.888 -} (0.347)$$

$$R^2 = 0.85$$

where

C_t = corn placed under support as percent of total production
C_{dt} = quantity delivered as percent of C_t
P_{1t} = corn price in November–May
P_{2t} = corn price in June–August
L_t = loan rate for period t
T = a time variable with 0 for 1948–60 and 1 for 1961–65

All coefficients for both equations are significant at the 0.01 level. Both equations were derived from aggregate data for the period 1948–63.

Price Expectations Model ● A simple learning model was initially specified for a price expectation formulation. It implies an expectation that price P_t, in period t, will be the same as price P_{t-1}, in $t-1$, plus a weighted correction factor:

$$P_t{}^* = P_{t-1}{}^* + \beta(P_{t-1} - P_{t-1}{}^*) \quad (8.7)$$

where

$P_t{}^*$ = expected price at period t
P_t = actual or realized price at period t
β = coefficient of expectations with $0 \leq \beta \leq 1$

Table 8.2 ● Corn: Price Support and Delivery Operations, 1948–65

Year beginning October	National average loan rate ($)	Price November-May ($)	Percentage of total production placed under support (%)	Price June-August ($)	Percentage of total production placed under support (%)
1948	1.44	1.20	16.2	1.21	90.0
1949	1.40	1.18	13.1	1.41	23.0
1950	1.47	1.55	2.0	1.63	2.0
1951	1.57	1.66	1.0	1.73	4.0
1952	1.60	1.47	14.0	1.47	90.0
1953	1.60	1.42	16.3	1.51	90.0
1954	1.62	1.38	9.6	1.37	97.0
1955	1.58	1.21	14.7	1.43	97.0
1956	1.45[a]	1.21	15.5	1.23	100.0
1957	1.29[a]	1.02	12.1	1.18	97.0
1958	1.24[a]	1.05	11.4	1.14	100.0
1959	1.12	1.00	13.8	1.08	87.0
1960	1.06	0.96	16.3	1.04	75.0
1961	1.20	0.97	18.2	1.03	94.0
1962	1.20	1.04	17.1	1.18	84.0
1963	1.07	1.10	10.6	1.13	29.0
1964	1.10	1.16	7.0	1.21	28.0
1965	1.05	1.12	6.4	1.27	27.0

Source: U. S. Dept. of Agriculture, Feed Situation no. 211, USDA ERS, November 1965.

[a] A weighted average of rates available to compliers and noncompliers.

The correction factor is a measure of past failure to predict price accurately.[6] However, a stochastic component of behavior is hypothesized and added to the price expectations model. This random element was included in the expectation function to reflect the impossibility of perfectly predicting the human choice process. Applying this notion to Equation (8.7), we obtain a revised price forecast, P_t^*:

$$P_t^* = P_{t-1}^* + \beta(P_{t-1} - P_{t-1}^*) + \beta|P_{t-1} - P_{t-1}^*|e \qquad (8.7a)$$

Setting

$$e' \equiv \beta|P_{t-1} - P_{t-1}^*|e \qquad (8.7b)$$

it follows by Equation (8.7), that

$$\tilde{P}_t^* = P_t^* + e'; \text{ and } e' \sim N(0, \sigma_{e'}) \qquad (8.7c)$$

The modification introduces a realistic aspect of variability among individuals with respect to their decision processes. It causes decisions to differ even for otherwise identical units using identical decision procedures. The validity of this or any other hypothetical model of price expectations should be investigated further. Halter and Dean have demonstrated how studying and testing such models might be accomplished through simulation techniques.[7]

Experimentation with the Micro-Simulator ● In addition to behavioral relationships, the micro-simulator includes accounting identities to summarize the operation of the first and update the status variables as farm operations progress through time. These identities include common accounting procedures such as summing of feed consumption (by feed and by class of livestock), grain bought and sold, labor hiring, production of crops and livestock, total operating costs, and gross and net revenue. The accounting routines also update inventories of grain and livestock.

As background for later application, some of the behavioral assumptions embodied in the micro-simulation model were tested and the sensitivity of the model was analyzed with respect to certain changes in parameters of the postulated decision-making processes. The purpose was to observe how changes in the values of certain parameters affect the

6. Heady discusses a variety of price expectation models. The present model can be viewed as a hybrid of his mean price model and random outcomes model. See Earl O. Heady, *Economics of Agricultural Production and Resource Use* (Englewood Cliffs, N.J.: Prentice-Hall, 1952), pp. 475–96.

7. A. N. Halter, and G. W. Dean, Simulation of a California Range-Feedlot Operation, California Agricultural Experiment Station, *Giannini Foundation Research Report* 282, 1965.

output of the model. Specifically, as noted above, several decision rules were assumed to represent the decision-making process. On a priori grounds, the parameters of these decision rules were assigned certain reasonable values. It was necessary to know whether and how changes in the values of these parameters would affect, in particular, average net revenue and average number of animal units on the farm during the period of analysis. The information gained from such an investigation afforded an insight into some important behavioral relationships of the model. The analysis suggested some propositions regarding the effect of changes in both the parameters and the decision rules upon the micro-simulator. It is beyond the scope of this chapter to provide a detailed discussion of the experiment.[8]

THE MARKET EQUILIBRIUM MODEL ● The macro-simulator is essentially an econometric submodel serving as the link between the simulated system and the rest of the economy. (See Fig. 8.2.) The endogenous inputs to this submodel are the aggregated outputs of the micro-simulator, and these in turn determine a set of overall outputs of the simulated system. These inputs are grain production and grain and livestock prices. The exogenous inputs of the econometric model are personal disposable income and the general price level of production factors (expressed by the index of items used in agricultural production). The outputs are predicted grain and livestock prices. The relationships of this submodel comprise an interrelated set of supply and demand schedules, and hence are referred to as the market. The prices which emerge from this model of the market are a set of equilibrium prices.

The econometric submodel is a modified version of Foote's four-equation model for the feed-livestock section.[9] The data used in estimating the parameters of the model are presented in Table 8.3. The model is specified in a form which permits a single-equation, least-squares estimation of the parameters.

Information on corn supply, livestock inventories, and corn fed to livestock is generated by a model representing only one region of the national economy, the Corn Belt, because the sample of farms was taken in that region. The outputs of the econometric model, however, are related to the national economy. This restriction requires that the econometric model utilize regional data in producing the average national prices. Such an approach is acceptable for two reasons. First, the Corn Belt is the major corn-producing region in the United States. It accounts for about 55 percent of the annual corn crop, and since it is a net corn exporting region, the Corn Belt accounts for about 60

8. Mordechai Shechter, Empirical Decision Rules for Agricultural Policy: A Simulation Analysis of the Feed Grain Program, Ph.D. thesis, Iowa State Univ., Ames, 1968.

9. Richard J. Foote, A Four Equation Model of the Feed-Livestock Economy and Its Endogenous Mechanism, *Journal of Farm Economics* 35 (1953): 44–61; idem, Statistical Analysis Relating to the Feed-Livestock Economy, *USDA Technical Bulletin* 1070, 1953.

Table 8.3 ● Basic Data for the Econometric Model

Year	(1) Corn Production Corn Belt (million bu)	(1) U.S. (million bu)	(3) Corn Belt as % of U.S. production (%)	(4) Corn Belt corn supply (million tons)	(5) AU(t) (thousand)	(6) PCD(t) ($ per bu)	(7) PL(t)	(8) PLPC(t)	(9) Q(t)	(10) CFED(t) (million tons)	(11) DPI(t) ($ billion)
1946	1,746	3,088	56.5	48.9	57,998	1.60	248	155	82	24.1	158
1947	1,192	2,392	49.8	33.4	55,464	2.16	329	152	80	20.5	172
1948	1,949	3,431	56.8	54.6	58,224	1.20	361	301	85	23.2	191
1949	2,048	3,760	54.5	57.4	61,362	1.20	311	259	88	26.9	187
1950	1,899	3,609	52.6	53.2	63,663	1.41	340	241	92	26.3	206
1951	1,832	3,370	54.4	51.3	62,307	1.44	409	284	92	26.6	225
1952	2,011	3,469	57.9	56.3	59,630	1.36	353	260	93	24.3	235
1953	2,111	3,652	57.8	59.1	58,740	1.35	288	213	96	25.1	250
1954	2,060	3,629	56.7	57.7	61,245	1.31	283	216	99	23.8	255
1955	2,252	3,909	57.6	63.1	62,946	1.19	246	207	99	25.2	271
1956	2,471	4,241	58.3	69.2	61,101	1.15	235	204	97	25.3	287
1957	2,544	4,466	56.9	71.2	59,954	0.94	275	291	99	26.6	305
1958	2,735	4,826	56.7	76.6	63,437	0.96	335	351	104	29.5	318
1959	3,146	5,350	58.8	88.1	61,401	0.91	313	344	102	31.6	337
1960	3,375	5,696	59.3	94.5	61,306	0.87	296	339	107	31.9	352

Sources: U.S. Dept. of Agriculture, Supplement for 1966 to Livestock-Feed Relationships, 1909–1965, USDA ERS Statistical Bulletin 337; U.S. Dept. of Agriculture, Agricultural Prices, USDA SRS Crop Reporting Board, June 1960; U.S. Dept. of Agriculture, Crop Production 1966, USDA SRS Crop Reporting Board, December 1966; U.S. Dept. of Commerce, Statistical Abstract of the United States, 1966, Bureau of the Census.

NOTE: Column heading symbols are defined in the text.

percent of all corn sold. These percentages have fluctuated very little in the past twenty years. Moreover, the yields of other feed grains tend to fluctuate in the same direction as those of corn, so that fluctuations in total feed grains production in both the Corn Belt and the United States are fairly accurately represented by year-to-year variations in Corn Belt corn production. The same argument applies to Corn Belt livestock production which has been an almost constant 37 percent of the national production over the past twenty years. Second, in subsequent testing of the reasonableness of the model, its predictions compared favorably with the observed behavior of the feed-livestock sector over the period of analysis. The results of this test are described below.

The Statistical Model ● The following symbols are used in the econometric model (t is a time subscript):

Q_t = the index of livestock and livestock products for sale and home consumption (1957–59 = 100)

DPI_t = disposable personal income

AU_t = number of grain-consuming animal units fed annually in the Corn Belt

PL_t = index of meat animal prices, January–December (1910–14 = 100)

$Pl_{t,7}$ = average corn price received by farmers, November–May[10]

$Pl_{t,1}$ = average annual corn price received by farmers

PCD_t = $Pl_{t,7}$ deflated by the index of prices paid in production

$CFED_t$ = corn fed annually in the Corn Belt

$SUPPLY_t$ = corn supply in the Corn Belt

$PLPC_t = \dfrac{PL_t}{PCD_t}$

The econometric model is expressed in terms of the logarithms of the variables

$$Q_t = 0.317 + 0.287 DPI_t + 0.537 AU_t \qquad (8.8)$$
$$(0.022) \qquad (0.147)$$
$$R^2 = 0.96$$

$$PLPC_t = 1.233 + 0.524 \frac{SUPPLY_t}{SUPPLY_{t-1}} - 0.686 Q_t + 1.780 CFED_t \qquad (8.9)$$
$$(0.191) \qquad (0.659)$$
$$R^2 = 0.81$$

10. The econometric model is best suited to predict the November–May price of corn. During this period corn prices mainly reflect the size of the previous October's crop. By June or July, the outlook for the next crop affects corn price level, and predicting corn price for that period becomes more complicated.

$$\frac{PCD_t}{PCD_{t-1}} = 0.004 - 0.778 \frac{SUPPLY_t}{SUPPLY_{t-1}} 0.301 \frac{PLPC_t}{PLPC_{t-1}} \tag{8.10}$$

$$R^2 = 0.93$$

More compactly, these equations are expressed in matrix form as

$$\begin{pmatrix} 1 & 0 & 0 \\ 0.686 & 1 & 0 \\ 0 & \dfrac{0.301PCD_{t-1}}{PLPC_{t-1}} & 1 \end{pmatrix} \begin{pmatrix} Q_t \\ PLPC_t \\ PCD_t \end{pmatrix}$$

$$= \begin{pmatrix} 0.317 + 0.287DPI_t\ 0.537AU_t \\ 1.233 + 0.524 \dfrac{SUPPLY_t}{SUPPLY_{t-1}} + 1.78CFED_t \\ 0.004 - 0.78 \dfrac{SUPPLY_t}{SUPPLY_{t-1}} PCD_{t-1} \end{pmatrix} \tag{8.11}$$

The left-hand side of Equation (8.11) constitutes a causal chain; namely, the coefficient matrix of the endogenous variables is completely triangular, with unit elements in the principal diagonal. The right-hand side contains exogenous variables (with respect to the econometric submodel). In this case we can apply the method of ordinary, single-equation least-squares to yield asymptotically unbiased estimates of the parameters.

Testing the Submodel ● Using 1961–67 data, the predictive power of the econometric model was tested by comparing the observed and predicted series of its outputs. This information, together with the data used in the testing, is given in Table 8.4. Predicted values were reasonably close to the observed values, and the model successfully predicted most of the turning points in the series.

OPTIMIZATION: RESPONSE SURFACE ANALYSIS ● A simulation model is basically an inductive process whereby experimental observations provide a basis for general assertions about the real system. In the first phase of this process numerical solutions of a simulation model are obtained for given alternative sets of policy decision rules, parameters, initial system conditions, and other exogenous data. The alternatives could arbitrarily be selected by the investigator. Or they could follow an ordered plan, one which would provide a means for a systematic study of the model response to the planned changes. The

Table 8.4 ● Comparison between Predicted and Observed Values, and Exogenous Data for the Econometric Model 1961–67

Year	Q	$\hat{Q}$	PLPC	$\widehat{PLPC}$	$PI(t,1)$	$\widehat{PI}(t,1)$	PL	$\hat{PL}$	PBEEF	$\widehat{PBEEF}$	PHOG	$\widehat{PHOG}$	SUPPLY(t)	AU(t)	CFED	DPI
	(1957–59 = 100)		($)		(1910-14=100)				($ per cwt)				(million bu)	(millions)	(million tons)	($ billion)
1961	107	107	305	350	1.08	1.02	299	311	20.20	20.40	16.60	17.90	3297.1	61.532	33.2	363.7
1962	111	110	316	·329	1.10	1.10	310	313	21.30	21.22	16.30	16.74	3142.5	63.041	32.7	384.4
1963	113	110	303	314	1.09	1.12	290	299	19.90	20.38	14.90	15.77	3237.8	62.271	31.2	402.5
1964	111	109	262	277	1.15	1.21	270	289	18.00	19.59	14.80	15.51	3055.2	58.753	29.7	431.8
1965	112	111	333	331	1.10	1.13	319	317	19.90	21.34	20.60	17.16	3231.9	57.681	31.9	469.1
1966	116	117	327	320	1.29	1.25	356	328	22.20	22.36	22.80	17.22	3040.4	61.500	33.1	505.3

Sources: U. S. Dept. of Agriculture, Livestock-Feed Relationships, 1909–1963, USDA ERS Bulletin 337; U. S. Dept. of Agriculture, Livestock Production Units, 1910–1964, USDA Statistical Bulletin 325; U. S. Dept. of Agriculture, supplement for 1966 to Livestock-Feed Relationships, 1909–1965, Bulletin 337; U. S. Dept. of Agriculture, Agricultural Prices, June 1960; U. S. Dept. of Agriculture, Crop Production 1966, December 1966; U. S. Dept. of Commerce, Statistical Abstract of the United States, 1966, Bureau of the Census.

NOTES: Predicted values are marked by "$\frown$" above the name of the variable. Column heading symbols are defined in the text.

system's behavior under these various conditions is traced and recorded. This experimental phase does not involve optimization.

In the second phase, the results of the experimental phase provide the data for research for an optimal policy. Statistical techniques are used for designing planned experiments with the simulation model and searching for its optimal solution. This method is called response surface analysis. The information thereby obtained (1) provides a better understanding of the analyzed policy and its impact on the simulated system; and (2) furnishes the policy maker with a set of optimal-decision rules which is usually much smaller than the set of all feasible rules.

The Policy Space ● As mentioned earlier, each simulation run was associated with a different decision rule and yielded specific values of the system's response variables. The policy decision rules considered relate to the Feed Grain Program. In the context of this model, the provisions of the Feed Grain Program are the parameters of the policy decision rules. These parameters constitute the elements of a policy space whose dimension is determined by their number. The policy space corresponds to the factor space of experimental design. The parameters are the factors, and the values of a parameter correspond to levels of a factor.

An example illustrates these concepts. Suppose the level of government grain stocks is an input, and the rate of support loan per bushel of corn is the output of a given decision rule. A market control mechanism could then be characterized by this decision rule in the following manner:

$$L_t = 0.90 \text{ if } S_{t-1} > S^*; \ 1.00 \text{ if } S_{t-1} = S^*; \ 1.10 \text{ if } S_{t-1} < S^* \qquad (8.12)$$

where

$$t = \text{a time period subscript}$$
$$L_t = \text{the loan rate in dollars per bushel}$$
$$S_t = \text{the level of stocks}$$
$$S^* = \text{a desired level of stocks}[11]$$

The step function, Equation (8.12), contains two parameters, S^*, and the parameter which specifies the step height which in this case is $0.10. Hence the policy space consists of two elements or factors. An example of a simpler decision rule is the following constant function:

$$L_t = \alpha 1.00 \qquad (8.13)$$

where α is the only parameter. A given decision rule may comprise a

---

11. S^* could represent the minimum level of stocks consistent with national security requirements, plus the amount of working stocks necessary for normal functioning of the market.

set of functions such as Equations (8.12) or (8.13), with each function relating to a different provision of the Feed Grain Program.

Four provisions of the Feed Grain Program were selected for the analysis, forming the elements of the policy space. The provisions were (1) minimum acreage of land diversion, (2) national average loan rate, (3) national average price support payment, and (4) payment rates on diverted land. Different combinations of the values of the provisions yielded different decision rules. In the language of experimental design there were four elements in the factor space, spanning $\prod_{i=1}^{4} n_i$ treatment combinations (decision rules), where n_i is the number of levels of the i-th factor (the value of the i-th provision). (The terms *factor, parameter,* and *provision* are used interchangeably in all subsequent discussion.) The levels associated with each factor are given in Table 8.5. In order to conform with established notation, capital letters denote a factor, and the numbers -1, 0, and $+1$ represent the levels of the factor. Most of the values which appear in Table 8.5 are within their actual 1961–67 range.

The Problem of Measurement ● It is first necessary to determine which response variables are to be selected to gauge the performance of the simulated system. On the basis of the Feed Grain Program's objectives, four response variables were chosen: average net farm revenue of all farms, average net farm revenue of participating farms, total corn stock accumulation in the period 1961–67, and total government costs during the same period.

NET REVENUE OF ALL FARMS. Average net farm revenue of the entire population of micro-simulator units is calculated as follows:

Let

$\bar{y}_R$ = mean income per farm in a given simulation run
y_{its} = net income of farm i, year t, simulation run s, $i = 1, \ldots,$
        n; $t = 1, \ldots, T$; $s = 1, \ldots, S$
w_i = a weight for farm i

then

$$\bar{Y}_R = \frac{\sum_s \sum_t \sum_i w_i y_{its}}{nTS} \tag{8.14}$$

NET REVENUE, PARTICIPANTS. It was assumed that the policy maker would be interested not only in the average farm income figure, but also in knowing how each decision rule affected the participating group. The policy maker probably would not select rules which penalized the vol-

Table 8.5 ● Provisions of the Feed Grain Program and the Level Specified for the Model

Provision	Factor	Levels of the factor		
		-1	0	+1
Minimum diversion, percentage of feed grains base	A	20	10	0
Price support loan rate ($ per bu)	B	0.95	1.025	1.10
Price support payment ($ per bu)	C	0.10	0.175	0.25
Diversion payment rate	D	0/50[a]	...	20/50[a]

[a]The first figure represents payment rate for minimum diversion. The second figure is the rate for above minimum diversion. Only two levels were specified for this factor.

untary participants. The net revenue per participating farm was calculated as follows:

Let

$\overline{Y}_R^P$ = mean income per participating farm in a given run

y_{its}^P = net income of participating farm i, year t, simulation run s,
$i = 1, \ldots, n_P; \; t = 1, \ldots, T; \; s = 1, \ldots, S$

n_P = the number of participating farms in year t

then

$$\overline{Y}_R^P = \frac{1}{TS} \, \Sigma_s \Sigma_t \, \frac{\Sigma_i w_i y_{its}^P}{n_p} \qquad (8.15)$$

STOCK ACCUMULATION. Each simulation run started with an initial stock level of 813 million bushels. This figure reflected the Corn Belt's relative share of total CCC-held stocks in October 1960. The model did not assume any sales of CCC stocks for export. The final value for each run was a gross figure representing the initial stocks plus accumulation minus sales in the domestic market.

PROGRAM COSTS. Total government costs include total land diversion payments, total price support payments, and storage charges on the accumulated stocks. These costs do not include administrative expenses associated with the operation of the loan program. The final figures are the cost of carrying out the program in the Corn Belt only.

The Problem of Sample Size ● Each simulation run yields a single observation for each of the four response variables. These observations are random variables because they are themselves functions of random inputs. Since the selection of an optimal policy is based on these observations, we are interested in increasing the precision of their measurements. Replication is a means of achieving this objective. By replicating the basic experiment, it may be possible to obtain a more precise estimate (a smaller error) of the mean effect of any factor of that experiment.[12] This is achieved when each sample observation is an average of several replications of the given policy alternatives. Each sequence in this investigation is equivalent to an experimental replication. Each run consists of several sequences. Operationally, each replication within a given run was associated with a different random series of normal variates and a different series of corn yields.

---

12. Pinhas Zusman, and Amotz Amiad, Simulation: A Tool for Farm Planning Under Conditions of Weather Uncertainty, *Journal of Farm Economics* 47 (1965): 574–94.

The optimal number of replications was determined by a method suggested by Cochran.[13] It incorporates both the problem of sample size and the cost of taking the sample.

Let

$l(z)$ = the loss (e.g., expressed as money cost or penalty) due to an error of amount z in the estimate

$f(z,n)$ = the frequency distribution of z

n = sample size (number of replications)

The expected loss for a given sample size is

$$L(n) = \int l(z) \ f(z,n) dz \tag{8.16}$$

Furthermore, let

$$C(n) = c_o + c_1 n \tag{8.17}$$

be the cost associated with taking a sample of size n, where c_o is the overhead cost, and c_1 is the cost per unit. If $l(z)$ is expressed in monetary terms, a reasonable procedure is to choose n to minimize $C(n) + L(n)$. The loss might be proportional to the absolute value of the error, namely, $l(z) = \lambda |\bar{y} - \mu|$ where $\bar{y}$ is an estimate of μ. Minimizing $C(n) + L(n)$ under this condition leads to the following expression for sample size:[14]

$$n = \left(\frac{\lambda s}{c_1 \ 2\pi} \right)^{2/3}$$

where s is the standard error of y. Hence, a preliminary estimate of σ, s, is needed in this case. A value of $s\bar{Y}_R \cong 1,000$ was obtained in a preliminary benchmark run of the model ($\bar{Y}_R$ = average net revenue per farm).[15] For $\lambda = 1$, and $c_1 = 75$,

$$n = \left(\frac{1000}{75 \ \sqrt{2\pi}} \right)^{2/3} \cong 3 \tag{8.18}$$

THE PROBLEM OF VALIDATION. Since results of the simulation runs were used in making policy recommendations, it is important to ascertain that these policy recommendations are derived from a model capable of

13. William G. Cochran, *Sampling Techniques*, 2nd ed., (New York: Wiley, 1963).

14. Schechter, Empirical Decision Rules for Agricultural Policy.

15. See the benchmark run column in Table 8.8.

predicting the real system to a reasonable extent. Various verification procedures are found in literature. Historical verification was used in this study. This procedure tests the degree of correspondence between data generated by the simulation model and the observed historical time series of the respective variables. In this way a measure of "goodness of fit" is obtained for the model *as a whole*. It should be noted however that this procedure is valid only when it reproduces the conditions (exogenous data, parameters, decision rules) which actually existed during the analysis period. The validation procedure in the circumstances is merely a null test. A model which fails this test would be suspect; however no strong statement can be made for the one which passes it.

The correspondence between the simulation model and the system it approximated was studied by observing the model's behavior under the Feed Grain Program's provisions which were in effect during the period from 1961 to 1967. One simulation run incorporating those provisions was carried out. It was designated the benchmark run, or run 0. The observed and the predicted values of a number of selected outputs are presented in Table 8.6, and Figures 8.3, 8.4, and 8.5. The output of the simulation model was based upon sample estimates "blown up" to represent regional quantities. It can be shown that the sample estimates are unbiased estimates of population totals at the level of the study area, but are not necessarily unbiased at the regional level. Therefore it is not surprising that the model was better in predicting the

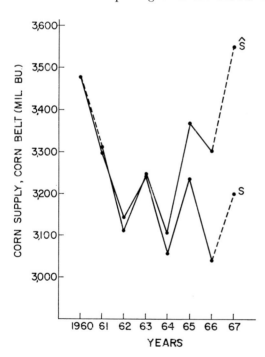

Fig. 8.3. Predicted $\hat{S}$ and observed S, corn supplies in the Corn Belt, 1961–67.

Table 8.6 ● Predicted and Observed Values of Selected Systems Outputs, 1961–67, Run O

Year	Average corn price		Livestock price index		Corn supply, Corn Belt		Animal units, Corn Belt		Percent of corn placed under support		Percent of corn delivered		Total payments	
	P^a	O^a	P	O	P	O	P	O	P	O	P	O	P^b	O
	($ per bu)		(1910-14=100)		(million bu)		(million units)		(%)				($ million)	
1961	1.08	1.03	267	299	3,312.3	3,297.1	54.9	61.5	25.4	18.3	79	97	645	772
1962	1.10	1.16	287	310	3,112.8	3,142.5	56.9	63.0	11.3	16.4	73	78	857	841
1963	1.09	1.12	294	290	3,243.2	3,237.8	57.6	62.3	11.5	9.8	58	13	1,058	843
1964	1.15	1.17	290	270	3,104.1	3,055.2	56.7	58.8	9.8	6.2	35	12	1,057	1,163
1965	1.10	1.16	294	319	3,367.7	3,231.9	56.6	57.7	8.6	5.3	26	0.09	1,239	1,391
1966	1.29	1.24	267	356	3,302.3	3,040.4	52.3	62.0	8.8	6.4	26	0.08	1,397	1,293
1967	1.20	1.03	266	336	3,548.5	3,447.0	53.1	61.2	0.0	10.4	0	23.50	1,312	865

Sources: U. S. Dept. of Agriculture, Livestock-Feed Relationships, 1909–1963, USDA ERS Bulletin 337;
U. S. Dept. of Agriculture, Livestock Production Units, 1910–1964, Statistical Bulletin 325;
supplement for 1966 to Livestock-Feed Relationships, 1909–1965; U. S. Dept. of Agriculture,
Agricultural Prices, June 1960; U. S. Dept. of Agriculture, Crop Production 1966, December 1966;
U. S. Dept. of Commerce, Statistical Abstract of the United States, 1966, Bureau of the Census;
U. S. Dept. of Agriculture, Farm Income Situation, USDA ERS, July 1968.

[a] P is the predicted value, O is the observed value.
[b] Corn Belt payments converted to national payments on the basis of the 1961 ratio between Corn Belt
and national payments.

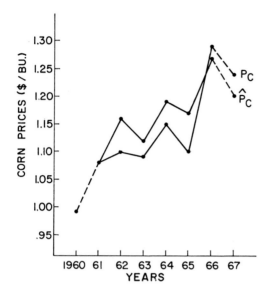

Fig. 8.4. Predicted $\hat{P}_c$ and observed P_c, average U.S. corn prices, 1961–67.

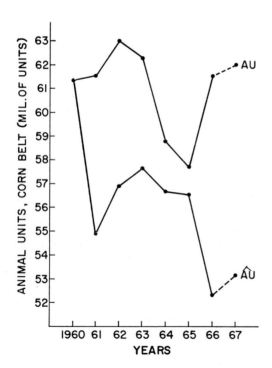

Fig. 8.5. Predicted $\hat{AU}$ and observed AU, number of animal units fed in the Corn Belt, 1961–67.

relative levels of the variables and turning points in their values than in predicting their actual values. (Owing to the very short time series involved no objective test for comparison was used.)

The model was best in predicting corn supplies in the Corn Belt (Fig. 8.3). As a result, the predicted U.S. average corn prices were also quite close to the actual 1961–67 values (Fig. 8.4). All turning points in the corn price series were predicted by the model. The model was fairly accurate in predicting relative changes in livestock inventories up to 1966 (Fig. 8.5). Thereafter, instead of an increase in number, it exhibited a continuation of the downward trend in inventories. This failure was probably a result of two interrelated factors. First, the actual livestock price index increased sharply from 1965 to 1966. This increase was influenced to a large extent by a strong upward trend in demand for meat, especially pork, associated with increased military procurements. The disposable personal income variable did not adequately reflect this demand expansion by the military. As a result, predicted livestock prices continued to decline until 1966 when the system responded to this predicted price trend with a decline in inventories, the result of pessimistic price expectations on the part of the farmers. The second reason for the decline in livestock inventories was associated with the model's underlying assumption of fixed levels for all livestock classes, except for hogs and beef. Poultry constituted a sizeable part of the inventory increase from 1965 to 1966. The model was not constructed to predict changes in this class of livestock.

The benchmark run yielded estimates very close to the percentage of corn placed under support, i.e., corn for which CCC nonrecourse loans were obtained (Table 8.6). However, the prediction equation for corn deliveries was rather sensitive to the ratio of market price to loan rate. As a result, a small deviation of predicted market price from its actual price caused a wide discrepancy between the predicted and observed values of corn deliveries. Nevertheless the model did predict the decline in deliveries from the very high levels in 1961–62 to the negligible quantities in 1965–67. In addition, there were still quantities of 1964–66 corn in the farm reseal program as of August 1967. Part or even all of this corn could eventually be delivered to CCC, raising the percentage figures indicated for this corn in the observed column of CCC deliveries.

The predicted values of total payments reflected the steady increase in government outlay for the Feed Grain Program. Except for 1961, there was an almost constant difference in the vicinity of $200 million between the predicted and the observed values. Part of this difference was a result of the inclusion of storage charges on CCC stocks in the predicted total payments. These charges were not included in the actual payments reported.

The preceding discussion leads us to conclude that within the period of analysis the present simulation model behaved in a reasonable manner. Thus it is a reliable tool for making relative comparisons among policy alternatives.

Response Surface Analysis ● In terms of experimental design our objective was to select a combination of factor levels which would maximize (or minimize) the selected response variables. This combination is the optimal decision rule with respect to a given response variable. Response surface techniques attempt to identify the factor levels which yield the extreme value of the response. The response of the simulated system can be represented by the *response function*.

$$\eta = \phi(x_1, x_2, \ldots, x_k) \tag{8.19}$$

where η is the response variable, and x_i is the level of the i-th factor. η represents the true value of the response corresponding to any particular combination of factor levels. It would be obtained in the absence of experimental error. Because of error the observed value, y, generally differs from the value of η. Combinations of factor levels correspond to points in a $k + 1$ dimensional space. The levels used in any set of trials are represented by a cluster of points whose configuration is the specific design of the experiment. This region is called the *experimental region*. The values of factors A, B, C, and D, given in Table 8.7, define the experimental region of this investigation.

Response surface analysis is usually carried out in two stages—exploration of the response surface, and determination of the optimum condition. In the first stage the investigator "maps" the experimental region and attempts to determine the general shape of the response surface. In the second stage he searches for the surface peaks. A sampling strategy specifies which sampling method should be used in each stage. Random or factorial sampling is usually employed in the first stage. The second stage involves a combination of one or more systematic sampling plans. The ability to carry out the experiment in stages is one of the main advantages of this technique. Rather than conducting one large and expensive experiment, several experiments on a lower scale are carried out. The results obtained in each stage provide the information needed for planning and executing successive experiments. Such a procedure is feasible only if the results of one experiment are quickly available, which is the case in computer simulation.

A commonly used strategy of response surface analysis in industrial experimentation suggests the following procedures:[16] In the first stage we attempt to approximate the response function within the experimental region by a first degree polynomial using a 2^k factorial experiment. Trials are carried out at a grid of points throughout the experimental region and the "height" of the response surface at these points is determined. Geometrically, the hyperplane, $\eta = \beta_0 + \beta_1 x_1 + \beta_2 x_2 + \ldots$, is fitted to the sample observations. Next, single factor or steepest

16. Owen L. Davies, (ed.), *The Design and Analysis of Industrial Experiments* (New York: Hafner, 1954).

Table 8.7 ● Basic Plan 3 for a $3^3 2^1$ Factorial Experiment

Trial number (run or treatment[a] combination)	Factor level			
	x_A	x_B	x_C	x_D
1	-1	-1	-1	0
2	1	0	0	0
3	0	1	1	0
4	0	0	-1	1
5	-1	1	0	1
6	1	-1	1	1
7	1	1	-1	0
8	0	-1	0	0
9	-1	0	1	0

[a]Treatments are combinations of factors A, B, C, and D, described in Table 8.5.

ascent method determines a new set of trials, i.e., additional sampling. The relative magnitudes and signs of the slopes, β_i, determine the direction of the steepest slope, or fastest "climb" toward the peak.

In the second stage the nature of the near-stationary region is determined by fitting a second degree polynomial. The grid method is again applied by performing a 3^k factorial experiment. The task then is to estimate a function, such as (for $k = 2$)

$$\eta = \beta_0 + \beta_1 x_1 + \beta_2 x_2 + \beta_{11} x_1^2 + \beta_{22} x_2^2 + \beta_{12} x_1 x_2 \qquad (8.20)$$

The true maximum, if it exists, can now be found, assuming that Equation (8.20) is an appropriate approximation of the response surface. The magnitudes of the factors which yield the highest point on this surface are estimates of their optimal values. The coefficients of the Equations (8.13) and (8.19) are estimated by the method of multiple regression. These coefficients are estimates of the main and interaction effects, except for a factor of proportion, in standard factorial analysis.

A complete analysis of the response surface was not possible in this investigation due to budgetary constraints, and first and second stages were combined by directly fitting a second degree polynomial. This treatment assumes that all interactions among factors can be disregarded, i.e., no coefficients for cross-product terms are estimated. Such a simplification is a trade-off price in obtaining more information about additional factors in the experiment. To the extent that not all interactions are zero, they are confounded with the estimated effects. A second simplification is the assumption that the topography of the response surface is relatively "smooth." Thus variation due to lack of fit is assumed to be small relative to experimental error, and most of the variability is due to the latter. This assumption was essential since an independent estimate of the experimental error was not available.

THE MAIN EFFECT PLAN. In terms of experimental design, the investigation required a plan which would enable the estimation of the main effects (single factor coefficients) in the most efficient manner. Three factors at three levels and one factor at two levels were considered, yielding a $3^3 2^1$ factorial experiment (Table 8.7). The selected plan permitted the estimation of the following polynomial:

$$\eta = \beta_0 x_0 + \beta_1 x_A + \beta_2 x_B + \beta_3 x_C + \beta_4 x_D$$

$$+ \beta_{11} x_A^2 + \beta_{22} x_B^2 + \beta_{33} x_C^2 \qquad (8.21)$$

where x_A, x_B, x_C, and x_D are the levels of factors A, B, C, and D, respectively, $x_0 = 1$, and eight independent coefficients, β_0, β_1, . . . , β_{33}, were estimated. The sampling plan involved nine sample observations, leaving one degree of freedom for the lack-of-fit test. (See below.) The plan specified a set of nine treatment combinations given in Table 8.8. Each row in Table 8.8 represents a treatment combination. For example, the last row includes factors A and D at their low levels, factor B at its intermediate level, and factor C at its high level.

The original values of the x's in Equation (8.21) are coded in the table, so that each x takes the values -1, 0, and $+1$ for a three-level factor, and 0 and 1 for a two-level factor. The relationships between the coded and original x values are:

$$\text{Factor A:} \quad x_A = \frac{-\tilde{x}_A + 10}{10}$$

$$\text{Factor B:} \quad x_B = \frac{\tilde{x}_B - 1.025}{0.075}$$

$$\text{Factor C:} \quad x_C = \frac{\tilde{x}_C - 0.175}{0.075}$$

$$\text{Factor D:} \quad x_D = \frac{\tilde{x}_D}{20}$$

where $\tilde{x}_A$ denotes the original values of factor A, etc.

Instead of fitting Equation (8.21) for the purpose of estimating the β's, it is more convenient to fit an equivalent expression. The design of Table 8.8 has the following properties:

$$\frac{\Sigma x_A}{9} = \frac{\Sigma x_B}{9} = \frac{\Sigma x_C}{9} = 0$$

$$\frac{\Sigma x_D}{9} = \frac{1}{3}$$

$$\frac{\Sigma x_A^2}{9} = \frac{\Sigma x_B^2}{9} = \frac{\Sigma x_C^2}{9} = \frac{2}{3}$$

Using these properties, the mean of η, $\bar{\eta}$, is calculated, yielding

$$\bar{\eta} = \beta_0 + \frac{1}{3}\beta_4 + \frac{2}{3}\beta_{22} + \frac{2}{3}\beta_{33} \tag{8.22}$$

Subtracting Equation (8.22) from Equation (8.21) yields

Table 8.8 ● Selected Response Variables of the Nine Decision Rules

Item	Run number[a]									
	0 (Benchmark)	1	2	3	4	5	6	7	8	9
Average annual net income per farm ($)	9,177	7,666	8,277	8,793	8,233	8,804	8,717	8,077	7,592	9,157
Standard deviation	1,063	891	976	1,019	958	1,020	1,024	953	897	1,067
Average annual net income per participating farm ($)	12,838	10,326	12,155	11,608	11,944	12,589	11,629	11,677	10,798	11,834
Stock accumulation at the end of 1967 (million bu)	1,236	1,033	1,612	1,569	1,406	1,293	1,351	1,721	1,071	1,193
Total government payment, 1961–67 ($ million)	2,480	1,139	2,280	2,772	1,917	2,248	2,968	1,865	1,221	2,563

[a]Each run or treatment is a combination of factors A, B, C, and D, described in Table 8.5 and Table 8.7.

$$\eta = \bar{\eta}x_o + \beta_1 x_A + \beta_2 x_B + \beta_3 x_C + \beta_4 \left(x_D - \frac{1}{3}\right)$$

$$+ \beta_{11}\left(x_A^2 - \frac{2}{3}\right) + \beta_{22}\left(x_B^2 - \frac{2}{3}\right) + \beta_{33}\left(x_C^2 - \frac{2}{3}\right) \tag{8.23}$$

or the equivalent form

$$\eta = \bar{\eta}x_o + \beta_1 x_A + \beta_2 x_B + \beta_3 x_C + \frac{1}{3}\beta_4(3x_D - 1)$$

$$+ \frac{1}{3}\beta_{11}(3x_A^2 - 2) + \frac{1}{3}\beta_{22}(3x_B^2 - 2)$$

$$+ \frac{1}{3}\beta_{33}(3x_C^2 - 2) \tag{8.24}$$

This equation yields an orthogonal matrix formed by the new coefficients of the β_i. The estimation proceeds as follows. Let Y be the vector of observations,

$$Y = (y_1, y_2, \ldots, y_9) \tag{8.25}$$

$$B = \left(\bar{\eta},\ \beta_1,\ \frac{1}{3}\beta_{22},\ \beta_3,\ \frac{1}{3}\beta_{33},\ \frac{1}{3}\beta_4\right) \tag{8.26}$$

The matrix of the transformed x's, X, is

$\bar{Y}$	x_A	$3x_A^2-2$	x_B	$3x_B^2-2$	x_C	$3x_C^2-2$	$3x_D-1$
1	-1	1	-1	1	-1	1	-1
1	1	1	0	-2	0	-2	-1
1	0	-2	1	1	1	1	-1
1	0	-2	0	-2	-1	1	2
1	-1	1	1	1	0	-2	2
1	1	1	1	-1	1	1	2
1	1	1	1	1	-1	1	-1
1	0	-2	1	1	0	-2	-1
1	-1	1	0	-2	1	1	-1

X =

Since $X'X$ is a diagonal matrix, the plan is orthogonal. A least-square estimator of B, denoted by $\hat{B}$, is

$$\hat{B} = (X'X)^{-1}X'Y \qquad (8.27)$$

We note that

$$\beta_0 = \bar{\eta} - \frac{1}{3}\beta_4 - \frac{2}{3}\beta_{11} - \frac{2}{3}\beta_{22} - \frac{2}{3}\beta_{33} \qquad (8.28)$$

by Equation (8.22), and that the estimate of $\bar{\eta}$, $\bar{y}$, is given by

$$\bar{\eta} = \bar{y} = \frac{\Sigma_i y_i}{9} \qquad (8.29)$$

The observed values of the four response variables in nine simulation runs are given in Table 8.9. The estimated coefficients of the polynomial function of these response variables and the regression analysis associated with the estimated coefficients are found in Table 8.10.

LACK-OF-FIT TEST. If the second degree polynomial, Equation (8.21), is a true representation of the general response function, Equation (8.19), then the lack-of-fit mean square would be an estimate of the experimental error variable, σ^2. However if the former is not an adequate approximation of the surface in the experimental region, then the residual sum of squares will be inflated by terms associated with this failure to represent the surface correctly. When an independent estimate of σ^2 is available, a comparison of the lack-of-fit mean square with this estimate provides a test for the goodness of fit of the second degree equation. Then a lack-of-fit mean square is substantially larger than the experimental error mean square which is a warning of poor approximation. However since approximating polynomials accounts for 98 percent of the variation in the four response variables, we suppose that the polynomial approximation is adequate. No exact statements (that is comparing the lack-of-fit variance with the experimental error, using an F-test) concerning the goodness of fit of this approximation could be made, and interpretation of the results should be made in this light.

ANALYSIS OF FITTED RESPONSE SURFACES. Following the estimation of the response surface, its extreme points are determined by differentiating with respect to the relevant factors. Generally in the presence of interaction and four factors, this procedure gives rise to a system of four equations in four unknowns, x_A^*, x_B^*, x_C^*, x_D^*, where the asterisk denotes the optimal value of the corresponding factor. Some factors—but not all, as expected for a first set of approximating trials—achieved an

Table 8.9 ● The Estimated Coefficients and Regression Analysis for Four Response Functions

Coefficients[a]	Net income all farms	Net income participants	Stock accumulation	Treasury costs
$\hat{\beta}_0$	8,140.56	11,837.38	1,361.09	1,788.85
$\hat{\beta}_1$	-92.63	118.62	194.03	193.73
$\hat{\beta}_{11}$	243.75	235.32	18.66	206.97
$\hat{\beta}_2$	282.97	520.26	187.95	259.55
$\hat{\beta}_{22}$	-280.67	-556.17	-64.35	-217.77
$\hat{\beta}_3$	448.45	179.03	-7.70	563.82
$\hat{\beta}_{33}$	216.36	-335.88	53.58	287.52
$\hat{\beta}_4$	324.48	671.28	-16.26	404.04
Components of sums of squares[b]				
Polynomial model	2,319,138	3,757,007	453,466	3,203,072
Lack of fit[c] (experimental error)	2,014	10,545	8,723	49,088
Total[d]	2,321,152	3,767,552	462,189	3,252,160

[a]Coefficient in left-hand column has quantitative effect shown in each of next four columns for the respective response variable.
[b]Degrees of freedom are indicated in brackets next to the component's name.
[c]Obtained by subtraction.
[d]Corrected for the mean.

Table 8.10 ● The Levels of Parameters Associated with Extreme Values of the Responses and the Value of the Response at These Levels, Optimal Parameters

Response	Criterion	$\tilde{x}_A$ (%) Max	Min	$\tilde{x}_B$ ($ per bu) Max	Min	$\tilde{x}_C$ (¢ per bu) Max	Min	$\tilde{x}_D$ (%) Max	Min	Net income all farms ($)	Net income participants ($)	Stock (million bu)	Costs ($ million)
Net farm income all farms	maximization	20[a]	8.1[b]	1.06[c]	0.95[b]	25.0[a]	10.0[b]	20[a]	0[b]	10,013[c]	12,590	1,293	3,133
Net farm income participants	maximization	0[a]	12.1	1.06[c]	0.95[b]	19.5[c]	10.0[b]	20[a]	0[b]	8,824	13,010[c]	1,633	2,840
Stock accumulation	minimization	0[b]	20[a]	1.13	0.95[a]	10.0[b]	18.0[c]	0[b]	20[a]	8,271	11,558	933[c]	1,771
Government costs	minimization	0[b]	14.7[c]	1.07	0.95[a]	25.0[b]	10.2[c]	20[b]	0[a]	8,004	10,259	1,084	988[c]

[a] Boundary and optimal values.
[b] Boundary value.
[c] Optimal value.

extreme value within the region. For example, taking the net income response equation,

$$y = 8,140.56 - 92.36\ x_A + 243.75\ x_A^2 + 282.97\ x_B$$

$$- 280.67\ x_B^2 + 448.45\ x_C + 216.36\ x_C^2 + 324.48\ x_D \quad (8.30)$$

and differentiating it with respect to x_B, we obtain

$$\frac{\partial y}{\partial x_B} = 282.97 - 561.34\ x_B \quad^{17} \quad (8.31)$$

Setting this expression equal to zero, the value of $x_B{}^*$ is

$$x_B^* = \frac{282.97}{561.34} = 0.504 \quad (8.32)$$

Using the coding equation for $\tilde{x}_B$, this value corresponds to a support loan of $1.06 per bushel.[18] Repeating this analysis for all response variables, maximizing the function in the case of net income and minimizing it for government cost and stock accumulation, optimal values for all factors were obtained (Table 8.10). However when the extreme value lay outside the experimental region, the proper boundary value was selected.

Net Farm Income Response Surface (All Farms) ●

MINIMUM DIVERSION LEVEL (x_A). Given the optimal values of all other factors, the response function is

$$y = \text{constant} - 92.63\ x_A + 243.75\ x_A^2 \quad (8.33)$$

with a *relative* minimum at $x_A = 0.19$ or, equivalently, $\tilde{x}_A = 8.1$ percent. This result suggests a tentative proposition regarding the impact of the parameter x_A. It is that, *ceteris paribus*, reduced diversion rates decrease net farm income up to this point, but beyond this level further reduction in diversion increases net farm revenue. Under these conditions, the policy maker has some flexibility in selecting the proper level of diversion

17. The extreme value of each variable can be determined independently of the others owing to the absence of cross-product terms in the fitted equations.

18. The function achieves a *relative* maximum with respect to this factor since the second derivative is negative. This is neither a necessary nor sufficient condition for the function y as a whole to reach a maximum at $x_B{}^*$. This condition can be determined only by evaluating the Hessian determinant of y.

above or below the minimum point. That is to say, if the objective is to increase farm income then, at $\tilde{x}_A = 8.1$ percent diversion, a change in x_A in either direction would accomplish it. The policy maker has therefore a certain degree of flexibility in selecting the proper level of this factor, knowing that he would increase net farm revenue whether the criterion required $\tilde{x}_A < 8.1$, or $\tilde{x}_A > 8.1$. However since the objective was to maximize y, the value in Table 8.10 corresponds to a boundary value of x_A.

PRICE SUPPORT LOAN (x_B). A *relative* maximum is located at $\tilde{x}_B = \$1.06$. This result suggests that x_B has a limited effect on farm income. Raising it beyond a certain point results in a decline in net farm income. This result could be attributed to the makeup of the sample. A majority of the farms in the south central region were classified as livestock farms. On these farms, more than half the annual gross income was earned by livestock enterprises. High support prices for corn tended to raise market prices as well, especially since CCC did not allow corn selling below a certain minimum price. The higher corn price meant higher feed prices in general and, at least in the short run, meant lower revenues from livestock whose prices fluctuated independently of the corn price. This explanation may account for some of the drop in income when the support loan rate was raised above $1.06.

PRICE SUPPORT PAYMENT (x_C). The relatively large coefficient of the linear term, compared with that of the quadratic term, suggests that a linear approximation might have been sufficient in the experimental region. This is evident in Figure 8.6 which depicts the topography of the response surface when x_A and x_D are held at their optimal levels within this re-

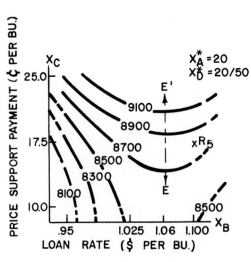

Fig. 8.6. Net revenue response surface.

gion. When $x_A^* = 20$, and $x_D^* = 20$, the net income surface becomes

$$y = 8{,}801.42 + 282.97x_B - 280.67x_B^2 + 448.45x_C + 216.36x_C^2 \qquad (8.34)$$

This is a case of a *minimax,* or a *saddle-point.* It can be seen in Figure 8.6 that while at $x_B^* = \$1.06$ there is a maximum with respect to x_B, the same point represents a minimum with respect to x_C. This surface suggests a continued search in the direction EE'. In explaining this result we should recall that the price support is a per bushel bonus to participating farms which is actually a form of direct subsidy. Therefore the higher the subsidy, the higher their income. To the extent that it did not adversely affect nonparticipants (apparently it did not within the stated range), price support payments increased average farm income as a whole. (See later qualification in discussion of x_C and participant income.)

DIVERSION PAYMENT (x_D). A large coefficient was associated with this linear term. As expected, net income increases with the payment for diverted land. The magnitude and sign of the β_4 indicates the general direction of search for a maximum. Whether the surface possessed a maximum with respect to x_D is a question to be settled by further investigation. The effect of x_D on the participant's income is in all cases similar to that of the price support payment, and the discussion need not be repeated.

Net Farm Income Response Surface (Participating Farmers) ●

MINIMUM DIVERSION (x_A). Unlike the case of the previous response variable, any decrease in minimum requirements for diversion increases the net income of participating farmers. This increase is due to expanded corn output at the supported price plus the direct subsidy. A participating farmer will only gain from a reduction in the minimum diversion level when all of his corn output is, in fact, protected by the equivalent of a government price insurance scheme.

LOAN RATE AND PRICE SUPPORT PAYMENT (x_B AND x_C). Differentiating the response function with respect to x_B yields the relevant equilibrium value

$$\frac{\partial y}{\partial x_B} = 520.26 = 1{,}112.34 \ x_B = 0 \qquad (8.35)$$

$$x_B^* = 0.468 \ \text{or} \ x_B^* = \$1.06$$

Similarly, for x_C, we obtain $x_C^* = 0.27$ or $x_C^* = 19.5$ cents.[19] Given the optimal values of x_A^* and x_D^*, y can be expressed in terms of x_B and x_C,

$$y = 12,862.60 + 520.26 \; x_B - 556.17 \; x_B^2$$

$$+ \; 179.02 \; x_C - 335.88 \; x_C^2 \qquad\qquad (8.36)$$

The value of y at this point is \$13,009.59. While the maximum with respect to x_B occurs at the same value of x_B as in the previous response surface (all farms), the present response surface also reaches a maximum with respect to x_C. This result is explained by increased participation due to higher subsidies per bushel. Additional participants probably come from the south central, beef-producing area. (Higher price support payments have provided an incentive toward increased participation of livestock producers.) However since the south central farms have lower average incomes than the cash grain farms of the north central counties, increased participation by the former group would effect a decline in average income of all participating farmers. Such a result is conceivable for other Corn Belt areas as well.

Stock Accumulation Response Surface ●

MINIMUM DIVERSION LEVEL (x_A). A corner minimum is located at $\tilde{x}_A = 20$. Lowering the minimum diversion level from 20 percent to 0 percent of the feed grains base has the expected effect of increasing the volume of surplus grain. Also note the very large linear effect relative to the quadratic effect, suggesting that the maximum is considerably outside the experimental region.

19. The necessary and sufficient conditions are satisfied

$$\frac{\partial^2 y}{\partial x_B^2} = -1,123.34 < 0$$

$$\begin{vmatrix} \dfrac{\partial^2 y}{\partial x_B^2} & \dfrac{\partial^2 y}{\partial x_B \partial x_C} \\[2ex] \dfrac{\partial^2 y}{\partial x_C \partial x_B} & \dfrac{\partial^2 y}{\partial x_C^2} \end{vmatrix} = \begin{vmatrix} -1,123.34 & 0 \\[2ex] 0 & -671.76 \end{vmatrix} > 0$$

PRICE SUPPORT LOAN AND PRICE SUPPORT PAYMENT (x_B AND x_C). The function reaches a relative maximum outside the experimental region, but close to its boundary ($\tilde{x}_B = \$1.13$), while attaining a corner minimum at $\tilde{x}_B{}^* = \$0.95$. The implication of the latter result is that control conditions approximating market equilibrium conditions would prove more effective in reducing surplus than conditions involving a higher degree of intervention.

The effect of x_C in conjunction with x_B is shown in Figure 8.7. The figure represents the hyperbola,

$$y = 1,; \ 85.72 + 187.95x_B - 64.35x_B{}^2 - 7.70x_C + 53.58x_C{}^2 \qquad (8.37)$$

given $\tilde{x}_A{}^*$, $\tilde{x}_D{}^*$. Along the line EE' (corresponding to $\tilde{x}_C{}^*$) the surface becomes increasingly steeper as it approaches the corner minimum. This is evident when the function is differentiated at two points, $\tilde{x}_B = \$0.95$ and $\tilde{x}_B = \$1.025$, along the line $\tilde{x}_C{}^* = 18$ cents. The partial derivatives are

$$\frac{\partial y}{\partial x_B} = 187.95 \text{ million bushels}$$

when $x_B = 0$

$$\frac{\partial y}{\partial x_B} = 187.95 + 128.70 \ x_B$$

$$= 316.65 \text{ million bushels}$$

when $x_B = -1$

This result suggests that the price support payment becomes less effective in surplus reduction after reaching a value of 18 cents per bushel.

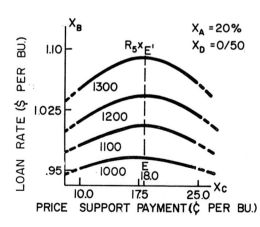

Fig. 8.7. Response surface for stock accumulation.

There are two explanations for this. The first, already mentioned, is associated with the group of livestock producers who may participate when grain price support payments increase to sufficiently high levels. Traditionally these farmers feed all or most of their feed grains. Therefore if they joined the program, corn stock accumulation need not decrease since the reduced livestock production would allow them to sell corn directly to CCC. When corn price is insured by a nonrecourse loan and buttressed with a subsidy, this course of action could be profitable to those producing a larger amount of grain for sale. The second explanation concerns the effect of price support payment on cash-grain producers who market corn directly as grain. Beyond a certain point higher price support payments stimulate cash-grain producers to intensify corn production.

DIVERSION PAYMENT RATE (x_D). The higher diversion payment rates cause a decline in stock accumulation by encouraging farmers to divert more land from production. However, the relatively small magnitude of the coefficient $\hat{\beta}_4$ suggests that this factor is not efficacious in reducing stock accumulation.

Government Costs Response Surface ●

MINIMUM DIVERSION AND PRICE SUPPORT PAYMENTS (x_A AND x_D). The surface corresponding to these factors, given the optimal values of x_B and x_D, is shown in Figure 8.8. The function is equal to $987.6 million at the minimum point, S, where $\tilde{x}_A{}^* = 14.7$ percent, and $\tilde{x}_C{}^* = 10.2$ cents. The existence of such a minimum suggests that the two decision rule parameters, x_A and x_B, *ceteris paribus,* have only a limited impact on reducing program costs. Raising price support payments beyond a certain point or lowering the minimum diversion requirement below another certain point increases government expenditures associated with the

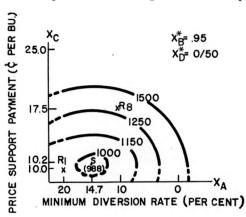

Fig. 8.8. Response surface for government costs.

program. The increase is projected through greater participation with the resultant increase in price support payments and diversion payments.

PRICE SUPPORT LOAN (x_B). The function attains a relative maximum at $\tilde{x}_B = \$1.07$, and a corner minimum at $0.95. The value of x_B at the minimum point again suggests that conditions which least interfere with market operations also would be least costly from the government's standpoint.

DIVERSION PAYMENT RATE (x_D). The sign and magnitude of this linear term implies that (1) changes in payment rate appreciably affect the program's costs, and (2) there is a direct relationship between the level of this factor and total program costs.

The Optimal Response Values ● When the optimization procedure was applied to each of the four response variables, four relative maximum or minimum points were identified, one for each surface. The points are listed in Table 8.10. (In addition, the table lists the values of the other three response variables, given the optimal levels of the parameters for that response.) The maximum or minimum values were obtained by evaluating the respective estimated response functions in terms of the optimal factor levels. Taking each variable independently, it is evident that some improvement has been achieved through the analysis in the levels of three out of four response variables. The results show a cut in cost of 67 percent and reduction in surplus accumulation of 46 percent below the lowest corresponding benchmark values of these responses. Similarly net farm income (all farmers) has been raised by about 10 percent. However only a slight improvement, 3 percent, is evident in net income of participants.

MARGINAL ANALYSIS OF THE RESPONSE SURFACE ● Several suggested approaches to further analysis of the response surface are now outlined. They involve two concepts of marginal analysis: marginal response and marginal rate of parameter substitution. The marginal analysis is applied in the neighborhood of the optimal combination. Such an analysis may be conducted for several reasons. After the experiment has been completed, the optimal combination may not be feasible because of unforeseen institutional or political constraints. In that case, the investigator would be interested in a combination which deviates least from the optimal one. Stated differently, we should prefer to move over a plateau rather than down a steep slope (if the objective is to maximize the response). Similarly situations can exist where it is not feasible to have every factor set at exactly its optimum level. Finally the surface may not have a true maximum in the region of experimentation. Nevertheless we may want to know the nature of the surface in regions of relatively high response.

Marginal Response ● Marginal response is the incremental change in the response variable resulting from a unit change in the level of a decision rule parameter. In terms of Equation (8.19) it can be approximated by

$$\frac{\Delta \eta}{\Delta \tilde{x}_i}, \quad i = A, B, \ldots.$$

This measure conveys quantitative information about the effectiveness of the parameter at a given point. We may consider, for example, the relation between the net farm revenue and the rate of price support payment (Fig. 8.6). When x_A, x_B, and x_D are at their optimal levels, the response function is

$$y = 8,872.74 + 448.45 \; x_C + 216.36 \; x_C^2 \qquad (8.38)$$

An increase of one cent, from 17.5 ($x_C = 0$) to 18.5 cents, had the following marginal response:

$$\frac{\Delta y}{\Delta \tilde{x}_C} = \frac{8,935.37 - 8,872.72}{1} = \$62.65$$

In other words, at the midrange of $\tilde{x}_C$, 17.5 cents, an increase of one cent in the price support payment rate would raise net farm income (all farms) by \$62.65. But when this rate is increased from 21.25 cents to 22.25 cents, the corresponding change in income is \$97.40. Therefore for the purpose of raising farm income, this particular parameter is about 60 percent more effective at its higher levels. (The function is evaluated in terms of the coded x_i. The marginal response involves the original values, $\tilde{x}_i$.)

Hence it is of interest to evaluate a unit change in a given parameter in terms of its effect on each of these responses using marginal response analysis. Doing this for one decision rule parameter, the price support loan rate, $\tilde{x}_B$, results in some interesting figures. When it is reduced from \$1.00 to \$0.99, the marginal response is a reduction of \$70.50, or 1 percent in average net farm income (all farms); a reduction of \$134.02, or more than 1 percent in average net farm income of participants; a decrease in stock accumulation of 33.39 million bushels, or 2.5 percent; and a cut in government costs of \$48.42 million dollars, or 2.3 percent. It is up to the policy maker to choose the proper course of action in this particular case. He would have to choose between maintaining incomes at their present levels or lowering them, thereby reducing surpluses and government costs.

Marginal Rate of Parameter Substitution ● Geometrically the marginal rate of parameter substitution is the numerical value of the tangent gradient of an isoresponse (or constant response) curve, or

$$\frac{dx_i}{dx_j} = - \frac{\partial y}{\partial x_j} \Big/ \frac{\partial y}{\partial x_i} \quad i \neq j; \ i, \ j = A, \ B, \ \ldots$$

We may consider, for example, the substitution of minimum diversion rates for support payment rates, and their relation to government cost. The policy maker might be confronted, due to unforeseen circumstances, with a situation in which he must deviate from the optimal combination. Furthermore we assume that he must choose a different point than S in Figure 8.6, yet he is restricted to the ranges $20 \leq \tilde{x}_A \leq \tilde{x}_A^*$, and $10 \leq \tilde{x}_C \leq \tilde{x}_C^*$. (Without these restrictions multiple valued combinations may arise.) When all other factors are held at their optimal levels, the response function is

$$y = 1,311.53 + 193.73x_A + 206.97x_A^2 + 563.82x_C + 287.52_C^2 \qquad (8.39)$$

Setting $y = 1,500$ and solving for x_C, we obtain an average rate of substitution in the above range of x_A and x_C,

$$\frac{\Delta \tilde{x}_C}{\Delta \tilde{x}_A} = -2 \text{ cents}$$

That is, on the average, it is necessary to lower the payment rate by two cents for each 1 percent decrease in the minimum diversion level. Information of this nature should prove quite valuable to the policy maker in determining the proper combination of parameters, i.e., choosing the best decision rule in the face of unforeseen additional constraints.

OPTIMAL RULES IN MULTI-RESPONSE SITUATIONS ● The design of a complex system usually involves more than one response measure. The policy maker should seek to obtain sufficient information on all these measures before selecting a decision rule. Once the information is presented to him however he must assign weights to the various responses. He must decide, for example, whether increasing farm income is more important than reducing government costs (unless these two variables are directly proportional to each other). Obviously, the most difficult problems concern variables which involve conflicting criteria. (Each response variable, or group of variables, could be associated with a particular segment of the socioeconomic structure such as the farm sector, the consuming sector, the government, and so on. The conflict then exists among the desires of these groups.) While we make no attempt to resolve these conflicts, we suggest below a couple of indices which could serve to clarify their exact nature.

A Graphical Representation of a Multi-Response Situation ● The responses corresponding to the nine decision rules (simulation runs) are plotted in Figure 8.9. The graph is based on the assumption that there exists a nonsingular transformation from the policy space to the response space. Each point represents one rule, identified by the number next to the point. Four responses are associated with each point. These are government cost, stock accumulation, net farm income, and participants' net farm income. In terms of the functional relationship which exists among the four responses, Figure 8.9 describes the contour lines of a surface whose height at any point is the net farm income corresponding to that point. A similar ray could be drawn for the net income of participants. The data for these maps are given in Table 8.8. The contour lines plotted in Figure 8.9 are approximations, since the number of sample points was not sufficient to indicate the exact nature of the surface.

Optimal Rules and Loss Coefficients ● It is also possible to plot the values of the responses of the four optimal rules (Table 8.10) in Figure 8.9. The points associated with the rules maximizing net income and participants' net income would then fall in the N-E quadrant of the graph. The points associated with the rule minimizing stocks and government costs would be in the S-W quadrant. Thus high incomes are also associated with high program costs and large surpluses, and vice versa. This is the nature of the conflict among the four optimal rules and is illustrated by the following results: Net farm income (all farms) associated with the stock-minimizing rule was 10 percent below the average income of the benchmark run. The income associated with the cost-minimizing rule was 13 percent below the benchmark run.

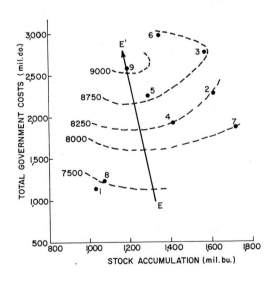

Fig. 8.9. Multi-response surface for stock accumulation, total government costs, and net revenue per farm.

Assuming that the benchmark run represented the actual conditions, then adopting any one of these rules would have entailed correspondingly lower incomes each year over a period of at least seven years (1961–67). It is highly questionable whether farmers as a group would have consented to such a prolonged drop in their net incomes.

Using the available information it is possible to state the conflict in precise terms of calculating the average potential income losses incurred in moving from the maximum net income rule to either the minimum stock rule or minimum cost rule. These are potential losses since it is assumed that the system is initially at the maximum income rule. We define the following symbols:

i = an index of an optimal rule
where i = 1 minimum stock rule
2 minimum cost rule
3 minimum income rule
4 maximum participants' income rule
s_i = stock level associated with optimal rule i
c_i = cost level associated with optimal rule i
y_i = income level associated with optimal rule i

and where rule i is represented by (s_i, c_i, y_i). Then the average potential loss incurred in moving from optimal rule i to optimal rule j, $L_{i,j}$ is

$$L(i,j) = \frac{y_j - y_i}{\left[(s_j - s_i)^2 + (c_j - c_i)^2\right]^{1/2}} \qquad (8.40)$$

Using the data of Table 8.10, the average loss of moving from (s_3, c_3, y_3) to (s_1, c_1, y_1) is 1.24. The loss of moving from (s_3, c_3, y_3) to (s_2, c_2, y_2) is 0.93. But the loss is only 0.33 if one moves from the minimum stock rule (s_1, c_1, y_1), to the minimum cost rule (s_2, c_2, y_2). It is also interesting to note that the largest loss, 2.65, is involved in moving from (s_3, c_3, y_3) to the participants' maximum income rule, (s_4, c_4, y_4). In practice however one would consider only such moves that at least would not hurt the participants more than they would hurt the entire farm group. This condition would be fulfilled in the present case. A move from (s_4, c_4, y_4) to (s_1, c_1, y_1) involves a loss of only 0.43. The corresponding figure for the move from (s_4, c_4, y_4) to (s_2, c_2, y_2) is 0.42. These figures are below 1.24 and 0.93 respectively.

Marginal Rate of Response Substitution ● Corresponding to marginal rate of parameter substitution, a similar concept is defined for analyzing optimal multi-response surfaces. Marginal rate of response substitution is likewise defined as

$$\frac{\Delta S}{\Delta C}\bigg|_{y_i = y_j = k} = \frac{s_i - s_j}{c_i - c_j} \, , \, i \neq j \, ,$$

where y, s, and c are defined as before, k denotes a constant, and i and j are the indices of two rules associated with a given iso-income line such as the broken contour lines in Figure 8.9. If the functional form of the surface is available, it would have been possible, using the above concept, to quantify the substitutional relationships between cost and stocks along a segment of the iso-income line.

To illustrate this concept, select rules three and five, which are located approximately on the same iso-income curve. Assuming that the curve is continuous and smooth, the average marginal rate of response substitution is

$$\frac{\Delta S}{\Delta C}\bigg|_{y = 8,750} = \frac{2,770 - 2,250}{1,570 - 1,290} = 1.85$$

This figure suggests that it is possible to reduce cost by an average amount of $1.85 million for each one-million-bushel reduction in surplus stocks along the indicated segment of the iso-income line. Such changes would not affect the level of income. Note that along this segment of the iso-income curve, the relationship between costs and stock is complementary. Hence decision rule three is obviously inferior to decision rule five. The information provided by the marginal rate of response substitution could be useful, for example, in decisions requiring small deviations from a given rule and simultaneously requiring the maintenance of a given level of income.

EFFICIENT RULES ● It has just been demonstrated that rule number three is inferior to rule number five. This result suggests that for a given surface it is possible to indicate a set of efficient rules. A rule is efficient in the present context if it is impossible to decrease cost by altering this rule without increasing stocks, and vice versa, while maintaining the same level of net income. The efficient rule has the property that

$$\frac{\Delta S}{\Delta C}\bigg|_{y = k} \leq 0$$

(Note that if the iso-income curve is an ellipse, both a concave and convex [to the origin] section of it will satisfy the inequality, but only one will be a locus of efficient rules by the definition.) The efficient rules in Figure 8.9 are contained in a wedge bordered on the right by the line $\overline{EE}'$. (Its boundary on the left could not be determined, owing to lack of observations in that region.) Only rules one, eight, and nine would qualify as efficient rules. The first two rules were characterized by low income, low surplus level, and low program costs. The last rule entailed a higher income level, moderate surpluses, but high levels of government expenditures.

GENERAL INTERPRETATIONS ● This was a pilot project designed to examine the feasibility and usefulness of a systems approach to policy making. Because of its exploratory nature, the work was conducted on a modest scale, necessitating a number of strong assumptions to simplify the investigation. Hence several reservations concerning the results obtained should be mentioned: Basic data for the experiment came from a restricted sample while the study developed methods in the framework of national policy. Expanded samples are needed to provide more complete information for meaningful models actually used in formulating policies. The model which simulated the farm management decision processes has limitations. The micro-simulator lacked sufficient sophistication and considered too few possible processes (as a result of the relatively small amount of information contained in the survey and the need to keep the exploratory model simple). The inadequate sample size severely limits the scope and reliability of the policy recommendations which can be based on this study. A complete sampling procedure, as described in the text, is required for an adequate analysis of the response surface.

The simulation model constructed in this study has flexibility and adaptability. Thus it could have been expanded to represent not only the production aspect of the agricultural sector, but also the varied facets of the rural sector. It could have incorporated the consumption activities of the family farm, the trade and service functions of the rural town, the actions of the local government, and the interactions which take place among the decision units making up the rural sector. In order to simulate such a system it would be necessary to conduct a comprehensive sample survey of these units. A population enumeration is not essential. Reliable results can be obtained from an adequate sample. Once such a simulation model is built it can be used continuously if the data are brought up to date. The model then could be the basis for policy recommendations as in this analysis. In addition, it could be used to facilitate and improve the testing of hypotheses about the behavior of individual decision units at various levels of aggregation. The proposed systems analysis approach to the socioeconomic problems of agriculture thus holds great promise.

Agriculture under Historic Programs, Reduced Technical Change, and Free Markets

THIS CHAPTER deals with the structure of agriculture under the environment of farm programs and markets for the past 40-year period. It deals particularly with the effect of various market and program conditions on net farm income and the demand for or use of major resource categories in U.S. farming. The resource categories of concern are labor, machinery, and buildings. The demand for or use of these resources is predicted from time-series data. Their quantities are then simulated under conditions as they prevailed over the period. The prevailing conditions included land retirement, farmer payments, support prices, and related programs over a large part of the period. Following these estimations, use of these resources is then simulated under alternative market and policy conditions. The alternative conditions simulated are those which suppose that (1) technical advance in agriculture was only half as great as actually realized, (2) free markets existed with no land retirement or other supply control programs, and (3) price support or government storage measures were not in effect.

After resource use or demand is predicted and simulated under the above three sets of conditions, estimates are made of price levels and farm income. Hence we examine what agricultural employment and investment in machinery and buildings might have been, had there been no public programs for agriculture, or had the rate of technical change been slower. Land retirement and other supply control programs in effect over much of the past 40 years represent an attempt to offset the output-increasing effects of farm technological advance. As indicated from the results in Chapter 3, the simulated conditions of a free market have net farm income expectations lower than under the conditions that have prevailed in recent years wherein supply has been restrained by land diversion, and direct payments have been used to bolster farm income. However, a simulated income is even greater than in recent years under conditions which suppose a slower rate of technical advance and less supply growth than occurred over recent decades.

The results in this chapter are considered to be largely of methodological nature and importance. Further work on the model used and incorporation of more detail (e.g., variables for biological inputs such as fertilizer, and consideration of public food aid programs) are needed before an analysis of this kind has great operational or practical importance. However, the results generated are in line with expectations of even further reductions in the farm work force under free market conditions and the decline of prices and farm income, until long-run equilibrium conditions would raise the levels of these two major variables.

This particular study has been made to analyze the basic nature of the farm problem. While the economic problems of agriculture have been directly those of commodity supply and price and income levels, fundamentally they are problems of resource demand and supply in relation to output and farm structural change. More basically, farm problems stem from economic growth which is reflected in declining real prices and increasing productivity of capital resources from nonfarm sources. Capital has been available to agriculture at sufficiently low real prices to result in large-scale substitutions of this resource for land and labor. The rapid adoption of capital inputs provides opportunities for growth in farm output and productivity, but if opportunities are few for moving excess labor resources from agriculture because of values, social attachments, skills, and other characteristics of farm people, the returns to farm labor remain depressed. How long this will continue depends primarily on the developing organization of agriculture.

The organization of agriculture is a reflection of parameters in the industry's structure. The organization is characterized by the numbers and sizes of farms, the size of the labor force, and the amount and kind of capital used. Knowledge of structural parameters is necessary to answer a number of fundamental questions relating to resource markets in agriculture. Whether or how soon returns in an agriculture free of government controls would eventually raise farm income per person depends on the responsiveness of farm workers to a fall in relative income and other price phenomena. The interrelationships of policies affecting national employment and farm labor mobility can be judged accurately only with knowledge of parameters in farm labor supply and demand functions. The demand and supply functions for a particular resource obviously are interrelated through resource prices, technical coefficients, and substitution rates, with the demand and supply functions for other resources. Thus the estimation of the basic structural parameters of demand and supply functions for other resources is also needed.

MODEL USED ● A major portion of the chapter is devoted to developing appropriate econometric models and deriving quantitative esti-

mates of structural parameters describing farm resource demand, farm
output, and income. The analysis includes an identification of the
variables affecting historic changes in farm investment demand on both
a national and regional basis, development of models describing the
aggregate demand for farm machinery, building investment and labor,
estimation of the parameters of the system from time-series data, and
use of the estimated parameters for simulating and projecting the national level of resources demand and farm income under the three alternatives outlined previously.

The regional analysis is based on the regions indicated in Figure
2.3. From a causal standpoint, many decisions in farming are interde-
pendent. For example, it is difficult to predict the number of hired
workers that will remain in agriculture, without estimates of farm
product prices, national unemployment, and factory wages. Important
farm input and output prices are determined by nonfarm variables such
as wage rates, national income, and population. The mobility of farm
labor is conditioned by the rate of national unemployment. Hence
overall models which include these nonfarm variables are necessary for
predicting farm income, output, efficiency, and resource employment.

NATIONAL MODEL ● The basic national model includes equations
explaining the stock of productive assets on farms, the aggregate production response of agriculture, the aggregate commodity supply of
agriculture, the aggregate demand for all farm commodities, net farm
income, farm machinery demand, farm motor vehicle demand, "other"
farm machinery demand, the total machinery supply function, farm
building demand, the total demand for farm labor, the total supply of
farm labor, and the separate demand for both hired and family labor.
The equations of the system are as follows in terms of the endogenous
variable to be predicted and the "predetermined" variables. The predetermined variables include those that have their values determined
outside the system and the lagged endogenous variables, for example,
$S_{Pt-1}{}^b$ and Y_{Ft-1}. (Definition of variables follows the equations.)

The stock of productive farm assets including money capital
$$S_{Pt}{}^b = f(Q_t{}^{s1}, S_{Pt-1}{}^b, T)$$

The aggregate production response function
$$Q_t{}^{s1} = f[(P_R/P_p)_{t-1}, S_{Pt}{}^b, G_t, W_t, A(t), T, C_t]$$

The aggregate commodity supply function
$$Q_t{}^{s2} = f(Q_t{}^{s1}, T)$$

The aggregate commodity price (demand) function
$$P_{Rt} = f(FCN_t, Y_{Dt}, Q_t{}^{s2}, G_t, P_{R't})$$

Definitional equations
1. Net farm income
$$Y_{Ft} = f[P_{R't}, T'(P_R/P_p)_t, S_{Pt}^b, (P_R/P_p)_t, Y_{Ft-1}, C_t]$$

2. Weighted net farm income
$$Y_{WFt} = (3Y_{Ft} + 2Y_{Ft-1} + Y_{Ft-1} + Y_{Ft-2})/6$$

The farm machinery market
1. The demand for all farm machinery
$$Q_{Mt}^D = f[(P_M/P_R)_{t-1}, A(t), ER_{t-1}, S_{Mt}, T]$$

2. The supply of all farm machinery
$$P_{Mt} = f(P_{ISt}, MSH_{t-1}, P_{NLt}, P_{Mt-1}, T)$$

3. The demand for farm motor vehicles
$$Q_{MVt}^D = f[ER_{t-1}, A_{Ft-1}, A(t), S_{MVt}, T]$$

4. The demand for other farm machinery and equipment
$$Q_{MEt}^D = Q_{Mt}^D - Q_{MVt}^D$$

The demand for farm building investment
$$Q_{BIt}^D = f(ER_{t-1}, LP_t, P_{Bt}, S_{Bt}, Y_{WFt-1}, C_t)$$

The farm labor market
1. The demand for total farm employees
$$Q_{TLt}^D = f[IMP_{t-1}, Y_{Ft-1}, P_{NLt}, A(t), (P_{TL}/TVBLA)_{t-1}, (P_M/P_{TL})_{t-1}]$$

2. The supply of total farm labor
$$P_{TLt} = f[P_{Mt}, A(t), P_{NLt}, U_{t-1}, Q_{TLt}^D, T, C_t]$$

3. The demand for hired farm employees
$$Q_{HLt}^D = f[A(t), A_{Ft-1}, P_{Mt}, (P_{TL}/TVBLA)_{t-1}, T, C_t]$$

4. The demand for family farm employees
$$Q_{FLt}^D = Q_{TLt}^D - Q_{HLt}^D$$

Endogenous Variables ●

Q_t^{S1} = Index of the quantity of farm products produced

Q_t^{S2} = Index of the quantity of farm products supplied

S_{Pt}^b = Index of the stock of productive farm assets at beginning of year

P_{Rt} = Index of the prices received by farmers for crops and livestock

Y_{Ft} = Net farm income

Y_{WFt} = Weighted net farm income for the last three years

Q_{Mt}^D = Quantity of total farm machinery demanded

Q_{MVt}^D = Quantity of farm motor vehicles demanded

Q_{MEt}^D = Quantity of other farm machinery and equipment demanded

P_{Mt} = Price index of farm machinery

Q_{BIt}^D = Value of investment for service buildings on farms

Q_{TLt}^D = Quantity of total labor demanded

P_{TLt} = Index of the farm wage rate

Q_{HLt}^D = Quantity of hired labor demanded

Q_{FLt}^D = Quantity of family labor demanded

Exogenous Variables ●

S_{pt-1}^b = Index of the stock of productive farm assets at the beginning of previous year

Q_{t-1}^{S1} = Index of the amount of farm products produced in previous year

T = Time

$(P_R/P_p)_{t-1}$ = Previous year's index of the ratio of prices received and paid by farmers

G_t = Government policy index for current year

W_t = Weather index for current year

$A(t)$ = Technological index for current year

C_t = Dummy variable representing structural changes before and after World War II, current year value

$P_{R't}$ = Current year wholesale price index, excluding food and farm products

FCN_t = Per capita food consumption index for the current year

Y_{Dt} = Personal disposable income for current year

T' = Index of production efficiency, (total output divided by total input)

Y_{Ft-1} = Net farm income in the previous year

Y_{Ft-2} = Net farm income two years in the past

Y_{Ft-3} = Net farm income three years in the past

$(P_M/P_R)_{t-1}$ = Index of the ratio of farm machinery prices to prices received by farmers in the previous year

ER_{t-1} = Equity ratio for the previous year

S_{Mt} = Index of stock of total farm machinery at beginning of current year

A_{Ft-1} = Cropland index for previous year

S_{MVt} = Stock of farm motor vehicles at beginning of current year

P_{ISt} = Price index for iron and steel in current year

MSH_{t-1} = Index of the amount of machinery shipped, lagged one year

P_{NLt} = Index of the nonfarm wage rate for current year

S_{Bt} = Stock value of service buildings on farms at beginning of current year

LP_t = Index of livestock production in current year

P_{Bt} = Index of prices paid for farm building materials in current year

P_{pt} = Index of the prices paid by farmers for aggregate inputs in current year

IMP_{t-1} = Index of mechanical power on farm for previous year

A recursive model constructed on a lag-causal ordering of the commodity markets and the causal structure of resource markets is used in the analysis. Least-squares regression techniques are used to estimate the parameters of the recursive model. Possible difficulties with the assumption of uncorrelated error terms in the recursive model were considered in the decision to use these techniques. Autocorrelated error terms exist in time-series data when the error term of one period is not independent of the error of previous periods. Johnson has indicated that when autocorrelated errors are present, the least-squares estimators remain unbiased and consistent but they are inefficient.[1] Autocorrelation may be caused by (1) omission of important variables resulting from either incorrect specification or deliberate omission of some variables due to the limited length of time-series data, (2) incorrect specification of the form of the relationship between economic variables, or (3) errors of measurement in the explanatory variables. There is a strong likelihood that an error of observation committed in one time period will be repeated in the next time period, and hence give rise to autocorrelated errors. Two generally accepted tests for autocorrelation are the Von-Neuman ratio and the Durbin-Watson test.[2] The Durbin-Watson test is used in this analysis. This d-statistic has been computed for all equations in the model. If the computed d-value is less than the tabular value of d_L (lower bounds), the hypothesis of random disturbance is rejected in favor of positive autocorrelation. If the computed d-value is greater than d_u (upper bounds), the hypothesis of random disturbances

1. J. Johnston, *Econometric Methods* (New York: McGraw Hill, 1963).

2. John Von-Neuman, Distribution of Ratio of the Mean Sucessive Difference to the Variance, *Annals of Mathematical Statistics* 12 (1941): 367–95; James Durbin and G. S. Watson, Testing for Serial Correlation in Least-Squares Regression, *Biometrica* 38 (1951):195–178.

is not rejected. If the computed d-value falls between d_L and d_u the test for positive autocorrelation is considered inconclusive.

When lagged endogenous variables are included as explanatory variables, the structural coefficients may be estimated as if autocorrelation were present. Koyck proposed a technique to obtain consistent estimators which depend on the assumption that the error term, u_t, is generated by an autoregressive scheme.[3]

$$u_t = \rho u_{t-1} + e_t$$

The assumptions are that u_t has a zero mean, a constant variance, e_t is not correlated with u_{t-1}, and there is no autocorrelation among the e's. Further, Koyck asumes specific values of ρ. Estimation by this technique is referred to as autoregressive least-squares. The cases in which an estimated coefficient (b′) is a consistent estimator of the real regression coefficient (b) have been outlined by Fuller who indicates that a more accurate estimate of b can be obtained if the value of ρ is known.[4] A simplified method for estimating ρ and the regression coefficients by an iterative process has been developed by Fuller and Martin and is used in equations of the national model of this study.[5]

REGIONAL MODEL ● Based on the underlying theory of the national model, the regional model includes approximately the same variables. However, fewer census data are available for the regional analysis, and modifications are made accordingly. The usual method employed in regression analysis of regional time-series data includes the estimation of separate regression equations for each region. Under this procedure the length of the series available for regional study would limit the total degrees of freedom (with reduction due to lags) to approximately sixteen. If we assume that four to six independent variables are needed to explain a substantial proportion of the variance of the dependent variable, the residual sum of squares from regression would be associated with approximately ten degrees of freedom. This number is insufficient for acceptable statistical results where a separate equation is used for each region. Hence the regional model includes all regions simultaneously in one equation (each resource, region, and year providing a separate observation). It is essentially a combination of analysis of covariance and multiple regression. With algebraic recombination of

3. L. M. Koyck, *Distributed Lags and Investment Analysis* (Amsterdam: North Holland Publ. 1954).

4. Wayne Fuller, A Non-Static Model of the Beef and Pork Economy, Ph.D. thesis, Iowa State Univ., Ames, 1959.

5. Wayne Fuller and James E. Martin, The Effects of Autocorrelated Errors on the Statistical Estimation of Distributed Lag Models, *Journal of Farm Economics* 44 (1961): 71–82.

certain intercept and dummy variables, the model is one of multiple covariance analysis with additional regression variables.[6] This model provides (1) an immediate statistical test for differences among regions and (2) inclusion of all regions in one equation with a larger number of observations. An underlying statistical assumption for this procedure is that observations from all regions are drawn from a common population. This however is an assumption which must be made if separate equations are estimated in the usual way and statistical tests performed between regional regressions. If there is no significant increase in the variance of variables, the relative increase in degrees of freedom for the residual sum of squares should increase the probability of obtaining good statistical results. More precise statistical results lend greater credence to subsequent economic analysis and interpretation.

Regional Demand for Total Farm Machinery ● The following regression equation (the expectation equation) is used for the ten production regions:

$$Q_{Mt}^D = b_o + \sum_{i=1}^{m-1} b_i + cQ_{Mt-1}^D + \sum_{i=1}^{m-1} d_i Q_{Mt-1,i}^D$$

$$+ eER_{t-1} + \sum_{i=1}^{m-1} f_i ER_{t-1,i} + g(P_M/P_R)_t + hT + U_t$$

where b_o is the overall intercept; b_i is the difference in intercepts between the i-th region and b_o, $i = 1, 2, \ldots, m-1$, and m is the number of regions (ten in this study). Q_{Mt}^D is the current investment in total farm machinery deflated by the wholesale price index; Q_{Mt-1}^D is the one-year lagged investment in total farm machinery deflated by the wholesale price index; d_i is the slope difference for Q_{Mt-1}^D between the i-th region and the m-th region given by c; ER_{t-1} is the equity ratio for the previous year; f_i is the slope difference for ER_{t-1} between the i-th region and m-th region given by e; $(P_M/P_R)_t$ is the index of the ratio of the farm machinery price to the price received by farmers for farm products (1957–59 $= 100$). T is the time trend, and is represented by the last two digits of the year. U_t is the error term.

The alternative stock adjustment equation for the total machinery demand is

$$Q_{Mt}^D = b_o + \sum_{i=1}^{m-1} b_i + cA(t) + \sum_{i=1}^{m-1} d_i A(t)_i + eER_{t-1}$$

6. J. T. Scott, Jr., The Demand for Investment in Farm Buildings, Ph.D. thesis, Iowa State Univ., Ames, 1965.

$$+ \sum_{i=1}^{m-1} f \text{ER}_{t-1,i} + g S_{Mt} + \sum_{i=1}^{m-1} h_i S_{Mt,i}$$

$$+ j(P_M/P_R)_{t-1} + kT + U_t$$

where $A(t)$ is the technological index; S_{Mt} is the stock value of the total farm machinery at the beginning of the year; the ratio $(P_M/P_R)_{t-1}$ is a one-year lag of $(P_M/P_R)_t$; and the remaining variables and coefficients are as defined in the preceding equation.

Regional Demand for Motor Vehicles ● The expectation equation for the demand for motor vehicles is

$$Q_{MVt}^D = b_o + \sum_{i=1}^{m-1} b_i + c Q_{MVt-1}^D + \sum_{i=1}^{m-1} d_i Q_{MVt-1,i}^D$$

$$+ e \text{ER}_{t-1} + \sum_{i=1}^{m-1} f_i \text{ER}_{t-1,i} + g(P_{MV}/P_R)_t + hT + U_t$$

The stock adjustment equation for the demand for motor vehicles is

$$Q_{MVt}^D = b_o + \sum_{i=1}^{m-1} b_i + c A(t) + \sum_{i=1}^{m-1} d_i A(t)_i + e \text{ER}_{t-1}$$

$$+ \sum_{i=1}^{m-1} f_i \text{ER}_{t-1,i} + g S_{MVt} + \sum_{i=1}^{m-1} h_i S_{MVt,i}$$

$$+ j(P_M/P_R)_{t-1} + kT + U_t$$

Q_{MVt}^D is the current investment in farm motor vehicles (including tractor, truck, and auto vehicles) deflated by the wholesale price index. $(P_{MV}/P_R)_t$ is the index of the ratio of the price of motor vehicles to prices received by farmers for farm products (1957–$59 = 100$); S_{MVt} is the value of the stock of farm motor vehicles at the beginning of the year.

Regional Demand for Total Farm Labor ● The regional demand equation for total farm labor is as follows:

$$Q_{TLt}^D = b_o + \sum_{i=1}^{m-1} b_i + c(\text{IMP})_{t-1} + d Y_{Ft-1}$$

$$+ \sum_{i=1}^{m-1} e_i Y_{Ft-1,i} + f P_{NLt} + g A(t) + \sum_{i=1}^{m-1} h_i A(t)_i$$

$$+ \; j\,(P_{TL}/TVBLA)_{t-1} \; + \; \sum_{i=1}^{m-1} k_i\,(P_{TL}/TVBLA)_{t-1,i}$$

$$+ \; 1\,(P_M/P_{TL})_{t-1} \; + \; U_t$$

b_o is the overall intercept, b_i is the difference between the i-th region and b_o (where $i = 1, 2, \ldots, m-1$), and m is the number of regions (ten in this study). $Q_{TLt}{}^D$ is the quantity of the total farm labor demanded; IMP_{t-1} is a one-year lagged index of the mechanical power on farms; Y_{Ft-1} is net farm income lagged one year; e_i is the slope difference for Y_{Ft-1} between the i-th region and the m-th region given by d. P_{NLt} is the index of the factory wage rate (1957–59 = 100); h_i is the slope difference for $A(t)$ between the i-th region and the m-th region given by g; $(P_{TL}/TVBLA)_{t-1}$ is the index of the ratio of farm wage rate to total value of buildings and land per acre, lagged one year (1957–59 = 100); k_i is the slope difference for $(P_{TL}/TVBLA)_{t-1}$ between the i-th region and the m-th region given by j; $(P_M/P_{TL})_{t-1}$ is the index of the ratio of farm machinery to farm wage rate (1957–59 = 100), lagged one year; and U_t is the error term.

Regional Demand for Hired Farm Labor ● The regional demand equation for hired farm labor is presented as follows:

$$Q_{HLT}{}^D = b_o + \sum_{i=1}^{m-1} b_i + cP_{Mt} + dA(t) + \sum_{i=1}^{m-1} eA(t)_i$$

$$+ \; fA_{Ft-1} \; + \; \sum_{i=1}^{m-1} g_i A_{Ft-1,i} \; + \; h\,(P_{TL}/TVBLA)_{t-1}$$

$$+ \; \sum_{i=1}^{m-1} j_i\,(P_{TL}/TVBLA)_{t-1,i} \; + \; kT \; + \; U_t$$

where $Q_{HLt}{}^D$ is the quantity of hired labor demanded and A_{Ft-1} is the index of cropland per farm in acres, lagged one year, with other variables and the relationships between the coefficients defined as in the demand for total labor.

Regional Demand for Farm Building Investment ● This equation is as follows:

$$Q_{BIt}{}^D = b_o + \sum_{i=1}^{m-1} b_i + cP_{Bt} + dS_{Bt} + eY_{WFt-1}$$

$$+ \sum_{i=1}^{m-1} f_i Y_{WFt-1,i} + gER_{t-1}$$

$$+ \sum_{i=1}^{m-1} h_i ER_{t-1,i} + jT + U_t$$

where $Q_{BIt}{}^D$ is the annual gross investment in productive farm buildings; P_{Bt} is the index of the price of farm building materials (1957–59 $= 100$); S_{Bt} is the stock value of productive farm buildings at the beginning of the year; T is the time trend; and U is the error term. Y_{WFt-1} is the lagged geometric average of the net farm income; f_i is the slope difference for Y_{WFt-1} between the i-th region and m-th region given by e; ER_{t-1} is the one-year lagged equity ratio; h_i is the slope difference for ER_{t-1} between the i-th region and the m-th region given by g. All variables are deflated by the wholesale price index.

Dummy and Time Variables in Regional Equations ● Phase plans shifts or substantial changes in all economic parameters occur in economic systems at certain times. They may occur between wartime and peacetime, or between economic booms and depressions. Ordinarily these types of discrete changes can be handled by using appropriate dummy variables in the regression equation. Dummy variables are included in the regional model and are used to permit changes in the intercept, in the slope coefficient, or in both as outlined by Suits.[7] They also are used in the cross-sectional analysis of this study to represent regional variation.

The suggested method for removing the time trend includes the use of orthogonal polynomials or inclusion of a function of time in the regression equation with the remaining explanatory variables.[8]

EMPIRICAL DATA USED ● The variables used, including their aggregation, are explained in this section. Limitations in research resources, lack of readily available data, and time restraints were the reasons for estimating the set of economic relationships based mainly on the theory of the firm but using aggregate data. Theil has suggested the methods for estimating macro-parameters by macro-variables formed from micro-variables, weighted to insure consistency.[9] May has outlined

7. D. B. Suits, Use of Dummy Variables in Regression Equations, *American Statistical Association Journal* 52(1957):548–51.

8. Gerhard Tintner, *Econometrics* (New York: John Wiley & Sons, 1963); Earl O. Heady and John L. Dillon, *Agricultural Production Functions* (Ames: Iowa State Univ. Press, 1961), pp. 108–94.

9. Henri Theil, *Economic Forecasts and Policy* (Amsterdam: North Holland Publ., 1958).

methods for consistent statistical estimation from simple available aggregations.[10] The grouping used by the U.S. Department of Agriculture in the sources outlined below conforms reasonably with these aggregation criteria. Reasonably consistent results are obtainable by simple aggregation if inputs are relatively homogeneous with respect to the variables which influence the economic relationship. Data limitations however required use of some input groups which were aggregated over types of farms and regions in violation of certain aggregation criteria.

Throughout this chapter, the main sources of data come from the regular series published by the U.S. Department of Agriculture supplemented by those published by the U.S. Department of Commerce.[11] The description of data follows. Unless otherwise stated, the data are available both for the nation and the ten production regions.

Q_{TLt}^D = Total farm employment (hired plus family) measured in million persons

Q_{HLt}^D = Demand for hired farm employees measured in million persons

Q_{FLt}^D = Demand for family farm employees measured in million persons

Q_{Mt}^D = Quantity of all farm machinery purchased (gross investment) by farmers in the current year, deflated, in millions of dollars. (Regional data are explained later)

Q_{MVt}^D = Number of motor vehicles purchased during the current year. The variable includes tractors, trucks, and the productive portion of automobile purchases (40 percent) (deflated value in millions of dollars). (Regional data are explained later)

Q_{MEt}^D = Amount of farm machinery and equipment purchases during the current year for productive purposes. The variable includes planting, harvesting, and tillage machines, farm wagons, sprayers, gas and electric engines, and dairying and haying equipment. Motor vehicles are excluded (deflated value in millions of dollars). (Regional data are explained later)

Q_{BIt}^D = Annual investment expenditures (gross investment) on new and remodeled farm buildings, in millions of dollars deflated by the wholesale price index

S_{Pt}^b = Beginning year stock of productive farm assets including farm real estate, less value of operator's dwellings;

10. Kenneth May, The Aggregation Problem for a One Industry Model, *Econometrica* 14 (1946): 285–98.

11. For a description of sources, see A. Y. Lin, Factor Demand in U.S. Agriculture, Ph.D. thesis, Iowa State Univ., Ames, 1967.

livestock; machinery; motor vehicles less 60 percent of the value of automobiles; stocks of feed crops held for subsequent use on farms, and working capital—in index form and deflated by the wholesale price index (1957–59 = 100)

Q_t^{S1} = Index of the farm output (1957–59 = 100)

Q_t^{S2} = Index of the volume of farm products marketed for consumption, nonfarm and government storage, and export

P_{Rt} = Index of the prices received by farmers for crops and livestock, deflated. Regional analysis uses the national data

Y_{Ft} = Total net farm income, deflated, including cash receipts, nonfarm income, and government payments minus production expenses, in millions of dollars

Y_{WFt} = Declining geometric average of the net farm income (deflated). $Y_{WFt} = 0.1667\ (3Y_{Ft} + 2Y_{Ft-1} + Y_{Ft-2})$

P_{TLt} = Composite farm wage rate, in index form deflated by the wholesale price index (1957–59 = 100)

P_{Mt} = Index of the current price of all farm machinery. Regional analysis uses the national data

P_{MV} = Index of the current price of motor vehicles. Regional analysis uses the national data

$\left(\dfrac{P_{TL}}{TVBLA}\right)_t$ = Index of the ratio of the composite farm wage rate to the total value of buildings and land per acre (1957–59 = 100)

$\left(\dfrac{P_M}{P_{TL}}\right)_t$ = Index of the ratio of the farm machinery price to the composite farm wage rate (1957–59 = 100)

MSH_{t-1} = Value of farm machines and equipment sold last year for domestic uses (deflated value in index form [1957–59 = 100]). Regional analysis uses the national data

IMP_{t-1} = Index of the stock of mechanical power and machines (1957–59 = 100), lagged one year. Regional analysis uses the national data

P_{Wt} = Wholesale price index. Regional analysis uses the national data

P_{pt} = Index of the prices paid by the farmers for items used in production, including interest, taxes, and wage rates with current value deflated by the wholesale price index. Regional analysis uses the national data

P_{Bt} = Index of the price paid for farm building materials (1957–59 = 100) (deflated by the wholesale price index). Regional analysis uses the national data

G_t = Index of the government agriculture policy. During those years when acreage allotment of production controls are in force, with flexible price supports, the value of -1 is given. If price supports are fixed, with rigid support of 85 percent or over, the value of $+1$ is given. For those years when soil bank and subsequent agriculture adjustment act provisions are in force, an additional -1 is given. The values are summed to form the index G_t

$\left(\dfrac{P_R}{P_p}\right)_{t-1}$ = Previous year's index of the ratio of prices received by farmers for crops and livestock to prices paid by farmers for items used in production, including interest, taxes, and wage rates. Regional analysis uses the national data

Y_{WFt-1} = Geometric average of the net farm income for the preceding three years, deflated and in millions of dollars

W_t = Stallings' index of the influence of weather on farm output

T = Time, an index composed of the last two digits of the respective years

T' = Index of productivity, the ratio of farm output to all farm inputs in the respective years

$P_{R't}$ = Wholesale price index other than food

FCN_t = Index of per capita food consumption (1957–59 = 100)

Y_{Dt} = Disposable personal income in millions of dollars deflated, for the United States in respective years

A_{Ft-1} = Index of cropland per farm in acres, lagged one year (1957–59 = 100)

$\left(\dfrac{P_{TL}}{TVBLA}\right)_{t-1}$ = Index of the ratio of composite farm wage rate to total value of buildings and land per acre, 1957–59 = 100, lagged one year

U_{t-1} = Preceding year's national rate of unemployment in percent

P_{NLt} = Index of the deflated nonfarm wage rate (1957–59 = 100)

C_t = Variable reflecting the once-for-all shift in structure. During the World War II period and prewar years the variable is zero; during the postwar period the variable is one

ER_{t-1} = Farmers' equity ratio, lagged one year. Computed from the total value of land and buildings divided by outstanding mortgage debt

P_{ISt} = Wholesale price index of iron and steel. Deflated by the wholesale price index (1957–59 = 100)

Y_{t-1} = Rate of interest of new farm mortgages, in percent, lagged one year. Regional analysis uses the national data

LP_t = Index of the gross production of livestock and livestock products (1957–59 = 100)

S_{Bt} = Stock value of farm buildings at the beginning of the year, excluding operators' dwellings. Millions of dollars deflated by wholesale price index (1957–59 = 100). Regional analysis uses the national data

S_{Mt} = Stock value of total farm machinery at the beginning of year. Millions of dollars deflated by the wholesale price index (1957–59 = 100)

S_{MVt} = Stock value of productive motor vehicles on farms (estimated as 40 percent of the total value) at the beginning of the year. Millions of dollars deflated by the wholesale price index (1957–59 = 100)

$\left(\dfrac{P_M}{P_{TL}}\right)_{t-1}$ = Ratio of the farm machinery price to the composite farm wage rate in index form lagged one year (1957–59 = 100)

$A(t)$ = Technological change index (1957–59 = 100). Computed as suggested by Kaneda[12]

$Q_{Mt,i}^D$ = Annual regional purchases (gross investment) of total farm machines in millions of dollars deflated by the wholesale price index. These figures were derived by dividing the stock value of total farm machines in a given region by the U.S. total stock values. This percentage was then multiplied by the total U.S. purchases to give a regional purchase figure. $Q_{Mt,i}^D = Q_{Mt}^D \cdot S_{Mt,i}/S_{Mt}$, where $S_{Mt,i}$ refers to stock value of total farm machines in the i-th region; S_{Mt} is the national stock value of total farm machines

$Q_{MVt,i}^D$ = Annual regional purchases (gross investment) of motor vehicles in millions of dollars deflated by the wholesale price index. These figures were derived in the same fashion as the $Q_{Mt,i}^D$. The S_{MVt} and $S_{MVt,i}$ data were from the same sources as S_{Mt} and $S_{Mt,i}$

$Q_{MEt,i}^D$ = Annual regional purchases (gross investment) of other farm machines in millions of dollars deflated by the wholesale price index. $Q_{MEt,i}^D = Q_{Mt,i}^D - Q_{MVt,i}^D$

$Q_{BIt,i}^D$ = Annual regional gross investment in farm buildings, in millions of dollars deflated by the wholesale price index.

12. Hiromitu Kaneda, Regional Patterns of Technical Change in U.S. Agriculture, 1950–1963, *Journal of Farm Economics* 49 (1967): 199–212.

Derived in the same fashion as the $Q_{Mt,i}{}^D$ using the ratio of regional stock value of farm real estate and national stock value of farm real estate

$Q_{Mt-1,i}{}^D$ = Annual regional gross investment for total farm machines, in millions of dollars, lagged one year and deflated by the wholesale price index. Data sources are the same as $Q_{Mt,i}{}^D$

$Q_{MVt-1,i}{}^D$ = Annual regional gross investment for farm motor vehicles, in millions of dollars, lagged one year and deflated by the wholesale price index. Data sources are the same as $Q_{MVt,i}{}^D$

$Q_{MEt-1,i}{}^D$ = Annual regional gross investment for other farm machines in millions of dollars, lagged one year and deflated by the wholesale price index where $Q_{MEt-1,i}{}^D$ $= Q_{Mt-1,i}{}^D - Q_{MVt-1,i}{}^D$

NATIONAL RESULTS, 1924–65 ● The following sections present empirical estimates of the functions previously outlined for the national model. The national model includes five equations explaining the aggregate commodity market and nine equations explaining the resource markets.

The Production Response Functions (Commodity) ● The production response function estimated with 1924–65 annual data is as follows: (The student t-value is presented in parentheses below each coefficient and the values of R^2 and d are indicated under the equation.)

$$Q_t{}^{S1} = -43.52882 + 0.123264(P_R/P_p)_{t-1} + 0.21986S_{Pt}{}^b$$
$$(3.25) \qquad\qquad (7.14)$$
$$+ 0.776164G_t + 0.248210W_t + 1.137410T$$
$$(1.58) \qquad (5.89) \qquad (16.81)$$
$$+ 0.119460A(t) - 2.534415C_t \qquad\qquad (9.1)$$
$$(2.01) \qquad\quad (-1.48)$$
$$d = 1.93^* \qquad R^2 = 0.99$$

The variable $Q_t{}^{S1}$ is the index of agricultural commodities produced. The coefficient of each variable is highly significant and has the expected sign. The hypothesis that the residuals are not autocorrelated is accepted in terms of the d-statistic, at the 1 percent probability level. (In the remainder of this study one asterisk on the Durbin-Watson d-statistic will indicate insignificant autocorrelation.)

The elasticity of $Q_t{}^{S1}$ with respect to $(P_R/P_p)_{t-1}$, computed at the 1924–65 mean is 0.17. (This is essentially a production response elasticity with respect to a one-year lag index of the parity ratio.) The elasticity with respect to the stock of investment in agriculture, $S_{Pt}{}^b$, is 0.33, and 0.15 with respect to the technological index, $A(t)$.

The variables in the equation provide the basis for estimating two general sources of increased output: (1) changes in the input levels associated with the variables $(P_R/P_p)_{t-1}$ and $S_{Pt}{}^b$, and (2) changes in the output due to $A(t)$. The technological index partly indicates the changes in output due to management and efficiency. With $A(t)$ at its 1965 value and other variables (investment inputs) at their 1924 value, the elasticity indicates that output would have been only 3.7 percent greater than the predicted 1924 output. (This computed contribution of technological improvements to agricultural production would have been greater if the output to input or productivity index of the U.S. Department of Agriculture had been used as the technological variable.) The productivity index combines effects of weather, management, and efficiency. Hence the effect of technological improvement separate from weather and management is hard to assess.

The estimated equation further predicts that output increased 27 percent from 1924 to 1965 as a result of a greater $S_{Pt}{}^b$. Thus the major portion of the increase in output from 1924 to 1965 is attributed to investment and technological improvements. Short-run price influences had a smaller effect on the secular increase in output.

Aggregate Commodity Supply Function ● The estimated commodity supply function using the time-series from 1924 to 1965 is as follows:

$$Q_t{}^{S2} = -12.19 + 0.61T + 0.78Q_t{}^{S1} \qquad (9.2)$$
$$\phantom{Q_t{}^{S2} = -12.19 +} (3.60) \qquad (6.93)$$

$$d = 1.73^* \qquad R^2 = 0.98$$

The variable $Q_t{}^{S2}$ is the predicted supply quantity (index) of agricultural commodities, including changes in inventories. The coefficients of the variables explain a high proportion of the annual variation in $Q_t{}^{S2}$. Using the 1 percent probability level as the criterion, the residuals are not autocorrelated.

The time variable, T, explains a significant portion of the annual variation of aggregate quantity supplied. The supply elasticity with respect to the time variable computed at the mean of T is 0.35, or less than half that for $Q_t{}^{S1}$ (0.81).

Aggregate Commodity Price (Demand) Function ● The estimated aggregate commodity price function using the annual data from 1924 to 1965 is as follows:

$$P_{Rt} = 220.9714 + 2.137803FCN_t + 0.117606Y_{Dt} - 1.101805Q_t{}^{S2}$$
$$(3.34) \qquad\qquad (2.08) \qquad\qquad (-4.02)$$

$$+ 2.449223G_t - 2.5506P_{R't} \qquad\qquad\qquad (9.3)$$
$$(1.56) \qquad\quad (-7.54)$$

$$d = 1.39^* \qquad\qquad R^2 = 0.93$$

All variables are significant at the 1 percent probability level and have the expected sign. The hypothesis of nonautocorrelated error terms is also accepted. All independent variables together explained 93 percent of the annual variation in commodity prices.

The variable $Q_t{}^{S2}$, the index of the supply of agricultural commodities, is among the significant variables in explaining the annual variation of commodity prices. The mean price flexibility of P_{Rt}, the index of commodity prices received by farmers, with respect to FCN_t, the index of per capita food consumption, is 1.96, and the estimated demand elasticity is 0.51.

The increasing level of disposable personal income, Y_{Dt}, and price supporting policy, G_t, have helped to maintain the level of agricultural commodity prices over time. The price flexibilities with respect to Y_{Dt} and G_t computed at the means are respectively 0.25 and 0.006. In contrast the level of the wholesale price index for commodities other than food has been moving opposite to the level of prices received by farmers. (However, the deflation of the index of prices received by farmers by the wholesale price index composed mainly of nonfood commodities might contribute somewhat to the negative sign.) The computed price flexibility with respect to this variable computed at the mean is −2.34.

The Stock of Productive Farm Assets Function (Commodity) ● The estimated function with annual time-series data for the period 1924–65 is as follows:

$$S_{Pt}{}^b = -8.39200 - 0.55111T + 0.719846Q_{t-1}{}^{S1} + 0.808353S_{Pt-1}{}^b \qquad (9.4)$$
$$(-1.71) \qquad (2.92) \qquad\qquad (1.12)$$

$$d = 1.74^* \qquad\qquad R^2 = 0.94$$

The coefficient for the lagged index of agricultural commodities produced, $(Q_{t-1}{}^{S1})$, is significant at the 1 percent probability level. The hypothesis that the residuals are not autocorrelated is also accepted.

By rearrangement of the terms in the stock adjustment model, the coefficient of $S_{Pt-1}{}^b$ can be interpreted as $1 - g$, where g is the adjustment coefficient, which is approximately 0.2 in this function. It indicates that the actual adjustment in inventories of productive farm assets during year t is some proportion, $g = 0.2$, of the desired or equilibrium changes in inventories.[13]

The long-run elasticity of demand for $S_{Pt}{}^b$ with respect to $Q_{t-1}{}^{S1}$ computed at the mean is 0.47. The amount of commodities produced thus plays an important role in determining the necessary adjustment in the total stock of productive farm assets. The long-run elasticity of $S_{Pt}{}^b$ with respect to the time variable, T, is only 0.20. The low elasticity and inconsistent sign of the time variable could result from the fact that most of the changes of $S_{Pt}{}^b$ over time have already been reflected through the changes of $S_{Pt-1}{}^b$ and $Q_{t-1}{}^{S1}$.

Net Farm Income Function (Commodity) ● The Y_{Ft} equation estimated for annual data from 1924 to 1965 is as follows:

$$Y_{Ft} = -38327.38 - 2768.483C_t + 214.3666P_{R't} + 100.641X_{Rt}$$
$$(-3.75) \qquad (2.36) \qquad (4.4)$$
$$+ 33.05465S_{Pt}{}^b + 101.0416(P_R/P_p)_t + 0.567146Y_{Ft-1} \qquad (9.5)$$
$$(2.28) \qquad (2.89) \qquad (7.95)$$
$$d = 1.82^* \qquad R^2 = 0.96$$

The price ratio, P_R/P_p, is included in several forms. One is the original form (P_R/P_p) and another is the form $[T'(P_R/P_p)]$ where T' is the productivity index (the ratio of total output to total input). The product of T' and (P_R/P_p) is denoted as X_{Rt} in the equation. The results indicate that a 1 percent increase in $(P_R/P_p)_t$ increases Y_{Ft} by 1.49 percent in the period 1924–65. A 1 percent increase in X_{Rt} increased Y_{Ft} by 0.68 percent.

An increase in $S_{Pt}{}^b$ contributes to an increase in Y_{Ft}. However, the coefficient for the shift in structure C_t indicates that Y_{Ft} declined more in real value over the postwar years than in prewar years.

Demand for Total Farm Machinery (Resource) ● The estimated demand function for total farm machinery is as follows:

$$Q_{Mt}{}^D = -3910.750 - 1.1915328(P_M/P_R)_{t-1} + 33.321269A(t)$$
$$(-0.44) \qquad (3.13)$$
$$+ 29.38883T + 132.5875ER_{t-1} + 0.0321888S_{Mt} \qquad (9.6)$$
$$(1.91) \qquad (3.47) \qquad (1.26)$$
$$d = 1.33^* \qquad R^2 = 0.90$$

All variables have the expected sign, and except for $(P_M/P_R)_{t-1}$ and S_{Mt} all variables are significant at the 1 percent probability level. (S_{Mt} is significant at the 5 percent probability level.)

13. Earl O. Heady and Luther G. Tweeten, *Resource Demand and Structure of the Agricultural Industry* (Ames: Iowa State Univ. Press, 1963), pp. 283–84.

The level of technology, $A(t)$, and lagged equity ratio are indicated to be most important variables in the demand for total farm machinery. Technological change has led to a rapid rise in the utilization of more machinery which has substituted for labor. A 1 percent improvement in technology is associated with a 1.6 percent increase in the demand for total farm machinery. The lagged equity ratio also is positively associated with the demand for total farm machinery.

The elasticity of demand for annual investment of total farm machinery with respect to $(P_M/P_R)_{t-1}$ is approximately -0.05 measured at the mean. Therefore farm machinery purchases are predicted to decline as the price of machinery increases relative to farm product prices.

The regression coefficient of S_{Mt} is the difference between the depreciation rate and the adjustment coefficient.[14] The average depreciation rate of total farm machinery has been computed, from a separate set of data, as 0.138.[15] Consequently the adjustment coefficient for total farm machinery is estimated at 0.106, implying that the average increment in total farm machinery investment has been approximately 11 percent per year of the beginning-of-year stock value of farm machinery.

Supply of All Farm Machinery (Resource) ● The estimated supply function for all farm machinery is as follows:

$$P_{Mt} = 11.95938 + 0.39262 P_{ISt} - 0.735667T + 0.003607 MSH_{t-1}$$
$$(3.46) \qquad (-2.23) \qquad (1.29)$$
$$+ 0.32623 P_{NLt} + 0.576885 P_{Mt-1} \qquad (9.7)$$
$$(1.94) \qquad (5.35)$$
$$d = 1.59* \qquad R^2 = 0.88$$

All variables except MSH_{t-1} are significant at the 1 percent probability level and have the expected sign. (MSH_{t-1} is significant at the 5 percent probability level.)

The price flexibility of machinery shipments (supply) computed from the equation is 0.02. Since it is near zero, the supply elasticity (1/price flexibility) is very large. This result is consistent with the hypothesis that machinery supply is highly elastic. Although Equation (9.7) indicates supply is less than perfectly elastic, it does indicate that price is relatively unresponsive to quantity changes in the short run. That farmers are price takers (quantity a function of price) and manufacturers are price setters can be inferred from this supply equation.

A variable which does significantly explain machinery prices is P_{ISt}. A 1 percent short-run increase in the iron and steel price is predicted to raise the machinery price by 0.34 percent. The result is realistic

14. Heady and Dillon, *Agricultural Production Functions.*

15. William A. Cromarty, The Demand for Farm Machinery and Tractors, *Michigan Agricultural Experiment Station Bulletin* 275, 1959.

since steel and iron are the important raw materials in farm machinery. Nonfarm wage rates affect the cost of machinery production, and the empirical results show that they have a very significant effect on the machinery price.

The short-run year-to-year variation in total farm machinery price is rather small. Hence the coefficient for the variable representing a one-year lag in farm machinery price is 0.58. The coefficient is significant at the 1 percent probability level.

The supply of farm machinery, analyzed as part of the recursive model, has a long-run price flexibility of 0.02. Thus supply prices are quite unresponsive to changes in quantity even in the long run, the most influential variable again being the price of iron and steel. A 1 percent long-run increase in the price of iron and steel is predicted to increase the supply price by 3.5 percent.

Demand for Motor Vehicles (Resource) ● Variables considered to be important influences on demand quantities of motor vehicles are the level of technology, the lagged one-year equity ratio, time, the lagged index of cropland, and the stock of motor vehicles on farms at the beginning of the year. The resulting equation for the 1924–65 period is

$$Q_{MVt}^D = -2138.35 + 17.76596A(t) + 83.28165ER_{t-1}$$
$$(2.41) \qquad\qquad (5.01)$$
$$+ 8.386136T + 3.918741A_{Ft-1} + 0.012950S_{MVt} \quad (9.8)$$
$$(0.73) \qquad\qquad (0.36) \qquad\qquad (0.35)$$
$$d = 1.22 \qquad R^2 = 0.84$$

All variables have the expected signs but the Durbin-Watson d-statistic falls in the inconclusive range, and T, A_{Ft-1}, and S_{MVt} have small t-values.

The variable representing the stock of motor vehicles is not significant in this demand equation, as compared to the significant influence of the stock value for the demand of total farm machinery. Although predictions based on the insignificant coefficient are weak, the adjustment coefficient for motor vehicles was computed at 0.10. This adjustment coefficient is as high as in the equation for the demand for total farm machinery. Table 9.1 includes elasticities of farm machinery and motor vehicle purchases for machinery price ratios, the technological index, time, and the equity ratio.

Demand for Other Farm Machinery and Equipment (Resource) ● The definitional equation of the demand for other machinery and equipment is as follows:

$$Q_{MEt}^D = Q_{Mt}^D - Q_{MVt}^D \qquad (9.9)$$

Table 9.1 ● Elasticities of Annual Gross Investment in Farm Machinery from 1924 to 1965 for Changes in Prices, $(P_M/P_R)_{t-1}$, Technology, A(t), Demand Structure, T, and Equity, ER_{t-1}

Inputs	Variables			
	$(P_M/P_R)_{t-1}$	A (t)	T	ER_{t-1}
Demand for total farm machinery	-0.049	1.58	0.62	0.52
Demand for motor vehicles	...	1.59	0.33	0.61

The demand for other farm machinery and equipment is treated as the residual, i.e., the demand for motor vehicles is subtracted from the demand for total farm machinery. (Estimation of the parameters was not undertaken since the equation is definitional.)

The total machinery demand equation can be used to predict that, had the farmers' financial or equity position of 1965 existed in 1924, total farm machinery purchases would have been 67 percent greater in 1924. More efficient methods of production, substitution of cheap operating inputs for farm labor and horsepower, improved management, and inflation permitted a slight increase in net farm income and a considerable improvement in the equity of farmers from 1924 to 1965, despite the rise in the ratio of $(P_M/P_R)_{t-1}$. An "acceleration" influence may be evident: Adoption of machinery in early years was partially responsible for the increased efficiency and improved financial position of farmers, thus permitting greater machinery purchases in later years.

Table 9.1 indicates that the major sources of increase in total machinery and motor vehicles demand have been the equity position of farmers, the level of technology, and structural changes represented by the time variable. Effects of technology are partially offset by the effects of price on the demand for total farm machinery. Undoubtedly the notable structural change embodied in the time variable is the continuous improvement in the quality and adaptability of machinery. Of course, the structural and financial categories are not entirely independent.

The nonfarm sector has performed an important role in farm mechanization. If the supply of farm machinery had not been elastic, increases in farm demand would have brought sharp machinery price increases, and farm mechanization would have progressed less rapidly. The fact that the machinery industry has supplied machines in quantities and qualities desired by farmers and at a relatively constant price elasticity is an important explanation of the rapid growth in farm machinery investment. In turn, the greater stock of machinery and its substitution for farm-produced power has been a significant element in raising productivity and reducing numbers of farm laborers.

Demand for Farm Building Investment (Resource) ● The deflated total value of real estate, Q_{BIt}^D, increased by 288 percent during the 1924–65 period. The increase is due largely to investment in building improvements including fences, windmills, and wells. In this study, the quantity demanded (annual gross investment of building materials) is specified as a function of prices, index of livestock production, interest rate, the stock of productive farm building assets, the three years' weighted average of the net farm income, and the structure variable for pre– and post–World War II years. All indexes are expressed as a percentage of the 1957–59 average.

The six independent variables [Equation (9.10)] in the following equation explain 87 percent of the annual variation about the mean of Q_{BIt}^D:

$$Q_{BIt}^D = 817.9438 + \underset{(6.20)}{375.2627C_t} + \underset{(4.56)}{34.1892ER_{t-1}} + \underset{(1.75)}{2.049107LP_t}$$
$$\underset{(-4.07)}{- 9.858559P_{Bt}} - \underset{(-1.82)}{0.004864S_{Bt}} + \underset{(3.70)}{Y_{WEt-1}} \qquad (9.10)$$
$$d = 1.27^* \qquad R^2 = 0.98$$

Coefficients of all variables except the index of livestock production are highly significant (at the 1 percent probability level). The signs of all the variables are consistent with theoretical expectations.

The weighted three-year average of net farm income is the most important variable. The variables representing the price for building materials and the stock of farm building also are highly significant. As mentioned for total farm machinery demand, the regression coefficient of the stock value of farm buildings, S_{BIt}, is the depreciation rate h minus the adjustment coefficient g.[16] Hence, the negative coefficient of S_{BIt} indicates that g exceeds h by 0.005. The exact depreciation rate is unknown (data are not available) but probably is considerably below the machinery depreciation rate. If the depreciation rate is 0.10, the the adjustment rate is $0.10 + 0.005 = 0.1005$. The levels of the adjustment coefficients are quite compatible with those for farm machinery demand.

According to Equation (9.10), the price elasticity of Q_{BIt}^D estimated at the mean is -1.0. The income elasticity of Q_{BIt}^D with respect to lagged three-year weighted average of the net farm income, Y_{WFt-1}, is 0.19.

Annual gross investment in building improvements in 1965 was 97 percent above the 1924 level. Three proposed causes of the increase are the equity ratio, the livestock production index, and the structural variable, C_t. If these variables are given 1965 values, the equation indicates that building investment demand in 1924 would have been 166 percent greater than it actually was. If building materials price, P_{Bt}, alone had been at the 1965 level in 1924, the quantity demanded would have been 70 percent less than it actually was in 1924. The index of livestock production can be used as a proxy variable for these changes and has a t-value for the equation which is significant at the 1 percent probability level. If livestock production had been at the 1965 value in 1924, other things being equal, demand for building investment would have been 34 percent above the actual level.

Structural changes have a broad range of physical and technological influences. Technological change for buildings has not been as dramatic as for farm machinery; nevertheless changes in methods of storing feeds,

---

16. Heady and Dillon, *Agricultural Production Functions.*

handling dairy cattle, etc., have influenced the demand for buildings. Influences tending to reduce farm numbers and replace labor with other resources also have a depressing impact on building investment. Some of these influences reduce demand while others increase demand, but the net influence according to Equation (9.10) is to shift demand to the right for postwar years.

With increases in agricultural production efficiency over time and with relatively stable input prices, farmers apparently improved their financial status sufficiently to increase purchases of building improvements by a sizeable amount. But the influence of trends in both building material prices and equity alone would have reduced demand by a net of about 25 percent up to 1965.

The analysis of demand indicates that a major portion of the increased annual investment in machinery and buildings may be explained by the level of technology, farmers' financial situation and slowly changing influences reflected by the time variable. For machinery, the major influences increasing demand were the improvement in farmers' financial status resulting from greater efficiency, lower relative prices of operating inputs, and structure and time variables (representing improvements in quality, adaptability, and convenience of durables). The structure and time variables also have important influences on the demand for other durable inputs included in this study.

Demand for Total Farm Labor (Resource) ● The demand for total farm employment is the aggregate of the demands for hired and family labor.

The estimated demand equation for total farm employment is as follows:

$$Q_{TLt}^D = 17640.22 - 17.87216IMP_{t-1} + 0.075626Y_{Ft-1}$$
$$(-1.90) \qquad\qquad (1.07)$$
$$- 63.44567P_{NLt} - 11.42658A(t)$$
$$(-9.26) \qquad\qquad (-1.05)$$
$$- 17.56882(P_{TL}/TVBLA)_{t-1} + 3.304025(P_M/P_{TL})_{t-1} \quad (9.11)$$
$$(-1.27) \qquad\qquad (1.20)$$
$$d = 1.62^* \qquad R^2 = 0.97$$

The lagged index of the price ratio of farm machinery to farm wage rates, $(P_M/P_{TL})_{t-1}$, is a significant explanatory variable. The positive coefficient suggests that total demand for farm labor declines in response to a fall in the relative price of machinery. This relationship suggests that machinery is substituted for labor with a relative decline in the machinery price. However, the long-run elasticity, measured at the mean for for total labor demanded with respect to this price ratio, is lower than expected. The computed elasticity is only 0.004.

Total farm labor demand has a large and negative quantitative relationship with the lagged index of the mechanical power on farms. A 1 percent increase in the index of the previous year's mechanical power reduces the current year's total labor demand by 1.11 percent, and an increment in modern farm mechanization has an even greater relative impact on farm labor employment.

Lagged net farm income, Y_{Ft-1}, has the expected positive relationships with total farm employment. Total employment in agriculture is predicted to expand with greater farm income in the previous year. This increment to the labor force is manifested mainly through an increase in family labor, rather than in the hired labor force.

Technological improvement, $A(t)$, has a significant (5 percent probability level) negative effect on demand for family farm labor and consequently on the demand for total farm labor. Technological improvement substitutes farm machinery for labor. A 1 percent increase in the technological index is predicted to reduce the demand for farm labor (number of workers) by 1.12 percent.

The lagged ratio of the farm wage rate to the price of land and buildings per acre, $(P_{TL}/TVBLA)_{t-1}$, has a negative effect on total farm labor demand. It is predicted that as the price of labor rises relative to the price of land and buildings per acre, the latter resources are substituted for labor (a "push" effect). A 1 percent increase in this price ratio causes total farm labor to decline by 1.5 percent in the following year.

The results also indicate that the wage rate for factory workers is a significant explanatory variable in total farm labor demand. A sustained 1 percent increase in P_{NLt} reduces total farm labor demand by 4.8 percent. This effect is one of "pull" exerted through migration to favorable nonfarm opportunities.

Supply Function for Total Labor (Resource) ● The supply function of total labor estimated with annual time series from 1924 to 1965 (all price indices deflated by the wholesale price index [1957–59 = 100]) is as follows:

$$P_{TLt} = 3.869360 - \underset{(-4.64)}{0.618736P_{Mt}} - \underset{(-0.41)}{0.045359A(t)}$$

$$+ \underset{(4.39)}{1.371446P_{NLt}} - \underset{(-6.24)}{1.211193U_{t-1}} + \underset{(1.66)}{0.003175Q_{TLt}{}^D}$$

$$+ \underset{(0.31)}{0.199450T} - \underset{(-0.27)}{1.372308C_t} \qquad (9.12)$$

$$\rho = 0.33 \qquad d = 1.53^* \qquad R^2 = 0.96$$

Although some coefficients are not significant at conventional probability levels, all display the expected signs. ρ is the autoregressive coefficient.

The long-run price flexibility with respect to labor demand computed at the mean is 0.42. This low price flexibility indicates that the labor demand or supply did not exert a significant effect on the farm wage rate. The nonsignificant effect on farm wage rates of farm labor demand or supply undoubtedly results from the excess labor supply in agriculture. Farm workers can be added to or subtracted from agriculture without noticeable effects on farm wage rates.

The negative coefficient for P_{Mt} also indicates that the relationship between labor and machinery is more competitive than complementary. P_{NLt} and U_{t-1} are both significant explanatory variables for the farm wage rate. A sustained 1 percent rise in P_{NLt} increases P_{TL} by more than 1 percent when U_{t-1} is at the 1924–65 average level.

As indicated by the positive coefficient of T, the real farm wage rate displays a rising trend over time. The structural variable, C_t, is insignificant in this function, but its effects on the farm wage rate are probably reflected in T.

The technological index, A(t), with the expected negative sign, has an elasticity with the farm wage rate of -0.06 (computed at the time-series mean). The substitutional effects of machinery for labor are again indicated.

Demand for Hired Labor (Resource) ● The estimated demand equation for hired farm employees is

$$Q_{HLt}{}^D = 3583.077 + 9.282995A(t) + 5.407297A_{Ft-1}$$
$$(3.85) \qquad\qquad (1.44)$$

$$+\ 0.804702P_{Mt} - 3.659986(P_{TL}/TVBLA)_{t-1}$$
$$(-0.26) \qquad\qquad (-2.26)$$

$$-\ 51.41593T + 188.4969C_t \qquad\qquad\qquad (9.13)$$
$$(-7.13) \qquad\quad (2.76)$$

$$\rho = 0.23 \qquad d = 1.65^* \qquad R^2 = 0.97$$

A number of variables reflecting agricultural resource prices influence the demand for hired farm employees. The index of the farm machinery price is one significant explanatory variable indicating a decline in hired labor demand in response to a fall in the price of farm machinery. The corresponding elasticity computed at the mean is 0.03.

The coefficient for the lagged index of the ratio of the farm wage rate to the price of buildings and land per acre is negative. It suggests that as the price of labor rises relative to the price of buildings and land, hired labor on farms declines.

The lagged index of cropland per farm, A_{Ft-1}, has a significant positive effect on the demand for hired farm labor. The corresponding elasticity of hired labor demand with respect to A_{Ft-1} is 0.18.

Although a significant variable, A(t) has a quite small positive coefficient as compared to its effect on the demand for total farm machinery and motor vehicles. Technological improvement has favored mechanization as a substitute for labor. While technological improvement has a significant negative effect on the demand for family farm labor (and consequently total farm labor) its effect on hired farm labor is less clear. On the one hand, improvements in technology increase labor efficiency and tend to encourage labor use. On the other hand, technological improvement substitutes farm machinery for labor. For hired labor demand, the substitution effect may have been partially offset by the migration of family labor and farm consolidation so that larger units remaining more often extend beyond family help.

The elasticity of hired labor demand with respect to time is —0.90. The demand for hired labor has declined over time as a result of substitution effects, but in other aspects the demand function has shifted to the right as indicated in the positive coefficient for the structural variable, C_t.

Demand for Family Labor (Resource) ● The demand for family farm labor is defined as follows:

$$Q_{FLt}{}^D = Q_{TLt}{}^D - Q_{HLt}{}^D \qquad (9.14)$$

Over 75 percent of the total farm labor demand (persons employed) in the 1924–65 period was represented by family labor. The demand (number of persons employed) for family labor is treated as the residual (total labor less hired labor). Thus parameters for family labor demand are not estimated, since the function is a definitional equation.

REGIONAL RESULTS, 1946–65 ● Regional demand estimates were obtained for all the resource markets.

Demand for Total Farm Machinery ● The equation for regional farm machinery demand is summarized in Table 9.2. The alternative stock adjustment equation was also estimated for regional machinery demand. However, the high multicollinearity among the stock value of farm machinery, the time trend, and technological index led to nonsignificance of the coefficients of many variables. Consequently the results of the stock adjustment model are not reported.

The regression results (Table 9.2) indicate that all variables were statistically significant. (The Durbin-Watson statistic also indicates significant autocorrelation.) The overall coefficients for the time trend, the ratio of farm machinery prices to the price received by farmers, and the one-year-lagged farm machinery investment were statistically significant. For the last variable, only the Delta States' coefficient differed significantly from the overall coefficient.

The overall coefficient for the lagged equity ratio is also significant

Table 9.2 ● Regression Equation and Related Statistics for Regional Total Farm Machinery Demand

Names of variables and statistics	Notation	Statistics & regression coefficients
Overall regression F ratio	F	379.886^a
Coefficient of determination	R^2	0.986
Durbin-Watson statistic	d	1.648^b
Overall intercept	b_0	-745.54 $(-4.40)^a$
Difference in the intercept for Lake States region	b_3	164.67 $(1.30)^c$
Difference in the intercept for Corn Belt region	b_4	321.94 $(2.65)^a$
Difference in the intercept for Northern Plains region	b_5	283.55 $(2.47)^b$
Difference in the intercept for Appalachian region	b_6	166.24 $(1.38)^c$
Overall time trend	T	14.72 $(4.59)^a$
Overall coefficient of Q^D_{Mt-1}	Q^D_{Mt-1}	0.867 $(3.34)^a$
Difference in the coefficient of Q^D_{Mt-1} for Delta States region	$Q^D_{Mt-1,7}$	0.690 $(-1.34)^c$
Overall coefficient of ER_{t-1}	ER_{t-1}	15.87 $(2.88)^a$
Difference in the coefficient of ER_{t-1} for Northeast region	$ER_{t-1,2}$	24.04 $(2.01)^b$
Difference in the coefficient of ER_{t-1} for Northern Plains region	$ER_{t-1,5}$	-9.67 $(-1.60)^c$
Difference in the coefficient for Appalachian region	$ER_{t-1,6}$	-9.44 $(-1.56)^c$
Overall coefficient for $(P_M/P_R)_t$	$(P_M/P_R)_t$	-2.56 $(-3.29)^a$

[a] Indicates coefficients significant at probability level $0 < P \leqslant 0.01$.
[b] Indicates coefficients significant at probability level $0.01 < P \leqslant 0.05$.
[c] Indicates coefficients significant at probability level $0.05 < P \leqslant 0.20$.

and has a positive effect on farm machinery demand. Regions which differ significantly from the overall coefficient are the Northeast, Northern Plains, and Appalachian regions.

Coefficients of variables for the ten farm production regions are presented in Table 9.3. While one aggregate regression was used to derive ten different regional equations, the coefficients are the same for

Table 9.3 ● Regression Coefficients for the Regional Total Farm Machinery Demand Equations

Region	Constant	Regression coefficients for			
		T	Q^D_{Mt-1}	ER_{t-1}	$(P_M/P_R)_t$
Pacific	-745.54	14.72	0.867	15.87	-2.56
Northeast	-745.54	14.72	0.867	39.91	-2.56
Lake States	-580.87	14.72	0.867	15.87	-2.56
Corn Belt	-423.60	14.72	0.867	15.87	-2.56
Northern Plains	-462.99	14.72	0.867	6.20	-2.56
Appalachian	-579.30	14.72	0.867	6.43	-2.56
Southeast	-745.54	14.72	0.867	15.87	-2.56
Delta States	-745.54	14.72	0.177	15.87	-2.56
Southern Plains	-745.54	14.72	0.867	15.87	-2.56
Mountain States	-745.54	14.72	0.867	15.87	-2.56

variables which were identical for all regions [T and $(P_M/P_R)_t$]. Elasticities for variables in these equations were calculated at the respective means and are reported in Table 9.4.

Results obtained from the regional estimates are consistent with those for the national function reported previously. The regional results further emphasize the lesser response in farm machinery investment with respect to the lagged equity ratio for the Appalachian and Northern Plains regions. As mentioned previously, areas suffering from chronic income depression, such as the Appalachian region, often are characterized by low assets and equity per family. A low-equity ratio generally leads to a low elasticity of farm machinery investment with respect to this variable.

Demand for Farm Motor Vehicles ● A stock adjustment equation was also fitted unsuccessfully for regional farm motor vehicle demand. High multicollinearity among stock values of motor vehicles, the technological index, and the time trend were present. For this reason, only the results for the expectation equation are reported (Table 9.5). The Durbin-Watson statistic indicated that the errors were not autocorrelated in the equation.

The overall coefficients for one-year-lagged investment, the lagged equity ratio, and the ratio of motor vehicle prices to prices received by farmers are statistically significant, and all have expected signs. For the lagged equity ratio, the regression results indicate a significant difference from the overall coefficient in the coefficients for the Northeast, Corn Belt, and Appalachian regions. Regional regression coefficients are the difference between overall coefficients and the regional coefficients.

To illustrate the broader aspects of the regression results, coefficients and variables for ten farm production regions (farm motor vehicles demand functions for all regions) are presented in Table 9.6. One aggregated regression equation was used to derive the ten different equations. Elasticities for variables in these equations were calculated at the respective means and are reported in Table 9.7.

The results obtained in the regional analysis again are consistent with the national analysis. However there is an inconsistent sign for the coefficient of the lagged equity ratio in the Corn Belt. The high value of the coefficient for the lagged farm machinery investment suggests that if multicollinearity were absent among the stock value of motor vehicles, the technological index, and the time trend, the stock variable (instead of the lagged investment variable) would yield statistically and economically more meaningful results.

Farm Buildings Investment ● The regression results reported in Table 9.8 include all variables of the farm building demand function which proved statistically significant. Insignificant autocorrelation is indicated by the d-statistic.

Table 9.4 ● Elasticities Computed at the Means of the Variables for Total Farm Machinery Demand

Names of variables	Notation	Elasticities
Time trend	T	2.610
Q^D_{Mt-1} for Pacific Region	Q^D_{Mt-1}	0.021
Q^D_{Mt-1} for Delta States Region	$Q^D_{Mt-1,7}$	0.006
ER_{t-1} for Pacific Region	ER_{t-1}	0.015
ER_{t-1} for Northeast Region	$ER_{t-1,2}$	0.023
ER_{t-1} for Northern Plains Region	$ER_{t-1,5}$	0.003
ER_{t-1} for Appalachian Region	$ER_{t-1,6}$	0.005
$(P_M/P_R)_t$ for Pacific Region	$(P_M/P_R)_t$	-0.727

Table 9.5 ● Regression Equation and Related Statistics for Regional Farm Motor Vehicles Demand

Names of variables and statistics	Notation	Statistics & regression coefficients
Overall regression F ratio	F	238.10[a]
Coefficient of determination	R^2	0.978[b]
Durbin-Watson statistic	d	2.130[b]
Overall intercept	b_0	-140.8 (-1.45)[c]
Difference in the intercept for Corn Belt	b_4	186.16 (2.54)[b]
Overall coefficient for Q^D_{MVt-1}	Q^D_{MVt-1}	65.01 (2.31)[b]
Overall coefficient for ER_{t-1}	ER_{t-1}	5.05 (1.43)[c]
Difference in the coefficient of ER_{t-1} for Northeast region	$ER_{t-1,2}$	14.13 (1.86)[c]
Difference in the coefficient of ER_{t-1} for Corn Belt region	$ER_{t-1,4}$	-6.24 (-1.28)[c]
Difference in the coefficient of ER_{t-1} for Appalachian region	$ER_{t-1,6}$	-4.82 (-1.23)[c]
Overall coefficient for $(P_{MV}/P_R)_t$	$(P_{MV}/P_R)_t$	-0.55 (-1.13)[c]

[a] Indicates coefficients significant at probability level $0 < P \leq 0.01$.
[b] Indicates coefficients significant at probability level $0.01 < P \leq 0.05$.
[c] Indicates coefficients significant at probability level $0.05 < P \leq 0.20$.

Table 9.6 ● Regression Coefficient for the Regional Farm Motor Vehicles Demand Equation

Region	Constant	Regression coefficients for		
		Q^D_{MVt-1}	ER_{t-1}	$(P_{MV}/P_R)_t$
Pacific	-140.8	65.01	5.05	-0.55
Northeast	-140.8	65.01	19.18	-0.55
Lake States	-140.8	65.01	5.05	-0.55
Corn Belt	45.36	65.01	1.19	-0.55
Northern Plains	-140.8	65.01	5.05	-0.55
Appalachian	-140.8	65.01	0.23	-0.55
Southeast	-140.8	65.01	5.05	-0.55
Delta States	-140.8	65.01	5.05	-0.55
Southern Plains	-140.8	65.01	5.05	-0.55
Mountain States	-140.8	65.01	5.05	-0.55

Table 9.7 ● Elasticities Computed at the Means of the Variables for Farm Motor Vehicles Demand

Names of variables	Notation	Elasticities
Ratio of machine prices to prices received by farmers	$(P_{MV}/P_R)_t$	-0.294
Lagged equity ratio for Pacific region	ER_{t-1}	0.055
Lagged equity ratio for Northeast region	$ER_{t-1,2}$	0.110
Lagged equity ratio for Corn Belt region	$ER_{t-1,4}$	0.003
Lagged equity ratio for Appalachian region	$ER_{t-1,6}$	0.002
Lagged investment	Q^D_{MVt-1}	6.220

Table 9.8 ● Regression Equation and Related Statistics for Regional Farm Buildings Demand

Names of variables and statistics	Notation	Statistics and regression coefficients
Overall regression F ratio	F	601.51[a]
Coefficient of determination	R^2	0.992
Durbin-Watson statistic	d	1.870[b]
Overall intercept	b_0	463.91 (9.22)[a]
Difference in the intercept for Corn Belt region	b_4	-42.12 (-1.59)[c]
Difference in the intercept for Appalachian region	b_5	-70.65 (-3.29)[a]
Overall time trend	T	-4.09 (-4.58)[a]
Price of farm building materials	P_{Bt}	-1.49 (-2.38)[b]
Stock value of farm buildings	S_{Bt}	0.00128 (2.09)[b]
Overall coefficient for Y_{WFt-1}		0.105 (4.82)[b]
Difference in the coefficient of Y_{WFt-1} for Northeast region	$Y_{WFt-1, 2}$	-0.100 (-3.24)[a]
Difference in the coefficient of Y_{WFt-1} for Lake States region	$Y_{WFt-1, 3}$	-0.089 (-3.92)[a]
Difference in the coefficient of Y_{WFt-1} for Corn Belt region	$Y_{WFt-1, 4}$	-0.040 (-1.85)[c]
Difference in the coefficient of Y_{WFt-1} for Northern Plains region	$Y_{WFt-1, 5}$	-0.89 (-3.98)[a]
Difference in the coefficient of Y_{WFt-1} for Appalachian region	$Y_{WFt-1, 6}$	-0.074 (-3.20)[a]
Difference in the coefficient of Y_{WFt-1} for Southeast region	$Y_{WFt-1, 7}$	-0.103 (-3.92)[a]
Difference in the coefficient of Y_{WFt-1} for Delta States region	$Y_{WFt-1, 8}$	-0.142 (-4.57)[a]
Difference in the coefficient of Y_{WFt-1} for Southern Plains region	$Y_{WFt-1, 9}$	-0.068 (-2.74)[a]
Coefficient of ER_{t-1} for Northeast region	$ER_{t-1, 2}$	11.31 (1.61)[c]
Coefficient of ER_{t-1} for Lake States region	$ER_{t-1, 3}$	7.56 (1.90)[c]
Coefficient of ER_{t-1} for Corn Belt region	$ER_{t-1, 4}$	9.53 (2.84)[b]
Coefficient of ER_{t-1} for Northern Plains region	$ER_{t-1, 5}$	12.05 (3.77)[a]
Coefficient of ER_{t-1} for Appalachian region	$ER_{t-1, 6}$	11.43 (3.55)[a]

Table 9.8 ● *(Continued)*

Names of variables and statistics	Notation	Statistics and regression coefficients
Coefficient of ER_{t-1} for Southeast region	$ER_{t-1,7}$	6.72 (2.05)[b]
Coefficient of ER_{t-1} for Delta States region	$ER_{t-1,8}$	7.61 (2.31)[b]
Coefficient of ER_{t-1} for Southern Plains region	$ER_{t-1,9}$	8.88 (2.61)[a]
Coefficient of ER_{t-1} for Mountain region	$ER_{t-1,10}$	5.53 (1.19)[c]

[a]Indicates coefficients significant at probability level $0 < P \leq 0.01$.
[b]Indicates coefficients significant at probability level $0.01 < P \leq 0.05$.
[c]Indicates coefficients significant at probability level $0.05 < P \leq 0.20$.

The overall coefficient for weighted net farm income (lagged one year) is positive. The regional coefficients (except in the Mountain region) indicate slightly different responses from the overall income effect.

While the overall coefficient for the equity ratio (lagged one year) was not significant, all regions except the Pacific have significant positive coefficients for this variable suggesting that the equity rate does serve as a variable influencing long-term investment in buildings. The coefficients for the time trend and farm building prices were significant and negative. Perhaps the time trend effect is associated with the decline in farm numbers. The stock value of farm buildings was also significant in explaining the annual gross farm building investment. The adjustment coefficients could not be computed because regional depreciation rates of buildings were unavailable.

The coefficients and variables for regional farm building demand functions are presented in Table 9.9. Again the functions for the ten production regions were derived from the overall function. Elasticities for these equations, calculated at the respective means, are reported in Table 9.10.

The more important explanatory variables include weighted net farm income, the equity ratio, time, the price for building materials, and the stock value of farm buildings. Regional differences with respect to response to the same variables for farm buildings investment were not significant.

Table 9.9 ● Regression Coefficients for the Regional Buildings Investment Functions

Region	Constant	Regression coefficients for				
		Y_{WFt-1}	P_{Bt}	T	S_{Bt}	ER_{t-1}
Pacific	463.91	0.105	-1.49	-4.09	0.00128	...
Northeast	463.91	0.005	-1.49	-4.09	0.00128	11.31
Lake States	463.91	0.016	-1.49	-4.09	0.00128	7.56
Corn Belt	421.79	0.065	-1.49	-4.09	0.00128	9.53
Northern Plains	463.91	0.016	-1.49	-4.09	0.00128	12.05
Appalachian	383.26	0.031	-1.49	-4.09	0.00128	11.43
Southeast	463.91	0.002	-1.49	-4.09	0.00128	6.72
Delta States	463.91	-0.037	-1.49	-4.09	0.00128	7.61
Southern Plains	463.91	0.037	-1.49	-4.09	0.00128	8.88
Mountain States	463.91	0.105	-1.49	-4.09	0.00128	5.53

Table 9.10 ● Elasticities Computed at the Means of the Variables for Farm Buildings Investment

Names of variables	Notation	Elasticities
Prices of farm building materials	P_{Bt}	1.370
Stock values of farm building	S_{Bt}	0.320
Lagged weighted income	Y_{WFt-1}	0.146
Y_{WFt-1}, Northeast region	$Y_{WFt-1,2}$	0.005
Y_{WFt-1}, Lake States region	$Y_{WFt-1,3}$	0.024
Y_{WFt-1}, Corn Belt region	$Y_{WFt-1,4}$	0.084
Y_{WFt-1}, Northern Plains region	$Y_{WFt-1,5}$	0.020
Y_{WFt-1}, Appalachian region	$Y_{WFt-1,6}$	0.058
Y_{WFt-1}, Southeast region	$Y_{WFt-1,7}$	0.003
Y_{WFt-1}, Delta States region	$Y_{WFt-1,8}$	0.074
Y_{WFt-1}, Southern Plains region	$Y_{WFt-1,9}$	0.046
Y_{WFt-1}, Mountain States region	$Y_{WFt-1,10}$	0.114
Time trend	T	2.160
Lagged equity ratio, Northeast	$ER_{t-1,2}$	0.097
Lagged equity ratio, Lake States	$ER_{t-1,3}$	0.071
Lagged equity ratio, Corn Belt	$ER_{t-1,4}$	0.048
Lagged equity ratio, Northern Plains	$ER_{t-1,5}$	0.159
Lagged equity ratio, Appalachian	$ER_{t-1,6}$	0.184
Lagged equity ratio, Southeast	$ER_{t-1,7}$	0.140
Lagged equity ratio, Delta States	$ER_{t-1,8}$	0.187
Lagged equity ratio, Southern States	$ER_{t-1,9}$	0.111
Lagged equity ratio, Mountain States	$ER_{t-1,10}$	0.080

Demand for Total Farm Labor ● The regression results in Table 9.11 include all statistically significant variables in the total farm labor demand equations. Autocorrelation was tested and found to be insignificant.

The overall coefficient for technological change was negative and significant at the 1 percent probability level. The regional differences for the same variable were significant but with positive signs. However, the regional regression coefficients—the differences between overall coefficients and the regional coefficients—had consistent negative signs.

Weighted net farm income (lagged one year) was tried as an explanatory variable but proved nonsignificant. The lagged ratio of composite farm wage rates to the total value of buildings and land per acre were negative and significant for the Northern Plains and Mountain regions. The sign for the Appalachian region was inconsistent. A positive relation between the lagged ratio of machinery prices and farm wage rates was indicated for the Northeast and Lake States regions, in contrast to the inconsistent sign for the Southeast.

The overall coefficients for nonfarm wage rates and lagged index of mechanical power were found to be significant and with consistent negative signs in explaining the demand for total farm labor.

To illustrate the broader aspects of regression results from the model, the coefficients and variables for regional total farm labor demand functions are presented in Table 9.12. One aggregate equation was used to derive the ten regional equations. Elasticities for variables in these equations, calculated at respective means, are reported in Table 9.13.

The important significant variables include the technological index, the nonfarm wage rate, the lagged index of mechanical power on farms, the lagged ratio of the composite farm wage rate to the total value of buildings and land per acre, and the lagged ratio of machinery prices to the farm wage rate.

Because results for the ten farm production regions show a close similarity to results from the previous national model, the general effects of each variable need not be reviewed. However, the regional analysis indicates that technological advance has had different effects among regions in reducing total farm labor demand. The negative effects of technology alone in reducing farm labor demand are indicated mainly for the Pacific, Southeast, and Mountain regions.

Demand for Hired Farm Labor ● The same analysis was applied in the regional demand for hired farm labor. However, as a result of high multicollinearity between the technological index, time, and the lagged ratio of farm wage rates to the value of land and buildings per acre, most of the coefficients were insignificant. Consequently the regional model for the hired farm labor was revised as follows:

Table 9.11 ● **Regression Equation and Related Statistics for Regional Total Farm Labor Demand**

Names of variables and statistics	Notation	Statistics and regression coefficients
Overall Regression F	F	$1,602.06^a$
Coefficient of determination	R^2	0.998
Durbin-Watson statistic	d	1.58^b
Overall intercept	b_0	3,371.98
		$(4.97)^a$
Difference in the intercept for Northeast region	b_2	-2,186.79
		$(-3.11)^a$
Difference in the intercept for Lake States region	b_3	-1,764.42
		$(-2.45)^b$
Difference in the intercept for Corn Belt region	b_4	-1,091.34
		$(-1.44)^c$
Difference in the intercept for Northern Plains region	b_5	-1,590.38
		$(-1.95)^c$
Difference in the intercept for Appalachian region	b_6	- 899.48
		$(-1.28)^c$
Difference in the intercept for Southeast region	b_7	- 949.52
		$(-1.39)^c$
Difference in the intercept for Delta States region	b_8	-2,119.45
		$(-3.09)^a$
Difference in the intercept for Southern Plains region	b_9	-1,699.32
		$(-2.41)^b$
Difference in the intercept for Mountain region	b_{10}	- 941.08
		$(-1.33)^c$
Overall coefficient of A (t)		-15.56
		$(-2.65)^a$
Difference in the coefficient of A (t) for Northeast region	$A(t)_2$	15.75
		$(2.68)^a$
Difference in the coefficient of A (t) for Lake States region	$A(t)_3$	15.40
		$(2.61)^a$
Difference in the coefficient of A (t) for Corn Belt region	$A(t)_4$	13.00
		$(2.13)^b$
Difference in the coefficient of A (t) for Northern Plains region	$A(t)_5$	16.45
		$(2.76)^a$
Difference in the coefficient of A (t) for Appalachian region	$A(t)_6$	12.96
		$(2.16)^b$
Difference in the coefficient of A (t) for Southeast region	$A(t)_7$	5.00
		$(2.54)^b$
Difference in the coefficient of A (t) for Delta States region	$A(t)_8$	15.70
		$(2.66)^a$
Difference in the coefficient of A (t) for Southern Plains region	$A(t)_9$	15.71
		$(2.66)^a$
Difference in the coefficient of A (t) for Mountain region	$A(t)_{10}$	1.56
		$(2.62)^a$
Coefficient of $(P_{TL}/TVBLA)_{t-1}$ for Northern Plains region	$(P_{TL}/TVBLA_{t-1}$	-4.01
		$(-1.53)^c$

Table 9.11 ● *(Continued)*

Names of variables and statistics	Notation	Statistics and regression coefficients
Coefficient of $(P_{TL}/TVBLA)_{t-1}$ for Appalachian region	$(P_{TL}/TVBLA)_{t-1}$	3.25 (1.29)[c]
Coefficient of $(P_{TL}/TVBLA)_{t-1}$ for Mountain region	$(P_{TL}/TVBLA)_{t-1}$	-5.30 (-2.27)[b]
Overall coefficient for P_{NLt}	P_{NLt}	-9.22 (-13.67)[a]
Overall coefficient for IMP_{t-1}	IMP_{t-1}	-1.85 (-2.96)[a]
Coefficient of $(P_M/P_{TL})_{t-1}$ for Northeast region	$(P_M/P_{TL})_{t-1,2}$	5.26 (1.49)[c]
Coefficient of $(P_M/P_{TL})_{t-1}$ for Lake States region	$(P_M/P_{TL})_{t-1,3}$	6.03 (1.69)[c]
Coefficient of $(P_M/P_{TL})_{t-1}$ for Southeast region	$(P_M/P_{TL})_{t-1,7}$	4.43 (-1.43)[c]

[a]Indicates coefficients significant at probability level $0 < P \leq 0.01$.
[b]Indicates coefficients significant at probability level $0.01 < P \leq 0.05$.
[c]Indicates coefficients significant at probability level $0.05 < P \leq 0.20$.

$$Q^D_{HLt} = b_o + \sum_{i=1}^{m-1} b_i + cP_{Nt} + dY_{Ft-1} + \sum_{i=1}^{m-1} eY_{Ft-1,i}$$

$$+ f(P_M/P_{TL})_{t-1} + \sum_{i=1}^{m-1} g(P_M/P_{TL})_{t-1,i} + U_t \qquad (9.15)$$

All variables are as described previously. All coefficients which were statistically significant are reported in Table 9.14.

The coefficients of all variables except Y_{Ft-1} for the Northeast region had the expected sign. Except for the Appalachian region there were no significant differences between the overall and regional functions. The Appalachian region showed a higher demand response for hired labor with respect to weighted net farm income and the ratio of farm machinery prices to farm labor wages.

Table 9.12 ● Regression Coefficients for the Regional Total Farm Labor Demand Equations

Region	Constant	A (t)	Regression coefficients for			
			$(P_{TL}/TVBLA)_{t-1}$	P_{NLt}	IMP_{t-1}	$(P_M/P_{TL})_{t-1}$
Pacific	3,371.98	-15.56	...	-9.22	-1.85	...
Northeast	1,185.19	0.19	...	-9.22	-1.85	5.26
Lake States	1,507.56	-0.16	...	-9.22	-1.85	6.03
Corn Belt	2,280.64	-2.56	...	-9.22	-1.85	...
Northern Plains	1,781.60	0.89	-4.01	-9.22	-1.85	...
Appalachian	2,472.50	-2.60	3.25	-9.22	-1.85	...
Southeast	2,322.46	-10.56	...	-9.22	-1.85	-4.43
Delta States	1,252.53	0.14	...	-9.22	-1.85	...
Southern Plains	1,672.66	0.15	...	-0.22	-1.85	...
Mountain States	2,430.90	-13.99	-5.30	-9.22	-1.85	...

Table 9.13 ● Elasticities Computed at the Means of the Variables for Total Farm Labor Demand

Names of variables	Notation	Elasticities
Technological index		
Pacific	$A(t)_1$	-0.180
Northeast	$A(t)_2$	0.273
Lake States	$A(t)_3$	-0.002
Corn Belt	$A(t)_4$	-0.017
Northern Plains	$A(t)_5$	0.014
Appalachian	$A(t)_6$	-0.010
Southeast	$A(t)_7$	-0.105
Delta States	$A(t)_8$	0.002
Southern Plains	$A(t)_9$	0.002
Mountain	$A(t)_{10}$	-0.367
$(P_{TL}/TVBLA)_{t-1}$ for Northern Plains region	$(P_{TL}/TVBLA)_{t-1,5}$	-0.076
$(P_{TL}/TVBLA)_{t-1}$ for Appalachian region	$(P_{TL}/TVBLA)_{t-1,6}$	0.024
$(P_{TL}/TVBLA)_{t-1}$ for Mountain States	$(P_{TL}/TVBLA)_{t-1,10}$	-0.152
Nonfarm wage rate	P_{NLt}	-1.057
Lagged index of power	IMP_{t-1}	-0.201
$(P_M/P_{TL})_{t-1}$ for Northeast region	$(P_M/P_{TL})_{t-1,2}$	0.067
$(P_M/P_{TL})_{t-1}$ for Lake States region	$(P_M/P_{TL})_{t-1,3}$	0.042
$(P_M/P_{TL})_{t-1}$ for Southeast region	$(P_M/P_{TL})_{t-1,7}$	-0.052

Table 9.14 ● Regression Equation and Related Statistics for Regional Hired Farm Labor Demand

Names of variables and statistics	Notation	Statistics and regression coefficients
Overall regression F ratio	F	205.32
Coefficient of determination	R^2	0.97
Durbin-Watson statistic	d	1.58^b
Overall intercept	b_0	407.04 $(\ 5.56)^a$
Difference in the intercept for Lake States region	b_3	-195.74 $(-1.57)^c$
Difference in the intercept for Northern Plains region	b_5	-254.51 $(-1.49)^c$
Difference in the intercept for Southeast region	b_7	-202.89 $(-1.45)^c$
Coefficient of Y_{Ft-1} for Northeast region	$Y_{Ft-1,2}$	-2.01 $(-1.61)^c$
Coefficient of Y_{Ft-1} for Appalachian region	$Y_{Ft-1,6}$	3.55 $(\ 1.75)^c$
Overall coefficient for P_{NLt}	P_{NLt}	-1.22 $(-2.14)^b$
Coefficient of $(P_M/P_{TL})_{t-1}$ for Appalachian region	$(P_M/P_{TL})_{t-1,6}$	1.78 $(\ 1.30)^c$

[a]Indicates coefficients significant at probability level $0 < P \leq 0.01$.
[b]Indicates coefficients significant at probability level $0.01 < P \leq 0.05$.
[c]Indicates coefficients significant at probability level $0.05 < P \leq 0.20$.

SIMULATION OF FARM INCOME AND RESOURCE DEMAND UNDER VARIOUS POLICY AND MARKET CONDITIONS ● A computer simulation model was used to evaluate the regression predictions against past resource demand behavior. No model is expected to fit the data exactly; the question is whether the residual errors are sufficiently small to be tolerable and sufficiently unsystematic to be treated as random. Among several approaches to historical verification, Cohen and Cyert suggest three general testing procedures in evaluating the "goodness of fit" of data generated by computer simulation experiments with actual time-series data.[17] One procedure, the method used in this chapter, is to regress the generated time series (predicted values) on actual time-series data, and then check whether the resulting equations have (1) intercepts which do not differ significantly from zero and (2) slopes which do not differ significantly from unity.

Simulation of the Historical Period and Model Validation ● In this study, the behavioral and definitional relations developed for the national model were rewritten in computer language. Given the time-series data for the exogenous variables and the values of the lagged endogenous variables at the beginning of the time period (1924), the endogenous variables for the entire historical period (1924–65) were then automatically generated, without any additional constraints, by the overall national recursive model. The generated time-series data were then regressed on the respective actual time series. The results are presented as follows where all variables are defined as previously:

$$\hat{S}_{Pt}^{b} = 6.03 + 0.95 S_{Pt}^{b} \qquad R^2 = 0.93$$

$$\hat{Q}_{t}^{S1} = 0.66 + 0.99 Q_{t}^{S1} \qquad R^2 = 0.99$$

$$\hat{Q}_{t}^{S2} = 1.82 + 0.97 Q_{t}^{S2} \qquad R^2 = 0.97$$

$$\hat{P}_{Rt} = 17.50 + 0.84 P_{Rt} \qquad R^2 = 0.95$$

$$(\hat{P}_{R}/P_{D})_{t} = 18.31 + 0.83 (P_{R}/P_{D})_{t} \qquad R^2 = 0.94$$

$$(\hat{Y}_{F})_{t} = 2{,}903.72 + 0.70 Y_{Ft} \qquad R^2 = 0.75$$

$$\hat{P}_{Mt} = 19.62 + 0.79 P_{Mt} \qquad R^2 = 0.75$$

$$\hat{Q}_{Mt}^{D} = 167.23 + 0.95 Q_{Mt}^{D} \qquad R^2 = 0.93$$

$$\hat{X}_{Rt} = 5.53 + 0.94\ X_{Rt} \qquad R^2 = 0.94$$

$$(\hat{P}_{M}/P_{R})_{t} = 14.69 + 0.82 (P_{M}/P_{R})_{t} \qquad R^2 = 0.91$$

$$\hat{Q}_{MEt}^{D} = 132.71 + 0.95 Q_{MEt}^{D} \qquad R^2 = 0.95$$

$$\hat{Q}_{TLt}^{D} = 236.16 + 0.96 Q_{TLt}^{D} \qquad R^2 = 0.96$$

$$\hat{P}_{TLt} = 2.48 + 0.97 P_{TLt} \qquad R^2 = 0.96$$

$$(\hat{P}_{TL}/TVBLA)_{t} = 2.07 + 0.98 (P_{TL}/TVBLA)_{t} \qquad R^2 = 0.95$$

$$\hat{Q}_{HLt}^{D} = -13.18 + Q_{HLt}^{D} \qquad R^2 = 0.98$$

$$\hat{Q}_{FLt}^{D} = 234.39 + 0.95 Q_{FLt}^{D} \qquad R^2 = 0.95$$

$$\hat{Y}_{WFt} = 2{,}908.36 + 0.71 Y_{WFt} \qquad R^2 = 0.77$$

$$\hat{Q}_{BIt}^{D} = 28.23 + 0.96 Q_{BIt}^{D} \qquad R^2 = 0.97$$

$$\hat{Q}_{MVt}^{D} = 70.74 + 0.91 Q_{MVt}^{D} \qquad R^2 = 0.89$$

$$(\hat{P}_{M}/P_{TL})_{t} = 7.07 + 0.91 (P_{M}/P_{TL})_{t} \qquad R^2 = 0.89$$

17. Kalman J. Cohen, and Richard M. Cyert, Computer Models in Dynamic Economics, *Quarterly Journal of Economics* 125 (1961): 112–27.

Out of the twenty variables tested, the coefficient of determination ranges from 0.75 to 0.99. Fifteen had values greater than 0.90. The intercepts vary from 0.66 to 2,908 depending on the different units of measurement for each variable. The slopes varying from 0.70 to 0.99 are considered to be quite close to unity. The production response function has the best fit, whereas the definitional net farm income function has the poorest fit.

As well as the schematic model used in Figure 9.1 the actual and predicted time series of the quantities demanded for five kinds of resources are presented in Figures 9.2 to Figures 9.8. As shown by these figures, the height and turning points are reasonably well predicted by the model. In general, the performance of the model in reproducing the historical period, considering the degree of accuracy needed for each variable, was deemed satisfactory.

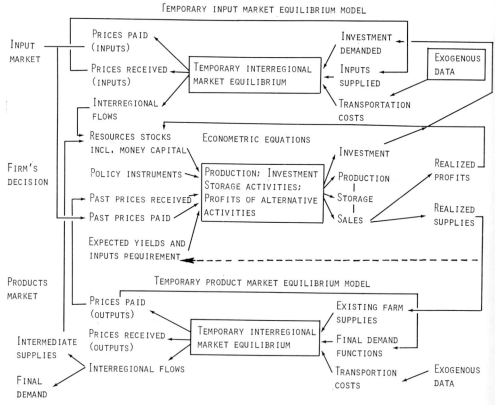

Fig. 9.1. *Schematic diagram of the economic structure of the resources demand and products supply.*

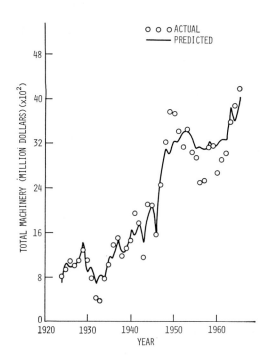

Fig. 9.2. Actual and pre-
dicted values of total farm
machinery purchases for the
United States.

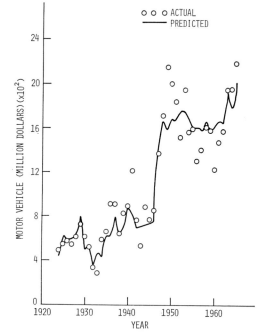

Fig. 9.3. Actual and pre-
dicted values of farm motor
vehicle purchases.

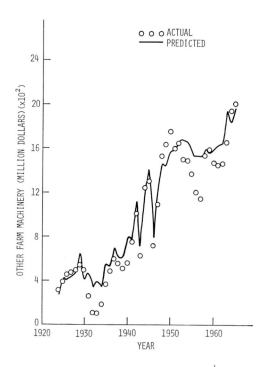

Fig. 9.4. Actual and predicted values of other farm machinery purchases for the United States.

Fig. 9.5. Actual and predicted values of farm building investment for the United States.

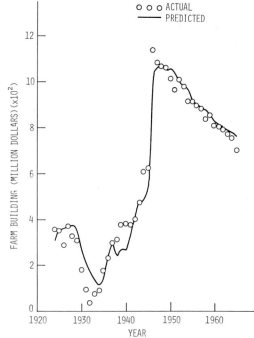

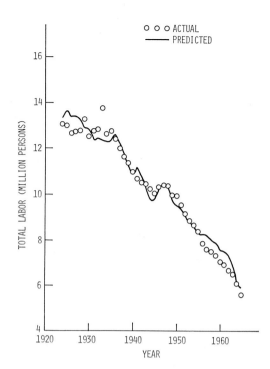

Fig. 9.6. Actual and predicted numbers of total farm employees for the United States.

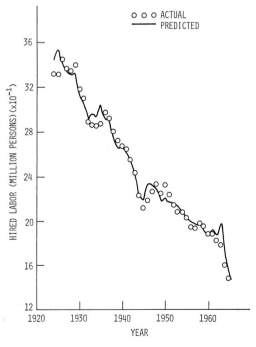

Fig. 9.7. Actual and predicted numbers of hired farm employees for the United States.

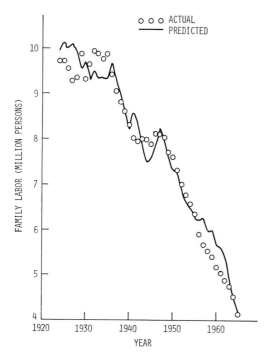

Fig. 9.8. Actual and predicted numbers of family farm employees for the United States.

Simulation of Alternative Historical Demands for Factors ● Total agricultural production in the United States increased rapidly over the past three decades. The index of production increased by 2½ times between 1930 and 1969. Total inputs in agriculture increased at a slower rate and the composition of the inputs changed markedly. The input of labor, historically the largest input, has been sharply reduced. Labor input declined from 13 million persons employed on farms in 1924 to 5.6 million in 1965. Capital input measured in real value rose and largely offset the decline in labor. The index (1957–59 = 100) of the stock value of productive farm assets rose from 110 in 1924 to 180 in 1965.

Past growth in agricultural production has not resulted from an increase in crop acreage. It resulted mainly from rapid technological advances and the addition and substitution of capital resources for both land and labor. Income has not increased apace with output because of the nature of demand for food products. The inelastic demand for farm products has limited the total U.S. gross farm income to a slow rise. With an elastic supply of inputs and farmers' increased demand or use of commercial inputs, in the absence of government programs the net short-run effect of using more efficient production techniques would have been a decrease in total national net farm income. Along with increased production of farm products, the inelastic supply of factors such as labor caused farm income to remain depressed.

Because of the magnitude of resource and commodity demand and supply conditions for agriculture, we now simulate conditions under which the rate of technical change would have been slower. What would the effect of a rate of structural change 50 percent lower than actual have been on the income and resource demand of agriculture?

Effect on Resource Demand ● As explained previously, the technological index was a significant explanatory variable in the production response function. The production response elasticity with respect to technology was computed as 0.15. Had technological advancement in agriculture increased at a rate only one-half the prevailing annual rate (3 percent), *ceteris paribus,* the problem of excessive supply of commodities in agriculture would have been reduced to some extent. Under the estimated parameters computed for the technological index A(t) and other variables, the demand for total labor would have increased and the demand for farm machinery would have decreased. These results emerge from simulation with the national recursive model. The simulated results for the demand of factors with the rate of technological change set at half the actual rate are presented in Table 9.15. Simulated results under a free market are included in Table 9.16. The demand quantities for all farm machinery, motor vehicles, total farm labor, hired farm labor, and building investment, are shown for selected years as simulated under the prevailing system in both tables. (The simulated results of these variables under the prevailing system are, as mentioned in model validation, highly consistent with the actual time series.)

Under a slower rate of technological growth, the demand for all farm machinery in 1965 would have been somewhat smaller than under prevailing conditions. On the other hand, simulated free markets indicate a somewhat larger farm machinery demand than under prevailing conditions. Under the conditions of free markets, it is predicted that the exodus of labor would have been greater (employment would have been smaller) and substitution of more machinery required than under prevailing conditions. The predicted or simulated results under the slower rate of technical change and free markets both show a lower motor vehicle demand than under prevailing conditions by 1965. Under a slower rate of change, fewer would have been needed; under a free market, there would have been fewer farm families to use them. Also, lower farm incomes are predicted to have dampened demand. A slower rate of technical growth would have resulted, in the sense of prediction and simulation, in a greater demand for family farm labor (i.e., a lowered rate of migration out of agriculture). However, free market simulation indicates a smaller 1965 demand for both family and hired labor than under conditions which prevailed. Building investment is predicted to be slightly larger under the restricted rate of technical advance mainly as a result of higher net farm income. For similar reasons, building investment demand is indicated to be lower under free market

Table 9.15 ● Simulated Results for Demand of Farm Machinery (Q_{Mt}^D), Motor Vehicles (Q_{Mt}^D), Total Farm Labor (Q_{TLt}^D), Hired Farm Labor (Q_{HLt}^D), and Building Investment (Q_{BIt}^D) under the Actual Rate and under a Lower Rate of Technological Change

Year	Q_{MTt}^D a	Q_{MTt}^D b	Q_{MVt}^D a	Q_{MVt}^D b	Q_{TLt}^D a	Q_{TLt}^D b	Q_{HLt}^D a	Q_{HLt}^D b	Q_{BIt}^D a	Q_{BIt}^D b
	($ million)				(thousand persons)				($ million)	
1924	714	714	441	441	13,370	13,370	3,442	3,442	312	312
1930	893	1,004	489	548	12,799	12,748	3,119	3,149	285	289
1935	1,169	720	620	380	12,357	12,511	3,045	2,921	150	148
1940	1,672	1,271	875	660	10,896	11,038	2,681	2,569	267	268
1945	2,148	2,128	723	723	9,780	9,795	2,184	2,178	553	555
1950	3,246	3,219	1,674	1,660	9,524	9,540	2,199	2,193	1,055	1,056
1955	3,111	3,182	1,584	1,622	8,267	8,245	2,020	2,039	920	920
1960	3,202	3,206	1,614	1,616	7,534	7,535	1,890	1,892	827	827

aSimulated results under the prevailing rate of technical change.
bSimulated results with technological changes at one-half of the prevailing rate but conditions of markets and farm programs at prevailing rates.

378

Table 9.16 ● Simulated Results for Demand of Farm Machinery (Q_{MTt}^D), Motor Vehicles (Q_{MVt}^D), Total Farm Labor (Q_{TLt}^D), Hired Farm Labor (Q_{HLt}^D), and Building Investment (Q_{BIt}^D) under the Actual and under Free Market Conditions

Year	Q_{MTt}^D a	Q_{MTt}^D b	Q_{MVt}^D a	Q_{MVt}^D b	Q_{TLt}^D a	Q_{TLt}^D b	Q_{HLt}^D a	Q_{HLt}^D b	Q_{BIt}^D a	Q_{BIt}^D b
	($ million)				(thousand persons)				($ million)	
1924	714	714	441	441	13,370	13,370	3,442	3,442	312	312
1930	893	893	489	489	12,799	12,799	3,119	3,119	285	285
1935	1,169	1,171	620	620	12,357	12,350	3,045	3,045	150	150
1940	1,672	1,674	875	875	10,896	10,855	2,681	2,682	267	262
1945	2,148	2,146	723	723	9,780	9,629	2,184	2,186	553	527
1950	3,246	3,245	1,674	1,674	9,524	9,423	2,199	2,201	1,055	1,034
1955	3,111	3,111	1,584	1,584	8,267	8,174	2,020	2,021	920	902
1960	3,202	3,207	1,614	1,614	7,534	7,502	1,890	1,891	827	819

NOTE: Estimates for the slower rate of technical change are included in Table 9.15.

aSimulated results under prevailing markets of technical change and farm programs.
bSimulated results under a free market and no farm programs.

379

conditions than under prevailing conditions. The fewer farms and reduced farm income under free market conditions could account for this difference.

Net Farm Income under Different Policy and Market Conditions ●
We now examine farm income under simulation conditions using the national recursive model. First we estimate income under the market, farm program, and technical conditions which actually prevailed in the 1924–65 period. The results are shown in column 2 of Table 9.17. These are not the results actually realized in each year, but are the results predicted from the model (and are highly consistent with the actual results of the year). Second, net income is simulated under the same conditions as prevailed in the period 1924–65, except that the rate of technological improvement is reduced one-half (column 3 of Table 9.17). Third, net income is simulated under free market conditions, with technological improvement at the rate actually realized in the 1924–65 period (column 4 of Table 9.17).

Direct measurement of income changes induced by government programs is difficult. In this study, the possible effects on resource demand and income were considered when government programs included these elements: (1) price support programs which altered both price relationships and the general level of farm commodity prices; (2) allotment or land retirement programs; and (3) direct payments.

The first two elements were combined to formulate the policy index, G_t, for estimating the structural parameters. During those years when acreage allotments or land retirement were in force with flexible price supports, a value of -1 was used. If price supports were fixed, with rigid support of 85 percent or over, the value of $+1$ was used. In years when Soil Bank and subsequent land control programs were in force, an additional $+1$ was used. The values were summed to form the index G_t. The values of G_t were set at their computed values in estimating columns 2 and 3 in Table 9.17.

In simulating the effects on income and resource demand under the prevailing conditions in the absence of government programs of the above types, the time series, G_t, was given zero values. Also, no direct government payments were included in net farm income. The results are those presented in column 4 of Table 9.17. One limitation of the free market analysis is its treatment of stocks. We simply assumed that stocks did not accumulate and hence no problem of stock liquidation existed for the last decade. Also, we had no method of offsetting the effects of government demand in international food aid in more recent years. Had it been necessary for a free market to absorb these quantities suddenly after they were accumulated, prices would have been even lower. However, the "free market" analysis supposes that stocks were not built up (i.e., the market operated continuously under "clearing conditions").

Table 9.17 ● Simulated U.S. Net Farm Income (Y_{Ft}) for Specified Years 1924–65

Year	Prevailing market conditions[a]	One-half rate technical improvement[b]	Free market[c]
		($ million)	
1924	10,854	10,854	10,854
1930	11,239	11,296	11,239
1935	7,605	7,790	7,303
1940	10,209	10,466	9,479
1950	15,193	15,229	13,768
1955	15,421	15,405	14,112
1960	13,772	13,787	12,504
1965	13,853	14,155	10,599

[a]Simulated net income under prevailing conditions of markets, farm programs, and technical change in the period 1924–65.
[b]Simulated net income with technological improvement at one-half the actual rate, but conditions of markets and farm programs the same as prevailed in the 1924–65 period.
[c]Simulated net income under a free market with no government programs and prevailing rates of technical change of the 1924–65 period.

The initial effects of support programs were to alter price relationships among commodities and maintain a higher level of product price than otherwise would have prevailed. The higher prices and government payments would have caused farm incomes under prevailing conditions to be above those of the free market by 1935. (Initial land diversion and related price support programs began in 1933.) As noted earlier, free market conditions assumed the absence of stock accumulation, as would have been expected under market-clearing conditions over the whole period. Had the stocks accumulated in the 1950s simply been dumped in returning to the free market, prices would have been considerably lower than under the programs in effect over the same period. (The difference between income under programs and a free market would have then been greater than shown.) With the passage of time and the growth of productivity, prevailing conditions of farm programs are estimated to have widened the margin of farm income over free market conditions. Net farm income, as indicated in Table 9.17, would have been substantially lower (4 to 30 percent) over the years, a result of the lack of direct payments from the government to farmers. But a slower rate of technical advance would have provided a growing income margin over prevailing conditions. The restrained supply against an inelastic demand is the explanation for this difference.

The simulated results under a slower rate of technological improvement (column 3 in Table 9.17) suggest that net farm income would have increased by 1 to 4 percent more than under the prevailing rate of technical advance. Under a slower rate of technological advance, commodity supplies would have been lower and prices would have been sufficiently higher to increase net farm income without direct payments.

In the absence of support programs, prices of resources with an inelastic supply to agriculture (such as total farm labor) would have declined relative to those with more elastic supplies (such as farm machines). Machinery prices are largely "cost determined" to agriculture; they have a relatively "flat" supply schedule. Changes in the ratio between resource prices and the reduction in net farm income would have caused important changes in the composition of resource demand. As indicated in Table 9.16, the demand for total farm machinery would have increased less than 1 percent annually, whereas the demand for total farm labor would have decreased from 1 to 8 percent annually. The demand for farm building investment also would have been lower as a result of the lower farm income under simulated free market conditions.

CONSISTENT RESULTS ● The analysis of farm structure and resource demand plus the simulation analysis just reviewed are consistent with results of Chapter 3 indicating that land diversion programs of the 1960s type and their related price support programs (including publicly assisted exports) caused farm income to be higher than expected under a free market. The results reviewed in this chapter are from a long-run model where it is supposed that farming would have a better chance to adjust to markets, and supplies and prices could "come into equilibrium" with demand. The results do show some relative price improvement over time under free market conditions, with the level approaching (being within the normal bounds of statistical confidence limits) that of prices under the prevailing conditions of farm programs. However, this comparability in price levels (even without accounting for the large publicly assisted exports in 1965) was not a great enough force to offset the magnitude of government payments to farmers for land diversion and consequent supply control by 1965.

While the results in this chapter are consistent with those of earlier chapters, showing that land diversion programs of the type in use in the 1960s and early 1970s provide a higher aggregate net farm income than expected under a free market, they do not indicate the relative magnitude of net income per farm. Also, all of the simulated models may be deficient in detail relating to input categories such as fertilizers, improved seeds, feeds, and breeds, and other biological variables. Models such as these should be developed before definitive predictions can be made of long-run effects of different program and market regimes.

CHAPTER TEN

Potentials for Improvements and Equity in Land Retirement Programs

THE STUDIES REPORTED in this book focus on the effects of different program alternatives, or variables related to them, on trade-offs in government costs, farm income, secondary community costs, distribution of benefits among farm strata, farmer participation, amount and location of land retirement, and similar quantities. Our goal has mainly been to determine how various effects in the "output set" compete with or complement each other as variables of the "input set" are changed. In this context, we attempted to provide additional data and detail on program alternatives in order that the responsible groups would have an improved basis for decisions on policy.

DISADVANTAGED GROUPS AND OPTIMAL RURAL POLICY ● These analyses omit many considerations which are important in public policy decisions. For example, we have not analyzed programs for those persons who have been and are being affected most negatively by the ongoing structural changes of agriculture; namely, persons with inadequate skills for nonfarm employment who are displaced from agriculture by advancing capital technologies and those persons of the nonfarm business and service sectors of rural communities whose economic opportunities decline with larger and fewer farms. Our commercial farm policies are designed to take care of persons who remain engaged in farming and would otherwise suffer as advancing technology finally reflects itself as a large market supply. But we have no real direct programs for those persons who are forced from farms and the rural community for the same reasons. Socially concerned people would surely ask: Are not these displaced persons and their welfare equally as important as those who stay to benefit from public program payments? Is it reasonable that some farmers, particularly owners of cotton land, receive payments in the hundreds of thousands of dollars when many agricultural workers who have extremely little salvage or employment value in other locations and industries are forced to leave farms?

While farm programs can be defended as a means of maintaining or achieving equity between food consumers and food producers, it must be emphasized that past and current policies do not assure equity among all groups of the rural community. A major benefit of existing programs in their effect on bolstering farm income and maintaining prices has been to bring capital gains to agriculture. Through price maintenance, technological advances and subsequent yield increases, and direct payments, farmland prices have advanced rather continuously for three decades. Cochrane placed the total capital gain to agriculture at $112 billion between 1940 and 1965 with the major share a result of public programs and agricultural development.[1] But as farmers have enlarged their units to realize these gains and take advantage of scale economies, the farm population and work force have declined to an extent that the capital loss to merchants and others in rural towns has been tremendous. While the surrounding countryside is characterized by increased land values and capital gains, the capital loss of many rural towns is expressed physically by empty store buildings with loose siding, teetering on the corner of their foundations, and former dwellings with crumbled chimneys and splintered windows.

Incomes of many other families in rural areas, especially in the commerce and service sectors of country towns, are low. These strata of rural people are faced with declining employment and asset values as big farms become bigger and diminish the labor force of the rural countryside. But whereas farmers have public mechanisms to maintain crop prices and increase land prices, and can claim larger government payments as they enlarge their land area, the local nonfarm workers who are displaced in this process have no similar set of programs. Why, if we have government programs to protect farmers from the devastating market effects of onrushing technology, do we not have parallel programs for their village neighbors and relatives whose local opportunities are being obliterated by exactly the same processes and forces? Under present rates of change, the towns serving as the centers of community activities and services may become so depleted that the remaining social and economic environment provides few positive pleasures to the larger farmers who remain amidst a greatly thinned farm population. Many towns and villages in rural areas are even now approaching this threshold.

In addition to workers displaced from farms and local nonfarm commerce and service personnel, a third disadvantaged group gains little or nothing from our sizeable government investment in agricultural

1. W. W. Cochrane, *The City Man's Answer to the Farm Problem* (Minneapolis: Univ. of Minnesota Press, 1965), p. 122.

programs. This group includes the chronically low-income families concentrated especially in mountainous, cut-over, and ethnic regions of agriculture. In contrast to highly commercial farmers and the two groups mentioned above, the source of their economic problems is not technology which substitutes (1) for land, increasing supply capacity and (2) for labor, reducing the demand for entrepreneurs and laborers in rural areas. Instead, it is the paucity of resources, education, and skills which they possess. The nation now has two large programs of investment to alleviate the ongoing or posed income problems of two specific segments of our society, namely, commercial farmers and the poor of urban centers. But the void is nearly complete with respect to the larger strata of rural population represented by workers displaced from farms, nonfarm people in small towns, and low-income farm families. Land retirement, supply control, commodity storage, foreign food aid, land set aside, commodity certificates, and payments or support price programs in their many alternative forms have virtually nothing to offer these groups as a means to compensate them for evaporating current economic activities or unfavorable future economic opportunities.

Hence if the purpose of *Future Farm Programs* were to analyze alternatives which are optimal across all economic and social strata of rural communities, it would not focus so greatly on land retirement and supply control programs. Instead it might even propose that shifts could be made from this conventional program format to one which better considers the outlook for all disadvantaged groups of rural communities. Its purpose however is the more restricted one of examining alternatives in land retirement, or land retirement as an alternative to other policies relating to supply, prices, and income in agriculture. Hence, it is not a comprehensive analysis of all farm policy alternatives.

OUTLOOK IN POLICY DEVELOPMENT ● The emphasis of this book is on land retirement because this mechanism has continuously been, and has prospects of remaining, the foundation of commercial farm policy for major field crops. We believe there are several reasons for this outlook.

The basic outlook for U.S. agriculture is largely the same for the 1970s as for the past decade. The farm sector can produce enough to bankrupt a large number of farmers if the full supply capacity is unleashed over a time period short of a decade. Expanded foreign demand has not absorbed enough producing capacity to offset advancing technology. The supply elasticity for credit and new capital technology is still so great that less mobile resources such as farm labor suffer depressed returns as demand for them declines. By contrast, the supply elasticity of farm labor, "sunk" capital in the form of buildings, and outdated farm technology and skills is so low that outward migration has not been fast enough to raise returns to levels found elsewhere in the economy. The relative concentration of poverty in agriculture is just as persistent today as it was a decade ago.

While it was known a decade ago, it is even more apparent now that in a nation with the large farm supply capacity of the United States, full employment, rapid economic growth, and inflationary factors have weak linkages with or little effect on farm commodity markets and agricultural income improvement. The linkages that do exist (aside from the conventional one where food as a raw material moves to the processing sector and a share of consumer food expenditures flows back to agriculture) have their greatest impact (1) in the generation of new capital technology which moves rapidly into agriculture, accentuating the decline in farm labor demand and the structural transformation of the farm firm and (2) in drawing labor out of agriculture to more remunerative employment elsewhere.

For practical and planning purposes the basic situation will continue, and economically appropriate and politically acceptable programs will be needed over a period longer than historically has been considered in farm policy acts and legislation. In addition, the public seems willing to finance income transfers and provide institutional means to assure a reasonable degree of equity for the aggregate farm industry. While a few scattered complaints are expressed, any organized or massive moves on the part of the public itself to lessen greatly the Treasury costs of farm programs and remove the modest restraints on supply are lacking. It is even possible that if an effective coalition were formed among farm organizations, rural communities, and farm operators, society at large would be willing to invest even more in achieving equity throughout the rural sector and in enlarging economic opportunities for its members.

Since the basic problems of commercial agriculture remain the same as in the past, there is a strong tendency for numerous farm groups to support a continuation of past program formats for meeting these problems. This is generally the result when a sector is surrounded by as many diverse and conflicting economic and political interests as is agriculture. Once a major policy has been initiated and become "bedded down" over a few years, competing interest groups tend to restrain any important or sudden departures from it. Political conflict makes it easier to add modifications here and there and continue with the same basic or general format. The ongoing basic policy format has not been considered "first best" by the current administration, the previous administration, or the majority of commodity and organizational groups that represent segments of agriculture and agribusiness. But in a game strategy context it is a "saddle point" which various political and economic groups are willing to accept "as one of the better of the worst outcomes that could happen." Perhaps for most groups concerned, ongoing policies based on the program elements surrounding land diversion are optimal to none but better than the potential pay-offs of numerous others.

Most importantly, it should be recognized that the policy "game" is played much more among commodity, agribusiness, and farm organization groups—each with its own minimax strategy—than among consumers, taxpayers, and farmers. With appropriate strategy shifts, it is likely that consumers (taxpayers) and the farm public could agree on other farm policies which could better guarantee market returns on resources used in agriculture, better guarantee equity and welfare within agriculture, and improve economic opportunities for those in rural communities who prefer either or both occupational and geographic migration.

Land Retirement and Land Capitalization ● With the need for farm programs demonstrated and generally agreed upon, and given the general public's willingness to finance them, it might seem best to simply maintain the same policy format for the next ten years—or even the next twenty if necessary. Under certain conditions of fund availability, this could be done with an important degree of peace between consumers (taxpayers) and the commercial farm public. However without these conditions the competition for funds may become more intense and the real value of present levels of transfer payments to agriculture may decline as (1) (a) a "lid" is held on the level of Treasury payments and farm commodity prices as other social and urban groups intensify their demands for improved economic and living conditions, and (b) inflation occurs and off-farm inputs or capital technologies continue to thrust up farm costs, or (2) small "chips" are broken from the block of farm program payments as marginal programs are eliminated over time. The present level of payments thus may serve largely as an "upper bound," a "constant quantity," to be capitalized into resources and redistributed among farmers in the market as they exchange these resources with the price premiums attached to them.[2] Research to date indicates a heavy capitalization rate on land values. While programs have raised commodity prices and income, land values have risen so that the ratio of land income to land price is no better than previously, and a new farm owner now can have fewer acres with the same investment. In other words, the same investment in fewer acres tends to give the same income as more acres from the same investment without programs would produce. Once payments become so capitalized, they have little income value in the gradual transition to a new generation of farmers. For example, if the public made a fifty-year contract with agriculture to provide it with $3.5 billion annually, the yearly payments would

2. For discussion of rates, extent, and magnitudes of capitalization, see Leroy Blakeslee, and Norman Whittlesey, Agricultural Production Control Programs with Mandatory Participation, *CAED Report* 35, Iowa State Univ., 1970; D. H. Carley, Acceptance and Results of the Acreage-Poundage Program for Georgia Flue-Cured Tobacco Growers, *Univ. of Georgia Agricultural Experiment Station Research Bulletin* 10, June 1967; Levi A. Powell, Clyde E. Murphree, and Charles D. Covey, The Income Implications of Acreage Control for Flue-Cured Tobacco Producers, *Univ. of Florida Agricultural Experiment Station Bulletin* 643, February 1962; James A. Seagraves and Richard C. Manning, Flue-Cured Tobacco Allotment Values and Uncertainty, 1934–1962, *Economic Research Report* 2, North Carolina State Univ., May 1967; F. H. Maier, et al., Sale of Flue-Cured Tobacco Allotments, *Virginia Agricultural Experiment Station Bulletin* 148; and T. W. Schultz, National Security, Economic Growth, Individual Freedom and Agricultural Policy, *CAED Report* 16, Iowa State Univ. 1962.

have no income benefits to the farm owners in forty-five years as payments became capitalized into land values. While income and capital values would decline if payments ceased, operators who received them at that time would have no more income than had they originally bought their resources at sufficiently lower prices. The value of present programs is to farmers (and their heirs) who were operating in the early period of their initiation (i.e., before they were fully capitalized into real estate values). And this is as it should be, since the programs were created for them. To remove programs from them not only would lessen their income but would also greatly reduce their asset values. In political reality, all major economic groups in our society react strongly when changes in legislation threaten large capital losses.

But in equal reality, it must be recognized that the capitalization process gradually reduces the realized value of farm programs built around land diversion and income transfers related to it. Although all evidence suggests that (1) problems of the current types will prevail in agriculture over the next one and likely two decades, and (2) the present generation of participants does benefit from existing land retirement and related programs, the eventual task is to create programs whose benefits do not become largely or fully dissolved through higher land values. Otherwise, the result is an annual transfer to agriculture from the Treasury of $3.5 billion or more which has no income benefit to the upcoming generation of farmers but serves only to hold a floor under the price of land. If reliance for controlling supply is to remain on land retirement with Treasury payments and price supports attached thereto, a complex question is: How can income benefits be maintained and capital losses prevented for the present generation of operators and owners while we eliminate extension of programs which benefit neither the general public nor the upcoming generation of farmers who respectively provide and receive government program payments over the long run?

Optimizing the Policy Mix ● Assuming that the above is a realistic environment within which farm programs must operate in the foreseeable future, how do we move toward some "operational goals" to better guarantee that (1) Treasury payments and price support benefits go continuously to farmers, rather than simply becoming capitalized into land values with neutral income effects for the future farm generation, (2) the consumer or taxpaying public better understands the need and purpose of farm and rural community programs, and places them on the same level of priority as equally pressing urban problems, (3) greater equity in program benefits is achieved for all sectors of farming and rural communities—not just transfers to large, expanding commercial farms with particular commodities such as cotton, and (4) economic opportunity is provided the farm and rural community populations on a par with other nonpoverty segments of the national economy?

An idealistic mix of policy elements could be suggested, as they have been in the past, to attain this combination of operational (i.e., nonultimate, generalized) goals. This mix could include these changes:

1. Divorce the benefits of Treasury payments and price supports from land or real estate resources and attach them to people or human resources. Established as "claims to equity" at some past or the present time, they would go with the individual and never become capitalized into land values. They could be realized rights equally for tenants as well as landlords, and they could move with families between farms, but only in terms of the orginal "human base" and not in terms of future land operated or volume produced. They could move off farms with the family, perhaps as an aid to mobility, and provide an income stream offsetting reduced land values for the landowner.

2. Exclude from eligibility for benefits any new entrant into farming, since from the standpoint of equity he has never realized past losses from publicly induced shifts in supply and could be considered to lack claim to public payments or mechanisms to offset them.

3. Convert the functions of the CCC solely to those of price stability and remove the overriding function of income transfer that it has served at times in the past. Perhaps an independent board paralleling the board of directors of the Federal Reserve System would be optimal for this purpose.

4. Improve the mechanism for gearing supply to domestic and export demand at levels which bring returns on resources and in agriculture more nearly in line with resource returns throughout the economy. The farm program format of the last forty years has not brought parity resource returns in this sense to more than a tenth of all farmers. It has not done so because the capitalization process converted payments into higher fixed costs for the next generation, because labor has been replaced at a faster rate than it migrated from agriculture, and because the substitution of capital technology for land pressed output forward faster than market demand, even though supply restraints were applied.

5. Increase investment in education, guidance, and vocational training for youth and younger members of rural communities, thus upgrading their competitive abilities and putting them on an equal footing in economic opportunities with the labor force in the rapidly developing urban centers and occupations.

6. Provide the consuming public a mix of commodities more in keeping with tastes and preferences associated with present levels of incomes as indicated by the magnitudes of price and income elasticities which exist in the United States. Encourage through program elements an expansion in production of those food commodities with greater elasticities and reduce price support levels on those commodities which act as inputs for these more elastic food items. These higher

support levels on input commodities act as a tax on production of more elastic items and slow their growth, as well as resulting in price levels to consumers which are high in relation to demand growth potentials.

7. Provide the tax-paying segments of society with a long-run solution to the problem for which they have rather steadily and willingly provided large funds in expectancy of a solution.

Numerous means could be suggested, and while they would be eagerly accepted by some farm groups, they would be equally opposed by others. Hence, while "idealized" means could be outlined readily, practical political realities are not likely to allow them in the near future.

Public Support and Nature of Agriculture ● All evidence points to the willingness of the public to continue farm programs which support and stabilize farm income and to improve resource returns in agriculture. Society at large will likely continue to provide programs and investments to retain some equity in agriculture if (1) workable means can be devised and agreed on by the many farm groups, (2) consumers are brought some "side benefits" from these investments and programs, and (3) the farm public establishes a closer linkage with the consumer and his needs, problems, and knowledge. Not only do past farm programs and large Treasury transfers indicate a willingness of the nonfarm public to support farm incomes at equitable levels, but precedent is also provided elsewhere in the economy. Means have been established, with prices or rates determined by boards and commissions representing the public and directly aside from the market, for guaranteeing market rates of resource return for such services and sectors as air transportation, communication, electricity, and other public utilities. To be certain, these provisions do not guarantee that every firm in these sectors will profit progressively, but in general they provide pricing procedures designed to return market rates on labor and capital resources for demand of given levels. Even for the services it provides, such as education, execution of law, police protection, roads, public buildings, and others, society expects the capital and labor resources involved to realize return levels equal to competitive alternatives. Although the attainment of market returns is with a somewhat distributed lag under inflation, it "meets the competition" through a pricing schedule reflected in contracts. There is no evidence that society prefers it to be otherwise, even though the process of providing appropriations is usually a step or two behind the growing population and demand. It does not ask teachers to subsidize education at a permanent sacrifice in income. It does not ask contractors to provide public buildings at a sacrifice in income on the labor and capital resources employed.

Given the existing precedents, it is reasonable to suggest that agriculture might turn its emphasis from parity in commodity price supports to parity in resource returns. Parity in resource returns is not appropriately reflected in the orthodox comparison of price indices for farm commodity and farm input prices. This comparison is not an adequate gauge because of the constantly and rapidly changing mix and productivity of the individual resources or cost items used in agriculture, and because of scale economies associated with larger farms. In fact agriculture could do worse than have itself given the pseudo-classification of "public good or utility," not only as a basis for priority in mechanisms which guarantee it market returns on its labor and capital but also because it is more nearly a "basic or fixed need" of consumers than are postal facilities, public roads, public utilities, or even educational services.

Food in minimum amount is a prior necessity in life in order that one may enjoy or benefit from the nonpriced and subsidized services provided through postal services, public roads, schools and recreational facilities, or public utilities whose prices have "stable floors and ceilings" which guarantee (lagged) market returns to resources. In a society with such high incomes and low supply prices for food commodities as the United States, and with so little of our total labor and capital resources required for food production, a minimum diet or choice of foods could be guaranteed all consumers. To have not yet guaranteed this condition, given the nation's level of wealth and economic development, is shortsighted in terms of consumers, food producers, and humanitarian concern. But the nation, in guaranteeing it, as it will eventually do, should not expect that farmers will supply this level of food at prices lower than required to provide market rates of return on the resources required to produce it. As it does for public services and utilities, we believe that society would readily provide farmers with parity or market returns on resources used in food production under certain conditions. It would be willing to provide prices and resource returns at this level as readily as it does for public services and utilities and allow farm groups to do it through market bargaining organizations, land retirement, or other means if farm organizations and commodity groups could only agree on the methods and conditions for doing so. Farming is a small sector as compared to the public sector, which accounts for nearly two-fifths of the gross national product, and the public sector much more nearly earns market rates of returns to the resources involved than does agriculture.

Farmer-Public Interaction ● As stated previously, the precedents of society and absence of organized resistance movements by individuals making up society suggest that attainment of market rates of returns on resources used under specified conditions in agriculture are reasonably possible. It would be useful however if the farm public exerted more effort to persuade consumers in this direction. Farm groups are among the few major producer organizations which tend to view consumers as their antagonists. Producers of other commodities follow an opposite strategy. They organize campaigns and conduct studies to learn the detailed preferences of their consumers. They extend continuous communication to convince the consumer that his life and happiness is interlocked with their commodity or service. This approach is quite foreign to producers of food, who often exchange erroneous concepts and heated blasts with consumers over the price of food. Farmers could benefit in strategies of other producers, and woo rather than war the consumer. They should be intensely concerned with consumer welfare where food is concerned. They should try to provide him with as much benefit and utility as possible, not only from food per se but also in knowledge of costs and returns in food production, processing and distribution, and in "spin-offs" from farm programs. They could try to convince the consumer that if he guarantees equitable returns throughout agriculture in public programs related to food production he also can gain from the expenditures involved.

Who should have been the first to discover and become shocked by the existence of undernourished people in the United States, concentrated especially in rural areas? Who should have discovered that city school lunch programs frequently provide food unwanted and wasted by students because it is not adapted to the preferences of particular ethnic groups or is inappropriately prepared? Farmers and their representatives. Instead it was urban people who did. We have large masses of land not needed for food production. But who is concerned about more of it being used for recreational purposes by urban consumers? Not farmers, but urban hunters and Isaac Walton League members who lead the fight to get land converted to wildlife and recreational areas.

This is not to propose that problems of surplus supply capacity and farm structural changes can be solved by eliminating malnutrition and increasing the amount of land for recreaion. However, it does indicate both the lack of communication of the farm public with the consuming public and the "opportunities foregone" in using food and land surpluses for services with high demand elasticities and to convince the dominant urban population that their investments in farm programs can bring benefits to the nonfarm public as well. An immediate reaction to the discovery of malnutrition in the countryside by urban representatives has been: Why should we pay large subsidies to rich farmers not to produce food and let poor people starve? Farm groups could have reacted by pressing for expanded food programs, recognizing that producing and supplying food is part of "doing their thing." After all, these same groups have strongly supported programs of shipping large quantities of foodstuffs overseas as a means of expanding demand. Such a reaction would have appealed to humanitarian feelings in both rural and urban society. The farm public should extend itself as a partner with the consuming public, warring with it less and engaging more its understanding and support through knowledge and arrangements to also provide the public with some tangible benefits from government farm programs.

The nonfarm population could be provided land for recreation, hunting, parks, city greenbelts, and similar purposes, at no incremental costs through existing programs. Over time, past programs have already provided payments for land retirement exceeding the market price of the land. All that is necessary is to acquire, on a voluntary basis even from older farmers who wish to retire with perhaps some premium payments to provide contiguous areas, land appropriately located under present program funding. The machinery and legislation for doing so already exist, but sufficient pressure for implementing and funding the programs has been lacking. Farm groups might well shoulder the burden by joining urban consumers in "a great partnership" in supporting programs under which both can gain. For some time, growth in agriculture has not been associated with expansion in cropland. Instead the reverse is true: output has grown as cropland was reduced. This same trend will hold true for the next several decades. Other uses for this land exist and the need should be made known. Outdoor recreation as a good with a high income elasticity ranks with health services, education, travel, clothing, and similar services. But whereas per capita consumption of other services with high income elasticities has increased greatly in the last two decades, the quantity of recreational land per capita is now no greater than it was twenty years ago, and the amount available per user has greatly declined. It is unrealistic that the amount of recreational land per capita should be static, and large numbers of persons should suffer malnutrition in a nation which has a surplus of both land and food and makes payments to have them nonused and nonproduced.

Public Support and Appropriations ● There are great possibilities for farm representatives to form an alliance with consumers (1) to view food production and consumption, land use, and government programs as a complementary set for the mutual benefit of all; (2) to use a combination of price mechanisms and government programs to bring, on the average, market rates of returns to resources used in agriculture while assuring progress and efficiency; and (3) to provide agriculture with stability and a greater share of the progress to which it greatly contributes, but frequently sacrifices because of a large number of small competitive producers, an inelastic demand, resources with low mobility under geographic isolation, and insufficient education and training facilities. It is unlikely that this alliance can be readily fashioned without guarantees of equity within agriculture from the programs. The fundamental basis for public agricultural policies is equity. Because of the inelastic demand for food and the high supply elasticity of new capital technology to agriculture, the absence of programs causes the farm sector to suffer reduced revenue and reduced employment while the consumer sector gains in a smaller outlay for food and a greater amount of resources to produce the other goods and services for which its income is partially released. Government programs can restore equity through price and payment mechanisms which protect farm income but allow declining real prices for food. One focus of U.S. society which will continue is greatly extended equity and economic opportunity for disadvantaged groups. In attempts to provide broader equity and opportunity, society at large will be examining transfer programs which are unrelated to production of public services and which contribute little to equity. It may annually chip $100 million here and there from programs (at least in real terms) that do not have these characteristics, in order that equity and opportunity programs elsewhere can be more appropriately funded. Persons and organizations looking for means to fund other pressing urban or societal programs typically take a glance at agricultural programs and propose a chip from this "mass of Treasury outlays" as a means of funding their own needs. A typical example in the statement in the recent Committee for Economic Development report, a report analyzing needs in fiscal and monetary policy and directly removed from appraisal of farm problems: We need to reduce our subsidies to agriculture on the simple basis that it is on the whole in excellent shape and is not threatened by any immediate collapse, whereas our cities are in grave danger.[3] The same prevailing "glance" is reflected in the statement of the chairman of the White House Conference on Food, Nutrition, and Health, that the group was troubled by large expenditures to prevent growing of food, but lack of similar funds to get rid of hunger.[4]

This is the continuous prospect which faces agricultural farm programs unless greater internal equity can be brought to them. And this minimum requirement in internal equity, at least over a decade, will not be sufficiently guaranteed by payment limits of $50,000. Under conditions of the past, some very large payments have gone to individual producers. The large payments have been concentrated around cotton production, but a few very large ones also have gone to producers of wheat and feed grains. Under the program structure, the major portion of Treasury payments has gone to larger producers, and smaller, low-income families have gained only modestly. Table 10.1 shows the distribution in 1964 among farmers with different market sales. The magnitude of market sales is highly correlated with farm size and larger farms can collect larger payments, if they participate, because they have a greater cropland base for diversion. However not all direct payments under programs of the 1960s and initial 1970s were

3. Committee for Economic Development, *A Stablizing Fiscal and Monetary Policy for 1970* (New York: Committee for Economic Development, December 1969), p. 11.

4. Robert Choate, Hunger in the U.S.: The Disgraceful Gap between Words and Action, *Des Moines Sunday Register and Tribune,* January 5, 1969, p. 8.

Table 10.1 ● Number of Farms and Government Payments by Sales Groups

Size of farms in market sales ($)	Number of farms (thousands)	Fraction of all farms (%)	Payments per farm ($)	Income farm payments (%)
20,000 or more	384	10.7	2,391	18.5
10,000-19,999	594	16.6	670	8.8
5,000-9,999	609	17.0	350	6.4
2,500-4,999	463	13.0	173	3.9
2,499 or less	1,523	42.6	51	1.2

Source: Earl O. Heady, Food, Agriculture and Public Policy, (New York: Random House, 1967), p. 16.

distributed for supplying land for retirement from crops. These payments also included direct income supplements. The income supplement proportion for 1968 was estimated by the Secretary of Agriculture as follows: 65 percent for cotton, 49 percent for wheat, and 11 percent for feed grains. Table 10.2 includes his summary of numbers of farmers receiving payments of various amounts. In cotton, the program representing the greatest proportion of compensation payments, 1.2 percent of the producers with payments over $20,000 received 27.6 percent of all government payments to cotton. The distribution was not nearly so heavily skewed toward large producers for feed grains and wheat.

To control production and support prices when land diversion is used as the supply control mechanism this disproportionate distribution of payments and producers is not necessary. Various estimates indicate that supply control could readily be attained with upper limits on payments of $10,000 or $20,000 to producers where land retirement is disbursed.[5] It is obvious for feed grains and wheat in Table 10.2 that around 94 percent of producers received less than $3,000 in payments but were recipients of the majority of the payments. Producers with over $10,000 got only 6.2 percent and 10.0 percent, respectively, of feed grains and wheat payments. In contrast, the 87.4 percent of the cotton producers with payments under $3,000 got only 27.8 percent of payments while the 3.4 percent of producers with payments over $10,000 obtained 44.7 percent of payments.

Existing supply control could be maintained with modest increases in Treasury costs even with payment limitations for feed grains and wheat. The situation would be somewhat different for cotton however since the funds here include large income supplements as well as payments for land diversion.

Somewhat in contrast, a regionally concentrated land retirement program based on whole-farm participation would require a distribution of payments in accordance with the amount of land supplied by each farm to cropland diversion. If the purpose of the program were purely that of supply control through land retirement, payment would need to be according to the amount of land retired. As shown in Chapter 5, the interregional distribution of payments would also shift greatly from the types of land retirement programs in effect in the 1960s and initial 1970s. However, without compensatory subsidies apart from payment for land retirement, the cost of attaining the specified level of supply control and price support would be much less. The extreme disparities existing under cotton programs of the 1960s would not prevail within the farm sector, even under a regionally concentrated

5. John A. Schnittker, Distribution of benefits from existing and prospective farm programs, pp. 89–104, in *Benefits and Burdens of Rural Development*, CAED (Ames: Iowa State Univ. Press, 1970); W. W. Wilcox, *Economic Aspects of Farm Program Payment Limitations*, Library of Congress, Legislative Reference Service 69–23855, Washington, D. C., November 1969.

Table 10.2 ● Distribution of Payments and Farmers, 1968 Program

Payments in excess of ($)	Cotton		Feed grains		Wheat	
	Producers (number)	Payments ($ million)	Producers (number)	Payments ($ million)	Producers (number)	Payments ($ million)
3,000	55,045	560.3	79,422	432.0	52,395	305.1
5,000	33,526	477.9	29,120	241.6	21,866	188.3
10,000	14,790	347.2	5,335	83.9	4,663	72.7
20,000	5,159	214.6	877	25.8	702	20.8
30,000	2,455	149.3	233	10.4	213	9.2
			(%)			
3,000	12.6	72.2	5.4	31.8	6.4	41.8
5,000	7.7	61.5	2.0	17.8	2.7	25.8
10,000	3.4	44.7	.4	6.2	.6	10.0
20,000	1.2	27.6	.1	1.9	.1	2.9

Source: C. M. Hardin, Secretary of Agriculture, Statement before the Subcommittee of the Senate Appropriations Committee, June 4, 1969.

land retirement program. The major problems of equity under regional concentration, supposing that farmers who shift their land permanently are fully compensated, would fall on nonfarm residents of the same rural communities where farms would have to be much larger and fewer, and commerce would be greatly lessened. Supposedly, an even greater amount than is saved in farm program payments would have to be appropriated to these persons if equity were to prevail.

MODIFICATIONS IN LAND RETIREMENT ● In the setting outlined earlier, we projected (1) the basic problems of agriculture and (2) continuation of public willingness to finance offsetting programs under certain conditions of equity. Given full knowledge of consumers and an alliance with them by food producers, we can expect market rate of return on resources used in food production as a standard criterion or goal and one which might be attained under these conditions. Numerous mechanisms could allow attainment of this goal, with the policy mix ranging over the farmer imposed supply control market mechanisms, direct payments to producers, and others. Under proper communication and alliance with consumers, agriculture might have whichever mechanism it could agree upon to provide market returns on resources, if equity and opportunity are also provided to the disadvantaged groups of the farm sector. However because of the competition and "game against each other" prevailing among commodity, organization, and agribusiness groups, the basic pattern of farm programs built around land retirement, direct payments, and support prices is likely to continue as an "equilibrium saddle point."

It is likely that farm programs extending to 1980 will be the current set with slight modifications, largely because political stalemates so require even though they are not optimal for many groups within and surrounding agriculture. Under the likelihood that this will be true, what improvements might be melted into this general pattern? Importantly, the stability or availability of Treasury-financed programs will require the increased equity already mentioned. Payment limits of $10,000 would allow supply control, with exceptions for cotton, at essentially present costs. Even a limit of $5,000 would allow an effective supply control program for feed grains and wheat under recent budget magnitudes with complete acceptance by the vast majority of farmers (since few participants receive amounts this large).

A second major improvement, even with the inflexibility of the present general program mix extended over the next 10 or 20 years, would be modifications to prevent the capitalization of program benefits into real estate values. The goal of farm programs has been to increase the stream of income in relation to the value of assets and resources used. However, the capitalization process causes the income stream to return to or approach the previous level. After the resources change hands through the market, the gains of the program are cancelled and the function of public expenditure is primarily to maintain asset values so that the new owner does not suffer a capital loss. This outcome could be eliminated most readily under the present general program format and level of Treasury payments by establishing a "base of equity payments" to all eligible farmers. The payment base of perhaps the average of the ten-year period, 1961–70, then would become an endowment for the farmer as an individual. He could move with it to another farm or expand his present farm, but it would not increase or decrease with the scale of the new farm. Tenants would have the same opportunity, but the payment would be fixed regardless of the farm and volume operated in the future. The farmer might even be allowed to take the endowment with him, perhaps at a reduced rate, if he moved from the farm before retirement age. Outside investors moving into agriculture would be ineligible for payments. Also, new or beginning farmers could be excluded from payments under the logic that they have no equity claims, since they have not farmed in the past and hence have not realized any actual or posed income losses through the rapid technological advance of farming and the low elasticity of demand for food. Or, in a vein suggested fifteen years ago and as now implemented in Holland and England, farmers who retire from farming early could start their social security benefits at an earlier age as a form of termination pay.[6]

A less effective modification which would allow society and the farm public to protect "family size" farms but would have a more delayed effect in separating payment benefits and land values is one which leaves the payment tied to the farm, but only for the existing operator. Supposing a fixed Treasury restraint which would be divided for the future, the program could work this way: The format could be the same as that of the present, but program eligibility would be limited to only the current operator and his farm. The payment would be a fixed amount, but only for this operator and farm in combination. An outside investor coming into agriculture and buying the farm would not receive the payment or be eligible for a similar one. Hence the land would have a greater value to the present operator than to an alternative owner. Suppose two farmers, A and B, participate in the program. Each receives a fixed payment for supply participation on his farm and is eligible for a stated level of price supports. Now A sells his land to B. B receives only the payment attached to his original farm and participates in price supports alone for that portion of output resulting therefrom. He does not receive the payment which formerly went to A, and the output he produces from A's farm must be sold at market prices. Under one alternative, if A dies or retires and his son takes over the farm, the son would not be eligible for the payments and price supports which formerly went with the farm. Hence

6. Earl O. Heady, Adaptation of Extension Education and Auxiliary Aids to the Basic Economic Problems of Agriculture, *Journal of Farm Economics* 39 (February 1957): 112.

all benefits would go to farmers who were actually engaged in the occupation at a given time (say the year prior to initiation of the program). The program, conforming to the basic format of current programs, could be voluntary as now, and those who select not to participate would not be eligible for future benefits. This would be true even if they enlarged their farms or created large estates by buying up the land of the initial participants.

The system would not prohibit larger farms. Any nonparticipant who could operate so efficiently as to pay the "own use value" of a farm to a participant could buy up land and establish a larger unit. However, the land would otherwise have greater value to the present owner and operator. (Alternatively, to offset the reduction in asset values, it would be possible to make a long-term contract with the present owner under which he would continue receiving the payments even though he sold the farm.) The transition to larger farms thus could be slowed but not prohibited. The retention of farming assets in family possession for the current generation would be strengthened. Outside investors (e.g., corporations) would not be prohibited from investing in agriculture, but land would have less earning capacity to them than to existing farm operators. Under program contracts, flexibility clauses could be incorporated (1) allowing adjustment in the benefits with changes in the general price index, and (2) allowing the government to buy up the contract under certain conditions of food emergency. With contracts extending over the operator's life and lack of inheritance rights, program benefits would gradually be wrung from land values. Upon death of a participant, funds from the given stock would be freed for gradual feeding into other types of farm programs under the emerging needs and long-run outlook of agriculture and society.

Farm families might claim that while the current operator realizes income maintenance under this program, a capital loss would be realized when the unit passes from one generation to the next. If this were not acceptable, the payment and price supports could be fixed to the farm and the family (rather than just the farm and the operator). If a son was farming with his father in the initial year of the program, he would be recipient to the same or a modified stream of benefits. But again, he could not sell his benefits, or if he enlarged his unit through rental or purchase, he would be eligible only for the initial mix of payments and price supports attached to the "home" farm. In this case, the advantage is given to the family and family farming. It does not prevent larger farms, corporate operations, and similar developments. Yet family farming would be greatly strengthened in comparison with present programs. Evidence suggests that current programs encourage larger farms and fewer workers in agriculture.[7]

One additional degree of flexibility may prevail even within the

7. Fred H. Tyner and Luther G. Tweeten, Simulation as a Method of Appraising Farm Programs, *American Journal of Agricultural Economics* 50 (February 1968): 66.

restraints of the current program set. Different rates of technological development, population growth, and consumer markets over the country cause considerable modification in the comparative advantage of commodities among regions. To an important extent, reallocations of production patterns are greatly restrained by existing programs. This situation prevails especially for crops such as cotton and soybeans. Several studies show that a crop pattern conforming to modern comparative advantage would modify importantly the spatial allocation of land use among many regions.[8]

The 1970s "set aside" programs insert some flexibility into crop patterns, especially in marginal areas where two or more different crops have close comparative advantage. The requirement for the farmer to "set aside" a given acreage but grow whichever crop he selects on the remainder allows some gradual and modest shifts. More important would be a gradual shift in the eligible cropland base among regions, while 5 or 10 percent reserve held by the Secretary of Agriculture could gradually be reallocated among regions. The pain of reallocation could be lessened by reducing payment rates to expanding farms and regions and increasing payment rates on the remaining acreage for those regions with declining bases. These differential changes would conform broadly to an equity pattern of payment distribution, since areas with declining advantage for particular crops typically are faced with a chronic depression of farm income while those with expanding advantage are characterized by well capitalized, progressive, and high-income producers.

EQUITY IN DISTRIBUTIONS ● The few illustrations outlined above suggest means, among many which could be mentioned, for overcoming certain limitations inherent in land retirement programs which have prevailed over the last forty years. Other changes could be suggested and the data of previous chapters provide information on tradeoffs in effects among alternative land retirement potentials—if we suppose that practical politics will require use of land diversion as the basic means of supply control and farm income maintenance for major field crops. While appropriately structured farm programs have an important equity basis, it is equally important that long-range land and resource conversion programs do not transfer the costs of farm structural adjustments from one group to another in society. It is unlikely that long-range programs will have economic and political acceptance if they provide gains to one group and demand sacrifices from another. There are numerous kinds of long-range land retirement programs which could make the producers of field crops as well or better off, im-

8. For example, see Earl O. Heady and Melvin Skold, Projections of U.S. Agricultural Capacity and Interregional Adjustments in Production and Land Use With Spatial Programming Models, *Iowa State Agricultural and Home Economics Experiment Station Bulletin* 539, August 1965; Ray Brokken and Earl O. Heady, Interregional Adjustments in Crop and Livestock Production, *USDA Technical Bulletin* 1936.

prove the position of taxpayers through lower Treasury costs, but transfer a burden to other farmers and to particular rural communities. Transformation of long-run land adjustment programs to achieve a reduction of grain production and an increase in grass and beef production would maintain or improve the position of the crop farmer at the expense of the cattle producer. Or to lessen the Treasury costs of programs through shifts which suddenly remove vast areas of crops from regions of lowest comparative advantage and allow them to concentrate in areas of greatest comparative advantage would cause merchants of the latter rural communities to gain at the expense of merchants in the former communities. Few would propose transfers of this type, since equity among commodity and regional groups of agriculture is equally as important and justifiable as equity between consumers and farmers at large. Given the stage of development and structure of consumer demand in the nation, it is not necessary that long-range land diversion and improved land use be attained through gain for one group at the expense of another group. In contrast with past and current programs, structuring can be so achieved with respect to rates of supply changes, timing of adjustments, and compensation to groups concerned, that no major group need make sacrifices. Even if these programs are applied so that slow changes are made in public costs, their rates of disturbance are small, and perhaps thirty years are required to bring economic balance and market returns or resources for farming, they could eventually be accomplished. We have already "been at farm programs" longer than this and still haven't attained or even approached this end.

Index

Accounting identities, 289
Acreage quotas, 51, 91, 93. *See also* Restraints in models
  analysis of effects, 138–40
  1980, 51, 88–99
  and trend exports, 88, 91
  and unsubsidized exports, 51
  use for bargaining, 136–40
Acreage restraint. *See* Restraints in models
Acreages
  annual land diversion (1970), 135, 267–72
  converted, 52
  and farmer bargaining power (1970), 125, 138
  feed grain program (1980), 84–85
  free market (1980), 53–55, 62–63, 69–70, 74–78
  free market (1970), 124
  historical trends, 6, 8, 229, 231
  long-term land retirement (1970), 125, 131, 134, 263–67
  long-term land retirement (1975), 147–49, 152, 156–57, 159–61, 165
  maximum diversion, percentages (1975), 197–202
  models, 27–31
  permitted, 278
  unlimited diversion (1975), 197–202
Agricultural policy
  considerations for planning, 24–25
  simulation model, Feed Grain Program, 275–77
Agricultural Stabilization and Conservation Service, 278–79
Agricultural trade
  grains, 227
  long-term trends, 227
Agricultural Trade Development and Assistance Act. *See* PL 480
Annual diversion programs, 110, 112, 114. *See also* Land diversion; Farm programs
Annual land diversion (1970), 125, 127–28, 135–37
Appropriations, farm programs, 394–95, 397

ASCS. *See* Agricultural Stabilization and Conservation Service
Autocorrelation, 331–32
Autoregressive least-squares, 332

Bargaining power, acreage quotas, 125, 127–28, 136, 138–40
  definition, 136, 138
Base of equity payments, 400
Basic commodities, legislation and funding, 3–4
Beef consumption
  in 1980, 46
  in 1970, 119–21
  in 1975, 145, 164, 178
Beef prices
  alternative prices (1975), 177
  with unrestricted and restricted government easement programs with grazing allowed (1975), 164
  with unrestricted and restricted government land purchase or rental programs (1975), 145
Beef production
  easement programs, 161, 165, 167
    restricted government, grazing allowed (1975), 161–63
    unrestricted government, grazing allowed (1975), 167–69
  projected demand (1975), 161
Break-even price calculations (BEP), 282

Capacity and resource requirements
  capital, 34–36
  crop acreages, 27–31
  crop yield trends, 38–43
  domestic consumption, 45
  estimates of export demand, 45, 49
  labor man-hours, 32–34
  production costs, 44–45
  product prices, 31–32
  projected levels of commodity demand, 45–49
  resource parameters, 36

Capital gains, result, 385–86
Capital input
  biological forms, 6
  fixed, 58
  mechanical forms, 6
  1900–70, 6
Capital-land substitution, 6, 10
Capital requirements
  acreage quotas (1980), 93, 96, 99, 102
  agriculture, 34–36, 58, 88, 210
  estimation of, 34–36
  feed grain program (1980), 88, 90
  free market (1980), 58, 65, 74, 78, 81
  livestock, 35
  machinery, 35
  real estate, 34
Capital technology
  commercial farm programs, equity basis,
    14–15
  consequences, 11
  crop acreage, 6
  crop output, 6–7
CCC. See Commodity Credit Corporation
Commercial farm programs, 14–16
Commodity Credit Corporation, 3, 234,
    277
  corn deliveries, 303
  farmers' decisions, 286–87
  PL 480 costs, 253, 255–56, 258, 260, 262,
    274
  possible future functions, 390
Commodity demand, 45, 49
Commodity production functions (1924–
    65), national model, 341–44. See also
    Models, national
Conservation Reserve Program, 6, 10, 135,
    148
  acreages, 124
  example, 220
  location, 155
  payments under, 277
Consuming regions, 28
Consumption per capita
  in 1980, 45–46
  in 1970, 118–21
  in 1975, 145, 178
Converted land. See Excess capacity under
    free market models
Corn
  deliveries to CCC, 303
  support prices, 314
  yield projections for 1980, 40
  yield projections for 1975, 148
Corn Belt
  and market equilibrium model, 290,
    292, 303
  and PL 480, 263
Cost function, 239–40
Costs, government
  annual diversion vs. long-term retire-
    ment programs, 118, 122–23
  annual land diversion (1970), 136–37

definition, 118, 122–23
food aid costs, 234–40, 250, 253–59
long-term land retirement (1970), 133–34
long-term land retirement (1975), 148,
    150–55, 157–58
maximum diversion, percentages (1975),
    184–86, 188–94
unlimited diversion (1975), 184–86, 188–
    94
Cotton
  acreages, 6, 53, 229, 266–67
  production trends, 6, 229, 267
  projected yield (1980), 41
  projected yield (1975), 148
  quotas, 56, 62–63, 65
Crop acreages, estimation by multi-
    regional linear programming model,
    27–31
Cropland, alternative uses, 159, 161
Cropland, retired. See also Diversion pro-
    grams; Idle acres; Land retirement
  acreage quotas, 91
  higher price levels, 194
  long-term programs, 133
  lower price levels, 188
  medium price levels, 191
Cropland Adjustment Program, 136
Crop production. See also Acreages; Mod-
    els
  estimation (programming model), 27–31
  historic trends, 227, 229, 231
  1970, 125, 135
Crops. See also names of individual crops
  historic trends, 6–7
  labor costs, 115, 117
  production costs, 44–45
  programmed prices (model), 31–32
  projections, 38–44, 114–16
Crop yield trends, 13, 38–43, 49–50

Decision-making
  loan and delivery, 286–87
  model, 281–82
  participation in programs, 282–84
Demand, domestic
  for 1980, 45, 48
  for 1970, 118, 245–46
  for 1975, 144, 176, 178
Demand, foreign
  for 1980, 45, 49
  for 1970, 126, 132, 138, 245–49
  for 1975, 144, 176, 178
Demand, price elasticity of, 124
Demand elasticities, 5
Demand estimates, domestic, 118
  farm buildings investment, 356, 362
  farm motor vehicles, 356
  hired farm labor, 365–67
  total farm labor, 365
  total farm machinery, 353–54, 356
Demand expansion, food aid, 225

Discriminant function, 283
Diversion programs. *See also* Cropland, retired; Idle acres
annual, 110, 112
historic, 6, 9
1970, 134–36
unlimited, 184
Durbin-Watson statistic, 353, 356
Durbin-Watson test, 331–32

Easement. *See also* Land purchase
alternative uses for, 159, 161
contracts, 159
definition, 143–44
Econometric models. *See* Models
Econometric submodel. *See* Macro-simulator
Efficient rules, multi-response situations, 324–25
Emergency Feed Grains Act, 106
Endogenous variables, 329–30
Excess capacity under free market models, 53, 55–56, 63, 65, 70–72, 84, 86, 97, 99
Exogenous variables, 330–31
Experimental region, 304
Export demand
commercial, 245
estimates of, 45, 49
noncommercial, 245
Export subsidies, 93, 97, 99

Farmer-public interaction, 392 94
Farm income
at different price levels, 187–88
from long-range retirement programs, 155, 170–72
losses, 222
under restricted grazing programs, 167, 170–71
under unrestricted grazing programs, 165
Farming, intensive vs. extensive, 220–22
Farm numbers
commercial, 207, 210
projections, 205, 207
Farm policy
acreage quotas as bargaining power, 136, 138
creation of bargaining board, 113
goals and objectives, 107–10
multi-year retirement, 113
problems of changing, 387–88
Farm problems, 4–5, 327
Farm programs. *See also* Models
alternative
easement program with grazing, restricted and unrestricted (1975), 144, 159, 161–70
land purchase, restricted and unrestricted (1975), 143, 156–59
long-term land rental, restricted and unrestricted (1975), 143, 147–55

maximum diversion, percentages (1975), 176, 182–202
unlimited diversion (1975), 176
analysis of compensation and welfare basis, 14–17
annual, cost of retirement per acre, 122–23
annual, strengths and weaknesses, 110, 112
data for national and regional models, 337–41
food aid and land retirement, 226
long-term alternatives, 143–44
model (1924–65), 371, 376–77
near-term alternatives, 113–14
public support and appropriations, 394–95, 397, 399
regional results (1946–65), 353–54, 356, 365, 367
types for 1980, 49–51
Farm size
economic pressures on, 215–18
for optimum use of machinery, 212–13
Feed Grain Program, 51. *See also* Feed Grain Program model
acreages (1980), 84–85
aims, 275–76
capital requirements (1980), 88, 90
data source, 278–79
diverted acreage decision, 286
idle acres (1980), 84, 86
labor requirements (1980), 88–89
land retirement under, 278
loan and delivery decision, 286–87
1980, 51, 84–88
participants (1961), 284
participation decision method, 282–84
price expectations model, 287–89
prices (1980), 86–88
Feed Grain Program model
analysis, 279–82
costs, 298
decision-making process, 281–82
interpretation, 325
lack-of-fit test, 310
main effect plan, 306–7, 309–10
marginal response, 320
net revenue, 296, 298
rate of parameter substitution, 320–21
response function, 304
response surface analysis, 304, 306
sample size determination, 298–99
stock accumulation measurement, 298
validation, 299–300, 303
Feed grains
acreages, 53, 63, 74, 84, 97, 263, 266
movement, 61–62
price elasticity, 124
yield (1980), 39–40
Fixed capital inputs, 58
Food
Asia, "green revolution," 5, 25

Food *(continued)*
    demand elasticities, 4–5, 109
    growth of demand, 5, 24
    public philosophy regarding, 392
    stable prices, 108–9
    unexpected world demand for, 5
Food Aid Act, 274
Food aid program. *See also* PL 480
    estimating net costs, 237, 239–40
    instrument of demand increase, 3
    international aid, 3, 109
    model, 240–44
Food production, foci of analysis, 26–27
Food Stamp Plan, 3
Free market
    definition, 53, 123
    long-term adjustment, 126, 129
    1980, 49, 52–83
    1970, 123–29
    short-term adjustment, 124, 126
    simulation, 377, 380, 382–83. *See also*
        Models, free market
Function, discriminant, 283–84

Government export programs. *See also*
        PL 480
    estimates of cost, 237, 239–49
    wheat, 231, 234
Grazing levels, 159
Grazing programs
    restricted, 165, 167
    unrestricted, 161, 165

Historical verification of data, 370–72

Idle acres. *See also* Cropland, retired; Di-
        version programs; Land retirement
    with acreage quotas (1980), 89, 91–93, 99
    with feed grain program (1980), 84, 86
Income. *See also* Farm income
    net farm, 110, 112, 380–82. *See also*
        Response surface
    rural areas, 385
Index of production (1930–69), 376
Indices
    crop output, 45
    multi-response situation, 321–24
Intermediate-term program, outlook, 140–
    41
Iso-income line, 324–25

Labor costs, equation, 115, 117
Labor man-hours, estimation (model), 32–
    34
Labor requirements, 88, 93, 99, 115, 117
    with acreage quotas (1980), 93, 95, 99,
        101
    with Feed Grain Program, 88–89

with free market (1980), 58, 65, 74, 78
Lack-of-fit test, 310
Lagged endogenous variables, 332
Lagged equity ratio, 345–46, 356
Land diversion
    annual programs, criticism of, 108–10
    instruments to control production,
        277–78
    payment, 315
Land purchase. *See also* Land retirement
    advantages, 150
    cost of program, 157–59
    resulting farm incomes, restricted par-
        ticipation, 152, 155, 157–59, 165,
        167, 170
    resulting farm incomes, unrestricted
        participation, 156–57, 161
Land rental programs, long-term. *See also*
        Land retirement programs
    restricted participation, 143–44, 147–48,
        150, 152
    unrestricted participation, 143–44, 147–
        48, 150, 152
Land restraints, model, 115
Land retirement. *See also* Cropland, re-
        tired; Diversion programs; Idle acres
    alternatives, 17–19
    annual land retirement (1970), 136–37,
        243–44, 256–59
    to bolster prices and income, 3
    community costs, 20–21
    to control supply, 3
    Feed Grain Program, 51
    historic trends, 6, 9
    long-term programs, 113, 130–32, 134
        acreages and crop production (1970),
            125, 131, 134
        acreages and crop production (1975),
            147–49, 152, 156–57, 159–61, 165,
            194–202
        definition, 130–31, 143, 176
        government costs (1970), 133–34
        government costs (1975), 148, 150–55,
            157–58, 161–63, 166–70, 184–86,
            188–94
        land retired (1970), 132–34
        land retired (1975), 148, 151–52, 154–
            58, 161–62, 165, 168, 182–84
        maximum diversion, percentages
            (1975), 182–84, 188–94
        net farm income (1970), 128, 134
        net farm income (1975), 152–53, 155–
            58, 165–67, 170, 187–88
        prices (1970), 127, 132, 134
        prices (1975), 145, 161, 164–65, 167, 176
        unlimited diversion (1975), 182–84,
            188–94
    outlook for future, 386–88
    parameters of farm price levels, 176,
        178–80
    payment levels to farmers, 181
    and PL 480, 10, 226

reasons for use, 18–19
relation to capitalization, 388–89
trade-offs, 19–21
types of programs, 19–21
uses of land, 130–31
Land retirement levels, acreages, 183–84
Land retirement programs. *See also* Land
  purchase
long-term
  alternatives, 143–44, 147
  commodity-selling activities (model),
    144, 146–47
  cost considerations, 134, 148, 150, 158,
    173–74
  objectives, 143
  parameters, 144
  policy implications, 170–73
  public decisions, 173–74
modifications needed, 399–402
operational goals, 389–91
payment rates per acre, 184–85
price levels analysis, 180–81
problems of equitable distribution,
  402–3
public support, 391–92
regional concentration, 397–98
Land retirement variables
competing and complementary, 21–23
input and output, 21
possible outcomes, 22–23
Linear programming models. *See* Models
Livestock price index, 303
Loan and delivery decision, 286–87
Loss coefficients, simulation model, 322–23

Macro-simulator, 279, 290, 292
Main effect plan, 306–7, 309–10
orthogonal matrix, 309–10
Malnutrition, U.S., 5
Marginal rate
of parameter substitution, 320–21
of response substitution, 323–24
Marginal response, 320
Market equilibrium model. *See* Models,
  market equilibrium
Mechanization
effect on labor requirements, 213, 215,
  223
relation to farm size, 212–13
Micro-simulator, 279, 281, 289–90
Minimax (saddle-point), 315
Minimum diversion level. *See* Feed Grain
  Program model
Models. *See also* Farm programs, alterna-
  tive
acreage restraint, 84–88, 91, 97
crop acreages estimated, 27–31
Feed Grain Program. *See* Feed Grain
  Program model
free market, 52–81. *See also* Free market
labor man-hours estimated, 32–34

long-term land retirement (1970), 130–
  34, 243–44, 253–56
market equilibrium, 290–93
measuring net cost of food aid shipments, 240–44
national, 328–32. *See also* National
  model
price expectations, 287, 289
production and location of major crops,
  27–31
product prices estimated, 31–32
real estate values estimated, 34–35
regional, 332–36. *See also* Regional
  model
short and intermediate policies, 115,
  117–18
simulation, 275–76
Model validation, 370–72
Multicollinearity, 353, 356, 365
Multi-regional linear programming. *See*
  Models
Multi-year land retirement, 113. *See also*
  Land retirement programs

National Agricultural Relations Board,
  proposed plan, 113
National model, 328–32
endogenous variables, 329–30
exogenous variables, 330–32
lagged endogenous variables, 332
results, 341–53
Net farm income
annual land diversion (1970), 128
farmer bargaining power (1970), 128,
  139–40
free market (1970), 126–29
long-term land retirement (1970), 128,
  134
long-term land retirement (1975), 152–
  53, 155–58, 165–67, 170
maximum diversion, percentages (1975),
  187–88
1924–65, 380–82
unlimited diversion (1975), 187–88

Optimal response values, 319–21
Optimal rules, multi-response situations,
  321–24
Optimization. *See* Response surface analysis

Parameters
crop yield trends, 38–43
policy space, 295–96
resource, 36–49
Parameter substitution, marginal rate of,
  320–21
Parametric programming techniques, 245,
  247–49

Parity, in resource returns, 391–92
Participation decision, 282–84
Payments, problem of equitable distribution, 402–3
Plan, main effect, 306–7, 309–10
PL 480
    background, 10, 225–26
    commodities, pricing, 260, 262
    comparison of net costs of shipments with alternative programs, 251, 253, 255
    cost recovery, 262
    costs
        annual land retirement with direct payments, 256, 258–59
        long-range land retirement with no restrictions, 251, 253
        long-range land retirement with restrictions, 255–56
        model to measure, 240–45, 247–49
    estimation of cost of food aid, 237, 239
    parameters, 245
    programs, relationship to stock levels, 274
    recipient countries, 249, 251
    restraints, 241, 242–44
    role in farm policy, 272, 274
    zero level of shipments, 247–48
Policies, short and intermediate
    formula, 118, 122
    government program costs, 118, 122–23
Policy programs
    history, 1930s–50s, 3–4
    new technologies, 4
Policy space, simulation model, 295–96
Price elasticity of demand, 124
Price expectations model, 287, 289
    stochastic component of behavior, 289
Price levels
    alternative, effect on net farm incomes, 187–88
    and alternative programs, 194, 197
    and distribution of government payments, 188, 190–91, 194
    government costs, sets of prices, 185–86
    and location of retired land, 188, 191, 194
    policy considerations, summary, 202–3
    production effects of different, 197, 200, 202
Prices
    acreage quotas (1980), 93–94, 99–100
    annual land diversion (1970), 127, 135
    farmer bargaining power (1970), 128, 139–40
    feed grain program (1980), 86–88
    free market (1980), 56–58, 65, 72–74
    free market (1970), 126–29
    hog, 167
    long-term land retirement (1970), 127, 132, 134

long-term land retirement (1975), 145, 161, 164–65, 167
    maximum diversion, percentages (1975), 176
    PL 480 commodities, guidelines, 260–62
    product, model, 31–32
    programmed, 86, 93, 99
    stability of, 108–9
    unlimited diversion (1975), 176
Price support, 277
    loan, 314, 319
    payments, 314–15
    PL 480 commodities, 248–49
Pricing coefficient (PC), 260, 262
Producing regions for major crops, 27
Production, effects of
    annual land retirement, 267
    limited long-range land retirement, 266–67
    unlimited long-range land retirement, 263
Production capacity, prospects, 99, 104
Production costs
    chemicals, 117
    crops, 44–45
    miscellaneous, 117–18
Production response function, 341–44

Quotas, acreage. See Acreage quotas

Ratio, lagged equity, 345–46, 356
Ratio estimates, costs, 44
Recreational land, 393–94
Regional model
    demands for machinery, vehicles, and labor, 332–36
    results (1924–65), 353–70
Regions
    consuming, 28
    producing, 27
Regression analysis, regional time-series data, 352
Regression equation, 286–87, 332–34, 356
    use of dummy variables, 39, 207, 336
Rents, programmed, 32, 34–35, 56, 65, 78, 88, 93, 99
Replication, 298–99
Resource functions (1924–65), national model, 345–46
Resource markets, regional demand estimates, 353–70
Resource parameters, cropland available, 36
Response function, Feed Grain Program, 304
Response substitution, marginal rate of, 323–24
Response surface
    analysis of fitted, 310, 313

government costs, 318–19
marginal analysis, 319–21
net farm income, 315–16
stock accumulation, 316–18
Response surface analysis, 293, 295–96, 298–300, 303–4, 306
Restraints in models
for crop acreages, 29–31
for evaluating land use, 239–40
supply control programs, 239–44
Retail business, total, 218–20
Rural areas, effects of structural adjustments on, 204–5
businesses, 218–20
population, 220–22
rural communities, 218–20, 222
size of farms, 215–18

Saddle-point. *See* Minimax
Sampling strategy, 3–4, 306
Short and intermediate policies. *See* Models. *See also* Policies, short and intermediate
Simulation, 276
Simulation analysis, national model, 382–83. *See also* Farm programs; National model
Soil Bank, 226, 234, 278
and acreage reserve, 106, 183
criticism of, 183
Soybeans
production areas, 52–53
yield projection (1980), 40
Stability, prices, 108–9
Statistical model, Feed Grain Program, 292–93
Stochastic component. *See* Price expectations model
Storage program, government, 140
Subsidy, export. *See* Export subsidies

Substitutions, 21–23. *See also* Trade-offs
capital for labor on farms, 210, 212–13, 215
Supply control, compensatory policies and food demand, 15–17. *See also* Land retirement
Supply control mechanisms, 123
annual land diversion programs, 114, 134–36
bargaining power of acreage quotas, 136, 138–40
Conservation Reserve Program, 6, 10
demand expansion, 234, 237, 239–40
free market. *See* Free market
Supply function equations, 345–46, 351–52
Surpluses, 83
Surplus supply capacity, possible solution, 393–94

Technological index, 342, 377
Technology
and crop production, 376–77
and farm industry, 107–8, 345, 348–50, 353
and rural communities, 223–24
Test, lack-of-fit, 310
Time-series data, 326, 331–32, 371–72
Trade-offs, 21–23, 173–74, 176. *See also* Substitutions

Values, optimal response, 319–21

Wheat
acreages, 6, 134, 229, 263, 266
estimates of production (1980), 38–39
export of, 231, 234
movement of, 58, 61
yields, 38–39